D1234829

The Distributional Effects of Environmental Policy

The Distributional Effects of Environmental Policy

Edited by

Ysé Serret and Nick Johnstone

National Policies Division, OECD Environment Directorate

Edward Elgar
Cheltenham, UK • Northampton, MA, USA

© OECD, 2006

All rights reserved. No part of this publication may be reproduced, stored in
a retrieval system or transmitted in any form or by any means, electronic,
mechanical or photocopying, recording, or otherwise without the prior
permission of the publisher.

Published by
Edward Elgar Publishing Limited
Glensanda House
Montpellier Parade
Cheltenham
Glos GL50 1UA
UK

Edward Elgar Publishing, Inc.
136 West Street
Suite 202
Northampton
Massachusetts 01060
USA

A catalogue record for this book
is available from the British Library

ISBN-13: 978 1 84542 315 5 (cased)
ISBN-10: 1 84542 315 1 (cased)

Printed and bound in Great Britain by MPG Books Ltd, Bodmin, Cornwall

Contents

Contributors

Ian J. Bateman is Professor of Environmental Economics in the School of Environmental Sciences at the University of East Anglia, UK. He is also Adjunct Professor in Agricultural and Resource Economics at the University of Western Australia, Perth. His principal research interests concern the economics of the environment, agriculture, forestry and risk with particular interest in the monetary valuation of preferences for public goods.

Christhart Bork worked as a research assistant at the University of Potsdam, Germany and finished his PhD in 2000. From 2000 to 2003 he was a staff member of the German Council of Economic Advisers. Since 2004 he has worked at the German Federal Ministry of Economics and Labour. His areas of interest include public economics, health economics and environmental economics.

Julii S. Brainard is a Senior Research Associate in the Centre for Social and Economic Research on the Global Environment (CSERGE) at the University of East Anglia, UK. She is particularly interested in the use of Geographical Information Systems for research in the field of environmental decision-making.

James T. Hamilton is the Charles S. Sydnor Professor of Public Policy at Duke University, Durham, NC, USA as well as a Professor of Economics and Political Science. He has written or co-authored six books as well as numerous articles in leading academic journals. He has received such awards as the David N. Kershaw Award from the Association for Public Policy Analysis and Management (2001), the Kennedy School of Government's Goldsmith Book Prize from the Shorenstein Center (1999) and Trinity College's (Duke) Distinguished Teaching Award (1993).

Nick Johnstone is Head of the Empirical Policy Analysis Unit at the OECD Environment Directorate, Paris. His current areas of interest include the analysis of public environmental policy, corporate behaviour and technological innovation. He has previously worked on environmental issues related to water supply and sanitation, transport and the energy sectors in both OECD and non-OECD countries.

Andrew P. Jones is a Senior Lecturer in the School of Environmental Sciences at the University of East Anglia, UK. He has interests in the role of the environment in determining human health and welfare, with geographical inequities forming a focus of his work.

Andrew A. Lovett is a Senior Lecturer in the School of Environmental Sciences at the University of East Anglia, UK. His research concerns the applications of Geographical Information Systems and statistical methods in the geography of health, landscape planning and visualisation, environmental economics and decision-making, and waste management.

Bengt Kriström is Professor of Resource Economics and Chair, Department of Forest Economics at SLU-Umeå, Sweden. His main research interest is applied welfare economics, in which pricing of non-market goods, green accounting and welfare analysis in equilibrium models are of primary interest.

David W. Pearce suddenly passed away on 8 September 2005. He was Emeritus Professor of Environmental Economics at University College London, UK. In a 40-year professional academic career he authored or edited over 50 books and contributed over 300 papers to academic journals. He was well known as the author or co-author of the 'Blueprint for a Green Economy' series of books. He received a UN Global 500 Award and a Lifetime Achievement Award from the European Association of Environmental and Resource Economists.

Ronald J. Sutherland is an independent consulting economist in Mathias, WV, USA. His main interests include government regulation, energy markets and investment analysis. His recent publications include estimating the benefits of restructuring an electricity market and determining resource adequacy in electricity markets.

Ysé Serret is a Policy Analyst in the National Policies Division, Environment Directorate at the Organisation for Economic Co-operation and Development (OECD), Paris. Her current areas of interest include the social and environmental policy interface, the use of instrument mixes for environmental policy and the better understanding of changing environment-related household consumption patterns.

y20

Book Title:

Preface

This book is a co-publication between Edward Elgar and the OECD Environment Directorate. It has arisen from the proceedings of an OECD workshop on the 'Distribution of Benefits and Costs of Environmental Policies: Analysis, Evidence and Policy Issues' held at OECD Headquarters, Paris, in March 2003. The workshop was organised by the National Policies Division, Environment Directorate, as part of the work programme on the 'Social and Environment Interface' which is one of the key priorities of the OECD's Environmental Strategy for the first decade of the twenty-first century.

The book builds upon earlier work undertaken by the OECD on the distributional effects of environmental policy, which has mainly concentrated on the financial impacts of the use of economic instruments. In contrast, the workshop and this book focus upon distribution impacts associated with both the distribution of environmental quality, and with the distribution of financial effects. Moreover, it looks at such impacts across a broad range of environmental policies.

The objectives of this book are threefold:

- to provide a conceptual framework to better understand the disparities in the distributional effects (environmental and financial) of environmental policy;
- to review empirical evidence on the distribution of environmental quality and in the distribution of financial effects of environmental policy; and,
- to assess the policy implications by reviewing some of the challenges facing policy-makers as they seek to design environmentally effective and economically efficient environmental policies, while ensuring that social concerns such as distributional effects are simultaneously addressed.

For their contribution to the fulfilment of these objectives – in addition to the authors of the book chapters – the editors would like to thank OECD government delegates to the Working Party on National Environmental Policies, as well as Christine Bae, Arno Bouwman, Paul Herrington, Hanneke Kruize, Susan Scott and Silvia Tiezzi.

On behalf of all of the contributors to this volume we would like to pay tribute to David W. Pearce, who suddenly passed away on 8 September 2005. David played an important role in the preparation of this publication, not least by providing a conceptual framework to analyse distributional issues associated with environmental quality. As with all of David's work, the insights provided and the clarity with which they are expressed serve as an inspiration to us all. More generally, David contributed to the work of the OECD Environment Directorate for more than thirty years, in the course of which he made significant contributions to environmental economics.

1. Distributional effects of environmental policy: introduction

Nick Johnstone and Ysé Serret

1. INTRODUCTION

The present volume is concerned with the distributional impacts associated with the introduction of environmental policies. The book focuses on distributional impacts according to economic status, which is admittedly only one vector by which to assess the distributional questions of a policy. Other possible criteria could include ethnicity, age, geographical or temporal distribution. Each perspective raises complex issues dealt with in a specific literature and can be the subject of a further study by itself. Given the richness of the topic addressed, the intention in the present volume is to centre the approach on distributional issues across one criterion in order to further develop the analysis and review the empirical literature.[1]

The basic unit of analysis applied in the chapters that follow is the household, with a focus on their relative wealth. However, different criteria can be applied as 'proxies' for wealth, such as household current income or lifetime income, household expenditures or expanded notions of wealth. Current annual income has generally been used as a proxy for households' wealth but such a measure is flawed because of its inability to reflect differences in household assets, life-cycle income effects, and other factors. However, while imperfect, it is a measure which is widely available. Where possible, other measures are sometimes used in the empirical studies discussed.

Concern with the distributional impacts of environmental policy according to socio-economic status arises in part out of a widespread fear that such measures can be regressive. This comes from two general perceptions (or perhaps misperceptions): poorer households pay disproportionately more of the financial costs associated with the introduction of environmental policies; and richer households receive disproportionately more of the benefits associated with improved environmental quality. Both of these assertions are controversial and the evidence about their validity is discussed in the chapters that follow. However, what is clear is that environmental policies have the potential to raise significant distributional concerns and, as policies become increasingly stringent, these concerns are likely to become more acute.

The book intends to widen the scope of previous analysis of the distributional effects of environmental policies in a number of ways, in particular by:

- Bringing together key aspects necessary better to understand and take into account distributional effects of environmental policy: theoretical analysis, empirical evidence and policy implications.
- Addressing concerns related to both the distribution of environmental quality and the financial effects of environmental policies.
- Adopting a comprehensive approach when looking at the distribution of environmental quality (environmental 'bads' and 'goods').
- Adopting a wide perspective when considering the distribution of financial effects of environmental policy by looking at the effects of different policy instruments, and not just economic instruments.
- Seeking to assess both the direct and indirect compliance costs, as well as taking into account effects arising through related markets (for example, public finance, labour markets, real estate markets).
- Adopting a wide geographical perspective when reviewing the empirical literature, in an effort to mitigate the strong geographical bias in favour of the United States, in particular with respect to the assessment of disparities in the distribution of exposure to environmental risks (for example, hazardous waste sites, toxic releases).
- Developing theoretically founded policy implications for the design and implementation of environmental policy, drawing in particular from the experience of OECD countries in addressing distributional concerns.

This introductory chapter will seek to contextualise the conceptual and empirical discussions in the chapters that follow by discussing some of the broad themes which run through the book, as well as some of the issues which underpin the evidence presented. First and foremost, discussions of distributional concerns cannot be divorced from the notions of 'fairness' which can underpin environmental policy (Section 2). Secondly, it is important to examine the relationship between issues of social equity and economic efficiency (Section 3), even though they are often treated separately in the policy assessment exercise. Thirdly, it is essential to have a clear understanding of the various channels through which the distributional effects of environmental policies can arise, not least because an analysis that focuses on the more evident direct effects can be quite misleading (Section 4). Fourthly, a closely related issue is the choice of policy instruments. The means by which – and the extent to which – distributional effects can arise from measures of equal stringency is affected by the characteristics of the policy measure introduced (Section 5). The chapter concludes (Section 6), with a brief overview of the coverage of the book.

2. DISTRIBUTIONAL IMPACTS AND NOTIONS OF FAIRNESS IN ENVIRONMENTAL POLICY

It is important to bear in mind the various objectives that can lie behind the widespread view that distributional issues need to be taken into account when introducing and assessing environmental policies. Since the overall distributional impacts of policies are reflected in terms of both financial effects and environmental effects, these cannot be examined in isolation. For public goods it is – almost by definition – impossible to ensure that the beneficiaries of a given policy are the same as those who bear the cost.[2] Even for local public goods it is rarely possible to restrict the cost implications of a particular environmental policy to its beneficiaries, and it is even more difficult to do so in a manner which reflects actual benefits received.

Thus, assuming that financial costs are borne more or less in proportion with levels of income, distributional concerns are likely to be perceived as less acute if the recipients of the environmental benefits live primarily in lower-income neighbourhoods rather than higher-income neighbourhoods. This is particularly important when there are significant differences in the incidence (in terms of affected populations) of environmental and financial impacts. Thus, it is the relationship between the two which will determine whether or not a given policy is perceived to be 'fair'.

With respect to the specific distribution of environmental quality, some conceptions of 'fairness' generally discussed in the literature to assess the distribution of environmental impacts include:[3]

- Equality of exposure to pollution or access to environmental amenities – for example, all households have the same level of exposure or access.
- Equality of environmental risk – for example, all households face the same level of risk, taking into account physiological and other differences.
- Progressive inequality – for example, systematically using environmental policy as a redistributional mechanism to favour poorer households.
- Procedural fairness – for example, ensuring that all households have the opportunity to express their environmental preferences effectively in the political sphere (such as through public hearings).

- Protection of 'basic' environmental needs – for example, ensuring that all households have access to a minimum level of environmental quality.
- Situational fairness – for example, ensuring that households continue to enjoy the level of environmental quality to which they have become accustomed (such as when their house was purchased).
- Preference-based notion of equity – in this approach a fair distribution may be one in which levels of environmental quality differ according to differences in demand for environmental quality.

Some of these notions are just elaborations upon one another. For instance, the distinction between equality of exposure and equality of risk is essentially one of measurement. The latter is a refinement on the former, entailing greater monitoring costs. However, the underlying motivation is likely to be similar. In other cases they are potentially complementary. For instance, a belief in the need for procedural fairness and preference-based notions of equity provides alternative means for the expression of demand. In the absence of market or policy failures, one or the other should be redundant.

However, the different principles may also represent different fundamental conceptions of fairness. For instance, the apparent regressivity of a particular policy will depend very much on whether a preference-based notion of equity or a physical risk or exposure notion of equity is adopted. As noted by Pearce (Chapter 2), depending upon the income elasticity of demand for environmental quality, a measure which appears to be regressive in terms of exposure levels may in fact be progressive when a preference-based notion of equity is applied. Thus, while some – but by no means all – studies (for example, Anderton et al., 1994a and 1994b; Brooks and Sethi, 1997; Millimet and Slottje, 2000; Kahn, 2001) indicate that pollution concentration levels are correlated with income, whether or not such a distribution is regressive according to preference-based notions would depend upon demand for environmental quality, and the evidence in this area is very limited (see for example, Hökby and Söderqvist, 2002; and Carson et al., 1995).

Thus, it is important to recognise these differences when trying to identify a government's objective with respect to a particular measure which seeks to redress some perceived distributional imbalance in environmental quality. For instance, policies which restrict the siting of hazardous waste facilities in neighbourhoods with high levels of poverty are more likely to be driven by an underlying belief in the need to protect access to a basic level of environmental quality for all households, than by a belief in preference-based notions of equity.[4] Indeed, the intention of such a policy may well be to override the revealed preferences of the affected community, a point which is taken up by Pearce (Chapter 2) as well as in the concluding chapter.

With respect to financial impacts, the issue is not significantly different from the effects of any public policy. Any policy will result in costs that are different across socio-economic groups depending upon their expenditure patterns, behavioural responses, employment opportunities and so on. Indeed, as emphasised by Kriström (Chapter 3), the main objective of all environmental policies is to change consumption and production patterns. As such, they will have, by their very nature, distributional impacts on households.

Whether or not such differences in impacts are 'fair' needs to be understood in the broader overall context of government policy with respect to the distribution of wealth. If it is assumed, as seems reasonable in the majority of cases, that the existing distribution of wealth in a given society prior to the introduction of a particular policy is considered not to be such as to necessitate additional redistribution policies above and beyond those which are already in place to meet these social objectives (that is, progressive income taxation, social welfare systems and so on), then the key issue is whether or not the distributional effects of the introduction of an additional policy (environmental or other) are 'marginal'.

However, as noted in Kriström (Chapter 3), even determining whether or not the effects are marginal depends crucially upon the 'proxy' for wealth used, such as household current income or lifetime income, household expenditures or expanded notions of wealth. Each has its own limits when looking at distributional issues. The empirical literature suggests that the definition retained may affect the results regarding the regressivity of environmental policy.[5] In short, conclusions about the distributional impacts of environmental policy in financial terms will differ according to the measure of income applied.

In the event that a particular environmental policy (that is, a carbon tax or a new pollution regulation) is thought to have non-trivial regressive impacts, then, for the sake of social justice, it is important to mitigate these impacts. However, this may not necessarily be done within the framework of the environmental policy itself. As discussed in the concluding chapter of this volume, it may be neither economically efficient nor environmentally effective to modify an environmental policy in order to meet social objectives. Indeed, modifications to the policy itself are unlikely to be the optimal means for addressing the distributional concerns.

Thus, in theory, environmental policy should not generally be the tool for addressing distributional issues, since there are other more suitable mechanisms. However, for political reasons it may be necessary to address the distribution of costs within the context of the environmental policy itself. For instance, the proposed BtU tax[6] in the United States and the petrol duty escalator in the United Kingdom were rescinded or reformed in part for distributional reasons. The introduction of countervailing policies with progressive impacts may not suffice to overcome such resistance, and the environmental policy will continue to be viewed as 'unfair'.

As such, the concept of fairness applied can have fundamental implications for the nature of interventions undertaken by public authorities, and on whether or not any intervention should be undertaken at all. Since the principles applied are rarely articulated at the time of introduction of a particular policy, this can lead to considerable confusion. Indeed, there is a strain in economics which cites the plethora and conflicting notions of fairness as reason enough to undermine it as a decision-making criterion (Kaplow and Shavell, 2002). While an extreme view, it does highlight the need to clarify the ultimate policy objective underpinning specific measures which are purported to address distributional concerns.

3.   THE RELATIONSHIP BETWEEN SOCIAL EQUITY AND ECONOMIC EFFICIENCY

Equity is, of course, only one criterion for assessing environmental policy. Other criteria set out in the OECD report on *Evaluating Economic Instruments for Environmental Policy* (OECD, 1997) include environmental effectiveness, economic efficiency, administration and compliance costs, public finance, dynamic effects and innovation, soft effects, such as those arising from the use of instruments on attitude and awareness, and other wider economic effects.

The tension which can exist between social equity and economic efficiency objectives is particularly important, and the issue is not fully resolved in the literature. Indeed, the debate is rarely engaged in the economic literature due to the use of 'Pareto Superiority' as the predominant means of policy evaluation in economics. Any policy or project in which everyone gains passes the test, and one in which everyone loses fails the test. However, as Kriström (Chapter 3) points out, almost all policies generate 'losers' and 'winners', and imposing the constraint that all must benefit from the introduction of each and every policy can only be an excuse for political paralysis.

In order to make the test of practical policy relevance, a number of conceptual refinements have been developed, perhaps most famously in the form of the Kaldor–Hicks criterion which states that a policy is 'welfare-improving' when the sum of benefits exceeds the sum of costs – that is, even if there are 'losers' from its introduction, a policy is socially beneficial if the winners can compensate the losers (see Johansson, 1993, for a discussion). Whether or not the compensation is actually paid is incidental to whether or not the Kaldor–Hicks criterion is in fact met. If it is hypothetically possible for the winners to compensate the losers such that both groups are net beneficiaries, that is sufficient.

Therefore, an environmental policy which brings considerable benefits to a small minority, but imposes lower overall costs on a large majority will satisfy the Kaldor–Hicks criterion since overall social welfare will have increased. In many cases this may be appropriate. For instance, if the initial distribution is 'optimal' and if the distributional effects of a given policy are marginal, it can hardly be administratively efficient to seek to ensure that such effects are addressed case by case with the introduction of each and every policy. The introduction of an advanced disposal fee on lead-acid batteries to cover disposal costs and environmental externalities will have distributional implications (because both the costs and the benefits are borne unequally), but these are not likely to be important enough to warrant the introduction of compensating measures.

However, there are cases in which the introduction of compensating measures is clearly required in order to ensure that the policy is acceptable. Even if the same population bears the financial costs and gains the environmental benefits, the distribution may be such as to make the measure politically infeasible or socially unacceptable. For instance, many OECD governments which have introduced environmentally-motivated energy taxes have simultaneously introduced compensating measures in order to reduce their regressivity. Since the effects were non-trivial, it was felt that such compensating measures needed to be part of the same 'policy package'.

In some cases, these 'compensating measures' are introduced through general reforms of tax policy. For instance, the revenue generated by an environment-related tax can be used to reduce tax rates for lower-income households, which would result in a more progressive fiscal policy in general. In other cases, it may be more directly targeted at those households which are most affected by the environmental policy – that is, lower-income rural households in the face of petrol taxes. The effects of such compensating measures on economic efficiency will be marginal as long as the incentive effects of the environmental policy remain untouched.[7]

In still other cases, governments may actually seek to marry improved social equity with economic efficiency. For instance, it has often been argued that lower-income households faced particular market failures (split incentives, information failures, credit market failures and so on) which prevented them from responding to environment-related residential energy taxes, and as a consequence complementary measures are needed to address such failures for distributional reasons (for an early discussion of these issues, see Brechling et al., 1991). Governments have sought to introduce compensating measures which not only address equity concerns but also increase economic efficiency by addressing such failures or barriers. This is discussed in the concluding chapter.

In other cases it may be possible to deal with the distributional impacts directly within the implementation of the policy instrument itself. For instance, it is frequently argued that one of the great advantages of tradable permits over other policy measures is the apparent separability of equity and efficiency objectives through the policy itself, via the initial allocation of permits. In this case, the pursuit of equity will not undermine efficiency objectives. Equity can be addressed in the initial permit allocation, and this will have no bearing on efficiency since efficiency is not affected by the way permits are allocated initially.

However, under certain circumstances this apparent separability breaks down. For instance, if the value of the permits has significant impacts on income levels and income elasticity of demand for the goods is non-linear then the allocation of permits will affect the aggregate level of demand for the environmental good. Only one specific distribution of permits will ensure that all agents have marginal costs equal to marginal benefits.[8]

In addition, for political reasons (including distributional concerns) many countries are actively considering using allocation mechanisms involving 'updating' in which current production and/or emission levels affect future permit allocations.[9] While this will likely come at a welfare cost, Böhringer and Lange (2005) point out that the magnitude of such costs will depend crucially upon whether or not the emissions trading scheme is 'open' or not. If the regulatory agency cannot take the overall allocation as given, different allocation rules will have different distributional *and* welfare implications.

Another area in which equity issues have been addressed directly within the policy measure itself is in the provision of environment-related public services where price discrimination on the basis of consumption levels is possible. For instance, through the use of escalating tariffs it is possible to reduce the regressivity associated with the imposition of user fees in the provision of water and sanitation services. While this is likely to have some impact on economic efficiency – particularly if tariffs are very low at low consumption levels – the incentive effects remain largely in place.

Moreover, there can be other 'public' motives to ensure minimum levels of consumption of environment-related public services. For instance, due to possible health externalities it may be economically inefficient to 'price' initial levels of service provision equal to the marginal environmental damages (environmental externalities and resource rents). At excessively low levels of consumption, private preferences may not reflect the public good benefits of reduced health externalities associated with higher levels of consumption.[10] In addition, even in the absence of such externalities there may be a widely-held social perception that basic levels of provision for all households are preconditions for maximising social welfare (see Johnstone et al., 2002a for a discussion).

In summary, the Kaldor–Hicks criterion can be interpreted as a way of allowing for the separation of equity and efficiency.[11] It can be seen as an argument for removing the burden of tackling distributional matters from the sphere of environmental policy. This may not, however, be politically feasible since – as noted above – the implementation of environmental policies is often constrained in practice by concerns over distributional matters. As such, if the effects on distribution are not trivial, then the mere 'possibility' of compensating poorer households may not suffice to justify a given policy intervention. Some compensating measure may need to be applied.

In addition to the potential impacts of environmental policies on the distribution of financial and environmental costs and benefits, it is also possible that the initial distribution of income will affect aggregate levels of demand for environmental quality for society as a whole (rather than for a given group of individuals). Moreover, it may also have an effect on the likelihood of this demand being effective, whether through public interventions or collective action.

On the one hand, if the income elasticity of demand for environmental quality is non-linear, then the initial distribution of income will affect aggregate demand. If, for instance, income elasticity of demand is convex, a more unequal distribution of income will lead to greater demand for environmental quality. Analogously, a concave income elasticity of the demand curve means that demand will be maximised at more equal distributions of income (see Boyce, 2003). As noted above, the evidence with respect to the income elasticity of demand for environmental quality remains an area requiring further empirical research (see Pearce in Chapter 2). Preliminary assessments of potential non-linearities in this relationship were undertaken by Kriström and Riera (1996), and they were unable to reject the possibility that the income–environmental quality relationship is non-linear.

On the other hand, there is a rich vein of literature which has examined the role of income distribution in encouraging or discouraging collective action to protect common property resources such as fisheries and pastureland. Olson (1965) argued that unequal distribution of income was likely to lead to greater conservation of common property resources for the simple reason that it was more likely that a small number of agents would be willing to bear a disproportionate share of the total costs of conservation in order to reap the benefits of conservation of the resource.

However, more recent literature is more ambiguous, finding that under plausible conditions a more equal distribution of wealth will lead to greater protection of common property environmental resources (Baland and Platteau, 1997; Dayton-Johnson and Bardhan, 2002). Drawing upon the insights of Becker (1983), Hamilton (Chapter 7) discusses issues of collective action in relation to the siting of hazardous waste treatment and disposal facilities.

4.   CHANNELS THROUGH WHICH DISTRIBUTIONAL EFFECTS OF ENVIRONMENTAL POLICIES CAN ARISE

The most evident (and often most important) channel through which the financial impacts of an environmental policy can arise relate to the effect of a given policy on the price of a good or service which is directly targeted by the policy measure. For example, the distributional effects of an environmentally-motivated fuel tax will depend upon how important fuel consumption is in the total basket of expenditures for low-income and high-income households. Similarly, the distributional effects of an energy efficiency standard for appliances will depend on the consumption and use of such appliances by households in different income brackets.

Indeed, the vast majority of existing empirical studies focus almost exclusively on the direct financial incidence of individual environmental policies. (Kriström, in Chapter 3, provides a review of recent studies.) In general, and for a wide variety of policy measures, such analyses reveal that impacts can be regressive. For instance, this is certainly true of carbon taxes. (See Brännlund and Nordström, 2004; and Cornwell and Creedy, 1997, for examples from Sweden and Australia respectively.)

However, this can provide misleading indications of the degree of progressivity or regressivity of the impacts of the policy. For instance, differences in behavioural responses of different income groups in the face of the introduction of a policy can affect the distributional impacts of the policy. On the one hand, substitution possibilities may differ markedly between different income brackets. On the other hand, price elasticities will differ in a relatively predictable manner depending upon differences in the share of affected goods and services in total expenditures across income levels. Ignoring such differences would overestimate the financial impact of the policy on low-income households relative to high-income households. In other cases, differences in behavioural responses may accentuate the distributional impacts.

West and Williams (2002) provide recent evidence on the implications of gasoline taxes on different income groups in the United States. They find that the price elasticity of the low-income quintile is approximately twice that of the high-income group. Sipes and Mendelsohn (2001) reach a similar conclusion. However, in a study of carbon taxes in Australia, Cornwell and Creedy (1997) find that low-income households have lower price elasticities. Thus, it is important to examine this on a case-by-case basis. For instance, in some markets substitution possibilities may be greater for high-income households, increasing their sensitivity to price changes. A thorough understanding of demand patterns across different socio-economic groups is essential.

In addition, it is important to take into account the indirect effects of environmental policies. Unless a given environmental policy only affects a final household good or service, there will be pass-through effects on downstream goods and services. Thus, a general energy tax (rather than a tax on residential energy use) will affect the costs of all goods and services in relation to their energy use.[12] Similarly, a technology-based standard to reduce biological oxygen demand in the production of pulp will affect the cost of stationery, books, newspapers and so on. (See Kriström, Chapter 3, for a discussion.)

In general, taking into account such input–output linkages appears to diminish the apparent strong regressivity (or progressivity) of at least some policies. The reason is intuitive and can be illustrated with the example of an energy tax. If the direct effects are significantly regressive due to the high importance of energy in the consumption basket of low-income households relative to high-income households, such effects will be mitigated to the extent that all other goods consumed which have energy inputs are consumed proportionally less in a relative sense by lower-income households.

In addition to the direct and indirect markets for the goods and services themselves, it is also important to take into account the effects produced through impacts on other markets and other public policy spheres. One of the most important issues relates to the impacts of a given environmental policy on the fiscal stance of the public authority. Some policy measures may have significant implications for public expenditures (for example, subsidies for investment in nature conservation or pollution abatement). Depending upon how the revenue is generated to finance such expenditures, impacts may be very different. Even direct regulations may necessitate significant expenditures on monitoring and enforcement.

However, some other measures may be net generators of government revenue. For instance, auctioned tradable permits or environment-related taxes can generate revenues in excess of any costs associated with policy implementation. In such cases, the means of revenue recycling can have significant implications for the distributional effects of a policy. Thus, recycling via reduced income taxes, corporate taxes or sales taxes will have a very different incidence for the distribution of impacts. This is an issue giving rise to lively discussion in the literature and some of the results are reviewed in Kriström (Chapter 3). Indeed, holding other factors constant, the means of recycling adopted may affect whether a policy is regressive or progressive. (See the aforementioned study by West and Williams, 2002; as well as Parry, 2004.)

Environmental policies affect different socio-economic groups not only as consumers and taxpayers, but also as wage-earners and shareholders. In some cases, the effects of environmental policies on employment markets, particularly in sectors directly affected by an environmental policy, may be more important than the distributional effects of policies in affected consumption markets (see OECD, 2003). Obvious examples relate to natural resource-based sectors. Because of the relative isolation and skill-specificity of employment opportunities in sectors such as forestry, mining and fisheries, it is sometimes argued that environmental policies in such sectors may have particularly important impacts on earning opportunities for those affected.

And, finally, environmental policies can have distributional implications through other markets in which the associated environmental improvement is, at least partly, embedded. In particular, for local public goods ('Tiebout goods'), the financial effects of environmental policies will not only be reflected in the cost of the policy measure per se, but also in the impact that the change in environmental quality has on other markets (see Pearce, Chapter 2 in the present volume). For instance, real estate prices are likely to be affected positively by the siting of an urban park in the neighbourhood and negatively by the siting of a disamenity such as a landfill site. (See Hamilton, Chapter 7, for a discussion of the latter case.)

It is important to take these impacts into account if a full assessment of the distributional impacts of a policy are to be determined. Taking the example of the urban park siting, the financial effect will be positive for local home-owners, as will the environmental benefits. However, it will be negative for tenants, and the non-monetised benefits in terms of access to the park may be of less value than any eventual rent increase. In such cases, there will be a natural 'sorting' in the affected markets with long-run impacts being very different from any short-run impacts (see Tiebout, 1956, for the original discussion).[13]

5. THE EFFECTS OF POLICY INSTRUMENT CHOICE ON DISTRIBUTIONAL IMPACTS

When examining the distributional issues related to the use of environmental policies, the literature generally focuses on the possible regressive impacts of economic instruments, especially taxes. In general it is felt that they are likely to have particularly regressive effects. In some sense, there is good reason – at least at first sight – for such an assumption. In the case of economic instruments (whether environment-related taxes or auctioned tradable permits), the rent associated with the use of the environment is received by the government.

However, in the case of direct regulation (whether technology-based standards or performance-based standards), the rents associated with the residual pollutants which continue to be emitted after specified abatement is undertaken are granted to the emitters themselves. In effect, in a partial equilibrium framework, the total costs of compliance under economic instruments have two elements (abatement costs and tax payments/permit purchases), while under direct regulation only the costs of abatement arise. This may accentuate the distributional impacts associated with the achievement of a given environmental target.

As has been noted above, this widespread belief in the greater potential for there being regressive impacts from the introduction of an economic instrument may be due in part to the focus on the 'direct' effects of the two classes of instruments. In particular, once the potential for revenue recycling is included in the analysis, it is much less clear that impacts are likely to be more regressive under the application of economic instruments. With the use of environment-related taxes or auctioned tradable permits the 'rents' which are granted to emitters under direct regulation can be used to offset any potential negative distributional impacts. Analogously, available evidence underlines how significantly the way of allocating permits affects the distributional impacts of tradable permits (auctioned versus grandfathered) (see Markandya, 1998; Cramton and Kerr, 1999; Dinan and Rogers, 2002;[14] Parry, 2004[15]).

Thus, whether or not a policy is regressive depends very much on the means of recycling applied. For instance, recycling via reduced income taxes will have very different effects from recycling via reduced value-added taxes. Indeed, the means of recycling can convert a policy from being regressive to being progressive. In a study of SO_2, carbon and NO_x policy, Parry (2004) finds that emissions taxes go from being progressive under 'proportional recycling' (that is, in proportion to ex ante tax burdens) to strongly progressive under 'lump-sum' recycling (that is, equal rebates to all households). (See Symons et al., 1994; Metcalf, 1999; and Bovenberg and

Goulder, 2002 for studies on the importance of the means of recycling assumed.)

The importance of the overall fiscal policy regime is also clearly evident with the use of environmentally-motivated subsidies. In this case, the distributional impacts will arise from the degree of regressivity or progressivity of the tax system used to raise the finance required to pay for such programmes. Interestingly, however, many subsidy programmes have been used to address both distributional and environmental objectives simultaneously. Examples include energy conservation subsidies or investment programmes to promote renewable energy. In the first case, at least, these policies are targeted directly at lower-income households. Thus, the subsidy is being used to address two objectives simultaneously – that is, internalisation of the environmental externality and distributional objectives. This is usually justified by the existence of significant market failures or barriers which increase the cost to low-income households and reduce their responsiveness to particular policy incentives. The efficiency of using subsidies in this way is a point taken up in the concluding chapter.

Another possible reason why there is a widespread belief that economic instruments have the potential to be more regressive than direct regulation is the transparency of their effects. Even if a market-based instrument and a direct regulation are targeted at the same environmental objective, the cost (and thus distributional) effects of the former may be more apparent. Taking the example of energy efficiency, it is possible to achieve given targets with a tax (encouraging the purchase and design of more efficient appliances) or through performance standards, mandating minimum levels of energy efficiency. The distributional effect of the former is quite transparent.

However, the effects of the latter are much less evident. As Sutherland (Chapter 5) points out, if low-income households have higher revealed discount rates than high-income households,[16] and if more energy-efficient appliances have higher capital/operating cost ratios than they would normally purchase, the effect of energy performance standards on appliances will be to override the temporal preferences of low-income households, restricting their options in the market with adverse effects on welfare.[17] More generally, when the indirect effects of both economic instruments and direct regulations on manufacturing and other sectors are taken into account, there is no reason to expect that the effects of the latter will be less regressive. (See Robison, 1985 for an early example of the application of input–output analysis to evaluating the distributional effects of direct forms of regulation.)

While infrequently assessed, liability for environmental damages can also have distributional implications. (See Ringquist, 1998; and Kanner, 2004, for discussions.) The distributional impacts of legal liability regimes are likely to vary widely depending upon the means by which damages are compensated in cases in which a firm (or other agent) is held responsible for adverse environmental impacts. In particular, the distributional impacts will not be the same whether damages are compensated on the basis of lost earnings or production losses, or according to fixed criteria set regardless of households economic status. What principles are applied varies widely across OECD countries, and differences are likely to be particularly important between civil law and common law regimes.

In short, all policy instruments have potential but different distributional impacts. To get a full picture of these effects, both direct and indirect channels through which they can arise are to be considered. Such an analysis tends to be easier to carry out in the case of taxes and auctioned tradable permits where the direct effects on household groups are generally more straightforward. However, even for taxes the case is complicated by the inclusion of indirect impacts, revenue recycling and behavioural adjustments. The fact that the distributional implications of taxes are particularly highlighted is probably due to their greater 'visibility' and should not be construed as an indication of their greater regressivity per se.

6. STRUCTURE OF THE BOOK

The first part of the book (Chapters 2 and 3) provides conceptual frameworks for assessing the distribution of environmental impacts and of the financial effects of environmental policies. It draws upon insights from environmental economics, welfare economics, public economics and political philosophy. It reviews the mechanisms through which the benefits and costs of environmental policies affect the individual household, and the reasons why such impacts are likely to be unevenly distributed.

The conceptual frameworks developed build on the framework for assessing the distributional implications of economic instruments used in previous work (OECD, 1994) and elaborate upon it by extending the analysis to include other forms of environmental policies. In addition, while many studies focus on the direct financial incidence of individual policies, this can provide misleading indications of the progressivity or regressivity of the impacts of the policy. As such, the analysis has been extended to include additional channels through which distributional effects arise (for example, indirect effects, differences in behavioural response by household type, the effects of policies on related markets such as real estate and labour markets).

Empirical evidence on the distributional implications of environmental policies is examined in the second part through selected case studies, including: ecological tax reforms in Germany (Chapter 4), regulatory approaches to residential energy efficiency (Chapter 5), exposure to noise in the United Kingdom (Chapter 6), and proximity to hazardous waste facilities in OECD countries (Chapter 7).

Chapter 8 examines the policy measures which have been introduced in OECD countries to address these distributional concerns. Building on this experience, the book reviews some of the challenges facing policy-makers as they seek to design environmentally effective and economically efficient environmental policies, while ensuring that social concerns such as distributional effects are simultaneously tackled. On the basis of the review and analysis of these key sets of issues to be addressed, policy implications are drawn.

NOTES

1. Thus, issues such as temporal inequality arising from distributional effects across generations is not covered. Similarly, distributional effects along racial-ethnic lines are not discussed. However, it must be recognised that there can be strong links between these different characteristics. As such, some of these other elements are addressed in cases where they are particularly strongly related to the distribution of household wealth and income.
2. It is the non-excludability and non-rivalry of consumption of public environmental goods that necessitates public policy interventions.
3. For a recent discussion of the principles of fairness underpinning different environmental policies in the United States, see Hsu (2004). Shoup (1989) provides a useful discussion of issues of fairness in allocation rules for public services such as water and sanitation.
4. Although such a policy is not necessarily inconsistent with a preference-based notion of equity if it is felt that there are market or policy preferences which prevent the expression of such preferences for low-income households.
5. In general, studies indicate that the regressive impacts of taxes are more limited in a lifetime context. For instance, a tax on gasoline appears less regressive than other analyses suggest when taken as a percentage of total consumption expenditures used as a proxy for lifetime income (Poterba, 1991). In a similar way, looking at the distributional effects of a shift in taxes on motor vehicle emissions, Walls and Hanson (1999) conclude that results depend heavily on the measure of income used and that the three vehicle pollution control policies examined are much less regressive when considering lifetime income than on the basis of annual income. Smith (1992) notes however that this conclusion may depend on a number of factors and that, in the case of energy and carbon taxation in the UK, the distinction makes little difference in distributional analysis.
6. In 1993, the Clinton Administration proposed a differential BtU tax on fossil fuels (a broadly-based general tax primarily on oils, gas and coal, based on the British Thermal Units of heat output).
7. Although there will be some loss of efficiency through the blunting of the 'output' effect of the policy – that is, demand for the goods and services affected will be greater than is optimal.
8. See Chichilnisky and Heal (1994) and Shiell (2003). See also McGuire and Aaron (1969) for a general theoretical discussion of the relationship between efficiency and equity in the supply of public goods.

9. For instance, in the context of the EU Emissions Trading Directive, the German Government's national permit allocation plan allows for ex post correction of allowances in the event of a substantial change in emission or production levels (see Böhringer and Lange, 2005).
10. Note that the importance of this only arises due to the discretionary nature of consumption of the environmental good.
11. The notion of separability refers here to the fact that the pursuit of equity does not undermine the efficiency goal and vice versa.
12. And depending upon substitution possibilities in production.
13. As noted in the concluding chapter below, this 'sorting' effect can have significant implications for the ability of a given policy to address distributional concerns. Efforts to site environmental amenities in lower-income neighbourhoods will ultimately be at least partially self-defeating as real estate prices rise in the face of such improvements. In effect, the government is in danger of 'chasing its own tail', in a futile effort to follow conditions in markets affected by its own policy interventions.
14. Examining the effects of a 15 per cent reduction in US carbon emissions under different allocation mechanisms, Dinan and Rogers (2002) estimate that the lowest-income households would be worse off under grandfathered permits while top-income households would be better off. The low-income households would be better off if, instead, the permits were auctioned with revenues recycled in equal lump-sum rebates for all households.
15. In an assessment of the distributional impacts of tradable emissions permits for carbon, SO_2 and NO_x in the US, Parry (2004) shows that grandfathered emissions permits can have a significant regressive effect as the rent ultimately accrues to shareholders.
16. A point which is supported by the empirical evidence. See Johnstone et al. (2002b) for a review.
17. Fisher (2004) points out that this result may not hold if the supply of appliances is not perfectly competitive.

REFERENCES

Anderton, D., A. Anderson, J. Oakes, M. Fraser, E. Weber and E. Calabrese (1994a), 'Hazardous Waste Facilities: Environmental Equity Issues in Metropolitan Areas', *Evaluation Review*, **18**(2), 123–40.

Anderton, D., A. Anderson, J. Oakes and M. Fraser (1994b), 'Environmental Equity. The Demographics of Dumping in Dixie', *Demography*, **31**(2), 229–48.

Baland, Jean-Marie and Jean-Philippe Platteau (1997), 'Wealth Inequality and Efficiency in the Commons', *Oxford Economic Papers*, **49**(4), 451–82.

Becker, G. (1983), 'A Theory of Competition among Pressure Groups for Political Influence', *Quarterly Journal of Economics*, **98**, 371–400.

Böhringer, Christoph and Andreas Lange (2005), 'On the Design of Optimal Grandfathering Schemes for Emission Allowances', *European Economic Review*, **49**(8), 2041–55.

Bovenberg, L.L. and L.H. Goulder (2002), 'Addressing Industry-Distributional Concerns in U.S. Climate Change Policy', working paper, Stanford University and Tilburg University. Available at http://weber.ucsd.edu/~carsonvs/papers/810.pdf.

Boyce, James K. (2003), 'Inequality and Environmental Protection', University of Massachusetts Amherst, Political Economy Research Institute Working Paper No. 51.

Brännlund, R. and J. Nordström (2004), 'Carbon Tax Simulations Using a Household Demand Model', *European Economic Review*, **48**(1), 211–33.

Brechling, V., D. Helm and S. Smith (1991), 'Domestic Energy Conservation – Environmental Objectives and Market Failures', in Dieter Helm (ed.), *Economic Policy towards the Environment*, Oxford: Blackwell Publishers.

Brooks, N. and R. Sethi (1997), 'The Distribution of Pollution: Community Characteristics and Exposure to Air Toxics', *Journal of Environmental Economics and Management*, **32**, 233–50.

Carson, R., R. Mitchell, M. Hanemann, R. Kopp, S. Presser and P. Ruud (1995), 'Contingent Valuation and Lost Passive Use Damages from the Exxon Valdez', Discussion Paper 95-02, Department of Economics, University of San Diego.

Chichilnisky, G. and G. Heal (1994), 'Who Should Abate Carbon Emissions? An International Viewpoint', *Economic Letters*, **44**(4), 443–9.

Cornwell, A. and J. Creedy (1997), 'Measuring the Welfare Effects of Tax Changes Using the LES: An Application to a Carbon Tax', *Empirical Economics*, **22**, 589–613.

Cramton, P. and S. Kerr (1999), 'The Distributional Effects of Carbon Regulation: Why Auctioned Carbon Permits are Attractive and Feasible', in Thomas Sterner (ed.), *The Market and the Environment*, International Studies in Environmental Policy Making, Cheltenham and Northampton, MA: Edward Elgar.

Dayton-Johnson, Jeff and Pranab Bardhan (2002), 'Inequality and Conservation on the Local Commons: A Theoretical Exercise', *Economic Journal*, Royal Economic Society, **112**(481), July, 577–602.

Dinan, Terry M. and Diane Lim Rogers (2002), 'Distributional Effects of Carbon Allowance Trading: How Government Decisions Determine Winners and Losers', *National Tax Journal*, **LV**, 199–222.

Fisher, Carolyn (2004), 'Who Pays for Energy Efficiency Standards?', Resources for the Future Discussion Paper 04–11.

Hökby, S. and T. Söderqvist (2002), 'Elasticities of Demand and Willingness to Pay for Environmental Services in Sweden', paper to 11th Annual Conference of the European Association of Environmental and Resource Economists, Southampton.

Hsu, Shi-Ling (2004), 'Fairness versus Efficiency in Environmental Law', Canadian Law and Economics Association Annual Meeting, Toronto, September.

Johansson, P.O. (1993), *Cost–Benefit Analysis of Environmental Change*, Cambridge: Cambridge University Press.

Johnstone, N. et al. (2002a), 'Environmental and Ethical Dimensions of the Provision of an Environmental Basic Need: Water and Sanitation Services in East Africa', in D.W. Bromley and J. Paavola (eds), *Economics, Ethics and Environmental Policy*, Oxford: Blackwell.

Johnstone, N., N. Caid and Y. Serret (2002b), 'Decision-making and Environmental Policy Design for Consumer Durables', OECD Monograph ENV/EPOC/WPNEP(2002)7/FINAL.

Kahn, M. (2001), 'The Beneficiaries of Clean Air Act Regulation', *Regulation*, Spring, 34–8.

Kanner, Allan (2004), 'Equity in Toxic Tort Litigation: Unjust Enrichment and the Poor', *Law and Policy*, **26**(2), 209–30.

Kaplow, Louis and Stephen Shavell (2002), *Fairness versus Welfare*, Cambridge, MA: Harvard University Press.

Kriström, Bengt and Pere Riera (1996), 'Is the Income Elasticity of Environmental Improvements Less than One?', *Environmental and Resource Economics*, **7**, 45–55.

Markandya, A. (1998), 'Poverty, Income Distribution and Policy Making', *Environmental and Resource Economics*, **11**(3–4), 459–72.

McGuire, Martin C. and Henry Aaron (1969), 'Efficiency and Equity in the Optimal Supply of a Public Good', *Review of Economics and Statistics*, **51**(1), 31–9.

Metcalf, G.E. (1999), 'A Distributional Analysis of Green Tax Reforms', *National Tax Journal*, **52**, 655–81.

Millimet, D. and D. Slottje (2000), 'The Distribution of Pollution in the US: An Environmental Gini Approach', mimeo, Department of Economics, Southern Methodist University, Dallas.

OECD (Organisation for Economic Cooperation and Development) (1994), *The Distributive Effects of Economic Instruments for Environmental Policy*, Paris: OECD.

OECD (1997), *Evaluating Economic Instruments for Environmental Policy*, Paris: OECD.

OECD (2003), *Synthesis Report on Environment and Employment*, OECD Monograph, ENV/EPOC/WPNEP(2003)11Final.

Olson, M. (1965), *The Logic of Collective Action*, Cambridge, MA: Harvard University Press.

Parry, I.W. (2004), 'Are Emissions Permits Regressive?', *Journal of Environmental Economics and Management*, **47**, 364–87.

Poterba, J.M. (1991), 'Is the Gasoline Tax Regressive?', *Tax Policy and the Economy*, vol. 5, Cambridge, MA: National Bureau of Economic Research, pp. 145–64.

Ringquist, E. (1998), 'A Question of Justice: Equity in Environmental Litigation', *Journal of Politics*, **60**(4), November, 1148–65.

Robison, H.D. (1985), 'Who Pays for Industrial Pollution Abatement?', *Review of Economics and Statistics*, **67**(4), 702–6.

Shiell, Leslie (2003), 'Equity and Efficiency in International Markets for Pollution Permits', *Journal of Environmental Economics and Management*, **46**, 38–51.

Shoup, Carl S. (1989), 'Rules for Distributing a Free Government Service among Areas of a City', *National Tax Journal*, **52**(2), 103–21.

Sipes, K. and R. Mendelsohn (2001), 'The Effectiveness of Gasoline Taxation to Manage Air Pollution', *Ecological Economics*, **2**(36), 299–309.

Smith, S. (1992), 'The Distributional Consequences of Taxes on Energy and the Carbon Content of Fuels', *European Economy*, Special Edition, 1, 241–68.

Symons, E., J. Proops and P. Gay (1994), 'Carbon Taxes, Consumer Demand, and Carbon Dioxide Emissions: A Simulation Analysis for the UK', *Fiscal Studies*, **15**(2), 19–43.

Tiebout, C. (1956), 'A Pure Theory of Local Expenditures', *Journal of Political Economy*, **LXIV**, 416–24.

Walls, Margaret and Jean Hanson (1999), 'Distributional Aspects of an Environmental Tax Shift: The Case of Motor Vehicle Emissions Taxes', *National Tax Journal*, **52**(1), 53–65.

West, Sarah and Roberton C. Williams III (2002), 'Estimates from a Consumer Demand System: Implications for the Incidence of Environmental Taxes', NBER Working Paper No. 9152.

PART I

Conceptual Frameworks and Literature Review

2. Framework for assessing the distribution of environmental quality

David W. Pearce

1. THE ISSUE

A sizeable empirical literature exists on the relationship between environmental quality and socio-economic groups within a nation's borders.[1] The hypothesis tested by this literature is that environmental quality is regressively distributed across socio-economic groups, that is, low-income groups are exposed to higher environmental risks than high-income groups. If this is true, and if the distribution across income groups is not freely chosen by those groups, then an issue of distributive equity arises. Regressive distributions could be deliberately chosen: it may be that low-income groups have a lower demand for environmental quality than high-income groups. Alternatively, higher levels of pollution may be connected with associated benefits – for example, lower property prices – that compensate those groups for higher environmental risk. But regressive distributions may also be the result of an unequal endowment of political power and limited ability to adjust to environmental risks. In so far as unequal political power explains the regressivity, an equity issue still arises. Even when power is fairly equally distributed, the public-good nature of many environmental goods, and hence the public-bad nature of the risks, may produce compromise allocations of the good that under-supply the good to higher-income groups and over-supply it to low-income groups, still producing an equity problem. These alternative explanations for regressivity of risks are explored in detail in Section 2.

From a policy standpoint, equity is a goal of social and economic policy in OECD countries. What constitutes 'equity' is not straightforward and the issue is not investigated in any detail further here. For excellent treatments see Young (1994) and Zajac (1995).[2] In the current context, an equitable outcome is taken to be one that produces an equal exposure to environmental harm, or the equal per capita endowment of environmental benefits, exposure and endowments being measured across income groups. Policy goals may then be formulated in terms of reducing inequality in exposure to harm, or increasing equality in the endowment of benefits. Both goals characterise the movement for environmental equity, more popularly known as environmental justice (EJ), that has assumed some importance in policy discussions in the USA and is now being discussed in European countries.[3] Unfortunately, what is meant by 'harm' and 'benefit' is itself not straightforward, an issue explored further in Section 2.

A second reason for being concerned with unequal distributions of harm is that they may be inefficient. This point is less obvious than the equity issue. Consider Figure 2.1 which shows a stylised linear dose-response function linking an environmental indicator, say ambient pollution concentration, C, to a 'damage' indicator, D (health damage, ecosystem damage and so on). Assume that the rich occupy land where $C = 10$ and the poor occupy land where $C = 40$. The average is then $C = 25$. Total damage is then given by $D = 1$ for the rich and $D = 4$ for the poor, that is, total $D = 5$. Equalising risks involves each group moving to locations where $C = 25$. Each then faces damage of $D = 2.5$ so that total damage is unchanged at $D = 5$. Now assume the dose-response function is non-linear and convex. Figure 2.1 shows that D for the rich is 1.2 and D for the poor is 8.0, making total damage 9.2. If risks are now equalised at $C = 25$, each group faces damage of 3.5, giving a total damage of 7. Aggregate damage is therefore reduced by equalising risks if dose-response functions are non-linear. This is the efficiency argument for equalising the distributive incidence of environmental hazards.

The purpose of this chapter is to provide a general conceptual framework for the analysis of the socio-economic distribution of environmental bads and goods. A 'bad' is the opposite of a 'good', so that pollution would

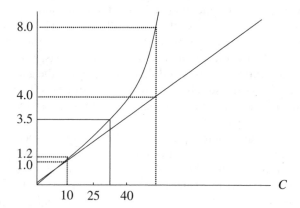

Figure 2.1   Efficiency and dose-response functions

be regarded as a bad, and pollution reduction as a good. This framework requires not only the setting-up of hypotheses about the existing distribution of environmental quality, but also a model to explain why that distribution comes about. The explanatory model is essential since the focus on regressivity (or otherwise) alone can be misleading if there are offsetting factors that compensate for the inequality of risks, or if inequality is freely chosen. Using this framework we first analyse the available empirical literature to see what evidence can be adduced for the hypothesis that the existing distribution of environmental bads is regressive – the 'environmental injustice hypothesis'. Second, we look at the evidence on the distribution of benefits from environmental policies. In this case there are no a priori expectations about the distribution of benefits: they may be progressive or regressive. Third, we investigate the relevance of accounting for the distribution of cost burdens along with the distribution of benefits of policies – the issue is whether it is the gross or net benefit (benefit minus cost) incidence that matters for policy. Fourth, we look at the issue of distribution from another perspective, namely whether the demand for environmental quality is 'income elastic' or not. If it is income elastic, the suggestion would be that improvements in environmental quality will tend to be biased towards higher-income groups since they demand more of it. Meeting varying demands for environmental quality is, of course, a sign of an efficient policy. But an equity issue may still arise if those demands are affected by the prevailing distribution of income. The argument may then be about whether the prevailing distribution of income is itself fair, or, if judged fair, whether there are some overriding moral principles that require an equal distribution of environmental quality: that is, income distribution could be fair but environmental quality distribution unfair. Finally, policy issues are addressed with the aim of seeing how far pursuit of equality of environmental endowments is consistent with efficient environmental and economic goals.

2. ENVIRONMENTAL JUSTICE AND ENVIRONMENTAL POLICY

The notion of environmental justice (EJ) is not straightforward. Roberts (2000) follows the Environmental Protection Agency (US EPA, 1998) in defining EJ as:

> [the] fair and equitable treatment of all people, regardless of race, ethnicity, income, national origin, or educational level in the development and implementation of environmental laws, regulations and policies. (Roberts, 2000, p. 537)

This definition tends to focus on the 'equal' impact of policy, whereas much of the EJ movement is concerned with not just this aspect of policy, but with the correction of any existing inequality of risks between income and racial groups. The only OECD country in which concern for environmental justice is mandatory is the USA. Other countries, however, provide guidelines on assessing the distributional impacts of policy measures and some of these guidelines have strong official backing.

2.1 The USA

Bowen (2002) traces the political history of the EJ movement in the USA, and notes that several empirical studies had a major influence on succeeding legislation – notably those by Bullard (1983), US GAO (1983) and the United Church of Christ (UCC, 1987).[4] Race as well as income was a major concern in these studies, the argument being that ethnic minorities are also unfairly exposed to environmental risks, in each case landfill sites with hazardous wastes. A further significant impetus to legislation were the '*NLJ* articles' (Lavelle and Coyle, 1992), a set of articles in the *National Law Journal* that charged the US EPA with discrimination against minorities and low-income areas when prosecuting violations of environmental law. It was alleged that lower penalties were applied to these areas, suggesting that EPA provided less environmental protection to them than to richer, white areas.[5]

In 1990, the US EPA established an internal working group to study the links between minority and low-income populations and environmental hazards. In 1992 the EPA established an Office of Environmental Equity to investigate EJ concerns and in the same year published a major report on the issue (US EPA, 1992). Formal EPA guidance was issued in 1998 (US EPA, 1998). In 1994 President Clinton enacted Executive Order 12898 which requires federal agencies formally to address issues of environmental hazards in low-income and minority communities. EO 12898 requires federal agencies to develop environmental justice strategies. Programmes, policies, planning and public participation procedures should be revised to:

> promote enforcement of all health and environmental statutes in areas with minority populations and low-income populations; ensure greater public participation; improve research and data collection relating to the health and environment of minority populations and low-income populations; and identify differential patterns of consumption of natural resources among minority populations and low-income populations. (EO 12898)

2.2 Other OECD

In the United Kingdom the Treasury has formalised central government advice on the treatment of different income groups in policy appraisal (HM Treasury, 2003). Any policy option must be analysed to determine whether impacts differ by socio-economic groupings. Depending on the judged significance of the distributional incidence, action may be required to modify the policy in question. Where formal analysis is called for, 'distributional weights' may be employed (for the theory and empirical illustrations see Sections 8.1 and 8.2 of this chapter). Such weights raise the social value of any unit monetary gain to low-income groups relative to other, richer groups. Such distributional weights can then be incorporated into a cost–benefit appraisal of the policy, this form of appraisal being that generally recommended for government policy. Annex 6 of the Treasury guidance provides more detail on the size of the weights to be adopted. Thus, those in the lowest quintile of relevant income would have their gains (or losses) multiplied by a factor of 1.8 relative to those on average income (these multiples hold for the value of the 'elasticity of marginal utility of income' of unity – see Sections 8.1 and 8.2 below). Those in the highest quintile would have their gains/losses multiplied by a factor of 0.4. The guidance further notes that, where the correction of social inequality is an explicit aim of policy, then the resulting weighted impacts can be further weighted to reflect the judgement that an extra unit of well-being to a low-income group is more valuable than it would be to a higher-income group.

In terms of policy, a number of OECD countries seek to make allowance for the incidence of environmental policy costs on low-income households. These allowances tend to reflect the judgement, sometimes backed by statistical evidence, that lower-income households have higher expenditures, proportionate to their incomes, for environmental services. Put another way round, some environmental expenditures constitute a higher proportion of low-income households' income compared to high-income households. Procedures used include establishing a 'consumption floor' below which no tax is levied, and having rising tariffs for consumption of the goods in question, effectively producing a cross-subsidy from richer to poorer groups. Examples of such measures are the Climate Change Levy in the UK which is not applied to households at all, and a lower rate of VAT on household energy bills than on other items subject to VAT, in Germany, where a 50 per cent rebate is provided on electricity taxes for storage heaters which tend to be used by low-income households; and the Netherlands, where there are exemptions for some low-income households from waste collection and sewerage charges (de Kam, 2002). Other examples are given in OECD (2001) and in de Kam (2002).

3.   THE CONCEPTUAL FRAMEWORK

3.1   The EJ Hypotheses

The hypotheses to be tested are (a) that the existing distribution of environmental 'bads' is regressive across income groups,[6] and (b) that environmental policy is distributionally biased against low-income groups. Hypothesis (a) probably more fairly describes the concerns of the EJ movement, but some of the literature is also concerned with hypothesis (b). As far as the first hypothesis is concerned, the expectation is that environmental risk, ER (which is to be defined shortly), declines with real per capita income (Y/N), as shown in the stylised function in Figure 2.2. Figure 2.2 is consistent with the 'environmental Kuznets curve' (EKC) referred to earlier (see note 1) and which is typically estimated across different nations. Figure 2.3 shows the full EKC that is usually postulated in the cross-country literature, and serves to highlight an immediate methodological issue. In Figure 2.3, the level of environmental risk ER^* is seen to be consistent with two different income levels $Y1/N$ and $Y2/N$. Thus, 'rich' and 'poor' could be exposed to the same level of risk, implying that there is no problem of environmental equity. However, as the $Y1$ groups improve their incomes so ER for them rises, while for the $Y2$ group it declines. Observation of equal risk exposure is not therefore sufficient to establish that there is no environmental inequity. The rate at which risk changes with respect to income change also matters. Very often, this two-part test is not carried out in the empirical literature.

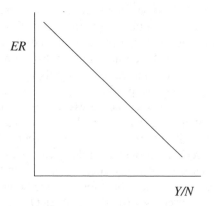

Figure 2.2   Income and environmental quality (linear relationship)

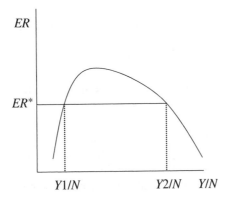

Figure 2.3   Income and environmental quality (non-linear relationship)

3.2   The Risk Unit of Account

The second methodological problem relates to the measure of environmental risk, *ER*. A distinction can be made between 'physical' risk measures and 'perceived' or 'preference-based' measures of risk. Physical risk measures tend to relate to some indicator of pollution or hazard such as ambient pollution concentrations or proximity to a landfill site. Preference-based indicators add a further 'layer' to the physical indicators by eliciting some measure of preference for or against the physical risk. It is easy to see that the two generic indicators could differ substantially. Attitudes to risk are known to vary substantially and if they varied directly with income it is possible that any one socio-economic group might not be overly concerned about exposure to risks. Moreover, if more exposed groups felt they were compensated in some way, for example, via lower property prices or closer proximity to employment opportunities, this may affect their preferences over risk.[7]

As far as the physical indicators of risk are concerned, the literature works with several different concepts:

(a)   Emissions
(b)   Net emissions
(c)   Ambient concentrations
(d)   Exposure
(e)   Health risk.

The differences between these indicators are important and it is far from clear that the literature using emissions can be relied upon in terms of scientific integrity. The following discussion attempts to explain why.

Consider two areas R and P, with the R area occupied by high-income (rich) groups and the P area occupied by the low-income (poor) group. Then, on the emissions measure of EJ, an environmental injustice occurs if $M_P > M_R$, where M is emissions, for example, tonnes of particulate matter. One hypothesis to explain this difference in emissions is that polluting industries locate in P rather than R areas in order to benefit from (a) lower wages and/or (b) lower political resistance to plant location. Both (a) and (b) are consistent with the polluting industries attempting to minimise costs. A hypothesis to explain the opposite result, that is, $M_P < M_R$ would be that emissions are functionally related to income, a situation consistent with solid waste generation for example.

The net emissions and ambient concentration, A, measures of EJ can be considered together. Net emissions in any area are equal to actual emissions minus any 'exports' of emissions to other areas, plus any imports from other areas. The net emissions concept corresponds more closely to an indicator of damage or risk to health or ecosystems. For any emission source, it is necessary to have a dispersion model to establish what part of emissions affects a given population. Obviously, net emissions are a better indicator than emissions since any region could emit significant pollutants but not impose local risks if those emissions are exported. Similarly, an area importing pollution could face high risks even though it produces a low level of emissions. Ambient concentration is a better measure still, since it will tend to be related to damage.

Exposure represents a further refinement on the concentrations measure. Exposure differs from concentrations in allowing for the behaviour of the population at risk. For example, if low-income groups work in outdoor occupations and high-income groups work in indoor occupations, lower-income groups will be more exposed to outdoor pollution even though ambient concentrations may be the same for both groups.[8] Similarly, the rich may be able to afford abatement measures such as double-glazing of windows to reduce exposure to noise. Access to medical advice and help may also vary with income groupings.

The final measure is total risk. This differs from exposure in allowing for personal characteristics of those exposed to risk, for example, nutritional status, predisposition to ill-health, income-related behaviour such as smoking and so on. By and large, it can be hypothesised that the poor will, other things being equal, be more at risk than the rich.

Overall, the measurement of the state of the environmental risk matters for the EJ hypotheses. Ideally, a measure such as exposure should be used, but ambient concentrations are likely to be the closest measure obtainable. What is clear is that an indicator such as emissions could be seriously biased. Box 2.1 summarises the various measures of environmental risk.

BOX 2.1   SUMMARY ENVIRONMENTAL
INDICATORS FOR USE IN
DISTRIBUTIONAL INCIDENCE STUDIES

Emissions

For any given area occupied by a given income class, compute the emissions of various pollutants. Usually this applies to air pollutants but also has meaning for solid waste (waste generation rather than emissions). Emissions are a limited indicator due to (a) failure to account for imports and exports of emissions, (b) exposure, (c) personal characteristics that may magnify or reduce risk of harm.

Concentrations

Net emissions (emissions − exports + imports) is an improvement on emissions, but concentrations, for example, parts per million (ppm) or ug/m^3, offer a better indicator still. Estimating concentrations requires direct measurement of ambient quality or an estimate of emissions combined with a dispersion model.

Exposure

Exposure to ambient concentrations allows for differences in activities among individuals, for example, timing of work, location of work, and hence is a better indicator of risk than concentrations. However, exposure data are often limited in their availability.

Risk

Personal risk is a function of exposure plus personal characteristics such as predisposition to environmental insults (for example, health state), plus other factors such as nutrition.

3.3   The Spatial Unit of Account

A significant part of the EJ literature concerns itself with the right way to measure the geographical unit of account. It has been found that results of empirical studies are sensitive to the geographical scale of the study, ranging from small areas to large ones, and to the spatial resolution of the information, for example, address codes, census tracts. In the US studies there is much debate about the use of SMAs (Standard Metropolitan

Areas), census tracts, and zip code areas, these ranging from the largest to the smallest area. The smaller the area the less likely it is that the pollution variable will have meaning, while the larger the area the more are localised inequities likely to be overlooked.

As noted above, it is not always valid to equate emissions with exposure to risk, so that procedures to integrate the various dimensions of the environmental hazard with the various dimensions of the population at risk can be important. The use of geographical information systems (GIS) is fairly recent but GIS has been applied to environmental equity issues – see, for example, Chakraborty (2001). In so far as GIS permits a better analysis of the data, more recent investigations using GIS are likely to be more reliable than the earlier studies which did not utilise the technique. As a general proposition, there are problems of assessing the validity of the various studies. One or two survey articles have made efforts to rank studies according to their scientific reliability, and choice of spatial unit figures prominently among the criticisms of various studies (for example, Bowen, 2002). Accordingly, it is important not to treat the empirical literature as if each contribution has equal scientific status.

3.4 'Rights'-based Distribution versus Preference-based Distribution

The physical indicator-based notion of EJ tends to involve a moral judgement to the effect that a regressive distribution of environmental quality is unfair. The moral benchmark for this judgement is that an equal distribution of environmental quality is just, and, in turn, the foundation for this judgement is that all individuals have an equal 'right' to environmental quality. In some of the EJ literature this is further interpreted as requiring that all individuals should be exposed to 'zero' environmental risk, an empirical impossibility.[9] The weaker, and more realistic, form of the moral judgement is that (a) different income groups should be exposed to the same or similar non-zero level of risk, and (b) the risks should in some sense be 'acceptable'. All income classes might be exposed to the same level of risk but if that risk is unacceptable, then equity is breached. Similarly, risks to different groups might be different but both risk levels might nonetheless be deemed acceptable. The notion of acceptability is not straightforward. What it usually means is that the environment should meet some standard of cleanliness set by law or public demand. This needs to be distinguished from a notion of acceptability whereby differential risks are significant, but the lower income group feels compensated by some other characteristic of their location (for example, employment).

Rights-based activists would tend to argue that, while such 'goals' may well be unrealistic, policy should nonetheless be aimed at moving towards them. However, there are several issues arising from the rights-based approach and these have all been raised in the EJ literature.

First, the distribution of any population is such that environmental quality per unit area will never be the same. People choose to locate where they do for many different reasons, so that adjusting environmental quality to be equal across all areas is very likely to be infeasible. Nonetheless, some environmental quality standards (for example, air quality) are often set so that minimum quality levels are achieved, that is, there is some notion of a threshold below which quality standards are deemed to be unacceptable.

Second, even if concentrations are equalised across areas, measures of exposure or total risk would probably not be equalised since these depend on human behaviour and prior characteristics.

Third, the rights-based approach tends to ignore costs. Equalising risks may well involve higher aggregate costs than if risks are differentiated. Equalising marginal costs of risk reduction would produce a minimum aggregate cost solution, but this would be consistent with risks varying location by location. While the rights-based approach would argue that risks and cost cannot be traded against each other, it remains the case that higher costs involve the sacrifice of other benefits that could be secured with the excess cost of risk equalisation. Those other benefits might also be the subject of an argument about 'rights', for example, rights to health care or education. Equity in environmental risks could be at the expense of forgone rights across the population to non-environmental benefits.

Fourth, rights-based approaches assume *either* that individuals exposed to risk share the same notion of environmental justice, *or* that individuals' preferences should be overridden because individuals are unlikely to be well informed about the nature of risks. Both assumptions can be tested through survey techniques which elicit individuals' attitudes to the environment and to environmental risks.[10] As long as individuals' preferences do not coincide with the notion of equal risk, then the rights-based approach will have policy goals that are quite separate from those emerging from a preference-based approach.

Fifth, if preferences are deemed to be relevant, then one procedure for measuring them is to elicit willingness to pay. But since willingness to pay is likely to vary directly with income, high-income groups will tend to have a higher willingness to pay than low-income groups for environmental risk reduction. Rights-based advocates will therefore tend to dismiss the relevance of willingness to pay measures of risk preference. Their position on non-monetised preferences may vary from rejection of any preference-based approach through to seeking non-monetised expressions of preference.

Finally, contained within the willingness to pay approach is the idea that expressions of willingness to pay could well take account of associated compensation for tolerating higher risks, for example, via lower property prices, employment opportunities and so on. This is the issue of self-selecting behaviour, that is, what is observed may be a set of individuals who have chosen to locate in low quality areas because they have traded off the associated costs with other benefits (Hite, 2000). This issue is complicated by the sequence of events that generate an environmental risk. For example, poor people living in an area that is developed for an airport may find themselves to be losers if property prices fall due to airport noise, pollution and congestion. But they could secure windfall financial gains if the airport attracts employment and the demand for housing rises. Those moving into the area after the airport is built could be compensated for any environmental problem through house prices, employment opportunities and so on. Higher-income groups might move out of the affected area, suffering a loss if property prices are depressed by the airport and experiencing a windfall gain if property prices rise.[11] Thus what matters is the net benefit or cost rather than just the cost of any risk. Adoption of a monetised preference approach to environmental equity can therefore quickly produce wholly ambiguous results, with a final judgement resting on detailed analysis of the welfare gains and losses for each group of individuals affected by the risk-creating activity.

At the heart of the different approaches to EJ is the familiar debate over economic efficiency versus equity. As will be shown shortly, iniquitous outcomes may well be economically efficient. The EJ movement selects equity as the relevant goal, usually completely disregarding efficiency.[12] The preference-based approach tends to assume efficiency is a 'higher' goal, the usual argument being that the creation of maximum social surpluses permits some of that surplus to be used to correct inequity. Somewhat surprisingly, little appears to be known about how individuals 'trade off' equity and efficiency. Atkinson et al. (2000) have shown how survey-based approaches to trade-offs between apparently competing principles of financial burden-sharing for environmental programmes can produce robust indicators of individual preferences. It remains to be seen how people trade notions of equity against changes in total net benefits from such programmes. It should also be noted that the rights-based approach is consistent with inequity being the result of economic forces that produce an efficient but inequitable outcome, and it is also consistent with inequity being a deliberate outcome of some exploitative process, including racism. The preference-based approach tends to assume away notions of exploitation of the poor or minority populations.

4.   WHY DOES ENVIRONMENTAL INEQUITY ARISE?[13]

This section describes alternative (although sometimes overlapping) explanations for the rise of environmental inequity.

4.1   Income Inequality and Tiebout Local Public Goods

The simple fact of income inequality is sufficient to produce differential environmental conditions faced by 'rich' and 'poor', provided environmental quality varies with spatial location. Since willingness to pay for environmental quality is itself a function of income,[14] then, regardless of the cost of supplying that quality, the rich will receive a higher level of quality than the poor. Figure 2.4 illustrates this simple proposition.

Implicit in this explanation is that individuals move location to equilibrate their demand for environmental quality with its cost of supply. The reason for this assumption is that environmental quality tends to have public good characteristics,[15] so that what is supplied to one group is automatically supplied to the other group within the jurisdiction of the public good. However, environmental quality can vary from location to location, so that, within any location space, environmental quality is a local public good, but environmental quality is not a pure public good across all locations. The notion that individuals with varying demands for local

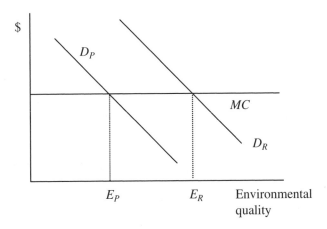

Note: D = demand; R = rich; P = poor; E = environmental quality; MC = marginal cost of supply.

Figure 2.4   Environmental quality as a local public good

environmental quality will spatially allocate themselves in this way is due to Tiebout (1956). Various EJ models stress either the 'push' factors, that is, for the rich, the presence of risk-creating activities as deterrents to residence, or the 'pull' factors, that is, the relative attractiveness of areas without risk-creating activities. Similar 'pull' factors will operate for the poor, since high risk areas may be areas with greater employment opportunities (Liu, 2001), tax revenue needs or lower priced property (Hite, 2000). In this respect, the models are not different to the basic Tiebout model above. However, non-economic models based on these push–pull factors tend to emphasise the feedback effects as well. As low-income groups migrate to high risk areas in search of the associated benefits, so high-income groups are further deterred from staying since they have preferences for locating in more homogeneous high-income areas (Been, 1994).

In what sense does an environmental equity problem arise with the Tiebout model? On the rights-based approach, rich and poor would have an equal entitlement to an acceptable level of environmental quality, and E_P in Figure 2.4 might be outside the range of 'acceptability'. On the preference-based approach, the difference between E_P and E_R would have a justification in the fact that both rich and poor have freely chosen their equilibrium, within the constraints set by their incomes. Indeed, it is possible that environmental quality differences are capitalised in some other good, such as property – see, for example, Brainard et al. (2003). If so, the poor would, other things being equal, face lower property prices than the rich, exactly compensating them for the lower environmental quality. Note also that, had the two groups the same income and the same tastes, then their demand curves for environmental quality would be coincident, and each would demand the same level of environmental quality. What some rights-based analysts are drawing attention to, therefore, is not so much the injustice of differing environmental quality levels, but the apparent injustice of different income levels: that is, it is the distribution of income they are objecting to. The contrasting outcomes of the two approaches amply illustrate the difficulty in defining what 'environmental justice' means. On the rights-based approach, an injustice remains. On the preference-based approach, there is no environmental injustice. The poor have the amount of the good they desire, as have the rich. As Been (1994) puts it: 'As long as the market allows the existing distribution of wealth to allocate goods and services, it would be surprising indeed if over the long run, LULU [locally undesirable land uses] did not impose a disproportionate burden upon the poor' (p. 1383).

Evidence that local public good disamenities are compensated for by differences in wages and house prices is provided in Blomquist et al. (1988). This study estimates a 'quality of life index' for urban areas of the USA and concludes that: 'compensation for location-specific, non-traded amenities takes place in both the labor and housing market and that the amount is substantial' (p. 105).

4.2 Income Inequality and Pure Public Goods

The Tiebout hypothesis cannot hold if the public good is 'global', that is, if the publicness extends across all feasible locations. Then, movement would not secure any change in environmental quality. Baumol (1972, 1974) and Baumol and Oates (1988) produce a theory of why a *form* of environmental injustice (as it would now be called) would come about in the case where environmental quality is a pure public good. Their approach is illustrated in Figure 2.5. Rich (R) and poor (P) have budget lines RR' and PP' respectively. These are drawn parallel to indicate that R and P face the *same price* of the public good E, environmental quality. Given their respective indifference curves, as shown, P would demand E_P of environmental quality, and R would demand E_R. Their respective equilibria are shown as C and A. Note that the similarity of the shapes of the indifference curves assumes that preferences are similar across the two income groups. However, since environmental quality in this case is a pure public good, whatever is supplied is supplied to both groups. What is supplied is therefore some compromise achieved by the political system. As shown in Figure 2.5, the quantity supplied, E, is roughly the average of the two demands, but, clearly, it could be closer to E_R or to E_P, depending on the

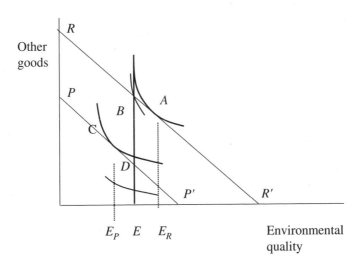

Figure 2.5   The Baumol–Oates model

relative political power of the two groups. But if E is supplied, then both rich and poor move to lower indifference curves than if each could have had the quantity they demanded (the Tiebout case). Their respective positions are given by D and B. The poor are now 'oversupplied' with environmental quality ($D > C$) and the rich are 'undersupplied' ($B < A$).

In what sense does the Baumol–Oates solution produce environmental inequity? In terms of the equity notions so far introduced, it does *not* produce environmental inequity. This is because both rich and poor receive the *same* level of environmental quality, E. The concept of equity here rests on the view that it is more unfair to make the poor pay for something they do not want (E_pE of environmental quality) than to fail to supply what the rich want (by the margin EE_R).[16] Moreover, this inequity is larger the closer E is to E_R, a result that might be expected if the rich are politically more powerful than the poor. In terms of Figure 2.5, P's willingness to pay for the 'excess' amount of the public good they receive is lower than the price they are being charged for it, while R's willingness to pay for the amount they fail to secure is greater than the ruling price. Expressed as a proportion of income, therefore, the poor are likely to have a larger welfare 'deficit' than the rich.

Once again, the analysis shows how difficult it is to define environmental equity: even if the rich and poor have access to the same level of environmental quality, a form of inequity can arise in so far as there are unmet preferences for the rich and 'forced' oversupply to the poor. Environmental benefits will tend to be distributed in a 'pro-rich' fashion.

The Baumol–Oates result is the outcome of market forces and the political system. Market forces alone, reflecting the prevailing distribution of income, can produce the result. But it is more likely that the unbalanced exercise of political power will bias the result further against the poor. To this end, the Baumol–Oates model combines market and political forces, the latter reflecting a degree of 'exploitation' of the poor by the rich.

Certain assumptions underlie the Baumol–Oates result. First, the preferences of R and P for the environment are assumed to be similarly structured. If the poor had strong preferences for the environment relative to those of the rich, then it is easy to generate the result that the poor get the right amount of environmental quality and the rich too much.[17] A further problem is that the analysis assumes rich and poor face the same price for the public good. But methods of financing the good may have a progressive structure, for example, income tax, whereby the rich face higher average taxes than the poor. Strictly, what matters is the marginal rate of taxation and this too could differ, being higher for the rich. If so, the budget lines in Figure 2.5 are no longer parallel, and it is possible to secure the opposite result to that shown in Figure 2.5.[18] Overall, however, the Baumol–Oates model provides an explanation for inequity in the specific sense of under and oversupply of the public good.

4.3 The Spatial Shifting of Externalities: Political Power and Inequity

It is widely argued that the Coase theorem (Coase, 1960) can be adapted to suggest that any risk-creating activity, say a factory or waste disposal site, will be located where environmental externalities are minimised (for example, Hamilton, 1993). The intuition is that the risky activity will be located in low-income areas because the willingness to pay to avoid the facility will be lower than in a high-income area. Hence firms with a choice of locations will choose that site where, if compensation had to be paid, the sums paid out would be the lowest. In fact, compensation pay-outs would be only one of a class of costs to the firm that would be minimised by siting in low-income areas. The model can be developed further to include political activity, the presumption being that low-income groups will not organise collectively in as efficient a way to oppose the risk activity, whereas high-income groups will. Thus, even without the notion of willingness to pay, a model of political collective action is sufficient to generate an efficient outcome – the externality will be minimised (Becker, 1983). These outcomes are illustrated in Figure 2.6. Figure 2.6 shows environmental damage along the horizontal axis and money on the vertical axis. The downward sloping line is the marginal profit curve ($M\Pi$) of the polluting activity, such that the firm will maximise profits when $M\Pi = 0$. The upward sloping curves are the marginal environmental damage (MD) curves in rich and

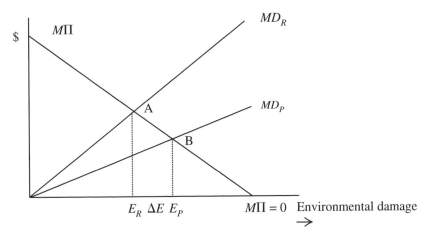

Figure 2.6   Coaseian bargains and environmental equity

poor locations, MD_R lying above MD_P due to income differences. Beginning with the assumption that the polluter has the property rights, the Coase theorem tells us that the two parties (rich or poor, and the firm) will bargain to achieve an optimal amount of externality. If there is only one possible location, this optimum is either A or B in Figure 2.6.[19]

Now consider the case where the firm can locate at either R or P and faces opposition from both communities. Because the firm owns the property rights, the sufferers must pay the firm not to pollute. Suppose the level of pollution is given by the fixed scale of economic activity which in turn is associated with pollution of ΔE.[20] Since the area under MD_R across the range ΔE is substantially higher than the area under MD_P, it follows that the rich can pay more to the polluter not to locate in their region. The polluting activity is located in P, the reduction in externality is given by the area under MD_P, and, importantly, the residual externality – the amount left over after the bargaining process – is given by area $x + y$. The externality is minimised but an environmental equity problem arises because firms' siting decisions will be systematically biased towards locating in poor areas. The poor will therefore be exposed to more risks than the rich.

Now suppose that the property rights rest with the sufferers. The starting point is now O, the origin. The polluter now has to pay the sufferers to secure any positive level of economic activity. At O he can compensate sufferers by more than their marginal damage and by less than his marginal profits. This process will continue until E_p is reached. But, clearly, at E_p the firm is involved in over-compensation to R, since it has gone beyond point A where $M\Pi = MD_R$. The firm pays out less compensation and has a higher total post-compensation profit level if it locates in P. Thus, in keeping with the Coase theorem, the firm locates in P regardless of the initial allocation of property rights. Once again, there is an environmental equity problem.

The previous argument effectively assumes that the firm operates with the same scale of activity regardless of whether it locates in P or R. But if a bargaining process does take place, then the natural equilibrium for that process is A if the location considered is R and B if it is P. In other words, the scale of activity by the polluter is also likely to vary between the two locations. Inspection of Figure 2.6 shows that, from an environmental point of view, locating in P is worse, since less reduction in environmental damage occurs at B than at A. From an efficiency point of view, however, locating at B remains an optimal solution since profits *minus* damage are maximised at B. The environmental equity problem remains.

Hamilton (1993, 1995) notes an important modification to the Coase–Becker argument above. This suggests that the regressive nature of risk-generating activity will be further aggravated by the lower likelihood of collective action by the poor. But, in contrast to the Coase–Becker model, this further reinforcement of the bias in siting decisions may be inconsistent with the result that the bias is optimal from an efficiency point of view. Essentially, the locations with the least political opposition may not be the locations with lowest willingness to pay to avoid the externality if willingness to pay is not truly 'revealed' in political activity. Whereas the Coase–Becker result assumes that both R and P organise themselves efficiently, Hamilton focuses on the probable differences in the ability of individuals to organise themselves. Even if willingness to pay to avoid the offending activity was the same in R and P, these differences in ability will show up as lower *expressed* political opposition.[21] A 'wedge' is driven between the (welfare) losses in P and the 'voice' expressing that welfare loss. Hamilton (1993) tests his model by observing that the siting of hazardous waste facilities in the USA between 1987 and 1992 is correlated with low voter turnout in elections. This result may not be consistent with the Coase–Becker outcome that overall social costs are minimised (or net benefits maximised, as in Figure 2.6). This is because the siting decision depends on expected externality costs multiplied by the probability that residents will effectively oppose the siting decision. Social costs could be higher in poor districts but, since the probability of translating those welfare losses into litigation, lobbying and so on is small, the effective cost to the firm is less. Hamilton (1999) shows that TRI (Toxic Release Inventory) plants with the highest toxic releases reduced their emissions more. As voter turn-out increased, so emissions declined. Other studies, for example, Arora and Cason (1999), also find that pollution is inversely correlated with proxies for political action: the stronger the voter turn-out or the proxy for voter turn-out, the less the emission level. In the USA this effect tends to work via the 'right to know' legislation concerning toxic releases.

It is possible to construct various models that produce similar results to the Coase–Becker outcome and the Hamilton outcome. For example, the rich are more likely to be able to move location than the poor. The rich are likely to be more mobile occupationally. Even if they fail to prevent a polluting activity being located in their area, they are more likely to be able to move away from the area once the siting has occurred. If so, the differences in mobility will act just like the differences in political activity – the poor will reside in more polluted areas than the rich.

A similar result emerges from models of behaviour when different income groups face a given environmental situation. For example, suppose the *existing* level of environmental quality is the same in a rich and poor area. Then the hypothesis is that the rich will engage in clean-up activities more than will the poor. So long as rich and poor occupy different locations, then an environmental inequity arises because the poor will then be exposed to more risk due to their inaction, while the rich will have cleaner environments.[22] However, if rich and poor occupy an area in which clean-up activities have public good characteristics, then the poor will benefit as free-riders from the activities of the rich. Such outcomes are consistent with everyone behaving in a self-interested manner, but there is some evidence to suggest that richer people may also behave more altruistically in this context, in line with a prediction of Olson (1965) – see, for example, Cardenas et al. (2002).

4.4 Environmental Discrimination

Differences in political power also occupy a central role in most political explanations of environmental inequity. These models tend to be qualitative and based on case studies of individual siting decisions and the various reactions to them by different groups of stakeholders. Political power is unevenly distributed across stakeholders, with minorities, low-income and immigrant communities having the least power. Inequity is then the outcome of a struggle for resources, where resources include clean environments, recreational facilities and the work environment (Pellow et al. 2001). Such struggles result from competing self-interests but also from racism and discriminatory attitudes among individuals and institutions. Testing hypotheses about discrimination is obviously complex and controversial. Much of the evidence in favour of the discrimination hypothesis is based on the *outcomes* of the relative burdens of environmental and other damages, that is, the fact of inequity is seen as evidence of discrimination. But the obvious problem is one of demonstrating discriminatory *intent*, something that is not easy to do in any quantitative manner. This perhaps explains the heavy reliance placed by environmental justice advocates on narrative case studies.

4.5 'Ecological' Explanations for Inequity

Ecological models tend to stress the dynamics of land use change and social grouping that takes place independently of any siting of risk-creating activities. Models are akin to invasion-succession sequences in standard ecology: incoming populations gradually expand and displace previous populations. If high-income groups believe that low-income groups lower property values and the social value of the community generally, then the higher mobility of high-income groups will lead them to move out of a given area. If low-income or ethnic minorities come into the area, the process of 'ghettoisation' might expand into surrounding areas. The presence of a risk-generating activity might then be accidental: what is observed is a post-siting decline in the average income level which then misleadingly appears to be associated with the activity (Liu, 2001). Put another way, the statistical association between low-income areas and higher risk activity, if it exists, tends to reflect baseline population dynamics rather than a causal process. Again, such models are not readily tested for in a quantitative fashion and resort is usually made to historical case studies to illustrate the sequence of events.

4.6 Conclusions on Explanatory Models of Environmental Inequity

While it is a simplification, the following proposition helps to fix ideas about the competing explanations for environmental inequity. Where the environmental good in question is a pure public good, the spatial nature of which traverses all relevant areas, there is no real possibility that environmental inequity, as defined by the EJ literature, will exist. Essentially, all income groups will be exposed to the same level of risk, ignoring any personal characteristics that make one group more disposed to the risk than other groups. That level of risk may be one associated with the economically optimal provision of the public good or the 'political' optimum brought about by competing demands for the good. However, as the Baumol–Oates public good model shows, there is a form of inequity in so far as any compromise supply of the good results in over-provision to the poor and under-provision to the rich. It is important to note, however, that the Baumol–Oates notion of inequity is not that adopted by the EJ literature.

In practice, few environmental goods are pure public goods. A great many of them take on the features of local public goods, so that the consumption of those goods varies by location. Tiebout-type models emphasise the fact that differences in income, and hence in willingness to pay, will set up migratory processes that will lead low-income groups to consume a lower quality environment than the high-income groups. Those non-economic models that stress push and pull factors tend to fit into this model as well, although they are arguably more elaborate in that they stress the cumulative effects of changing population characteristics on the migration process.

Political explanations for any low-income–high risk association can also be fitted into the general Coase–Becker framework which stresses the role played by anticipated costs to a firm locating in a given area. Such costs – for example, litigation, transactions costs – are likely to be higher in high-income areas where the ability to organise and lobby against a siting decision is higher. As shown, independently of the allocation of property rights, the Coaseian process produces outcomes which will tend to site the offending facility in a low-income area. The Coase–Becker model is a 'positive' explanation of why this outcome occurs, but it also has normative content in suggesting that the result is, in any event, optimal from an economic efficiency standpoint. As noted earlier, what is efficient may not be equitable, and there is no 'meta principle' to determine whether equity is more or less important than efficiency. Understandably, therefore, the EJ literature is sharply divided on the importance of efficiency. Hamilton's (1993) work does sound a caution about Coaseian outcomes being efficient if true willingness to pay by low-income groups diverges from expressed political opposition.

What might be called the 'market dynamics' approach to equity therefore acknowledges that outcomes may be inequitable but that the inequity is a direct result of inequality of incomes. If the prevailing distribution of income is itself optimal, then, as the quotation from Been (1994) suggests, there will be unequal exposure to risk. What much of the EJ literature is therefore contesting is the optimality of the prevailing income distribution. Unequal risks are simply the outcome of unequal incomes.

Finally, care has to be taken to distinguish positive and normative issues. Much of the literature tries to explain why inequity arises, and this is an exercise in positive analysis. However, these analyses are nonetheless driven by the implicit or explicit judgement that unequal exposure to risks is unfair, and that is a normative judgement.

5.   THE EMPIRICAL EVIDENCE ON ENVIRONMENTAL INEQUITY: PHYSICAL MEASURES

The extensive literature on physical measures of environmental inequity is primarily American. Caution therefore needs to be exercised in supposing that, even if the American literature has a consensus finding, the finding can be generalised to other OECD countries.

The various studies use different approaches, resulting in different indicators of inequity. Studies focusing on landfill/hazardous waste sites tend to take a socio-economic indicator, say income per head or per household and compare it to 'with' and 'without' site locations. If, for example, locations with sites are systematically associated with lower incomes than locations without sites, then this would be regarded as evidence of environmental inequity. The degree of risk is typically not measured, that is, the risk takes a [0, 1] measure: either there is a site or there is not. Results may then be formulated as 'poorer people are X times more likely to be located near to a risky site than are rich people', where 'poor' and 'rich' themselves need to be defined. Air quality studies, on the other hand, have continuous data that can be compared to socio-economic information. Results are presented in various forms. Areas may be classified as 'low' air quality and 'high' air quality based on the continuous data, reducing the location characteristic to a [0, 1] form again. More elaborate use of continuous data often involves regressions of the form:

$$Poll = aA + bB + \ldots + rR + yY$$

where *Poll* is pollution, *a..y* are coefficients, *A*, *B* are explanatory factors other than race (*R*) and income (*Y*). If *y* is negative and statistically significant, there would be evidence of income inequity. Many studies simply report correlations between pollution and income (race). A few studies report indicators such as 'poor persons per square kilometre' and correlate this with pollution. An indicator of the form 'pollution per unit income' appears not to be reported in any study, but a 'pollution elasticity' is reported by Kahn (1998) and Khanna (2001). Kahn finds an inverted 'U' curve (that is, an EKC – see Section 3.1) for vehicle emissions in California. As median household income increases so pollution at first increases and then decreases. Khanna finds the opposite result for the same data, that is, a 'U'-shaped curve linking pollution and income per head.

Section 4 suggested some plausible combinations of market and political forces that could give rise to environmental equity, where inequity is defined as the poor being exposed to greater environmental risks than the rich. This section reviews the empirical literature. In so doing, we make the assumption that, unless specific errors in the studies have been pointed out, all studies are equally valid. This is a strong but unavoidable assumption. Most of the empirical literature emanates from the USA where, as noted earlier, the environmental justice movement has a strong foothold in political discourse and in legislation. Limited information appears to exist for other countries.

5.1 Europe

Table 2.1 shows the evidence for Europe. While the evidence is very limited, the data for the UK suggest that the *existing* distribution of risks is biased towards the poor. For the spatially wider public goods, such as air pollution control, policy to reduce those risks would therefore be 'pro-poor'. For locally confined risks, for example, from waste sites, the outcome would depend on the specific targeting of policy towards the areas of risk. It should be noted however that several of the UK studies use *emissions* as the relevant pollution indicator, imparting an unknown degree of error to the results.

Table 2.1 Social incidence of environmental damages in Europe

Study	Pollutant or hazard	Finding
McCleod et al., 2000, England/Wales Uses GIS	SO_x, NO_x, PM_{10} *concentrations*	Pollution negatively associated with lower social class index, that is, inequity exists, but rich in SE England exposed to higher pollution than poor in other regions.
Pye et al., 2001, UK, Uses GIS	NO_2, PM_{10} *concentrations*	Weak positive correlation between pollution and social deprivation. Clean air policy simulations benefit the poor most.
Friends of the Earth, 2001, UK	Carcinogenic factory air *emissions*	Highest emissions occur in most socially deprived areas.
Walker et al., 2000, UK	Hazardous substances – accident risk	Risk correlated with ethnic minority population concentrations.
Stevenson et al., 1998, UK	Road traffic emissions	Respiratory illness correlated with emissions and low income.
Bateman et al., 2002, Birmingham, UK Brainard et al. 2002	Air pollution	Pollution correlated with ethnicity even when income controlled. Income relationship regressive.
Bateman et al. (Chapter 6, this volume)	Noise	Noise levels and socio-economic deprivation very weakly correlated. Very weak association between noise and ethnicity. Night-time noise correlated with deprivation.
Brainard et al., 2003, Birmingham, UK	Green space	Income relationship regressive.
Mitchell and Dorling, 2003, UK	Air pollution – nitrogen dioxide	Income relationship regressive.
Walker et al., 2003, UK	Flood risk, Integrated Pollution Control (IPC) sites, air quality	Tidal flood risks regressive; fluvial flood risks progressive; IPC sites regressive; air pollution regressive.
Kruize and Bouwman, 2003, Netherlands	Noise, air pollution, green space, safety risks, waste facilities	All risks regressively distributed other than aircraft noise.

5.2   North America

Tables 2.2 and 2.3a/2.3b look at the far more substantive North American evidence.[23] Table 2.2 deals with the early American studies and Table 2.3a with more recent studies. A review of early studies is provided in Cutter (1995) and of early and late studies in Bowen (2002). Hamilton (Chapter 7 in this volume) provides an extensive review that focuses on hazardous waste. The very early studies all related to air pollution, other than the Berry (1977) volume which covered many forms of pollutant. The general finding was that damage was higher the lower the income level, but with qualifications shown in Table 2.2. In the 1980s the focus shifted to hazardous waste sites, and in the 1990s (Table 2.3a) coverage included toxic releases, waste sites and air pollution, particular targets of the environmental justice movement. It is important to note that several of the early politically influential studies (for example, UCC, 1987; US GAO, 1983) have been severely criticised.[24]

Use of the Toxic Release Inventory is interesting because of the way different authors have treated the data. Some studies simply aggregate pollutants in the TRI regardless of their difference in toxicity (Perlin et al., 1995; Millimet and Slottje, 2002), and this could be inconsistent with what should be risk-based exposure indicators. Some authors seek to weight the individual releases by some measure of toxicity (Brooks and Sethi, 1997; Arora and Cason, 1999). The extent of bias from using unweighted data is not easy to gauge, although Millimet and Slottje (2002) argue that weighting provides little value-added since the chemicals probably do not vary much by toxicity. The TRI is also an emissions inventory rather than an exposure inventory, whether toxicity is allowed for or not, and it was noted earlier that this is a potential distortion of the exposure-impact relationship.

The Millimet–Slottje analysis requires discussion because it utilises an imaginative approach to policy implications. First, they find substantial inequity in the prevailing distribution of pollution. Second, they further decompose pollution into releases to land, water and air. For 1997 (1998 was an unusual year, see Table 2.3a) air emissions accounted for over half of the 'inequality' of social burdens, land for about 30 per cent and the remainder by water and underground releases. An interesting finding is that policy designed to reduce land and underground emissions is *inequality-reducing* at both county and state level, but that comparable policy on air emissions *increases inequality*. This finding contrasts with much of the EJ literature. Third, the analysis also estimates an 'environmental welfare function' in order to investigate the trade-off between pollution and inequality (pollution reductions being treated as increases in *income*).[25] The aim of this function is to explore the trade-offs in contexts where, as found for air pollution, pollution declines but inequality rises. Clearly, any such

Table 2.2   Social incidence of environmental damages in the USA: early studies

Study	Pollutant or hazard	Finding
Freeman, 1972	TSP, SO_x in 3 cities, *concentrations*	Low-income groups have higher pollution within cities, but relationship breaks down across cities.
Zupan, 1973 New York City New York Met area	SO_x, TSP *concentrations* CO, SO_x, TSP *emissions*	Pollution correlated with low incomes.
Harrison, 1975	CO, NO_x, O_x *concentrations* Benefits of auto-emissions control policy	Pollution reductions unrelated to income in metropolitan areas. But pro-poor benefits in urban areas.
Berry, 1977	PM_{10}, SO_x Chicago, *concentrations* PM_{10}, SO_x in 12 cities, *concentrations* Noise, solid waste	Low- and middle-income groups bear higher pollution. Low-income groups bear higher pollution. Unclear.
Asch and Seneca, 1978	PM_{10}, NO_2, SO_x *concentrations*, 23 states	(Generally) low-income groups bear higher pollution burden.
Harrison and Rubinfeld, 1978	Air pollution, Boston	Air pollution improvements pro-poor.
Bullard, 1983	Hazwaste sites, Houston	Black residents more exposed to sites. Study severely criticised by Been, 1994 and Bowen, 2002.
US GAO, 1983	4 hazwaste sites in SE states	Sites correlated with black populations and poverty. Criticised by Bowen, 2002.
UCC, 1987	Hazwaste, national level	Sites correlated with black and minority populations. Severely criticised by Bowen, 2002.
Rose et al., 1989	Environmental damage from surface mining, Virginia	Damage distributions compared to income gains from mining. Lower-income households bear greatest net losses.

*Table 2.3a   Social incidence of environmental damages in the USA:
recent studies*

Study	Pollutant or hazard	Finding
Brajer and Hall, 1992, California	O_3 and PM_{10}	Pollution correlated with low incomes, black and Hispanic communities. Criticised as 'poor' research by Bowen, 2002.
Mohai and Bryant, 1992	Hazwaste sites in Detroit	Distance to site regressed on race and income. Inequality confirmed. Severely criticised by Bowen, 2002.
Zimmerman, 1993	Hazwaste sites, nationwide	Hispanics and blacks correlated with sites but no link to income.
Burke, 1993	TRI releases, *emissions*, Los Angeles county	Minority status and low incomes correlated with emissions.
Anderson et al., 1994 Anderton et al., 1994a Anderton et al., 1994b	TSDF sites, nationwide	1980 sites not inequitably distributed by race/ethnicity but some evidence of income inequality. 1990 sites more inequality by income. There is 'almost no support for the general claim of environmental inequity'. Goldman and Fitton, 1994, find a race link if zip codes are used.
Perlin et al., 1995	TRI releases, *emissions*	Emissions positively associated with *higher* incomes, but also with ethnic minority presence.
Glickman and Hersh, 1995	Toxicity-weighted TRI releases, and storage of hazardous substances, Allegheny county, Pittsburgh	Proximity to hazards mainly affects low-income groups. Mortality risks far less clearly related. Warn against generalisations.
Bowen et al., 1995	TRI releases, *emissions*, Cuyahoga county (includes Cleveland)	Reverse link between race and emissions at census tract level but positive link at county level.
Kriesel et al., 1996	TRI releases, *emissions*	Results depend on specification of model, for example, race and income inequality exists only when they are included in model, but do not exist when other variables added.
Yandle and Burton, 1996	Hazwaste sites, Texas	Correlation with low-income white areas.

Table 2.3a   (continued)

Study	Pollutant or hazard	Finding
Cutter et al., 1996	TSDFs, S. Carolina	No association at census level, some indication of sites being in higher-income white areas otherwise.
Boer et al., 1997	TSDFs, Los Angeles county	Minorities linked to sites but not income.
Brooks and Sethi, 1997	Toxicity-weighted TRI releases, *emissions*	Low-income, low education, minority populations correlated with pollution. These groups have benefited most from improvements.
Bae, 1997, Los Angeles	O_3, CO, NO_2, SO_2, PM_{10}, Pb *concentration* exceedances above standards	Existing risks borne more by poor, therefore benefits of policy pro-poor.
Been and Gupta, 1997	Hazwaste sites	New sites 1970–94 were *not* located in African-American areas. But evidence of Hispanic bias. No correlation with poverty.
Hockman and Morris, 1998	Hazwaste sites and incinerators, Michigan	Race correlated with sites, especially incinerators.
Hamilton and Viscusi, 1999	Hazwaste: superfund priority list	Non-white populations disproportionately represented near sites. Income regressively related.
Arora and Cason, 1999	TRI, *emissions*, US-wide, zip code level	Non-whites, low incomes and unemployment correlated with TRI especially in SE areas, and especially in non-urban areas. Demographic variables proxy for political action, inversely correlated with TRI.
Hite, 2000	Landfills in Franklin county, Ohio	Evidence of racial inequity but no evidence of income inequity. See text for discussion.
Millimet and Slottje, 2002	TRI, *emissions*	Uses Gini measure of pollution inequality across and within states. 1988–97 substantial inequality exists but stable over time at both levels. 1998 saw rise in both levels of inequality. Reduced air pollution *increases* inequality.

Table 2.3a (continued)

Study	Pollutant or hazard	Finding
Kahn, 2001, California	CO, NO_2, O_3, SO_2, PM_{10} *concentrations*	Apart from O_3, poor experience higher pollution than rich. Poor have experienced a relatively greater improvement in air quality 1980–98.
Haynes et al., 2001, Cuyahoga, Cleveland	TRI releases, *emissions*	Higher releases correlated with Hispanic population and low housing values, but doubts about findings.
Chakraborty, 2001	Accidental releases of extremely hazardous substances, Hillsborough county, Florida	Non-white population and poverty linked to number of releases.
Atlas, 2001	TSDFs, national	No pattern of TSDFs or their risks being inequitably concentrated in disproportionately minority or low-income areas.

Note: TRI = Toxic Release Inventory; TSDF = Transfer, storage and disposal facilities.

Table 2.3b Social incidence of environmental damages in Canada

Study	Pollutant or hazard	Finding
Handy, 1977, Hamilton, Ontario	Air pollution: dust and sulphates	Income negatively associated with pollution, that is, inequity.
Jerrett et al., 1997, Ontario	National Pollution Release Inventory	Income *positively* correlated with pollution, that is, no inequity.
Harrison and Antweiler, 2002	National Pollution Release Inventory	No association between releases, transfers and income.

trade-off has to incorporate some measure of inequality-aversion and the model is tested for varying levels of aversion. Ignoring 1998, the level of 'environmental welfare' increases over time, even when fairly high degrees of inequality-aversion are incorporated.[26] Finally, Millimet–Slottje produce some partial tests for the 'compensation hypothesis' introduced in Section 2. In their case they investigate whether wages vary with pollution, so that damages from pollution may be offset (at least partially) by higher wages. They do find evidence for this effect. The Millimet–Slottje study is considerably more sophisticated than the vast majority of contributions to the EJ literature since (a) it shows that prevailing inequality in pollution incidence does not necessarily translate into the finding that reducing pollution will reduce inequality; (b) it makes an explicit attempt to investigate the trade-off between reduced pollution and increased inequality; and (c) it provides some evidence for the compensation hypothesis.

The other study that adopts a strikingly more realistic approach to the environmental justice issue is Hite (2000). The reason for this is that the results emanate from a random utility model in which individuals choose location characteristics so as to maximise personal 'utility'. As noted above, simply observing the location of risky installations and correlating that location with population characteristics fails to account for any trade-offs that individuals may make between the risk and other characteristics of the area. The differences in approach tend to produce a divide in the empirical literature. Whilst perhaps a simplification, 'rights-based' authors favour the statistical association measures, and 'preference-based' authors favour the trade-off or compensation approach.

5.3 Conclusions on Environmental Equity Using 'Physical' Indicators

Summarising the findings of the literature in Tables 2.1 to 2.3 is difficult. First, studies vary widely in their modelling sophistication. Second, choice of spatial unit is, as a number of the studies point out, crucial, with results being rendered invalid or less firm once the spatial unit is changed. Third, many of the studies take a 'snapshot' of the existing state of racial or income incidence of pollution risks, and do not ask how a general pollution-reducing policy might affect the different social groups. Fourth, as noted earlier, those that do look at both the snapshot and the directional change in inequality in light of policy measures produce some varying results. It is not always the case that, if inequality exists, it is reduced by reducing pollution generally. Fifth, and contrary to the generalisations in the literature, the studies that link risky installations with population characteristics are not at all unanimous in finding evidence of environmental inequity. Sixth, and perhaps the most important conclusion, the major part of the empirical literature makes no reference to any trade-offs in siting decisions by households. Risks may therefore differ by social group, but there is then no information on the possibility that those risks are offset by other location characteristics. The two most sophisticated studies – Millimet and Slottje (2002) and Hite (2000) – suggest that such trade-offs do occur. Finally, the literature is geographically extremely biased, with all but a handful of studies coming from the USA. There is no way of knowing if the results from these studies would be replicated in other OECD countries.

6. THE BENEFITS OF ENVIRONMENTAL IMPROVEMENT: THE INCOME ELASTICITY OF 'DEMAND' FOR ENVIRONMENTAL QUALITY

Sections 4 and 5 explored the most widely studied aspect of environmental equity, namely, the extent to which poor people live in areas where environmental quality is lowest and risks highest. A recurrent theme was the differing approaches to defining inequity. The 'rights-based' approach focuses on physical indicators of risk, or potential risk. The economic, or 'market dynamics' approach focuses on the extent to which individuals find themselves in situations in which the costs of environmental quality to them are out of line with the benefits to them. In this section we explore a much smaller literature which addresses the issue of whether or not environmental policy benefits the rich or the poor, respectively summarised by asking whether policy is pro-rich or pro-poor. In contrast to much of the discussion in Sections 4 and 5, the issue is not whether the status quo condition of the environment is regressively or progressively distributed, but whether incremental change to that status quo benefits one group more than the other. There are two strands to this literature: (a) efforts to analyse the benefits (and costs) of specific pieces of legislation to assess their pro-poor or pro-rich characteristics and (b) efforts to measure the income elasticity of 'demand' for environmental quality.

6.1 Policy Costs and Benefits

Several studies have estimated the monetary value of environmental policy benefits, and have then sought to allocate these benefits across income groups. The relevant magnitude is then WTP_i/Y_i, where i is the ith income group. A number of studies have sought to estimate the (marginal) costs to different income groups, for example, by looking at the tax system to see what the likely incidence is of the finance needed for the policy measure. If both benefit and cost incidence was estimated, then it would be possible to compute the net benefits of environmental policy as a fraction of income, that is $(WTP_i - C_i)/Y_i$. If WTP/Y is rising with income, then this is evidence that the income elasticity of WTP is greater than unity, and the good is 'pro-rich' (see Section 6.2). Nonetheless, many of the original studies do not make an explicit statement about income elasticity.

6.2   Income Elasticity of 'Demand' for Environmental Quality

It is widely hypothesised that environmental quality is a 'luxury good' or an 'elitist good' so that extra provision of environmental quality will benefit the rich more than the poor (McFadden, 1994). Interestingly, this assumption has not been widely tested and appears to reflect some casual observations about the nature of the people who participate in environmental protests and organisations. To understand better how this proposition might be tested, it is necessary to investigate the notion of the income elasticity of 'demand' for environmental quality. To begin with, assume that it makes sense to speak of some 'quantity' of the environment, E. The possible relationships between E and income, Y, are shown in Figure 2.7, in terms of an elasticity known as the income elasticity of demand. This is defined as:

$$\eta = \partial E \cdot Y / \partial Y \cdot E$$

The focus of interest is on the heavy-lined curves. The extremes, where $\eta = 0$ and ∞ are shown just for comparison. It is easy to see that the income elasticities are related to another measure, namely the ratio of E to Y. For example, if $\eta < 1$, then the ratio E/Y falls as Y increases, as shown in Figure 2.7 by the slopes of the dotted lines. The full set of relationships is shown in Box 2.2.

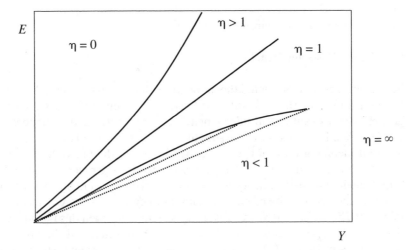

Figure 2.7   Income elasticities of demand

BOX 2.2   INCOME ELASTICITIES OF DEMAND
           AND EQUITY CONCEPTS

Nature of good E		Income elasticity	E/Y (as Y rises)	Equity
Normal	Luxury	> 1	Rises	Pro-rich
Normal	Unit η	$= 1$	Constant	
Normal	Necessity	$0 < \eta < 1$	Falls	Pro-poor
Inferior		< 0	Falls	Pro-poor

Box 2.2 shows that the income elasticity of demand could be used to classify environmental goods according to whether they are pro-rich or pro-poor.[27] The basic rule is that benefits are pro-rich if the income elasticity is greater than unity (Carson et al., 2001).

Because of the nature of environmental commodities, the *quantity* demanded is often not observed. Hence it is not possible to estimate income elasticities of demand on a systematic basis. What is observed is a different elasticity, the income elasticity of willingness to pay, abbreviated to the 'income elasticity of WTP'. This magnitude is given by:

$$\omega = \partial WTP \cdot Y / \partial Y \cdot WTP$$

The relationship between the income elasticity of demand and the income elasticity of WTP is not determinate. Observations of ω do not enable us to infer observations of η. Any environmental good, E, may, for example, have a $\eta > 1$, but a ω greater or less than unity (Flores and Carson, 1997). To see this, rearrange the equation for η as:

$$Y / \partial Y = \eta \cdot E / \partial E$$

and substitute this into the equation for ω to give:

$$\omega = \eta . \partial WTP \cdot E / WTP \cdot \partial E$$

Note that $\omega < 1$ is quite compatible with $\eta > 1$, so that a good that is a 'luxury good' can have an income elasticity of $WTP < 1$ (Flores and Carson, 1997).[28]

BOX 2.3   SUMMARY OF INDICATORS OF EQUITY IMPACTS OF POLICY

Measure	Explanation
E_i/Y_i	Physical 'burden' of pollution by income group.
WTP_i/Y_i	Monetary value of environmental policy benefits as a fraction of income. If this rises with Y, then $\omega > 1$.
$(WTP_i - C_i)/Y_i$	Monetary value of NET environmental policy benefits as a fraction of income. If this rises, then the elasticity of *net WTP* (consumer surplus) exceeds unity.
η	Income elasticity of DEMAND.
ω	Income elasticity of WILLINGNESS TO PAY.

Which is the relevant concept for classifying environmental goods? Both concepts convey useful information, but it has been argued that, since the focus of most environmental policy is on public goods that have some quantity constraint, the second concept, ω, is more relevant (Flores and Carson, 1997).[29] Section 7 looks at some of the evidence.

Box 2.3 summarises the various indicators of equity that emerge from the literature which utilise either some measure of demand, or some measure of willingness to pay.

7.   THE EMPIRICAL EVIDENCE ON ENVIRONMENTAL EQUITY USING MONETISED MEASURES

7.1   Income Elasticity of WTP

There are two potential sources for empirical estimates of ω, the income elasticity of WTP. The first is studies of the benefits, and the costs as well, of specific policy measures. Such studies tend to estimate benefits on the basis of the *benefits transfer* technique, that is, borrowing unit values for pollutants from other studies. The second relies on primary non-market valuation studies. The two most useful valuation techniques that permit estimation of an income elasticity are (a) travel cost and (b) contingent valuation. In each case it is necessary to identify a *valuation function*, that is, a function linking WTP to independent variables which must include income if ω is to be estimated. Hedonic property price studies appear to be a third, but, as noted in Pearce (1980), hedonic property prices are very likely to have built into them an *assumed* income elasticity of unity. Hence, income elasticities cannot be derived from these studies. Benefits transfer studies are common but invariably are presented in a manner that makes inferring income elasticities impossible since unit values are averages taken from one or more 'primary' studies. A few studies attempt to allocate the benefits across income groups. No studies appear to be available which estimate the magnitude $(WTP - C)/Y$.

Evidence of the income elasticity of WTP and the income elasticity of demand is not substantial. The early literature is summarised in Pearce (1980). Kriström and Riera (1996) provide an exploratory investigation into valuation studies based on the contingent valuation approach (CVM) to environmental goods and, more recently, Hökby and Söderqvist (2001) have assembled evidence from Swedish CVM studies. Table 2.4 reports estimates of ω.

One other possibility for gaining some insight into income elasticities is to look at national environmental expenditures and relate them to GNP. Expenditure is, of course, not the same as WTP, the latter exceeding the former by any consumer surplus. McFadden and Leonard (1993) suggest that, as the share of environmental expenditure tends to rise with GNP, the income elasticity must be greater than unity. Pearce and Palmer (2001) actually estimate the expenditure elasticity for European Union countries and arrive at an elasticity of 1.2, consistent with the McFadden and Leonard hypothesis.[30] Hanemann (1996) notes that national elasticities greater than unity could easily be consistent with household elasticities less than unity, especially as there is some evidence to suggest that elasticities are not constant over ranges of income.

The general impression from Table 2.4 is that the income elasticity of WTP for environmental change is less than unity, and numbers like 0.3–0.7 seem about right. The exception to this basic rule is the paper by Sieg et al. (2000) which, however, adopts an entirely different approach to the other studies. It involves a general equilibrium model of house price response to discrete change in air quality in Southern California. The resulting elasticities of around 4 are therefore interesting in suggesting that it is important to model distributional impacts in a general equilibrium framework.

7.2   Income Elasticity of Demand

Evidence of the income elasticity of *demand* is difficult to derive from non-market valuation studies. This is because studies tend not to consider contexts in which price and quantity combinations are varied. Hökby and

Table 2.4   Non-market valuation benefit studies: elasticity of WTP (ω)

Study	Income elasticity of WTP	Comment
Gianessi et al., 1977, compliance with 1970 Clean Air Act, USA	0.35–0.87*	Monetised benefits by income group based on *benefits transfer*.
Harrison and Rubinfeld, 1978, US clean air standards	1.00	Derived from a *hedonic property* price model and hence probably constrained to unity (see text).
Nelson, 1978, noise in the US	1.00	Derived from a *hedonic property* price model and hence probably constrained to unity (see text).
Harris, 1979, UK noise	0.20–0.40	Based on *CVM*.
Walters, 1975, UK airport noise Heathrow Gatwick	 1.89–3.20 2.09–2.62	Suspect results due to assumption that house prices are a proxy for permanent income. Akin to a *hedonic property* model, using estate agents' valuations of depreciation.
Kriström and Riera, 1996, 6 CVMs: Finland, France, Norway, Netherlands, Spain, Sweden	Probably less than 1	Evidence not conclusive, based on inspection of WTP equations in Six *CVM* studies.
Hökby and Söderqvist, 2001, 21 estimated CVM equations in Swedish valuation studies	Range −0.71 to 2.83 Mean = 0.68 Median = 0.46	*CVM*. One elasticity is negative. Four out of 21 elasticities > 1 16 elasticities in range 0.20–0.91.
Imber et al., 1991, Kakadu conservation zone, Australia	0 0.20	Zero is the figure reported in Imber et al. but the study carries a critique by Hanemann suggesting this is incorrect. Kriström and Riera rework the valuation equations to get 0.2.

Table 2.4 (continued)

Study	Income elasticity of WTP	Comment
Carson et al., 1995, Exxon Valdez tanker spill in Alaska	0.28	*CVM*
Santos, 1998		
Landscape change, UK	0.20	*CVM*
Landscape change, Portugal	0.30	*CVM*
Meta analysis of landscape studies	0.57	*Meta analysis*
Loehman and De, 1982, avoidance of respiratory symptoms, Florida	0.26–0.60	*CVM*
Jones-Lee et al., 1985, accidents	0.40	*CVM*
Biddle and Zarkin, 1988, occupational risk	0.70	*CVM*
Viscusi and Evans, 1990, health status	1.10	*CVM*
Sieg et al., 2000, air quality, S. California	4.2–4.7	*General equilibrium* model of property price changes.

Note: * Estimated by author from data in the original.

Söderqvist (2002) pool data from several studies of the WTP for reduced marine eutrophication in the Baltic Sea. The 95 per cent confidence interval for the estimates of η is 0.71–1.49, with a point estimate of 1.1. Using a restricted form of relationship between η and ω (see note 29) the value of η is 0.51.

7.3 Conclusions on Income Elasticity

Overall, while the evidence is limited, the general thrust of the literature is that, for individual goods, the income elasticity of WTP is less than unity. The recent empirical work tends to support Pearce's (1980) suggestion that the impression that environmental quality is an 'elitist' good is not justified.

The implication for policy is that environmental policy is probably biased towards benefiting the poor rather than the rich.

8.   THE POLICY IMPLICATIONS

Quite what policy implications follow from an analysis of income-pollution relationships will depend on how the empirical evidence is perceived. As we have seen, the evidence is :

(a)   Generally confined to the USA, but with some ambiguous evidence from the UK.
(b)   Probably leaning towards the view that *existing* environmental quality and income are negatively correlated in many cases.
(c)   But with many caveats about the geographical generalisability of such findings.
(d)   With many caveats about the extent to which any findings can be generalised across all pollutants and all environmental assets.
(e)   No clear findings with respect to the distributional impacts of *changes* in environmental quality.
(f)   The fairly firm finding that the income elasticity of willingness to pay is less than unity.

The main *methodological* finding has to be that by far the major part of the empirical literature on distributional incidence fails to account for any compensatory mechanisms that may exist in locational decisions. The economic theory literature is careful to point out the potential importance of such factors. For example, locating in a more polluted area produces well-being losses that may be, at least partially, compensated by lower prices for other goods such as housing. The *policy* relevance of this finding depends on how the distributional issue is perceived. As noted earlier, much of the environmental justice movement would not regard compensatory factors as being relevant to policy, since some form of 'equal' risk exposure is regarded as a non-tradable right. The more economically-oriented approach would argue that these compensatory mechanisms need to be accounted for.

However, in so far as policy-makers *are* (or should be) concerned with environmental equity, certain policy implications can be stated.

8.1   Factoring the Distributional Impacts into Decision-making

The most obvious implication is that the social incidence of policy measures needs to be factored into decision-making. On the basis that all decisions involve *some* form of comparison between costs and benefits, a decision rule would require that benefits exceed costs in the aggregate, *and* that the distributional incidence of (net) benefits should be 'acceptable'.[31] What constitutes the degree of acceptability will depend on the form of 'social welfare function' adopted by decision-makers. For example, a Rawls-type social welfare function (SWF) would sanction a policy only if its benefits accrue to the least well-off in society. Rawls (1971) argued that the distribution of resources between people is just if and only if it offers the same opportunities to all members of society. If there is inequality, resources must be distributed so that the most disadvantaged in society are favoured. This amounts to maximising the well-being of those who are most disadvantaged, that is, maximising the minimum well-being, or 'maximin'. The 'reasonableness' of this rule is revealed by imagining that everyone is in an original state and no one knows to which state of well-being they will be assigned (the 'veil of ignorance') by some policy change. Since each individual could be assigned the worst state, everyone will vote for a rule that protects the worst off. Rawls's approach is 'consequentialist' because it focuses on the outcome of a set of rules rather than on the idea of justice as 'process'.[32] A Rawlsian SWF is usually written:

$$SW = \min (U_1, U_2, \ldots, U_N)$$

which means that the well-being of society is determined solely by the well-being of the individual with the lowest level of well-being. This SWF is strongly egalitarian. It is easy to imagine any number of variants of such rules, for example that the greater proportion of benefits should accrue to the poor rather than the rich.

8.2 Distributional Incidence and Cost–Benefit Analysis

It is possible to 'adjust' cost–benefit analysis to allow for distributional incidence in a different way. To understand the implications it is first necessary to consider the SWF that is usually embodied in cost–benefit analysis. The 'classical utilitarian', 'purely utilitarian' or Benthamite SWF is adjusted here to allow for environment:

$$SW = U_1(x_1, e_1) + U_2(x_2, e_2) + U_3(x_3, e_3) + \ldots + U_N(x_N, e_N)$$

U = utility = welfare = well-being
$1 \ldots N$ = people in society
x = quantity of consumption goods
e = quantity of environmental goods

We would expect $\dfrac{\partial U_i}{\partial x_i} > 0, \quad \dfrac{\partial U_i}{\partial e_i} > 0$

This SWF assumes that there is *equal marginal utility of consumption (income)*, that is, additions to x and e are valued equally by the various individuals. This means the social decision-maker is indifferent to *who* gets the gains (rich or poor, for example, or future generations versus present generations). This is the basic SWF underlying the general practice of cost–benefit analysis subject to a modification shortly to be introduced about what happens when there are losers as well as gainers. It assumes U increases with x; that U increases with e (or decreases with p); that we can measure U; that we can add up the various U_is, and that social welfare increases with individual welfare.

In practice, virtually all policies involve some people gaining and some losing (for example, taxpayers) so that the SWF looks more like:

$$SW = U_1(x_1, e_1) + U_2(x_2, e_2) - U_3(x_3, e_3) - U_4(x_N, e_N)$$

Cost–benefit analysis embodies the Kaldor–Hicks compensation principle[33] which says that a policy is desirable if it brings about a positive change in social welfare, ΔSW ($\Delta SW > 0$) and that this condition is met if

$$[\Delta U_1(\cdot) + \Delta U_2(\cdot)] > [-\Delta U_3(\cdot) - \Delta U_4(\cdot)]$$

Distributional concerns can be allowed for by assigning weights to the various gains and losses to produce a 'generalisable utilitarian' SWF or 'weighted sum of utilities' SWF:

$$SW = a_1 \cdot U_1(\cdot) + a_2 \cdot U_2(\cdot) + a_3 \cdot U_3(\cdot) + \ldots + a_N \cdot U_N(\cdot)$$

Here the weights are given by the a's. There are various ways of deriving such weights. The first rule is simply to set

$$a_i = \frac{\bar{Y}}{Y_i}$$

where Y is income and $\bar{Y}$ is average income. The effect is to 'equalise votes' as if each person had the same average income. Thus, a poor person who has 60 per cent of the average income would have a weight of $1/0.6 = 1.67$, and a rich person with twice the average income would have a weight of 0.5. This is a crude rule that turns out to be a special case of a more general rule – see below.

The second rule sets the value of a by adjusting for the elasticity of the marginal utility of income. The relevant formula is then

$$a_i = \left[\frac{\bar{Y}}{Y_i} \right]^{-\varepsilon}$$

where ε is the elasticity of the marginal utility of income function. This function links extra utility (well-being) to extra income and is usually assumed to take on a constant elasticity form. Since ε measures the social weight to be attached to changes in different levels of income, it is also a measure of *inequality-aversion*.

The weight is shown here for individual i relative to the average income but it can be computed for any benchmark income. For example, one might set $a = 1$ for the richest group or person, and then express the weights on the other individuals' utility relative to this rich group (the rich person's Y would be substituted for average income in the above equation). Note that the conventional SWF in cost–benefit analysis is now a special case of this new SWF in which the a's equal unity.

What this shows is that cost–benefit analysis does not *have* to assume that the prevailing distribution of income is 'optimal'. CBA can be flexible in allowing for different SWFs.

Weighted approaches can secure very different results to 'conventional' CBA. Consider the following very simple examples.

	Gain	Loss	Net gain
Group A	+10	−4	+6
Group B	+2	−6	−4
Aggregate gain	+12	−10	+2

In the first example above we illustrate conventional CBA. Group A secures net gains measured by WTP of +6 but group B has net losses (perhaps measured by WTA) of −4. Overall, the gainers can compensate the losers with a net final gain of +2. CBA would approve of this policy. Even though the losers might be poor and the gainers rich.

Now let $a_B = 1.6$ and $a_A = 1.0$, then the weighted gains will be:

	Gain	Loss	Net gain
Group A	+10	−4	+6
Group B	+2 × 1.6 = +3.2	−6 × 1.6 = −9.6	−6.4
Aggregate gain	+13.2	−13.6	−0.4

The weighted approach now rejects this policy.

The value of ε is debated in the literature. An excellent survey is given by Cowell and Gardiner (1999). There it is concluded that a 'default' value of ε is unity with the range being from 0.5 to 4.0. However, values such as 4 imply a quite dramatic degree of inequality-aversion. To see this consider two individuals, rich and poor, with utility functions of the form:

$$U_i = \frac{Y_i^{1-\varepsilon}}{1-\varepsilon} \quad i = R, P$$

The ratio of the two *marginal* utilities is given by:

$$\left[\frac{Y_P}{Y_R}\right]^\varepsilon$$

Suppose $Y_R = 10\,Y_P$. The range of social values is shown below, corresponding to various values of ε.[34]

$\varepsilon =$	0.5	0.8	1.0	1.2	1.5	2.0	4.0
Loss to R as a fraction of gain to P	0.31	0.16	0.10	0.06	0.03	0.01	~0

What this tells us is that at $\varepsilon = 4$, the social value of extra income to R is zero. At $\varepsilon = 1$, a marginal unit of income to the poor is valued ten times the marginal gain to the rich. At $\varepsilon = 2$, the relative valuation is 100 times. On this 'thought experiment' basis, then, values even of $\varepsilon = 2$ do not seem reasonable. A value of $\varepsilon = 1$ does seem feasible. Overall, looking at the implied values of ε in savings behaviour and at the thought-experiment above, values of ε in the range 0.5 to 1.2 seem reasonable.

8.3   Equity Weighting in Practice: An Example

The importance of equity weighting in cost–benefit analysis can be illustrated by considering estimates of the social cost of greenhouse gases.[35] If a cost–benefit analysis of climate change control was being considered, it would be necessary to estimate the global damage done by climate change and compare it to the costs of control. A survey of the estimates of damage can be found in Pearce (2005). Since a disproportionate share of the damages accrues to developing countries (relative to GNP) there is a strong case for equity weighting. To illustrate how equity weighting affects global damage estimates, we employ the SWF introduced previously:

$$D_{WORLD} = D_R \cdot \left[\frac{\bar{Y}}{Y_R}\right]^\varepsilon + D_p \cdot \left[\frac{\bar{Y}}{Y_P}\right]^\varepsilon$$

where R=rich and P=poor and D is the monetary value of damage. Crude estimates of the relevant magnitudes are then D_R=$216 billion and D_P=$106 billion, for $2 \times CO_2$ (Fankhauser, 1995); Y_R=$10,000 and Y_P=$1,110; and $\bar{Y}$ =$3,333.[36] Substituting in the equation above produces estimates of world damage of:

unweighted	$ 322 billion
weighted, ε = 0.5	$ 307 billion
weighted, ε = 0.8	$ 343 billion
weighted, ε = 1	$ 390 billion
weighted, ε = 1.5	$ 600 billion

It can be seen that the value of ε matters a great deal. If ε=0.5, there is little change to the unweighted estimates of damage. If ε=1, there is a 20 per cent increase in global damages, and if ε = 1.5 damages rise by nearly 100 per cent. If damages are doubled, then the benefits from avoiding climate change are also doubled, with formidable implications for the amount of action that would be taken to control climate change.

8.4   Cost–Benefit Analysis and Income Elasticity of WTP

Sections 6 and 7 discussed the notion of the income elasticity of willingness to pay, ω. Leaving aside the issue of equity weighting discussed in Section 8.2, the value of ω can be extremely important in practical cost–benefit analysis. For example, to appraise an investment in environmental conservation requires not only that the benefits be estimated for the near future but over the longer run as well. But over the longer run population may grow, in which case the total benefits of the conservation investment will grow[37] at the rate of population growth. This effect is often not factored into actual cost–benefit studies. But if incomes grow with time then WTP is also likely to grow: indeed, this is what an income elasticity of WTP measures. Hence there needs to be a second adjustment to the benefit stream. The final formula to account for population effects and income elasticity is:

$$\frac{B_t}{B_{t-1}} = [1 + \omega \cdot y + p]$$

where the expression on the left-hand side is the growth rate of total benefits, y is the rate of growth of per capita income, and p is population growth. To illustrate the effects, assume population growth is zero, that income grows at 3 per cent per annum and that ω is 0.3, a result that is consistent with the empirical survey in Section 7. Then benefit growth would be $0.3 \times 0.03 = 0.01$ or 1 per cent per annum. For an investment with a 50-year time horizon, the effect would be to add 65 per cent to the estimated benefits.

8.5   Fiscal Policy and Environmental Distribution

Environmental damage may be successfully tackled through policy measures such as environmental taxes and regulations. However, those measures may themselves have distributional implications. Thus poorer households may not only suffer more exposure to environmental harm, but the means of reducing the harm may also impact more heavily on them relative to their incomes. Clearly, there are various potential combinations of the distribution of harm and the distribution of the policy costs. In the worst case, damage may be regressively distributed and policy costs may also be regressively distributed. If damage is 'progressive', that is, suffered mainly by the rich, a similar equity issue will arise if the poor pay disproportionately more than the rich to resolve the problem. In such circumstances, policies need to address both the cost and benefit sides of the picture. As indicated earlier, many OECD governments already embody distributional concerns in their development of fiscal measures for the control of environmental damage, with various measures being used to lower the cost incidence on the poor: rebates, zero charges, reduced charges, compensation measures and so on. The central conclusion is that addressing the distributional incidence of environmental damages (benefits) is not sufficient. Care has to be taken also to address the incidence of the policy costs as well.

8.6   Summary of Policy Implications

The policy implications of the analysis of distributional incidence issues can be summarised as follows:

(a)   The social distribution of *existing risks* gives rise to equity concerns that many would argue need to be remediated by targeted action to improve environments in areas where low-income and vulnerable groups exist. These remediation policies may or may not be influenced by the extent to which environmental risks are offset by other gains from locating in higher risk areas.

(b)   The social incidence of *new policy measures* is a legitimate cause for concern in decision-making. At the very least, an analysis of who gains and who loses from policy measures is required. Methodologies exist for adjusting conventional cost–benefit criteria to account for equity impacts. Depending on the accepted measure of inequality-aversion within a society or across nations, the effects of equity weighting can be substantial. It is important to assess the distributional incidence of the benefits *and* the costs of environmental policy.

(c) The social incidence literature produces estimates of the income elasticity of willingness to pay for environmental improvement. Contrary to popular belief, this income elasticity is almost certainly below unity. Such income elasticities need to be factored into cost–benefit studies of environmental impacts. Again, the choice of the 'right' value can have significant effects on the outcome of a cost–benefit appraisal.

(d) Care has to be taken that active discouragement of the siting of polluting activities in low-income or ethnic minority areas does not harm employment prospects in those areas. The views of people in the relevant areas need to be sought. This places a premium on policies that generate full information about development prospects and their associated risks: the poor tend to have less access to information compared to the rich. One risk is that some 'non-users' will be active politically in trying to prevent developments from being sited in particular areas. Care needs to be taken to ensure that these activists are representative of local people who are directly affected and who face the real trade-off between development and environmental risk. There may also be detrimental environmental effects – for example, 'brownfield' sites might be avoided because of a fear of environmental injustice, with the result that new development shifts to greenfield sites where amenity values may be very high. In the same vein, policies designed to improve the environments of poor areas may force up rents and property prices, giving rise to longer term forces that encourage the poor to move out of the area and the rich to move in ('gentrification'). In short, 'pro-poor' policies need to be evaluated carefully for their second and third round effects.

(e) Finally, where distributional effects are significant and a matter of serious concern, some of the proceeds from environmental taxes may be earmarked for allocation to improvement policies in poor areas.

NOTES

1. The cross-national literature is ignored here. The relevant empirical literature is encapsulated in the notion of an 'environmental Kuznets curve' (EKC) which traces out relationships between environmental quality (or resource use) and real income per capita. While it is usually characterised as taking on the shape of an 'inverted U' curve – with environmental degradation or resource use at first rising with income growth and then

falling – the empirical evidence is in fact more ambiguous than is generally supposed. See Harbaugh et al. (2000). The EKC function usually takes the form $E_{it} = a + b \cdot Y_{it}/POP_{it} + c \cdot (Y_{it}/POP_{it})^2 + \varepsilon$, where E is environmental degradation, Y is real income, POP is population, ε is an error term, i is location, t is time, and a,b,c are parameters to be estimated. Note that we also ignore the literature that deals with distribution of environmental goods across 'economic' groups – consumers and producers for example.

2. An excellent classification of equity concepts can also be found in Carraro (2002).

3. There are many strands to the EJ literature and they extend way beyond the empirical investigation of the social incidence of environmental costs and benefits. One relates to the ethical underpinnings of the techniques used to assess environmental justice. A significant issue, for example, is whether individuals have some natural right to a 'clean' or 'zero risk' environment and, if so, what status is then appropriate for procedures such as risk assessment in which risks are explicitly traded against costs of risk reduction and against non-environmental benefits. This literature is not explored in this chapter, other than tangentially. For extensive discussion see the special issue of *Human and Ecological Risk Assessment*, Volume 6, No. 6, 2000, especially the papers by Goldman, Sexton, Simon and Foreman. It should also be borne in mind that the EJ literature is itself a sub-set of a larger literature that analyses inequalities in health and access to public goods generally, the argument being that poorer people tend to have lower health status, lower life expectancy and so on. This substantial literature is not considered here. For a review see Wagstaff and van Doorslaer (2000). The *British Medical Journal* (http://bmj.com) has carried a large number of articles on health and inequality, as has the *Journal of Policy Analysis and Management*.

4. Bowen (2002) regards all these studies as being of comparatively low scientific quality.

5. The '*NLJ* articles' are themselves the subject of a detailed debate as to the validity of the allegations – see Ringquist (1998) and Atlas (2002). Much of the debate relates to the source of information – the EPA's Civil Enforcement DOCKET database – and the ways in which researchers have interpreted it. Ringquist suggests the *NLJ* allegations are false. Atlas also finds serious fault with the *NLJ* analysis but additionally suggests Ringquist's results are invalid due to misuse of the DOCKET database.

6. For the rest of the chapter we confine attention mainly to income groups, but a significant part of the literature is concerned with racial groups as well. In so far as race and income tend to be correlated, it can usually be taken that findings related to income also hold for racial groupings, but not always.

7. The 'environmental justice' movement tends to disregard the preference-based approach since it sees equality of risk exposure as a 'right' that cannot be traded. Such 'lexical' orderings are the subject of a fairly extensive literature in environmental economics. In this case, however, the argument is further divided according to whether the advocates themselves have lexical orderings on behalf of those at risk, or whether those at risk have the lexical orderings. As several authors note, this makes distinguishing ideology from good research difficult.

8. The importance of measures of exposure as opposed to concentration is stressed by Smith (1988). Note that the example given in the text could work the other way: indoor pollution may vary directly or inversely with income.

9. The first law of thermodynamics is sufficient to show that zero risks are impossible, even if they can be thought of as desirable, which itself is a dubious judgement. See Wildavsky (1995).

10. This argument holds independently of how preferences are measured, for example, there is no presumption that preferences are measured by willingness to pay to avoid risks.

11. These arguments in the context of airport noise are presented in some detail in Walters (1975).

12. We take efficiency to mean the maximisation of net social benefits or the minimisation of net social costs, where benefit and cost derive their meaning from individuals' preferences as measured by willingness to pay or willingness to accept.

13. In discussing the various modes of causation we do not consider the notion, conveyed

in significant parts of the EJ literature, that inequity is the result of racism. Racial prejudice will produce inequity between income groups, the focus of this report, if minority groups are correlated with low incomes, as tends to be the case. Omitting a discussion of racism as a causal factor is not intended to downplay its potential importance. For a discussion see Pellow et al. (2001).

14. We investigate just what this relationship is in Section 8.

15. We take a public good to be one that, if provided to R would also be provided to P, without R being able to prevent P from securing the good. These are the attributes of joint consumption (non-rivalry) and non-exclusion.

16. In Figure 2.5, the poor's willingness to pay is given by the slope of their indifference curve at D, and this is less than the price of the public good, shown by the slope of the budget line. The rich's willingness to pay exceeds the price at B.

17. Such a case would be illustrated by making the indifference curve of the poor very steep and that of the rich very shallow.

18. Baumol and Oates (1988) attach little importance to this case but this may reflect the nature of marginal taxation in the USA. Marginal tax rates do vary significantly in other countries. Note that the compromise supply of the public good is now assumed to be the outcome of a political bargain based on post-tax bargaining functions rather than pre-tax ones.

19. A or B is an optimum because $M\Pi = P - MC = MD$, where P is price and MC is the marginal cost of producing the polluting good. On rearrangement, $P = MC + MD = MSC$, where MSC is marginal social cost. Implicit in this analysis is the assumption of perfect competition. Bargaining when there is imperfect competition is more complex: see Pearce and Turner (1990).

20. ΔE has been drawn so that E_p is both the resulting level of environmental degradation and the optimal level with respect to MD_p. This is just to avoid the diagram becoming overcrowded with lines and symbols and has no other significance.

21. *Why* these differences in collective organisation exist is yet another major question of interest, but not one pursued here.

22. There are obvious 'moral' issues here. If the poor *choose* not to opt for clean-up and the rich do, the preference-based approach would conclude that the outcomes are optimal. The EJ movement, however, would argue that the inability or unwillingness to organise is itself a function of the initial income inequality and hence the poor should be helped in some way to organise themselves. Indeed, much of the EJ movement is concerned with exactly this process.

23. Goldman (1994) has pointed to the US bias in EJ studies, calling for similar studies in other countries.

24. Table 2.3a does not pretend to be comprehensive as there are many studies of the kind listed, varying in sophistication. Studies have been chosen according to a rough check on the number of citations.

25. The 'environmental welfare function' is given by $EW = -Y^*(1 + G)$ where Y^* is mean income and G is the (income) Gini coefficient.

26. On measures of inequality-aversion, see Section 8.

27. We could equally well say environmental policy that improves the environment is 'regressive' if the benefits are pro-rich and 'progressive' if benefits are pro-poor. But different writers use regressive and progressive in different ways, for example, pro-poor benefits are sometimes called 'regressive', so pro-rich and pro-poor seem better in this context.

28. There is a special case where there is only one public good and individuals differ in their incomes but not in preferences. Then it can be shown that $\omega = \eta/p$ where p is the price elasticity of demand (Ebert, 2000). To classify goods as pro-rich or pro-poor in terms of η, then, would require knowledge of ω and p.

29. The arguments are complex, but the basic difference is that the supply of a public good is exogenous to consumers, whereas consumers choose the amount they consume of a private good. Full details can be found in Hanemann (1991) and Flores and Carson (1997).

30. However, McFadden and Leonard (1993) wrongly infer from this that *any* income elasticity of *demand* must be greater than unity.
31. There is nothing new in this proposal. For example, it formed the basis of an extensive debate about the foundations of welfare economics in the 1950s. The *locus classicus* is Little (1950).
32. A significant part of the EJ literature is concerned with process justice. Process approaches argue that justice is defined by agreement over the rules, regardless of what the outcome of those rules is.
33. The transition obscures a switch from 'ordinal' utility in the Kaldor–Hicks world to cardinal utility. This is not discussed here.
34. The ratio of incomes between R and P has been chosen to illustrate *international* differences in real income per capita. The ratio would be far smaller for analysis of a policy *within* an OECD country. Across OECD countries the ratio could reach 7, the ratio for the USA compared to Mexico.
35. Note that the value of ε enters a cost–benefit analysis in two ways: as a measure of inequality-aversion across different income groups if the costs and benefits are equity weighted, and as a component of the social time preference rate as a discount rate, that is, inequality-aversion through time. This underlines the importance of choosing the 'correct' estimate of ε.
36. We take rich countries to be OECD countries, poor to be everyone else.
37. Assuming the asset is a public good and that there are no 'congestion effects', that is, the greater the number 'consuming' the good, the lower is the well-being of the existing users as the number of users expands. Strictly, such goods are 'club goods' as opposed to public goods.

REFERENCES

Anderson, A., D. Anderton and J. Oakes (1994), 'Environmental Equity: Evaluating TSDF Siting over the Past Two Decades', *Waste Age*, **25**, 83–100.

Anderton, D., A. Anderson, J. Oakes, M. Fraser, E. Weber and E. Calabrese (1994a), 'Hazardous Waste Facilities: Environmental Equity Issues in Metropolitan Areas', *Evaluation Review*, **18**(2), 123–40.

Anderton, D., A. Anderson, J. Oakes and M. Fraser (1994b), 'Environmental Equity. The Demographics of Dumping in Dixie', *Demography*, **31**(2), 229–48.

Arora, S. and T. Cason (1999), 'Do Community Characteristics Influence Environmental Outcomes? Evidence from the Toxic Releases Inventory', *Southern Economic Journal*, **65**, 691–716.

Asch, P. and J. Seneca (1978), 'Some Evidence on the Distribution of Air Quality', *Land Economics*, **54**, 218–57.

Atkinson, G., F. Machado and S. Mourato (2000), 'Balancing Competing Principles of Environmental Equity', *Environment and Planning A*, **32**, 1791–806.

Atlas, M. (2001), 'Safe and Sorry: Risk, Environmental Equity, and Hazardous Waste Management Facilities', *Risk Analysis*, **21**, 939–54.

Atlas, M. (2002), 'Rush to Judgement: An Empirical Analysis of Environmental Equity in US Environmental Protection Agency Enforcement Actions', mimeo, Department of Political Science and Public Administration, North Carolina State University.

Bae, C.-H. (1997), 'How Los Angeles' Air Quality Policies Benefit Minorities', *Journal of Environmental Planning and Management*, **40**(2), 235–60.

Bateman, I., A. Jones, A. Lovett, I. Lake and B. Day (2002), 'Applying

Geographical Information Systems to Environmental and Resource Economics', *Environmental and Resource Economics*, **22**(1–2), 219–69.

Baumol, W. (1972), 'Environmental Protection and the Distribution of Incomes', in OECD (ed.), *Problems of Environmental Economics*, Paris: OECD, pp. 67–73.

Baumol, W. (1974), 'Environmental Protection and Income Distribution', in H. Hochman and G. Peterson (eds), *Redistribution through Public Choice*, New York: Columbia University Press, pp. 93–104.

Baumol, W. and W. Oates (1988), *The Theory of Environmental Policy*, 2nd edition. Cambridge: Cambridge University Press.

Becker, G. (1983), 'A Theory of Competition among Pressure Groups for Political Influence', *Quarterly Journal of Economics*, **98**, 371–400.

Been, V. (1994), 'Locally Undesirable Land Uses in Minority Neighbourhoods: Disproportionate Siting or Market Dynamics', *Yale Law Journal*, **103**, 1383–422.

Been, V. and F. Gupta (1997), 'Coming to the Nuisance or Going to the Barrios? A Longitudinal Analysis of Environmental Justice Claims', *Ecology Law Quarterly*, **24**, 1–56.

Berry, N. (1977), *The Social Burdens of Environmental Pollution*, Cambridge, MA: Ballinger.

Biddle, J. and G. Zarkin (1988), 'Worker Preferences and Market Compensation for Job Risk', *Review of Economics and Statistics*, **70**(4), 660–66.

Blomquist, G., M. Berger and J. Hoehn (1988), 'New Estimates of Quality of Life in Urban Areas', *American Economic Review*, **78**(1), 89–107.

Boer, J., M. Pastor, J. Sadd and L. Snyder (1997), 'Is there Environmental Racism? The Demographics of Hazardous Waste in Los Angeles County', *Social Science Quarterly*, **78**, 793–810.

Bowen, W. (2002), 'An Analytical Review of Environmental Justice Research: What Do We Really Know?', *Environmental Management*, **29**(1), 3–15.

Bowen, W., M. Salling, F. Haynes and E. Cyran (1995), 'Toward Environmental Justice – Spatial Equity in Ohio and Cleveland', *Annals of the American Association of Geographers*, **85**(14), 623–40.

Brainard, J., A. Jones, I. Bateman, A. Lovett and P. Fallon (2002), 'Modelling Environmental Equity: Access to Air Quality in Birmingham, UK', *Environment and Planning A*, **34**, 695–716.

Brainard, J., I. Bateman and A. Jones (2003), 'Accessing Urban Park Locations: Contrasting Equity of Access with Economic Efficiency Measures', mimeo, University of East Anglia, CSERGE.

Brajer, V. and J. Hall (1992), 'Recent Evidence on the Distribution of Air Pollution Effects', *Contemporary Policy Issues*, **X**, April, 53–71.

Brooks, N. and R. Sethi (1997), 'The Distribution of Pollution: Community Characteristics and Exposure to Air Toxics', *Journal of Environmental Economics and Management*, **32**, 233–50.

Bullard, R.D. (1983), 'Solid Waste Sites and the Black Houston Community', *Sociological Inquiry*, **53**, 273–88.

Burke, L. (1993), 'Race and Environmental Equity: A Geographic Analysis in Los Angeles', *Geographic Information Systems*, October, 44–50.

Cardenas, J., J. Stranlund and C. Willis (2002), 'Economic Inequality and Burden Sharing in the Provision of Local Environmental Quality', *Ecological Economics*, **40**, 379–95.

Carraro, C. (2002), 'Climate Change Policy: Models, Controversies and Strategies', in T. Tietenberg and H. Folmer (eds), *The International Yearbook of Environmental and Resource Economics 2002/2003*, Cheltenham, UK and Northampton, MA: Edward Elgar, 1–65.

Carson, R., R. Mitchell, M. Hanemann, R. Kopp, S. Presser and P. Ruud (1995), 'Contingent Valuation and Lost Passive Use Damages from the Exxon Valdez', Discussion Paper 95–02, Department of Economics, University of San Diego.

Carson, R., N. Flores and N. Meade (2001), 'Contingent Valuation: Controversies and Evidence', *Environmental and Resource Economics*, **19**, 173–210.

Chakraborty, J. (2001), 'Acute Exposure to Extremely Hazardous Substances: An Analysis of Environmental Equity', *Risk Analysis*, **21**(5), 883–94.

Coase, R. (1960), 'The Problem of Social Cost', *Journal of Law and Economics*, **3**, 1–44.

Cowell, F. and K. Gardiner (1999), 'Welfare Weights', Report to the UK Office of Fair Trading, available at www.oft.gov.uk/NR/rdonlyres/.

Cutter, S. (1995), 'Race, Class and Environmental Justice', *Progress in Human Geography*, **19**(1), 111–22.

Cutter, S., D. Holm and L. Clark (1996), 'The Role of Geographic Scale in Monitoring Environmental Justice', *Risk Analysis*, **16**, 517–26.

de Kam, F. (2002), 'Issues Paper', in OECD, *Implementing Environmental Fiscal Reform: Income Distribution and Sectoral Competitiveness Issues*, COM/ENV/EPOC/DAFFE/CFA(2002)76Final, Paris, OECD.

Ebert, U. (2000), 'Environmental Goods and the Distribution of Income', Department of Economics, Discussion Paper V-199–00, Oldenbourg: University of Oldenbourg.

Fankhauser, S. (1995), *Valuing Climate Change: The Economics of the Greenhouse*, London: Earthscan.

Flores, N. and R. Carson (1997), 'The Relationship between Income Elasticities of Demand and Willingness to Pay', *Journal of Environmental Economics and Management*, **33**, 287–95.

Foreman, C. (2000), 'Environmental Justice and Risk Assessment: The Uneasy Relationship', *Human and Ecological Risk Assessment*, **6**(6), 549–54.

Freeman, A.M. (1972), 'The Distribution of Environmental Quality', in A. Kneese and B. Bower (eds), *Environmental Quality Analysis*, Baltimore: Johns Hopkins University Press, pp. 243–80.

Friends of the Earth (2001), *Pollution and Poverty – Breaking the Link*, London: Friends of the Earth.

Gianessi, L., H. Peskin and E. Wolff (1977), 'The Distributional Implications of National Air Pollution Damage Estimates', in F. Juster (ed.), *The Distribution of Economic Wellbeing*, Cambridge, MA: Ballinger, pp. 201–26.

Glickman, T. and R. Hersh (1995), 'Evaluating Environmental Equity: The Impacts of Industrial Hazards on Selected Social Groups in Allegheny County, Pennsylvania', Discussion Paper 95–13, Washington DC: Resources for the Future.

Goldman, B. (1994), *Not Just Prosperity: Achieving Sustainability with Environmental Justice*, Washington DC: National Wildlife Federation.

Goldman, B. (2000), 'An Environmental Justice Paradigm for Risk Assessment', *Human and Ecological Risk Assessment*, **6**(6), 541–8.

Goldman, B. and L. Fitton (1994), *Toxic Wastes and Race Revisited: An Update of the 1987 Report on the Racial and Socioeconomic Characteristics of Communities with Hazardous Waste Sites*, Washington, DC: Center for Policy Alternatives.

Hamilton, J. (1993), 'Politics and Social Costs: Estimating the Impact of Collective Action on Hazardous Waste Facilities', *RAND Journal of Economics*, **24**(1), 101–25.

Hamilton, J. (1995), 'Testing for Environmental Racism: Prejudice, Profits, Political Power?', *Journal of Policy Analysis and Management*, **14**, 107–32.

Hamilton, J. (1999), 'Exercising Property Rights to Pollute: Do Cancer Risks and Politics Affect Plant Emission Reductions?', *Journal of Risk and Uncertainty*, **18**(2), 105–24.

Hamilton, J. and W.K. Viscusi (1999), *Calculating Risks? The Spatial and Political Dimensions of Hazardous Waste Policy*, Cambridge, MA: MIT Press.

Handy, F. (1977), 'Income and Air Pollution in Hamilton, Ontario', *Alternatives*, **6**, 18–24.

Hanemann, M. (1991), 'Willingness to Pay and Willingness to Accept: How Much Can They Differ?', *American Economic Review*, **81**, 635–47.

Hanemann, M. (1996), 'Theory versus Data in the Contingent Valuation Debate', in D. Bjornstad and J. Kahn (eds), *The Contingent Valuation of Environmental Resources: Methodological Issues and Research Needs*, Cheltenham, UK and Northampton, MA, USA: Edward Elgar, 38–60.

Harbaugh, W., A. Levinson and D. Wilson (2000), 'Re-examining the Empirical Evidence for an Environmental Kuznets Curve', NBER Working Paper 7711, Cambridge, MA: National Bureau of Economic Research, Inc.

Harris, A. (1979), 'Is Quiet a Luxury Good? A Survey Approach', *International Journal of Social Economics*, **6**, 177–88.

Harrison, D. (1975), *Who Pays for Clean Air?* Cambridge, MA: Ballinger.

Harrison, K. and W. Antweiler (2002), 'Incentives for Pollution Abatement: Regulations, Regulatory Threat and Non-governmental Pressure', mimeo, University of British Columbia.

Harrison, D. and D. Rubinfeld (1978), 'Hedonic House Prices and the Demand for Clean Air', *Journal of Environmental Economics and Management*, **5**, 81–102.

Haynes, K., S. Lall and M. Trice (2001), 'Spatial Issues in Environmental Equity', *International Journal of Environmental Technology and Management*, **1**(1), 17–31.

Hite, D. (2000), 'A Random Utility Model of Environmental Equity', *Growth and Change*, **31**, 40–58.

HM Treasury (UK) (2003), *The Green Book: Appraisal and Evaluation in Central Government*, London: HM Treasury, www.hm-treasury.gov.uk.

Hockman, E. and C. Morris (1998), 'Progress towards Environmental Justice: A Five-year Perspective on Toxicity, Race and Poverty in Michigan, 1990–1995', *Journal of Environmental Planning and Management*, **41**(2), 157–76.

Hökby, S. and T. Söderqvist (2001), 'Elasticities of Demand and Willingness to Pay for Environmental Services in Sweden', paper presented to 11th Annual Conference of the European Association of Environmental and Resource Economists, Southampton.

Imber, D., G. Stevenson and L. Wilks (1991), 'A Contingent Valuation of the Kakadu Conservation Zone', Resource Assessment Commission, Research Paper No. 3, Canberra.

Jerrett, M., J. Eyles, D. Cole and S. Reader (1997), 'Environmental Equity in Canada: An Empirical Investigation into the Income Distribution of Pollution in Ontario', *Environment and Planning A*, **29**, 1777–800.

Jones-Lee, M., M. Hammerton and P. Philips (1985), 'The Value of Safety: The Results of a National Sample Survey', *Economic Journal*, **95**, 49–72.

Kahn, M. (1998), 'A Household Level Environmental Kuznets Curve', *Economics Letters*, **59**, 269–73.
Kahn, M. (2001), 'The Beneficiaries of Clean Air Act Regulation', *Regulation*, Spring, 34–8.
Khanna, N. (2001), 'The Income Elasticity of Non-point Source Air Pollutants', Working Paper WP0110, Economics Department, New York: Binghampton University.
Kriesel, W., T. Centner and A. Keeler (1996), 'Neighborhood Exposure to Toxic Releases: Are There Racial Inequities?', *Growth and Change*, **27**, 477–99.
Kriström, B. and P. Riera (1996), 'Is the Income Elasticity of Environmental Improvements Less Than One?', *Environmental and Resource Economics*, **7**, 45–66.
Kruize, M. and A. Bouwman (2003), 'The Distribution of Benefits and Costs of Environmental Policies: A Case Study on the Distribution of Environmental Impacts in Rijnmond Region: The Netherlands', paper presented to OECD Workshop on the Distribution of Benefits and Costs of Environmental Policies: Analysis, Evidence and Policy Issues, Paris: OECD.
Lavelle, M. and M. Coyle (1992), 'Unequal Protection: The Racial Divide on Environmental Law', *National Law Journal*, 21 September, S1.
Little, I.M.D. (1950), *A Critique of Welfare Economics*, Oxford: Oxford University Press.
Liu, F. (2001), 'Dynamics and Causation of Environmental Equity, Locally Unwanted Land Uses, and Neighbourhood Changes', *Environmental Management*, **21**(5), 643–56.
Loehman, E. and E. De (1982), 'Application of Stochastic Choice Modeling to Policy Analysis of Public Goods: A Case Study of Air Quality Improvements', *Review of Economics and Statistics*, **64**(3), 474–80.
Loomis, J. and R. Walsh (1997), *Recreation Economic Decisions: Comparing Benefits and Costs*, State College, Pennsylvania: Venture Publishing.
McCleod, H., I. Langford, A. Jones, J. Stedman, R. Day, I. Lorenzoni and I. Bateman (2000), 'The Relationship between Socio-economic Indicators and Air Pollution in England and Wales', *Regional Environmental Change*, **1**(2), 78–85.
McFadden, D. (1994), 'Contingent Valuation and Social Choice', *American Journal of Agricultural Economics*, **76**, 689–708.
McFadden, D. and G. Leonard (1993), 'Issues in the Contingent Valuation of Environmental Goods: Methodologies for Data Collection and Analysis', in J. Hausman (ed.), *Contingent Valuation: A Critical Assessment*, Amsterdam: Elsevier.
Millimet, D. and D. Slottje (2002), 'Environmental Compliance Costs and the Distribution of Emissions in the USA', *Journal of Regional Science*, **42**(1), 87–105.
Mitchell, G. and D. Dorling (2003), 'An Environmental Justice Analysis of British Air Quality', *Environment and Planning*, **35**, 909–29.
Mohai, P. and B. Bryant (1992), 'Environmental Racism', in P. Mohai and B. Bryant (eds), *Race and the Incidence of Environmental Hazards: A Time for Discourse*, Boulder, Co: Westview Press, pp. 163–76.
Nelson, J. (1978), 'Residential Choice, Hedonic Prices and the Demand for Urban Air Quality', *Journal of Urban Economics*, **5**, 357–69.
OECD (2001), *Environmentally Related Taxes in OECD Countries: Issues and Strategies*, Paris: OECD.

Olson, M. (1965), *The Logic of Collective Action*, Cambridge, MA: Harvard University Press.

Pearce, D.W. (1980), 'The Social Incidence of Environmental Costs and Benefits', *Progress in Resource Management and Environmental Planning*, **2**, 63–87.

Pearce, D.W. (2004), 'The Social Cost of Carbon and its Policy Implications', *Oxford Review of Economic Policy*, **16**(3), 362–84. Reprinted with amendments and extensions in D. Helm (ed.), *Climate Change Policy*, Oxford: Oxford University Press.

Pearce, D.W. (2005), 'The Social Cost of Carbon and its Policy Implications', in D. Helm (ed.), *Climate Change Policy*, Oxford: Oxford University Press, pp. 99–133.

Pearce, D.W. and R. Turner (1990), *Economics of Natural Resources and the Environment*, Hemel Hempstead: Wheatsheaf.

Pearce, D.W. and C. Palmer (2001), 'Public and Private Spending for Environmental Protection: A Cross-country Policy Analysis', *Fiscal Studies*, **22**(4), 403–56.

Pellow, D., A. Weinberg and A. Schnaiberg (2001), 'The Environmental Justice Movement: Equitable Allocation of the Costs and Benefits of Environmental Management Outcomes', *Social Justice Research*, **14**(4), 423–39.

Perlin, S., R.W. Setzer, J. Creason and K. Sexton (1995), 'Distribution of Industrial Air Emissions by Income and Race in the United States: An Approach Using the Toxic Release Inventory', *Environmental Science and Technology*, **29**, 69–80.

Pye, S., J. Stedman, M. Adams and K. King (2001), 'Further Analysis of NO_2 and PM_{10} Air Pollution and Social Deprivation', Report AEAT/ENV/R/0865, Culham: AEA Technology.

Rawls, J. (1971), *A Theory of Justice*, Oxford: Oxford University Press.

Ringquist, E. (1998), 'A Question of Justice: Equity in Environmental Litigation', *Journal of Politics*, **60**(4), November, 1148–65.

Roberts, S. (2000), 'Environmental Justice: Examining the Role of Risk Assessment', *Human and Ecological Risk Assessment*, **6**(6), 537–40.

Rose, A., B. Stevens and G. David (1989), 'Assessing who Gains and who Loses from Natural Resource Policy: Distributional Information and the Public Participation Process', *Resources Policy*, **15**(4), 282–91.

Santos, J.M.L. (1998), *The Economic Valuation of Landscape Change: Theory and Policies for Land Use and Conservation*. Cheltenham, UK and Northampton, MA: Edward Elgar.

Sexton, K. (2000), 'Socioeconomic and Racial Disparities in Environmental Health: Is Risk Assessment Part of the Problem or Part of the Solution?', *Human and Ecological Risk Assessment*, **6**(6), 561–74.

Sieg, H., V. Kerry Smith, H.S. Banzhaf and R. Walsh (2000), 'Estimating the General Equilibrium Benefits of Large Policy Changes: The Clean Air Act Revisited', NBER Working Paper 7744, Cambridge, MA: National Bureau of Economic Research, Inc.

Simon, T. (2000), 'In Defense of Risk Assessment: A Reply to the Environmental Justice Movement's Critique', *Human and Ecological Risk Assessment*, **6**(6), 555–60.

Smith, K. (1988), 'Air Pollution: Assessing Total Exposure in Developing Countries', *Environment*, **30**(10), 16–20, 28–35.

Stevenson, S., C. Stephens, M. Landon, S. Pattendon, P. Wilkinson and T. Fletcher (1998), 'Examining the Inequality and Inequity of Car Ownership and the Effects of Pollution and Health Outcomes such as Respiratory Disease', *Epidemiology*, **9**(4), 29 (Abstract only).

Tiebout, C. (1956), 'A Pure Theory of Local Expenditures', *Journal of Political Economy*, **LXIV**, 416–24.

UCC (United Church of Christ) (1987), *Toxic Wastes and Race in the United States. A National Report on the Racial and Socio-Economic Characteristics with Hazardous Waste Sites*, New York: UCC – Commission on Racial Justice.

US EPA (Environmental Protection Agency) (1992), *Environmental Equity: Reducing Risk for All Communities*, EPA/230-R-92-008, Washington DC: US EPA.

US EPA (Environmental Protection Agency) (1998), *Final Guidance for Incorporating Environmental Justice Concerns in EPA's NEPA Compliance Analysis*, Washington DC: Government Printing Office.

US GAO (General Accounting Office) (1983), *Siting of Hazardous Waste Landfills and their Correlation with Racial and Economic Status of Surrounding Communities*, Washington DC: GAO.

Viscusi, W.K. and W. Evans (1990), 'Utility Functions that Depend on Health Status: Estimates and Economic Implications', *American Economic Review*, **80**(3), 353–74.

Wagstaff, A. and E. van Doorslaer (2000), 'Income Inequality and Health: What Does the Literature Tell Us?', *Annual Review of Public Health*, **21**, 543–67.

Walker, G., J. Fairburn and K. Bickerstaff (2000), 'Ethnicity and Risk: The Characteristics of Populations in Census Wards Containing Major Accident Hazard Sites in England and Wales', Occasional Paper 15, Department of Geography, University of Staffordshire.

Walker, G., J. Fairburn, G. Smith and G. Mitchell (2003), 'Environmental Quality and Social Deprivation', R&D Technical Report E2-067/1/TR, Bristol: Environment Agency.

Walters, A. (1975), *Noise and Prices*, Oxford: Oxford University Press.

Wildavsky, A. (1995), *But Is It True? A Citizen's Guide to Environmental Health and Safety Issues*, Cambridge, MA: Harvard University Press.

Yandle, T. and D. Burton (1996), 'Re-examining Environmental Justice: A Statistical Analysis of Historical Hazardous Waste Landfill Siting Patterns in Metropolitan Texas', *Social Science Quarterly*, **77**, 477–92.

Young, H. Peyton (1994), *Equity in Theory and Practice*, Princeton, NJ: Princeton University Press.

Zajac, E. (1995), *The Political Economy of Fairness*, Cambridge, MA: MIT Press.

Zimmerman, R. (1993), 'Social Equity and Environmental Risk', *Risk Analysis*, **13**, 649–66.

Zupan, J. (1973), *The Distribution of Air Quality in the New York Region*, Baltimore, MD: Johns Hopkins University Press.

GLOSSARY OF CONCEPTS

As several technical concepts are used in this chapter, and after being introduced are summarised by a single statistic, this glossary summarises them.

Income elasticity of demand

This is the change in the *quantity* demanded of some environmental asset in response to a small change in *income*. It is given by the formula:

$$\eta = \partial E \cdot Y / \partial Y \cdot E$$

where E is the quantity demanded, Y is income.

Income elasticity of willingness to pay

This is the change in the *willingness to pay* for some environmental asset in response to a change in *income*. It is given by the formula:

$$\omega = \partial WTP \cdot Y / \partial Y \cdot WTP$$

where WTP is willingness to pay.

Price elasticity of demand

The price elasticity of demand is the change in the *quantity* demanded with respect to a change in the *price* of the environmental asset. It is given by the formula:

$$p = \partial E \cdot P / \partial P \cdot E$$

where P is price and p is the price elasticity.
  Under certain circumstances: $\omega = \eta / p$.

Income elasticity of pollution

Some authors use the notion of an 'income elasticity of pollution' which is defined as the percentage change in pollution for a given percentage change in income. Note that, despite the similarity in appearance, this is not the same as the income elasticity of demand, but refers more to the supply of pollution at different income levels. Clearly, however, the notion could reflect demand forces:

$$d = \partial E_S \cdot Y / \partial Y \cdot E_S$$

where E_S is the ambient concentration of pollution.

3. Framework for assessing the distribution of financial effects of environmental policy

Bengt Kriström

The primary fact of economics is the production of wealth. The division of the product among those who create it is secondary in logical order, and in a sense, in importance. Yet the most important subject of thought connected with economy is distribution. (J.B. Clark, 1894, Palgrave Dictionary of Economics)

1. INTRODUCTION

By its very nature, environmental policy must have distributional impacts. Because the essential purpose of environmental policy is to change consumption and production patterns, there will inevitably be 'winners' and 'losers' among the economy's households and firms. Indeed, the daily drama of environmental policy typically involves making hard choices rather than implementing 'win–win' policies. Witness the sometimes acrimonious protests against gasoline tax increases, or the occasionally unfriendly reception of a decision to preserve a natural resource; in any realistic setting, environmental policy imposes both gains and losses. Yet, the environmental economics literature has focused primarily on efficiency. We know much less about how the fruits of environmental policy are distributed in society, than how to design efficient policies.

The tide is now turning and distributional concerns are returning to the frontlines of economic research: a vigorous new strand of the macroeconomics literature explores the income distribution–growth nexus,[1] modern welfare economics stress the importance of scrutinising the distribution of impacts, for example, in the recent literature on assessing the benefits and costs of public programmes,[2] a dynamic and growing literature on the distributional impacts of trade liberalisation in multiregional settings has recently begun the task of quantifying the equity dimensions.[3]

There are other examples and they all display the fact that economists increasingly confront equity issues directly, notwithstanding a tradition of perhaps keeping at least an arm's-length distance to them. Perhaps the most cogent reason for being concerned with environmental policy and distribution is that an understanding of distributional impacts allows the shaping of policy packages that are more likely to be accepted by the public. Either disregarding distributional impacts as 'a necessary evil' or being stifled by them appear to be unnecessarily extreme positions. Yet, while economic theory provides a crisp and useful working definition of an efficient environmental policy, it cannot claim to offer a final resolution of just what a 'fair' environmental policy entails. Rather, it offers a structured way of thinking about distributional issues and suggests ways of disentangling them empirically.

This chapter elaborates on the OECD (1994) framework for understanding the financial distributional impacts of environmental policy. It presents a survey of some relevant work in the area that has become available since 1994 and a structure for distributional analysis that places additional emphasis on the indirect channels. The fact that an economy consists of a set of mutually dependent markets adds some twists to the distributional analysis which we highlight here. There are important connections between the economy and the environment as well, but they are not treated fully in the chapter. We will, however, propose a framework that at least in principle includes such linkages. Our discussion is framed against a backdrop of a large number of policy instruments, ranging from incentive-based instruments to 'softer' policies such as information strategies. Our story is heavily bent towards what is known about incentive-based measures, because it is in this area that we have the bulk of empirical evidence and experience.

The structure of the chapter is as follows. Section 2 briefly pins down a set of key conceptual issues, such as the definition of a welfare-improving environmental policy and just what it is that should be distributed (annual income or lifetime income are two alternatives). Section 3 unravels our elaboration of the 1994 framework. We progressively introduce additional linkages between markets and begin by examining different policy instruments at the individual household or firm level. We then proceed to a one-market analysis. For example, restricting the use of gasoline through higher taxes or otherwise will increase the price of gasoline and we assume that the price increase affects no other market. The distributional impacts depend on how firms are able to pass costs on to consumers at one particular market. In the second stage, we allow the repercussions to be felt through a particular sector of the economy. In certain cases, limiting the analysis to one sector is natural. The sector analysis very clearly shows how a policy generates 'winners' and 'losers', as the impacts cascade through the markets of the sector. It also brings out the useful point that it is sometimes important to take market dependences into account when designing environmental policy. In addition, it suggests circumstances under which one can be satisfied with a less complex (in terms of dependences across markets) analysis. The third stage is general equilibrium analysis, which knits together all the markets of the economy and brings additional advantages to the analysis of environmental policy. For example, keeping track of the budgetary impacts when environmental taxes (or revenues from permits) are added into an existing tax system is greatly simplified with this approach, not least if the policy is supposed to be revenue-neutral. Combining the framework in three stages as suggested here goes some way to understanding the mechanics of adjustment. We then suggest how an integrated framework for distributional analysis can be developed that includes economy–environment interactions, by putting it all together in a social accounting matrix (SAM). Section 4 looks at policy responses. These include tax exemptions (household/firm), limited grandfathering of permits and other ways of sacrificing some efficiency gains for equity reasons.[4]

2.   KEY CONCEPTUAL ISSUES

Three conceptual issues underlie many discussions of distributional effects of environmental policy. The first is the definition of cost. It will be useful to first view the costs as opportunity costs from the production side. This helps mapping out some of the basic assumptions made in the empirical studies surveyed. Let us make clear at once that we abstain from looking at win–win policies.[5] In so far as such policies exist, they should be implemented (and herein lies a controversial identification issue, but we finesse it here). Next we ask just what should be meant by a welfare-improving environmental policy, given the starting point that this is the basic purpose of environmental policy. Standard economic theory tells us to move forward with a policy that has sums of benefits exceeding sums of costs, although this (Kaldor–Hicks) criterion invokes a particular view on distributional matters. We present arguments for and against the use of this criterion. In our view, efficiency and equity cannot be easily separated, which is a basic tenet of this widely-used criterion. Finally, we ask what it is we should measure in distributional studies, a question that is by no means trivial. Traditionally, income is used as the unit for comparison of policies but there are some interesting alternatives that occasionally lead to modified conclusions (primarily regarding the regressive impacts of an instrument).

2.1 The Cost of Environmental Policy

To fix ideas and summarise some of the key points that will be made hereafter, a capsule summary of the costs of environmental policy is presented
in Figure 3.1.

Figure 3.1 portrays the cost of improving environmental quality from
some level Z^0 to another level Z^1. The cost is here taken to be the loss in
income (or national product). There are alternative measures of opportunity costs, but the important point is that we assume away free lunches.[6] An
efficient policy takes the economy from Z^0 to Z^1 at minimum cost in terms
of income. This cost will be distributed across the households and firms of
the economy in particular ways not captured in the figure. The minimum
cost is depicted as one where the economy smoothly adjusts, that is, we
follow the production possibility as suggested in the figure. The minimal
cost is the income loss $GDP^0 - GDP^1$. A substantial number of models are
now available that analyse the costs of environmental policy. These models
are typically based on calculating the costs of environmental policy as

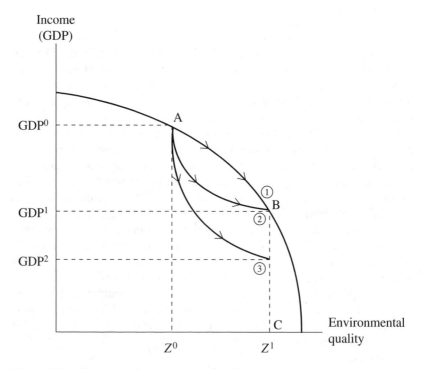

Figure 3.1   The cost of environmental policy

suggested by the move labelled ①. Much of our discussion will circle around gross costs, conceptualised in this way.

While environmental policy could entail unemployment of labour and impose other adjustment costs, these costs are seldom quantified in distributional studies. Indeed, the real world consists of heterogeneous firms and households, each with different possibilities to adjust to new policies.[7] During a certain amount of time, we can expect to find various transition problems throughout the adjustment from Z^0 to Z^1. This is depicted by the curve ②, in which the policy imposes 'transition costs'. A certain fraction of the economy's resources is not utilised during the adjustment process. When firms are closed, labour (and other resources) becomes temporarily unemployed. Yet, the goal is reached efficiently in the end. While the empirical evidence is scant on the distributional impacts of environmental policy, we know even less about how the transition costs are distributed. Finally, we illustrate a possibility in which the policy goal is reached, but the cost to the economy is higher than implied by an efficient policy. This is the curve labelled ③ in the figure. A bulk of empirical evidence suggests that incentive-based instruments are more efficient than regulations, so that the latter are more often associated with developments suggested by ③. Consequently, the total costs of regulations are likely to be higher, but scarcely anything is known about the distributional impacts. We will return to this point.

While Figure 3.1 does not show who wins and who loses from reaching the environmental goal, it illustrates a number of useful ideas. As stressed by OECD (1994), a policy has to be assessed against a fixed baseline. There are two basic 'fixed points' to use in a distributional study. We can compare the consequences of a policy relative to the status quo, that is, the point A in the figure. Alternatively, we can compare across policies, given that the goal is Z^1.[8] We can easily extend the figure to include the development of the economy over time, and use a baseline scenario as the fixed 'point' of comparison.

If the move from Z^0 to Z^1 imposes gains to some individuals and losses to others, the immediate question that arises from an economic point of view is in which sense the move is welfare-improving. In other words, in a cost–benefit assessment some mechanism has to be invoked that weighs benefits and costs together. In the next section, we discuss interpretations of what a welfare-improving policy entails and then turn to the question of how to make this idea operational.

2.2 Welfare-improving Environmental Policies

The basic purpose of environmental policy is to find (and impose) welfare-improving changes of resource allocation. Following Dasgupta et al. (1995), there are two ways of assessing changes in aggregate well-being (or welfare). One would be to measure the value of changes in the constituents of well-being (utility and freedoms), and the other would be to measure the value of the alterations in the commodity determinants of well-being (goods and services that are inputs in the production of well-being). For measurement purposes, the authors propose an index – which turns out to be a 'greener' version of national product – that has the following property: small investment projects which improve the index are at once those that increase aggregate well-being. They abstract, however, from distributional issues.

If a policy is a boon to some households and a burden to others, one must, in general, weigh these (utility) gains and losses together. In economic theory, it is assumed that there exists a distribution of utilities across households that is judged (by a social planner) to be better, worse or equivalent to some other distribution. How to implement this idea in practice is a vexing issue that has transcended much of economic thought. The so-called Kaldor–Hicks criteria make it operational by defining all policies with sums of benefits exceeding sums of costs as socially beneficial.

A common way of measuring benefits (welfare change) is to use the maximum willingness to pay a person attaches to, let us say, an environmental improvement.[9] One then compares the sum of benefits with the sum of the costs. If the sum is positive, the policy is welfare-improving.[10] These criteria are in wide use, not least in environmental policy analysis. For example, they cut through essentially all the literature on the 'double dividend' issue, because most evaluations compare the total benefits with the costs of revenue-neutral tax swaps. Furthermore, the bulk of the voluminous literature on environmental valuation invariably compares the total benefits with the total costs.[11] It is rather difficult to find examples where the Kaldor–Hicks criteria are not used to define a welfare-improving policy.

A standard interpretation of the Kaldor–Hicks criteria holds that a policy is socially worthwhile if, potentially, the winners could compensate the losers.[12] Whether or not compensation is actually paid is a separate matter to be decided upon by others, that is, the political system.[13] One can interpret this compensation idea as a way of separating efficiency and equity. Put simply, make the cake as big as possible and consider the cutting of the cake as a separate (and in principle unsolvable) distributional issue. Note that the separation idea is a basic tenet of investment theory. Choosing investments with the largest present value makes the cake as big as possible and the cake can be cut at will by a perfect capital market; it affords any combination of present and future consumption.[14]

2.2.1   Environmental issues and the separation between equity and efficiency

Turn now to environmental issues and the compensation criteria. Suppose that a dam construction necessitates the removal of a home. The home-owner's preferences are such that his willingness to pay for living in his current home is his income, that is, he cannot bear the thought of relocating. We can ask how much he is willing to pay for not having the dam, and check to see if this sum covers the net profits the construction company would have made from its investment. However, we can also ask what compensation the home-owner requires for accepting the project. This compensation is infinitely high in this example. Under this compensation criterion, the project cannot be worthwhile. The result of summing the benefits and the costs of the dam construction depends on the distribution of property rights in the status quo.[15] Several ways out of these kinds of dilemmas have been proposed, yet it is clear that the separation of efficiency and equity may not always be the most palatable assumption to make.[16] A report by Herrington (2003) provides a very useful illustration of the issues involved when trying to separate equity and efficiency in the case of water services.

The separation between equity and efficiency has been a controversial topic in some discussions about global warming policies. According to Chichilnisky and Heal (1994), one cannot separate efficiency from equity in a global permit trade market, implying that the prices of permits vary across regions (reflecting the equity/efficiency trade-off). The reason is that one is dealing with a global public good. An alternative view, based on the separation idea, holds that efficiency requires one single market price of carbon permits, because this translates to equal marginal abatement costs in all sources (and hence minimised costs). The resulting equilibrium will, for any initial distribution of permits, map into a set of 'winners' and 'losers'. Provided that unlimited transfers between countries are available, such transfers can be used to confront the distributional issues. The fact that one is dealing with a public good does not matter, according to, for example, Sturm (1995). Yet, a moment of reflection suggests that the initial distribution of carbon permits is likely to be a major issue when trying to implement a global permit market. While the efficiency properties of permit markets are useful, the underlying distributional concerns remain a major hurdle for the implementation of such markets.

Return now to the practical questions of finding welfare-improving environmental policies. As we have seen, the Kaldor–Hicks criteria remain the workhorses in cost–benefit analysis. They are insensitive to the distribution of 'winners' and 'losers'. In other words, the Kaldor–Hicks approach entails putting the welfare weights equal to one for each individual (so that only the sums matter). This particular choice can be motivated in several ways, for example, by assuming that the prevailing income distribution is optimal. There is no objective way to choose weights; however, any choice reflects a particular view about how welfare should be distributed in society.[17] A number of useful possibilities are explored in the chapter by David Pearce (see Chapter 2). The counter-argument to weighting benefits and costs, attributable to Hotelling in the 1930s, is that if policies were based on sums of benefits and costs, we would all be better off on the average. In some cases we lose, in others we win, but on the average everybody will be better off.

Whichever argument one chooses to support, there seems to be little to lose from detailing the distributional aspects of environmental policy change. Highlighting the distributional impacts of any policy often provides useful information per se. Further, recent developments of empirical methods for public programmes emphasise, as noted above, the need for detailing the impact on the distribution of outcomes. Empirical methods widely used in environmental economics are particularly suitable in this context, for example, contingent valuation surveys (because data on losses and gains are assembled at the individual level).

As a practical matter, it is often found that improvement of environmental quality provides small benefits to many, but imposes large costs on a few. This is amply documented in the literature. A useful survey appears in Chapter 7 in this volume by James Hamilton on siting of 'undesirable objects'. There is similar evidence in the literature on natural resource conflicts. High-profile issues include the spotted owl controversy in the United States. Some estimates suggest that the benefit of saving the spotted owl is about US$30 per American, while the cost is localised to the forest industry in the north-western USA.[18]

To sum up: conventional analysis of the costs and benefits of environmental policy is based on summing these items. We argue here that information about how these benefits and costs are distributed will often be useful, notwithstanding the thorny issue of weighting them together.

2.3 What is to be Distributed?

The Environmental Protection Agency[19] suggests that studies of environmental policy measures should include an assessment of: (i) firms' revenues and costs, (ii) public sector revenues and costs, (iii) regions, (iv) growth, employment, competitiveness (at the national level), and (v) population (income, ethnic groups, men/women, children). To this we could add the intertemporal dimension, although this lies beyond the scope of the present chapter.[20] One also needs measures that answer directly the question of how equity is affected by a policy change. This, in turn, calls for a definition of equity, of which there are many. In order not to get trapped into the intricacies of a philosophical debate that extends over many centuries, the approach taken here is to discuss measures that can serve as descriptors of equity.[21]

2.3.1 Descriptors of equity

Horizontal equity means that 'equals should be treated equally', so that, for example, individuals with the same income should pay the same income tax and receive the same benefits.[22] Vertical equity is a principle that implies 'unequal treatment of unequals'. A person with no income should not pay the same tax as a person with income. Tietenberg's (1996) survey shows that environmental policy in the United States conflicts with both equity criteria in several cases. Tietenberg (p. 471) concludes that vertical equity criteria have been violated in the sense that 'the net benefits have been disproportionately received by the well-to-do people'. Horizontal equity criterion has, in part, been violated, because people in the same income category have received different net benefits. For air pollution, urban residents have gained more than those in rural areas, the latter possibly with net negative benefits.

Perhaps the most often used descriptor of the distributional impacts of environmental policy is whether or not policy is regressive or progressive (a subset of vertical equity criteria). In most cases in the environmental economics literature, regressive implies that the cost share decreases with income. The opposite is true for progressive impacts. In order to appreciate these definitions, let us take a closer look at what a proper notion of 'cost share' entails and then discuss the concept of income in more detail.

The cost of environmental policy is often based on standard measures of real income changes found in the welfare economics literature; compare, the willingness to pay measures discussed above. These measures include the fact that households may adjust consumption patterns in response to policy change. Any measure of cost that does not allow for this is flawed from an economic perspective.

Turning to income, one must stress that there are many concepts of income; indeed, the very question of just what income is has been a topical subject in economics for at least a century.[23] Comprehensive income measures, such as the so-called Haig–Simmons measure of income (consumption + net change in worth) may well lead to other conclusions regarding regressivity than income from work. Within a certain income group we could find a student with a bright future, a person being temporarily unemployed, a rich retiree and so on and so forth.

The upshot of this is, as Poterba (1991) shows, that taxes on gasoline appear much less regressive when taken as a percentage of total consumption expenditures (this is the proxy for lifetime income).[24] However, Smith

(1992, p. 250) notes that this conclusion depends on the institutional arrangements regarding the length of low-income spells. He finds that the distinction between annual income and lifetime income makes little difference for UK data, in distributional analysis of energy and carbon taxation.[25] In short, conclusions about the distributional impacts of environmental policy are not necessarily robust towards the used concept of income. This conclusion is borne out by experience from the literature on the burden of taxation which suggests that 'The choice of income measure clearly affects both the estimated distribution of taxes by income class and the effect of reform proposals' (Atrostic and Nunns, 1990, p. 382).

Finally, whether or not environmental policy is regressive or progressive also depends on additional assumptions. Whalley (1984) shows how alternative incidence assumptions, that is, how the tax burden is shifted backwards and forwards across markets 'can determine whether the tax structure appears to be progressive or regressive' (Atrostic and Nunns, 1990, p. 377).

2.3.2 Other ways of describing distributional impact

While income is ordinarily used to assess distributional impacts, there are a number of other possibilities that will be briefly mentioned here.

- Environmental quality
- Wealth, broadly defined

It may be of interest to determine how a policy changes environmental quality across the population.[26] Primarily in the United States, there is a long-standing debate on environmental equity involving, inter alia, siting issues, for example, whether or not the siting of environmentally detrimental facilities like power plants is biased against particular ethnic groups. In Europe, there is a recent discussion about 'environmental space'. In both cases, concepts of equity are related to environmental quality, not income. For a recent discussion of these issues, see Martinez-Alier (2002).

Following recent developments of economic theory, the distribution of wealth, broadly defined, could serve as a starting point for a distributional study. Thus, one scrutinises how the distribution of broadly defined assets, including real capital, human capital and social capital are affected by policy changes. See Dasgupta (2001), Heal (1998) and Heal and Kriström (2005) for further discussions about expanded notions of wealth.

In conclusion, there are good arguments for broadening the set of descriptors quite independently of what concept of fairness is being adopted.

3. FRAMEWORK FOR DISTRIBUTIONAL ANALYSIS OF ENVIRONMENTAL POLICY

We unlock our amendments to the 1994 framework by proceeding in a sequential fashion. We begin by examining impacts of environmental policy at the household/firm level. We then examine how a subset of households and firms interact in one particular market and proceed to analyse the interaction of a subset of markets in a given sector. Finally, we end at the level of the economy, in which all markets interact.

3.1 Checklist Summary of OECD 1994 Framework

Let us begin by summarising the framework proposed in the OECD (1994) study in terms of the proposed checklist for distributional analysis (Box 3.1). We elaborate certain aspects of this framework and add some fresh empirical insights that have been gained since 1994.

BOX 3.1   CHECKLIST-SUMMARY OF
FRAMEWORK FOR DISTRIBUTIONAL
ANALYSIS IN OECD, 1994

1. Benchmark for comparison (for example, (i) status quo or (ii) comparative analyses of different policies to reach a given goal).
2. Government revenue? (Whether or not an instrument generates revenue is important for distributional impact analysis).
3. Initial impacts (determination of the initial impacts of the measure).
4. Selection of relevant groups for analysis (useful to include analysis beyond the traditional income distributional analysis, for example, small business impacts, geographic differences).
5. Final impacts analysis. (Long-term impacts on income groups and transitional impacts on worker. Steps include determining (change in compliance) costs; transitional costs for workers; effects of price changes on consumers and firms; firms' profits; government revenues; summarise for various groups.)
6. Available options for mitigation or compensation (advantages and disadvantages).

In principle, the OECD framework can be applied for understanding the following types of environmental policies (Russell and Powell, 1999, p. 309):

1. Prohibition (of inputs, processes or products)
2. Technology specification (for production, recycling or waste treatment)
3. Technological basis for discharge standard
4. Performance specification (discharge permits)
5. Tradable performance specification (tradable permits)
6. Pollution charges
7. Subsidies (lump sum for capital cost, or marginal (as the self-finance deposit-return))
8. Liability law provisions
9. Provision of information (to polluters, investors, consumers, activists)
10. Voluntary agreements

A cursory glance at this list suggests that the distributional impacts of different instruments depend on the choice of measure for analysis. If one compares a uniform environmental tax with a site-specific regulation, the former instrument will equalise the marginal cost across sources. This is not necessarily the case for a regulatory measure. A distributional study comparing these two instruments might conclude that the regulatory instrument is more costly, yet in a broader perspective the price for reducing environmental damage in the right places might be worth paying. An environmental tax, for example, is not ideally suited for cases when the damage varies geographically. In such a case, regulations may in practice also be easier to implement, given the complexities of introducing environmental taxes that vary geographically.

3.2 Individual Households

We begin with the household and first look at costs and very briefly comment on the benefits of environmental policy. We focus on the costs of environmental policy, even though it is clear that the distributional impacts of natural resources policy may be very important. A framework for analysing the distributional impacts of resources policy is developed in Rose et al. (1988).

As a first-order approximation, one could define the cost of, for example, an environmental tax by looking at the price change only (for a relevant good); one multiplies the price change by the current consumption level. Such measures will be recognised from popular press coverage as new, or changed, taxes. This is an upper bound, because households invariably are price-responsive and cut their consumption. A lower bound on the cost can be obtained by taking the consumption level after adjustment and multiplying this by the price change. This is an underestimate of the true economic cost, because it assumes that the household attaches no value to the consumption that gets lost in the adjustment. To calculate the lower bound one has to estimate what the new consumption level will be. The upper and lower bound calculated in the way suggested will always bound the true economic cost, which is the loss in consumer surplus. Bounding the costs in this way is sometimes useful, not the least because it invokes minimal assumptions, relative to the way consumer surplus calculations are often made.

It is to be noted that two households with the same consumption level and the same income may well adjust differently to higher prices. There are many reasons for this (one household might not be able to switch to public transportation mode, for example), but we highlight the fact here that two households may simply have different preferences, yet their observable characteristics are the same. The consumer surplus approach to defining cost takes different preferences into account. A vegetarian and a meat consumer with identical economic characteristics presumably have different views on a meat tax. When analysing the distributional impacts of such a hypothetical tax across income groups, it is clear that we need to base the economic cost of this policy on a measure that includes differences in preferences, as well as other pertinent differences between households.

To fix ideas, consider the many ways in which a household may be affected by changes of aspiration levels in environmental policy.

- *The price of a 'directly linked' good is affected*   For example, a carbon tax will raise the price of fossil fuels. Thus, transportation and heating costs are directly affected. These will, in turn, vary across households in several dimensions, including preferences, income, the prices of other goods, regionally and so on.
- *Prices of other goods change*   The household will also be affected as the relative prices of other goods are affected, following market adjustments.
- *Income from work*   Increased stringency of environmental policy may lead to significant losses of income, at least in the short run, as some firms are shut down.
- *Other income may be affected*   Because households are owners of all firms, profits affect household income. In addition, income from certain natural assets may also be affected by natural resources policies, for example, changes in forestry laws or zoning restrictions.
- *Households may be compensated*   Household net income depends on the structure of the prevailing tax system. Revenues from environmental taxes and permit auctions must, in one way or another, be

---

**BOX 3.2   EARLIER STUDIES ON THE
DISTRIBUTIONAL EFFECTS
OF ENVIRONMENTAL POLICY**

Insights from the earlier literature (until about 1985) have been summarised as follows:

- Environmental damage is regressively distributed
- Environmental benefits are progressively distributed
- The regressive impacts are amplified by indirect links between markets
- The net cost of environmental policy is regressive

Note: See Zimmerman (1986, p. 96). These conclusions have, to some extent, been modified. See especially Chapter 2 in this volume by David Pearce on environmental benefits.

---

returned to the economy. Several options have been scrutinised, for example, reduced payroll taxes, VAT and lump-sum returns. Each choice maps into different distributional consequences. A quantitative regulation provides no income and therefore no ways of returning to the economy what is basically a scarcity rent. These issues are discussed below.

- *Environmental benefits*   These are valued differently by different households, depending on preferences, income and prices of various goods and services. See David Pearce (Chapter 2 in this volume) for a detailed discussion.

In a complete study, the benefits and the costs would be analysed in an integrated way and the incidence of net benefits would be the focal point. It will be useful to keep the limited objective pursued here in mind when contemplating how the fruits of environmental policy are spread across an economy's households. (Box 3.2 considers some insights from earlier studies.)

3.2.1   Empirical findings at the household level

Several studies focus on the regressive/progressive nature of carbon taxation. Brännlund and Nordström (2004), Cornwell and Creedy (1997), Symons et al. (1994) and Tiezzi (2001) are examples from Sweden, Australia, England and Italy of household studies. The Australian and

Swedish studies confirm the view that carbon taxes are regressive.[27] This, however, depends to some extent on how the tax revenues are returned to the economy. Symons et al. who limit their study to carbon taxation of driving fuels is an example of this. For American data, Sipes and Mendelsohn (2001) find a regressive pattern in the case of a gasoline tax, but another US study by West and Williams (2002) on gasoline taxation suggests that a lump-sum return may actually make the tax package progressive. For Denmark, the comprehensive study by Klinge-Jacobsen et al. (2001) also suggests that gasoline taxation may be progressive. Walls and Hanson (1999) stress the difference between annual income and lifetime income, as discussed above. Kriström et al. (2003) shed some light on how carbon sequestration affects the regional distribution of income, under the assumption that a carbon market is available. They calculate net forest growth at a regional level in Sweden. The results show, as expected, a very significant difference compared to current climate policy, which entails taxing carbon. Using the sequestration option implies significant gains for rural areas, that is, those that lose most on the current policy. Examples of recent distributional studies at the household level are contained in Table 3.1.

We might add to Table 3.1 some of the insights from papers presented at the OECD conference to which the present chapter was a contribution. Bork (Chapter 4 in this volume) studies ecological tax reform in Germany in a microsimulation model that includes data on 51 537 taxpayers and 1339 variables. This remarkably rich data set is used to explore the cost of tax reform. He finds a result that is now familiar: ecological taxes (for example, taxes on motor fuels) are regressive. The model assumes no repercussions in any market, let alone responses at the individual level. Consequently, our discussion above suggests that we can interpret the results as upper bounds (at least in terms of the price increases of goods). As duly noted by Bork, the model 'is a suitable instrument to analyse first-order effects of a reform or a reform proposal'. We will explore how models that allow for repercussions introduce additional subtleties in the analysis of distributional impacts in Sections 3.4 to 3.6 below. Brainard et al. (Chapter 6 in present volume) provide an exhaustive analysis of how urban noise pollution affects different groups in Birmingham, UK. They include several dimensions, for example, deprivation, race and age, in their analysis. Interestingly, there seems to be a correlation only between the level of socio-economic deprivation and exposure to noise.

3.2.2 Behavioural response, price elasticity and income

The cost to a household of environmental policy measures depends to a large extent on substitution possibilities. It is sometimes held that environmental policy imposes unequal burdens, because people in upper-income

Table 3.1 The costs of environmental policy, examples of empirical studies at the household level

Authors	Title of study	Type and source of data	Notes on approach	Principal finding
Roberts et al. (1999)	'The Distributional Impacts of Fuel Duties: The Impact on Rural Households in Scotland'	Combination of questionnaire, interviews, travel diaries and focus groups. Five areas in rural Scotland. Car transportation focus of analysis.	Analysis of responses. Not based on econometric modelling. No elasticity estimates.	'in rural areas, increased fuel duties are unlikely to achieve their desired objective of reducing environmental pollution. Most rural households will not adjust their travel patterns . . . the tax is not only inequitable but also inefficient' (p. 287).
Rajah and Smith (1993)	'Distributional Aspects of Household Water Charges'	Family Expenditure Survey (FES) England and Wales, financial year 1984–85. Includes detailed information about 7000 households.	Data indexed to 1991–92 levels. Water consumption estimated by econometric model using other survey data. Examines five different water pricing schemes.	Regressive impact for examined pricing schemes. Finds 'a potential value of a system of non-metered water charges that closely proxies household water consumption' (p. 108).
Cornwell and Creedy (1997)	'Carbon Taxation, Prices and Inequality in Australia'	Official data on carbon emissions by industry and fuel type for financial year 1989–90. Household expenditure	Analysis of the carbon tax needed to meet the Toronto target, that is, a reduction of	The carbon tax is found to be regressive, but 'transfer payment can be adjusted to compensate for the

	pattern from 1984 Household Expenditure Survey.	Australian carbon emissions by 20% up to 2005, 1988 being the base year.	regressivity of a carbon tax without decreasing total revenue' (p. 35).
Klinge-Jacobsen et al. (2001)	'Fordelningsvirknin gen af energi- og miljöavgifter' [Distributional impacts of environmental and energy charges]	Expenditure surveys, national accounts, environmental and socio-economic data from comprehensive database [Lovmodel].	Analysis of direct and indirect distributional effects on households of energy and environmental taxes.	In Denmark, 'taxes on petrol and registration duties for cars are progressive . . . most other environmental taxes are regressive' (p. 7).
Tiezzi (2001)	'The Welfare Effects of Carbon Taxation on Italian Households'	Monthly Italian household data from 1985:1–1996:12. Five household types (no. of adults + two age groups if 1 or 2 adults). Six consumption goods.	Econometric model (AIDS). Simulated introduction of carbon tax, with progression, 1997–2000.	'the presumed regressivity of carbon taxation is not sustained. This might be due to the fact that the reform has mainly hit transport fuels, whereas heating prices have increased relatively less' (p. 12).
Brännlund and Nordström (2004)	'Carbon Tax Simulations using a Household Demand Model'	Household expenditure data 1985, 1988, 1992 (12 000 obs) combined with quarterly macroeconomic price quantity data 1980:1–1997:4.	Econometric model (QIADS). Carbon tax with three replacement options. Labour tax, VAT and subsidy to public transportation.	Regressive. Urban/rural dimension, rural households mostly affected.

Table 3.1 (continued)

Authors	Title of study	Type and source of data	Notes on approach	Principal finding
West and Williams (2002)	'Estimates from a Consumer Demand System: Implications for the Incidence of Environmental Taxes'	1996–98 Consumer Expenditure Survey. State-level price information.	NBERs TAXSIM model to calculate marginal and average tax rates for workers. Econometric Model (AIDS).	'increasing the gas tax is generally regressive, but that this depends greatly on how the revenue is used . . . a lump sum transfer to households more than offsets the regressivity of the gas tax, and thus in this case, increasing the gas tax is quite progressive' (p. 6).
Sipes and Mendelsohn (2001)	'The Effectiveness of Gasoline Taxation to Manage Air Pollution'	Contingent valuation type of survey. Hypothetical questions on gasoline price increase (personal interviews). Los Angeles and Connecticut, Nov 1999–Feb 2000. N = 221 (200 usable responses), 336 (300) respectively.	Econometric model. With and without interaction effects. Finds low income elasticity (0.1–0.2), perhaps attributable to the way data were collected.	'Even if the income elasticity estimates in this paper are low, a tax on gasoline would most likely fall on the poor' (p. 309). Argues that tax on transportation results in significant welfare losses with small environmental improvements.
Kriström et al. (2003)	'Fördelningseffekter av Miljöpolitik' [Distributional	Survey study of N = 1000 rural/urban household sample.	Rudimentary analysis of willingness to pay	Rural households (a minority) are willing to

effects of environmental policy]	Rudimentary cost–benefit analysis of increasing/ decreasing wolf population.	for increase/decrease of wolf population.	pay more for decreasing the wolf population than urban population is willing to pay for increasing it.
Walls and Hanson (1999)	'Distributional Aspects of an Environmental Tax Shift: The Case of Motor Vehicle Emissions Taxes'	1018 household sample from US Department of Transportation 1990 Nationwide Personal Transportation Survey (NPTS). Includes detailed household and household-owned vehicle information. Emissions data from remote sensing data set of 90 000 vehicles.	Tabulation of annual fees as percentage of annual and lifetime income; current registration fee, vehicle-miles travelled (VMT) fee and emissions fee. Revenue-neutral reforms, replacing current vehicle registration fees (these are based on value of vehicle).	Income: 'Our results are heavily dependent on the measure of income we use . . . our three fees appear regressive and reducing motor vehicle registration fees does not completely offset the problem.' Lifetime income: 'All of the fees appear regressive, but much less so than on the basis of annual income' (p. 63).
Kriström et al. (2003)	'Fördelningseffekter av Miljöpolitik' [Distributional effects of environmental policy]	Data on net forest growth in Sweden and gross carbon tax payment in different counties.	Calculation of carbon sequestration from forest net growth (gross carbon = 6 ton/capita, net carbon = 1 ton/capita).	If forest owners were paid for carbon sequestration, significant net transfers from comprehensive carbon taxation. Net gainers: rural, forest-rich areas. Net losers: urban areas.

brackets have more options to adapt (by moving to another location, for example).[28] Johnstone and Alavalapati (1998, p. 16) observe that higher-income households will tend to have a higher price elasticity for household fuels. They go on to observe that such patterns are further aggravated by potential market failures. If there are insulation measures with high returns, low-income households could face particular difficulties on imperfect capital markets; they may not be able to borrow to the same extent as other types of households. This reinforces the regressivity of environmental policy. It is therefore of interest in a distributional study to examine the price sensitivity across income groups. Let us approach this question by looking at some ways of explaining this with some basic economics insights. We then discuss some empirical evidence on this issue.

In their study of gasoline taxes, Sipes and Mendelsohn (2001, p. 304) observe that 'Traditionally, economists have assumed that price elasticities are the same for everyone'. From the simplest possible demand structure, that is, a demand curve linear in price and income (and other characteristics), it follows that the price elasticity decreases with income (as long as higher income increases demand). Intuitively, this seems like a reasonable characterisation of consumer behaviour in general. The greater our income, it is not unnatural that our demand would be less price-elastic.

A drawback with the linear demand curve is that it is not quite consistent with demand theory, even though it is an often used approximation. Using demand curves that are consistent with economic theory, one can show that price elasticity, income elasticity and substitution elasticity are closely linked (in the two-good case, price elasticity is a weighted sum of the income and substitution elasticities, the weight being the budget share). Under certain assumptions, the variation of the price elasticity mainly comes from variations in the elasticity of substitution, that is, how difficult it is to substitute between goods from the consumer's point of view, from a good that becomes more expensive. We would then interpret higher price elasticity as an indicator of a higher elasticity of substitution.

A third way to approach possible varying elasticities is via a theory developed by Ragnar Frisch. A key parameter in this theory is what is called the Frisch parameter. It is the elasticity of the marginal utility of income.[29] Frisch famously argued that it has values of about -10 for the 'very poor' ranging all the way up to -0.1 for the richest part of the population. According to Frisch's ideas, the price elasticity varies inversely with the Frisch parameter, if the budget share is constant. This line of inquiry then suggests that for goods with constant budget share, price elasticity will be lower, as we move from higher to lower income.

So what does the empirical evidence tell us about this issue? First of all, the evidence is relatively scant. There are, of course, many studies of household demand, but relatively few that focus on environmental policy in the dimension of interest here. Cornwell and Creedy (1997, p. 30), in their analysis of carbon taxation in Australia, find that 'for goods on which lower-income earners spend a relatively higher proportion of their budget, the lower-income earners have relatively lower price elasticities compared with higher-income earners, and therefore have less scope for substitution'. Sipes and Mendelsohn (2001) suggest, on the other hand, that higher income decreases price elasticity for gasoline consumption.[30] West (2004) studies instruments for vehicle pollution control, that is, a gas tax, a size tax and a newness subsidy. The author examines price responsiveness by income deciles and finds that lower-income households reduce miles to a larger extent than wealthier households; low-income households have higher price elasticities for gasoline. She finds that the newness subsidy is regressive, while a tax on gas or miles is progressive over 'the bottom half of the income distribution'. This result is due, inter alia, to the fact that lower-income households do not own cars to the same extent.

Johnstone and Alavalapati (1998) examine price elasticities for food, citing the quite common result that food consumption is not particularly price-responsive. A very stable relationship exists between income and the food budget share, showing that it decreases with increasing income (Engel's law). Given the differences in budget share between 'rich' and 'poor' households regarding food, environmental taxes on agriculture will then tend to be regressive. The fact that agriculture is subjected to various subsidies could be seen in this light. This will be further discussed in Section 3.3. The study by Brännlund and Nordström (2004) on the distributional impacts of carbon taxation finds very small differences between price elasticities across income groups. Their results are, to some extent, a consequence of the particular empirical model used.

In conclusion, the empirical findings often depend on the structure of the model used in the analysis. We are therefore forced into something of an impasse. Neither theory nor empirics allow a robust conclusion about how price elasticities vary across income groups in the case of environmental goods.

3.3 Individual Firms

Let us now move to the second 'player' at the first level of analysis, that is, the individual firm. As we have noted above, there is a close link between the household and the firm, because firms are owned by households. Consequently, while we will be discussing how firms are affected by environmental policy, the distributional effects are not independent of ownership structure in the economy. Indeed, lower profits are passed on to owners of the firm in terms of lower returns on their invested capital. Furthermore, the extent to which environmental policy affects employment is of course of much relevance to households. In short, while the firm is a logical unit of analysis, we are mostly interested in the distributional impacts on the households of the economy. In the following, these impacts are sometimes referred to indirectly and we occasionally proceed as if 'the firm' had independent interest in our analysis of distributional issues.

Environmental policy affects the firm through prices on inputs and output, but also its technology, depending on the specifics of regulation. In some cases, environmental regulations also include the level of production. Consider a simple example, in which an environmental tax is levied on an input of production, a common example in countries where such taxes are used. There are two effects at the level of the firm. First a substitution effect at every given level of production. The relative price for the taxed input is higher, so the firm substitutes away from this input. Under the weak assumption of cost minimisation, this substitution will be observed quite independently of ownership structure. For example, domestic heating plants in Sweden conform to this behaviour; see Brännlund and Kriström (2001). Because of the particular ownership structure (that is, the plants are owned by the municipality), profit maximisation is not possible and prices are set to average cost.

The slightly stronger assumption of profit maximisation implies an output effect; the profit-maximising firm will lower its output in response to an input tax. Substitution possibilities depend on the particulars of the technology. In some cases, such as in the metallurgy sector, it is impossible to reduce carbon emissions by substitution in the process of making steel from iron. This may explain why process emissions are often completely exempted from, for example, carbon taxes.

From a distributional perspective, there is a difference between a regulatory measure and an incentive-based instrument at the level of the firm. Without environmental policy, the firm will expand emissions until the marginal benefit is zero; the firm is provided one input for free. A regulation of emissions is a constraint on the use of this free input. For example, suppose the firm used 20 units in the status quo and a regulation stipulated a maximum use of 10 units. The cost to the firm of the quantitative regulation is the difference between the levels of profits with and without regulation. Suppose, instead, that a tax was imposed on this input such that the goal of 10 units is reached. The difference is now that the firm will have to pay a tax on the remaining emissions, that is, 10 units (Figure 3.2). Clearly, from the point of view of the firm, the regulatory measure is preferred, because profits must be higher.

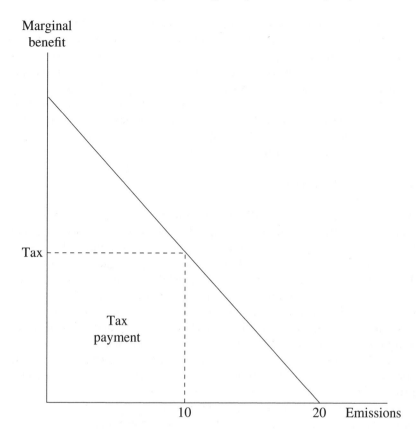

Figure 3.2   Difference between a regulation and an environmental tax from a firm's point of view

One can take the view that the tax-cum-regulation discussion is simply a debate about how the scarcity rent should be distributed. The rent can be distributed to households via the tax or remain with the firm's owners under a regulation. There is potentially a long-run difference regarding the number of firms at the market level, which we will return to in the next section.

We can also examine emission permits from the point of view of the firm. If the permits are grandfathered to the firm, this means that the scarcity rent stays with the firm, according to the discussion above. Alternatively, if the permits are auctioned, the rent will be captured by the seller of permits, so that the revenues are returned to the taxpayers. Thus, from a distributional point of view, auctioned permits are equivalent to taxes. From the firm's perspective it also follows that a regulatory measure is equivalent to a grandfathered permit.

An environmental subsidy could be constructed in several ways. There are subsidies for capital investment as lump sums or those that affect revenues or costs at the margin. Subsidies can thus be constructed as investment tax credits, accelerated depreciation for pollution control equipment, but arguably also via energy tax exemptions. Wind power is subsidised in several ways in certain countries (for example, Denmark and Sweden). From the firm's point of view, a subsidy can be viewed as a negative of a tax, and much the same analysis applies. A difference arises at the market level, and we return to this in the next section.

3.4   Individual Markets

A more stringent environmental policy will affect the cost of production and therefore the price households pay for the good or service they buy from the firms. Indeed, sooner or later the costs for environmental improvements will be passed on to the households through higher market prices. This impact is quite independent of the particular instrument used to reach the environmental goal. Put simply, there are no free lunches. The analysis in this section shows how markets adjust to environmental policy, how costs are passed on and it provides a glimpse of firms' dynamics. Thus, in addition to showing how the market price of a good will be affected (and hence the cost of consumption), the analysis also suggests employment effects, as workers become (temporarily) unemployed when (and if) certain firms exit the market.

Let us illustrate how an optimal environmental policy imposes distributional effects, in terms of affecting the firms in a given market. Recall that we assume no impacts on any other market. Suppose for simplicity that social damage is proportional to the level of production. We impose an environmental tax, here as a tax on production. In the upper panel of Figure 3.3, we illustrate how firm 1 exits the market, while firm 2 remains in the market, albeit with lower profits. In the lower panel we show how these mechanisms come into play at the market level. Thus, we add the demand side, along with the social cost of the negative externality associated with production. Consumer price increases while the firm's net price is lower; the difference is the tax paid per unit of product. The environmental policy is optimal, because the price is set to social marginal cost (rather than private marginal cost, as in the status quo).

We may well note that the policy is optimal in the sense that the sum of the benefits exceeds the sum of the costs. Figure 3.3 shows that (an optimal) environmental policy must have distributional impacts. Firms will stay or exit the market, depending on the particulars of technology choices made earlier. Households face a higher market price, lose jobs in the exiting firms

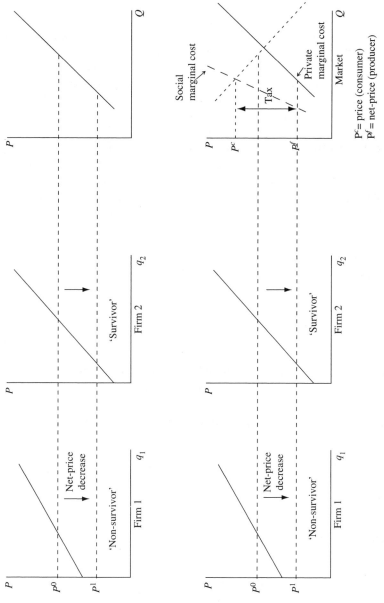

Figure 3.3 Distributional effects of environmental policy at the market level

and are exposed to a lower rate of return on the factors that they own in this particular market.

3.4.1　Differences between instruments

It is of some interest in a distributional study to disentangle how the unavoidable costs for environmental quality improvement vary across policy instruments. Even if the total cost is the same across instruments (which is quite unlikely in practice), it is not necessarily the case that environmental taxes, permits or quantitative regulations impose the same burden across households and firms. We therefore use the ideas above to study distributional impacts of instrument choice, assuming again that the repercussions stay within the market under study.[31] Thus, we simplify by leaving out the details of the individual firms and simplify further by assuming constant costs. The latter assumption means that there will be no impacts on firms' profits; competition assures that any excess profit will be absorbed by entry of new firms. Consider the following instruments, introduced to reach the target:

- Environmental tax
- Permit trading (grandfathered or auctioned)
- Regulation
- Environmental subsidy

Table 3.2 and Figure 3.4 summarise the distributional impacts of different policy instruments.

A number of simplifications have been used to make Figure 3.4 as tidy as possible. Note that we have assumed that all instruments bring about

Table 3.2　Distributional impacts of different policy instruments (a partial equilibrium view)

Policy	Consumer	Firms	Tax revenues	Environmental benefits
Environmental Tax	$-(2+3+4)$	0	$2+3$	$4+5+6$
Grandfathering of permits	$-(2+3+4)$	$2+3$	0	$4+5+6$
Auction of permits	$-(2+3+4)$	0	$2+3$	$4+5+6$
Regulation	$-(2+3+4)$	0	0	$4+5+6$
Environmental subsidy	$-(2+3+4)$	$2+3$		$4+5+6$

Note: Numbers correspond to areas in Figure 3.4. See Fullerton (2001) and OECD (1994) for additional details.

exactly the same improvement in environmental quality. This is a rather strong assumption in the case of price instruments, given that it is more difficult in practice to reach a target with an environmental tax. The cost of reaching the target is also the same across the instruments. As we have argued, this assumption does not square well with the evidence; economic instruments are typically more efficient. We here allow prices to change explicitly at the level of the market, so that the economic costs are split between sellers and buyers in proportion to their price elasticities. Because households own the firms, one may again argue that this distinction between firms and households is quite meaningless, yet there is at least a pedagogical advantage of keeping the distinction here.

The gain to society from the environmental quality improvement is area 4+5+6 and in this case the differences between the instruments are the financial distributional effects. Beginning with the environmental tax, consumers lose areas 2+3+4, a loss that can be mitigated by returning the tax revenues 2+3 to them. Consumers must pay a part of the cost of

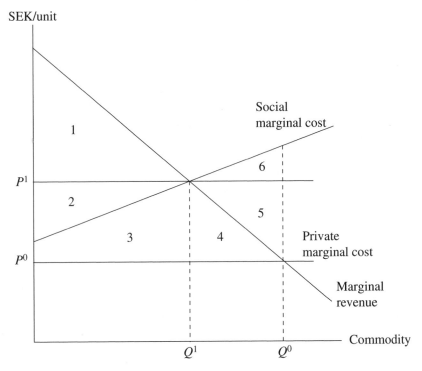

Figure 3.4   Distributional impacts of different policy instruments

improving the environment via price increases that arise when firms pass on the tax.

Auctioning permits is equivalent from a distributional point of view to using a tax in this example. A grandfathering of permits again simply means a transfer of rents from consumers to firms (the area 2+3). A regulation nets no tax revenue, so provides no revenues that can be used for compensatory reductions of taxes (or increases in subsidies).

3.4.2 Long-run effects

Intuitively, there could be a difference between these cases over the long run. If the rent is captured by firms rather than taxed away, this will attract resources to the regulated sector (relative to the tax case or auctioned permits), such that one can expect a larger number of firms in the long run under a regulatory scheme. Some economists have therefore argued that consumers benefit from emission limit regulations since one expects relatively higher output and therefore lower prices; see Helfand (1999) for a review. Note, however, that these resources are 'stolen away' from other parts of the economy; the relatively higher output requires resources that must be taken from somewhere. Thus, other goods may well become relatively more expensive. It should also be noted that a grandfathering scheme could make entry to the sector more difficult than otherwise. The long-run impact of grandfathering is therefore not clear.

Let us sum up the discussion so far. From a distributional perspective there are differences between policy instruments. We take the view here that the differences are mainly how the rent is distributed. Grandfathering leaves the rent with the firms receiving the permits, while, for example, taxes turn the rent over to households.

3.4.3 Notes on subsidies

Turn now to subsidies. The firms are given a subsidy such that they are induced to abate an amount equivalent to a fulfilment of the target. A subsidy has to be paid by taxes. If it is financed in a non-lump sum manner, this invokes additional social costs.[32] The distributional financial implications of a non-lump sum tax increase, say the VAT versus the income tax, will be touched upon below (albeit in a different context, when we discuss revenue recycling). The long-run impacts of subsidies are of particular interest. The celebrated Baumol–Oates (1988) result holds that emissions may actually be higher in the long run under a subsidy scheme. The reason is that the subsidy attracts additional firms into the sector. While each firm emits less, the sum of emissions may actually be larger.

Given the importance of subsidies and their close link to environmental issues, a few additional comments will be made about them. Some subsidies can be labelled 'environmentally harmful', although this label has no exact definition. Agriculture receives significant subsidies in many countries (in numerous ways) and ordinarily does not pay its external cost, so the use of this label is motivated in this case. As noted by O'Brien and Vourc'h (2001, p. 7), 'Removing the special treatment of the agricultural sector – concerning especially its effects on water pollution and the price it pays for water – would be a major step towards improved policy consistency.' It is not difficult to find other examples of 'harmful subsidies', see, for example, the list compiled by Panayotou (1998, p. 69), who notes four advantages of phasing them out: freeing up budgetary resources, improving economic growth, removing a progressive instrument (arguing that such subsidies generally favour the rich) and promoting environmental quality.

Pursuing distributional objectives through (directly or indirectly) subsidising certain activities has additional drawbacks. Let us consider a somewhat intricate example when income distributional objectives conflict with other objectives. Leaded fuels have been subsidised (in at least one country) on distributional grounds with the argument that only the high-income earners could afford cars that run on the non-leaded fuel. This sort of subsidy confuses the role of prices as signals of scarcity with the income distributional objective. The subsidised fuel is less expensive at the pump, but the societal cost (which includes the negative externalities) has to be picked up by somebody. Ironically, this burden might well fall disproportionately on the group that was financially favoured.[33] Moreover, lead has an effect on learning ability. Consequently, a very real cost of the subsidy might well fall on children, which certainly is an unintended side effect.

To sum up: from an environmental economics perspective, subsidies should ordinarily be used when an activity is associated with a positive externality. In other cases, subsidies may lead to unintended effects such as higher rather than lower emissions. It is important to take a comprehensive look at the total economic impact of a subsidy scheme. Getting the prices wrong, as the 'harmful environmental subsidies' suggests, implies a misallocation of resources and may well lead to unintended distribution of the total social cost, notwithstanding other distributional objectives.

3.4.3   The empirical evidence: a cross-instrument comparison
Regarding the empirical findings across instruments, the evidence is scant. To OECD (1994) and Tietenberg (1996), we might add that Markandya (1998, p. 469), in his survey of distributional issues in environmental policy, argues that permit markets in the United States are beneficial for households in lower-income brackets. Helfand (1999, p. 229) discusses some empirical examples that support the notion that distributional concerns

tend to favour the use of standards over taxes. Her examples include cases when the price of certain goods becomes relatively lower.

We have little by way of empirical information regarding the distributional impact of information programmes, let alone their relative efficiency. The same is true for voluntary agreements. To this one could add certain kinds of tax differentiations that normally do not enter the environmental economics literature. Recently, there have been a number of proposals on VAT differentiation, for example, lower VAT on ecologically-labelled goods. Evidence is scarce on the distributional impacts of 'ecological' VAT differentiation. An informed guess would be that such a reform might well be progressive, presuming that the budget share for eco-labelled goods is increasing in income. (Box 3.3 offers a comparison between economic instruments and alternative measures.)

3.5 Different Market and Ownership Structure

In the standard analysis of environmental policy, as well as in our analysis above, markets are typically assumed to be competitive. We therefore close this section by commenting briefly on other kinds of market structures. The case is certainly empirically relevant (consider water regulation and district heating plants, both containing many examples of monopolies). As a benchmark we compare the two extreme solutions, the competitive market and the monopoly market. In the long run, prices will be forced down to minimum average cost if the market is competitive. Not so in the monopoly case (assuming now that a monopoly is allowed to maximise profits), when prices will be higher. In the intermediate case when the market is an oligopoly, the market price will be found somewhere in between those two extremes.

If we allow the ownership structure to include publicly-owned companies, impacts of environmental policy depend on the assumed objective of the public company: profit maximisation, cost minimisation or some other objective (like covering average variable cost). From an efficiency perspective, prices should be set at marginal (not average) cost. When average costs are declining in the relevant market interval, marginal cost pricing means that the company makes a loss. Conversely, rising average costs imply that the company makes a profit using marginal cost pricing. Either way, the company may not be allowed to make profits and must set price to average cost. Consequently, depending on the cost structure, average cost pricing implies either lower or higher prices, compared to efficient pricing. In turn, this will have distributional consequences.

It is possible to invoke a pricing rule that takes on any efficiency–equity trade-off directly, as in Feldstein (1972). His idea implies different pricing rules for necessary and luxury services. As we have seen, if there are negative

---

BOX 3.3   ECONOMIC INSTRUMENTS VERSUS
           ALTERNATIVE MEASURES AND THE
           REGRESSIVITY ISSUE

Are standard economic instruments in environmental policy
necessarily more regressive than the alternative policy measures?
As we have seen, there is ample evidence that environmental
taxes are regressive (with the caveat that this really depends on
how the tax revenues are recycled). But alternative policies, such
as energy conservation programmes (with indirect environmental
benefits), may certainly be a boon to richer households and a
burden to the less well off. This, at least, is what Sutherland (1994)
finds in his study of electric utility demand side management
(DSM) programmes. Such programmes involve various efforts to
affect household's consumption of electricity. They may include
load management technologies, rebates to investment in alternative energy sources, insulation measures and so on and so forth.
In short, they can be viewed as subsidies that affect electricity consumption. These subsidies more often than not end up in the
hands of richer households in Sutherland's study, notwithstanding
the fact that low-income earners live in less energy-efficient
housing (and may therefore enjoy relatively larger electricity
savings). In short, richer households participate more frequently
in the subsidy programmes. The flip side of the coin is that the
costs of DSM are picked up by all consumers, not least the non-
participating poorer households; hence the regressivity. To summarise, while economic instruments in environmental policy are
often found to have regressive impacts, alternative policies are by
no means immune to such distributional impacts.

---

externalities one must tread lightly and consider the total social cost of pursuing distributional objectives via the price system.

3.6   Interrelated Markets at the Sector Level

Because markets are interrelated, environmental policy may have impacts
in several markets not directly affected by a policy measure. This means
that the distributional impacts of environmental policy become somewhat
more subtle. When markets adjust and the impacts cascade throughout the

economy, any policy measure may generate 'winners' and 'losers' in ways not always transparent initially. It is natural to begin by analysing a given sector of the economy, assuming that repercussions mostly stay within the sector. Thus, we will show how a policy targeted on one industry in a given sector generates 'winners' and 'losers' within the sector, proceeding again with the implicit assumption that these benefits and costs will sooner or later end up in the hands of the households. Mapping gains and losses from industries in a sector to corresponding financial impacts on households is, in principle, not difficult. We need to know the distribution of ownership and 'who works where'. Such information can be collected in a social accounting matrix (SAM), which is our proposed way of putting the suggested framework together. We will return to the SAM after having completed our household-firm, market, sector and 'whole economy' analysis.

A concrete example will be useful. Suppose we are contemplating a tax on chlorine input to the pulp and paper industry. For simplicity, we limit the discussion to forest owners, sawmills and the pulp and paper industry. A moment of reflection reveals that the chlorine input tax will be a boon to sawmills, while forest owners are bound to make losses. The pulp and paper industry will shift some of the cost of the tax backwards in the supply chain and pay a lower price for the pulpwood; the higher consumer price on chorine lowers the demand for pulpwood input. Given a lower demand for pulpwood, it will then be relatively more profitable for the forest owner to sell additional quantities of saw wood to sawmill owners. This, in turn, will tend to depress the price of logs. Consequently, forest owners will suffer lower profits; the same is true for the pulp and paper mills, while profits increase in sawmills because a key input has become less expensive. The lower demand for pulpwood will depress its price and affect the demand for chlorine in 'a second round' of market repercussions. In turn, we find that the environmental tax on chlorine does not bite in quite the same way as when we had no interconnections between markets. The reason is that market repercussions affect another input when pulpwood becomes less expensive.

Thus, there are two 'losers' and one 'winner'. The losing forest owner and the winning sawmill owners are disconnected from the environmental policy goal of reducing chlorine emissions. Relative to the analysis that did not take the relationships in the sector into account, the environment is also a 'loser'. This is because emissions of chlorine will be relatively larger, compared to the standard partial equilibrium analysis. It is clear that a distributional analysis focusing only on the cost of the environmental policy to the pulp and paper industry, that is, an analysis following the lines described earlier in the paper, paints a too limited picture.

To illustrate the approach, we use the example in Brännlund and Kriström (1996). They view the forest sector as consisting of forest owners,

Table 3.3   Effects on Swedish pulpwood and saw timber volumes and prices from a 5 SEK/kg tax on chlorine (percentage changes)

Pulpwood volume	Saw timber volume	Pulpwood price	Saw timber price
−0.40	1.50	−4.8	−2.0

Source: Brännlund and Kriström (1996).

sawmills and pulp and paper industry and study a chlorine tax, using the framework above. The effects on the forest owners and the sawmills of a chlorine tax, in terms of pulpwood and saw timber prices and volumes, are illustrated in Table 3.3.

As expected, the pulpwood volume is reduced; the demand from pulp and paper industry is lowered by the chlorine tax. The empirical results confirm our intuition; forest owners find it more profitable to supply more saw wood, hence the increase of saw timber volume. Pulpwood price is lowered essentially because of the lowered demand from pulp and paper mills while saw timber price decreases as a consequence of increased supply. From this we conclude that forest owners' profits will decrease and (owners of) saw timber mills enjoy a higher profit. However, the emissions of chlorine will be higher than that predicted with the no-repercussions assumption.

We can summarise the distributional impacts by using the concept of the 'observed' demand curve. It makes it possible to represent all market repercussions in a single diagram, which depicts the demanded quantities of a good. Thus, for all possible configurations of prices in the economy we plot a curve relating the price and quantity of the good in question. An example is given in Figure 3.5.

To explain Figure 3.5, let us continue with our chlorine example (the argument is, of course, completely general). Suppose that the demand curve for chlorine is initially given by D^0 in Figure 3.5, and the price of chlorine is initially w^0. The industry will thus consume chlorine at point A. A tax on chlorine, resulting in price w^1, reduces chlorine demand to point B in the figure. Without repercussions on other markets, the analysis is exactly equal to the partial equilibrium case. Thus, the distributional analysis of Figure 3.3 is a special case of our more general model. When the price of pulpwood decreases, the demand for chlorine will shift outward to D^1. The observed demand for chlorine will then be at point C.

The effect on profits in the partial equilibrium case is given by the area bounded by prices w^0, w^1 and the demand curve, that is, the area $1 + 2$. The total change of profits in all markets in the sector is given by the area bounded by the observed demand curve, that is, $1 + 2 + 3 + 4$. Consequently,

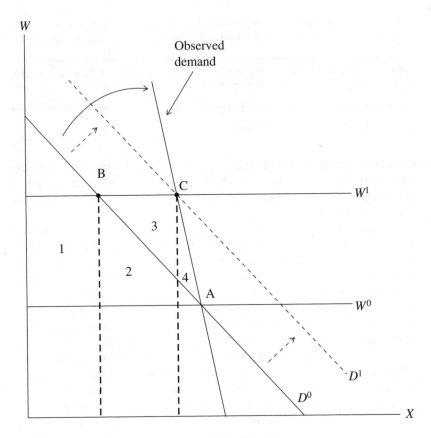

1+2 = profit change without
market repercussion

1+2+3+4 = profit change in
whole sector

Figure 3.5   Distributional analysis and market repercussions;
the 'observed' demand curve

the difference between the partial and sector analysis boils down to how
much the observed demand is pivoted to the right. In turn, the extent of
this pivot depends on the specifics of each market in the analysed sector.
An important parameter is the cost share of the targeted input. If the
cost share is small, a partial equilibrium analysis often provides a useful
first-order approximation.[34] In such cases, the analyst may conveniently

disregard the market repercussions and therefore simplify the distributional analysis substantially.[35]

This framework can be used to analyse different kinds of environmental
policies when market linkages are of interest. We illustrate this by considering an exemption from a general energy tax. If renewable energy
sources are 'subsidised' in this way, it will have an impact on the competitiveness of all sectors that compete for the same basic input. It has been
argued that in a forest-rich country, subsidising forest residues will have no
impact on other actors using the wood resource as an input. This is plainly
not true, because it depends on the relative profitability of using wood
resources in various activities. If energy inputs other than biomass to district heating plants are taxed, the plant will substitute towards less expensive inputs. If these inputs are labelled wood residues, pulpwood or even
saw wood does, in principle, not matter. Only the relative profitability is of
interest; it might well be cheaper to use saw wood as an input rather than
oil, if the latter is taxed sufficiently highly.

3.7 Interrelated Sectors: Economy-wide Models

The final step of the analysis is to allow all markets in the economy to interact. In a general equilibrium model, the economy is interpreted as a system
of mutually dependent markets. A change which at a first glance only seems
to affect one market, can in practice affect all markets in the economy (see
Box 3.4). This perspective has several advantages. Experience shows that
many indirect and complex relationships are revealed that otherwise can be
difficult to disentangle with alternative approaches.

Consider a carbon tax as an example. Companies with increased costs
will shift some of these costs on to the buyers of their products. If agriculture uses a significant amount of fossil fuels and experiences a carbon tax
increase, parts of this increase will be shifted towards slaughterhouses
and others that demand agricultural products. The cost of distributing the
goods on roads will also increase, costs that sooner or later will have to
be paid by the households. Analogously, should the proceeds from the
carbon tax be used to cut labour taxes, it is reasonable to expect that goods
that are relatively 'labour-intensive' will fetch a relatively lower price. Prices
on haircuts and consulting services may therefore fall. Such reductions will
end up in the hands of the households, much in the same way as households
in the end must pay the costs of higher taxes. With this perspective, it is
again clear that the distributional implications of environmental policy
can be rather subtle. Furthermore, it is sometimes very useful to allow for
links between (all) the actors of the economy, when carrying out distributional studies.

Computable General Equilibrium (CGE) models are often used for empirical work. Such models are useful for several reasons. For example, there are many advantages with a model where revenues and expenditures of different agents are treated in a consistent way. It is useful when assessing 'who wins' and 'who loses' from green tax reform. For one thing, one is able to shed light on the interaction between different tax bases. Thus, if fossil fuels are subject to an energy tax and a carbon tax, increasing the latter tax will lower the revenues generated by the former. In turn, it may no longer be possible to lower a distortionary tax to the extent planned 'initially'. A carbon tax change can also affect the value added tax and other tax revenues. In principle, such tax interaction effects can easily be handled within the general equilibrium framework.

To sum up: because an economy consists of interrelated markets, implying in any realistic economy a set of interdependent tax bases, we sometimes need a general equilibrium perspective to be able to unravel the distributional consequences of environmental policy. Disregarding such links can be defended, as we have seen, in cases where the environmental reform is taken to be 'small' relative to the size of the economy.

Some of the limitations with applying these models need to be mentioned. Most current CGE models focus on the cost side. In other words, they shed light on how firms and households adjust to permutations of the tax system and the cost this entails (see Figure 3.1). Few models include the environmental benefits in a consistent manner (if at all). An exception is Sieg et al. (2001), who study the benefits of environmental improvement in a general equilibrium framework. They show with an example from Los Angeles how environmental improvements affect the housing market. This has distributional implications, for example, the low-income households will have to pay a higher rent induced by the environmental improvement. Over the long run, this often changes the distribution of income in a certain area, as low-income earners can no longer afford the increased cost of living caused by environmental improvements.

Some of the uncertainties that by necessity arise should also be mentioned. In particular, the models build on demand and supply schedules whose shapes cannot be known with certainty. One cannot, ex ante, know exactly how consumers and companies will react to a change in the tax system. If the demand and supply schedules are specified incorrectly in the model, this source of error can be propagated in the model, which further complicates predictions about the level of different variables. Finally, CGE models seldom include a full description of prevailing tax systems which is a drawback in certain cases, not the least when interpreting the regressivity/progressivity of revenue-neutral tax reforms.

There are many examples of models where the economy and ecological systems interact. For example, there are several models highlighting inter-actions between the climatic system and the economic system, but they ordinarily do not include distributional issues.[36] Some models portray how environmental deterioration impacts productivity, so that, for example, increased acidification lowers productivity, as in Bergman and Hill (2000). Including such linkages is of independent value that sometimes yields useful insights in a distributional analysis. Consider, for example, the dis-tribution of property rights over a natural resource such as lichen. These are the main fodder for the domesticated reindeer in northern Scandinavia and can be found only on old (that is, ready-to-cut) trees. In order to portray how changes of forest policy affect reindeer husbandry, it is useful to obtain some understanding of the links between lichen and forest growth. The change in the stock of lichen is a function of the number of old trees, itself a function of the state of the relevant markets and the pre-vailing regulatory framework. Changing the current property rights such that reindeer owners have the right to cut lichen has significant distribu-tional implications, as the study by Parks et al. (2001) shows. Bostedt (2002) argues that there exists a policy choice such that reindeer owners' and forest owners' losses are minimised, relative to the prevailing (forestry-based) distribution of property rights. There is a 'middle way', involving some restrictions on cutting. Disallowing cutting of old trees, or allowing for 'tree mining' are options of less merit, according to Bostedt's (2002) calculations.

This case also illustrates the financial implications of co-benefits arising from the introduction of environmental policy. This would arise if a given environmental policy (that is, a carbon tax) generates ancillary environ-mental benefits (that is, reduced local air pollutants) in addition to the direct benefits (that is, reduced carbon emissions). If the ancillary impacts are themselves subject to regulation, the cost implications associated with the reduced emissions need to be included in the analysis. For instance, if local air pollutants are subject to a tradable permit system, permit prices will fall subsequent to the introduction of the carbon tax, resulting in cost savings. See Box 3.5.

Table 3.4 summarises the results from a number of economy-wide models where distributional concerns have been included in the analysis. The models we discuss are essentially conventional economic models, where certain aspects of energy goods or the like have been highlighted. Environmental policy in most applied general equilibrium models is no different from analysis of ordinary tax policy.

Table 3.4 Distributional impacts of environmental policy in economy-wide models

Authors	Title of study	Type and source of data	Notes on approach	Principal finding
Metcalf (1999)	'A Distributional Analysis of Green Tax Reforms'	1994 Consumer Expenditure Survey with adjustments: (1) for medical spending; (2) matching the national accounts aggregates on income and consumption; (3) corporate tax payments attributed to households.	Uses an input–output model. 10% decrease of income tax base, matched by increase of various environmental taxes.	'It appears from this analysis that any distributional concerns about the greater use of environmental taxes can be addressed through a careful menu of tax reductions that are targeted to low-income households' (p. 672).
Labandeira and Labeaga (1999)	'Combining Input–Output Analysis and Micro-Simulation to Assess the Effects of Carbon Taxation on Spanish Households'	Input–output table and consumer expenditures for 1994.	Carbon dioxide tax in consumption and production.	Neutral effect.
Bovenberg and Goulder (2001)	'Addressing Industry-Distributional Concerns in US Climate Change Policy'	13 production sectors 17 consumer goods, year = 2000.	Dynamic General Equilibrium model, 2000–80: 'fairly realistic treatment of US tax system . . . detailed representation of energy production and demand'.	Distributional impacts of carbon policy can be neutralized at low efficiency costs. For example, only 13% of carbon permits must be freely provided to prevent losses to fossil fuel industries.

BOX 3.4   THE EFFECTS OF ENVIRONMENTAL
POLICIES ON RELATED MARKETS
THROUGH CHANGES IN
ENVIRONMENTAL QUALITY

Environmental policy, like any other policy, may have effects on various markets, for example, certain asset markets. For example, *if* reduction of 'acid rain' has a beneficial effect on the current and future state of forests, this will have an impact on profits in the forest sector. A large literature documents the relationship between housing prices and environmental quality.[37] Roback (1982) is particularly interesting, because she disentangles links between different markets; changes of environmental quality have effects on the labour market. Furthermore, there is a large literature on the links between health and environmental quality. Health-related costs include direct medical expenditures and production losses as well as personal suffering. An example is Künzli et al. (2000), who estimate that 40 000 people die every year from the effects of air pollution in three European countries (Austria, France and Switzerland). A general finding from studies on the external costs of air pollution is that chronic (that is, total) mortality dominates. In the case of the ExternE programme, about 80 per cent of the particulate matter, sulphur dioxide and nitrogen oxides external costs can be attributed to chronic mortality.[38] A recent study by Pope et al. (2002) provides a link between external health costs and certain demographic factors using US data on individuals within an ongoing prospective mortality study (starting 1982). While they present estimates of relative risks across socio-economic factors, income is not included among those. There is some support for the notion that external costs fall disproportionally on the poorer part of the population; see Johnstone and Alavalapati (1998) (for a review of older literature, see Zimmerman, 1986). Chapter 2 by David Pearce has more on this.

As an aside, it can be mentioned that there are studies that explore links between the shape of the income distribution and health status; an uneven income distribution implies higher health costs according to Lynch et al. (1998). For a critical overview of this literature, see Gravelle (1998). Deaton (2003) provides a useful summary of the literature from an economic perspective.

BOX 3.5   CO-BENEFITS OF ENVIRONMENTAL POLICY

A number of papers estimate the co-benefits from environmental policy, that is, any reduction of environmental pressure that originates from other sources than the one targeted in a specific policy. A survey of work on climate policy appears, for example, in Bye et al. (2001). They include eleven studies in their survey, displaying very significant variations (from US$ 2 to $508/ton of carbon, in 1996 prices). These differences depend on methodology and coverage. Some studies include a wide range of pollutants, while others limit themselves to two pollutants. Models also differ in terms of the benefits included. Some studies are limited to health benefits, while others include recreational values, traffic and vegetation. Kverndokk and Rosendahl (2001) survey the same literature with focus on the Nordic countries, the UK and Ireland. They conclude that the ancillary benefits are in the same order of magnitude as the costs. Burtraw et al. (2001) claim that the ancillary health benefits from a US$ 25/t carbon tax in the US is about US$ 12–14.

While the co-benefits from environmental policy tend to paint a more positive picture of the net costs of a particular action, some care in interpretation of the results is warranted. To see this, let us make an analogy with two private goods, a computer and DVDs. If the price of computers decreases, we expect that the demand for DVDs increases. However, as long as the price of DVDs is constant, we cannot add the resulting increase in consumer surplus for DVDs. This would be a kind of double-counting of the benefits to consumers of less expensive computers. Indeed, if we increase the number of consumer goods, we can, by a judicious choice of them, find that decreasing the price of computers provides a very substantial 'co-benefit', in terms of increased consumer surplus for other goods (assuming constant prices on goods other than computers). Turning to environmental issues, consider the case of sulphur and carbon emissions. Suppose both types of emissions are taxed. Consider an increase in the carbon tax and assume that the sulphur tax is set correctly in the status quo. If we increase the carbon tax there will be less carbon emissions but also a co-benefit of reduced sulphur emissions. Because there is also a cost associated with reducing sulphur emissions, it is quite possible that adding both benefits would be an overstatement of the net benefits to society of the carbon policy. In the case of DVDs, it is true that the demand for them will increase, but if prices are constant, this benefit is exactly balanced by the costs of adding resources to their production. In summary, it would seem prudent to interpret co-benefits carefully when thinking about the costs and benefits of environmental policy. Lutter and Shogren (2002) argue that the ancillary benefits of carbon reductions suggest that we need a 'tradable permit tariff' on carbon if one actually wants to include ancillary benefits of climate change. This is because the ancillary benefits imply a wedge between the marginal benefits of reducing carbon emissions and the marginal costs (in a market for carbon, price will equal marginal costs, but the price is an underestimate of the marginal benefit if there are ancillary benefits). The co-benefits actually transform a global problem to one that includes local problems, hence the wedge. Without the co-benefits, the benefit of carbon reduction is independent of where this reduction takes place.

Most studies of environmental taxation in models that allow for market repercussions conclude that such taxes are regressive. The sample of studies shown above suggests that there exist options for reducing unwanted distributional impacts by targeted measures. For example, Bovenberg and Goulder (2001) calculate that a carbon dioxide tax can be introduced in US industry without significant distributional impacts, should the tax be combined with exemptions or grandfathering. We will return to a more detailed discussion about the possibility of how different revenue-replacement instruments can be used to mitigate distributional concerns (see Section 4).

3.8 Putting it all Together

Depending on the objectives of a particular study of distributional issues, one may choose to use any of the methods displayed in the previous sections of this chapter. Yet, there is a certain advantage of having a method for consistent data handling that could serve as a starting point for empirical enquiries, no matter which particular set of models a given problem seems to require.

The basic building block is a SAM – a Social Accounting Matrix – which can be used to summarise the data in a compact way. The national accounts can be viewed as a particular SAM, in which pertinent data about the economy are collected into a matrix. A SAM is typically an aggregation of data, so that income and outlays for a particular group of, for example,

Table 3.5   A Social Accounting Matrix (SAM)

	X	Y	Welfare	Budget constraint
Good X	100		−100	
Good Y		100	−100	
Welfare			225	−225
Labour (L)	−25	−75		100
Capital (K)	−75	−25		100
Environment (EN)			−25	25

households are displayed. This is because it is useful to obtain a bird's-eye view of the policy under consideration, such that the various links between the economy (and the environment) are easy to see. The consistency imposed by a SAM on the data often allows one intuitively to disentangle important indirect effects of policy change. Rose et al. (1988) use an essentially SAM-based approach to study the link between income distribution and natural resource use.

There are many ways to construct a SAM. Consider a simplistic example, portraying a number of pertinent dimensions of our analysis. Presume that two goods X and Y are produced using inputs K and L. Thus, $X = f(K,L)$ and correspondingly for Y, where $f(K,L)$ is a production function. The household is endowed with K and L, which they sell in the respective markets. Income is the return on these assets. We also assume that environmental quality is valued positively by households and we include environmental quality in the asset base. Constructing a SAM for this economy requires finding data on production, income and the value of environmental quality, each in monetary terms. For the sake of illustration, a set of numbers has been put in Table 3.5.

The first column shows the value of production in X and the cost of inputs K and L. The first row suggests that the consumer produces 'welfare' by consuming what the X sector produces. The second row–column pair displays this information for the Y sector. Note that X is capital-intensive and Y is labour-intensive (X buys 25 units of labour and 75 units of capital; Y buys 75 units of labour and 25 units of capital). Household ('full') income is made up of capital, labour and environment endowments, as suggested by the last three rows and the final column. For the typical analysis of financial distributional effects, income is defined over market assets only. The example here suggests a generalisation of the income concept which may or may not be relevant in a given distributional study.

In order to carry out a distributional analysis, it would be a straightforward matter to disaggregate the household account into informative subsets.

In other words, we can put a magnifying glass on the household account and break it into homogeneous groups across income. For example, one may want to assemble data on rural/urban households and scrutinise distributional issues in this dimension. The SAM would display, for example, differences in endowments and consumption patterns and different preferences regarding environmental quality, together with a snapshot of sector technologies.

A SAM is not a model, so that the imposition of a structure in terms of a model is a separate activity. There are numerous ways of providing a structure that enables one to map the consequences of environmental policy onto a SAM. Input–output analysis is one possibility, non-linear models in the CGE tradition offer another approach. The SAM serves as a framework and a focal point for analysis. A team of economists could focus on how to impose the various economic structures (production and utility functions), while natural scientists could help in forming opinions about the link between the ecological and economic systems. In our simplistic example, the latter would involve discussion of the link between environmental quality and production in, say, the X sector. A policy change directed towards the externality has impacts on the whole economy and the complex sequence of direct and indirect effects can, in principle, be disentangled. This includes the direct and indirect effect of taxes which we have touched upon and will return to below.

Dasgupta (2001, p. 201), in a developing country context, discusses how forest concessions in the uplands of a watershed could result in damages for low-income farmers downstream (via siltation, increased incidence of flooding and so on). If the forest merchant is not charged for the externality inflicted, one effectively subsidises forest-cutting at the expense of the potentially poor farmers and fishermen. Eventually, the income losses would show up in the standard account, but the SAM approach provides a vehicle for shedding light on market and non-market links in a direct way. Thus, while we are mainly concerned with the financial distributive effects of environmental policy, we believe that there is merit in including non-market goods and services in this discussion.

The SAM framework proposed here is closely linked to the literature on 'green accounting'. Over the past 30 years several countries have developed their own set of 'green' accounting systems via their statistical offices; and international organisations such as the OECD, the World Bank and EUROSTAT have contributed to the development of 'greener' accounts. The UN, through its statistical office, has developed an extensive System of Environmental and Economic Accounts (SEEA) that complements and extends the System of National Accounts (SNA). In principle, these efforts provide a consistent information system that allows a broad set of analyses to be made. The theoretical underpinning for the structure of such a system has been set out in Dasgupta et al. (1995), yielding a rather different structure compared to that suggested in the SEEA. A recent survey of the literature appears in Heal and Kriström (2005). It should be noted that there is a wide range of different proposals and the literature has not yet converged on the final structure of environmental accounts, let alone the appropriate SAM for analysing environment–economy interactions. This is essentially because the proposals appear to be addressing different questions. While the SEEA can be viewed as an expansion of the SNA and its Keynesian connotations, the proposal in, for example, Dasgupta et al. (1995) has a different measurement objective: welfare change (as approximated by a linear index called NNP). The purpose here is not to discuss the subtleties of green accounting, but rather to indicate the usefulness of a SAM as a starting point for environmental policy analysis.

4.   POLICY RESPONSES

There are a number of policy options available that can be used to confront unwanted distributional impacts. Barde and Braathen (2002) identify three general kinds of measures; *mitigation, compensation* and *tax shifts*. Mitigation includes changing the structure of taxation (for example, lower rates, exemptions related to the income level), compensation could include lump sum or targeted subsidies and tax shifts would involve the reduction of other taxes (for example, labour taxes).

Let us begin by noting that the impacts of environmental policy depend on whether it targets a private good (say a petrol tax), or whether the policy is directed towards investment in, for example, a municipally-owned sewage treatment plant. However, we will focus mostly on market goods and discuss a number of those options, including various special forms of regulations:

- Using various tax replacement options
- Using various exemptions and grandfathering policies
- Using subsidies and special kinds of regulations

4.1   Tax Replacement Options

Because revenues from taxes or auctions must eventually be returned to the economy, such instruments can all be discussed under some replacement option. In general, the superior replacement rule is 'no earmarking', because it provides maximum flexibility. Thus, whatever the most important need happens to be at a certain point in time, the 'no earmarking' rule ensures that tax resources can be allocated to their most beneficial end. There seem to be small advantages from introducing fixed earmarking rules, assuming that tax revenues are used prudently under a more flexible scheme. Yet, there are quite a few proposals on just how the revenues are to be recycled, including earmarking them for energy saving investments, R&D in pollution control, environmental tax exemptions and perhaps most prominently lowering labour taxes. These issues have been discussed at great length in various recent OECD documents (see Barde and Braathen, 2002, for references), so we can be relatively brief here.

Several proposals originate in the literature on the 'double dividend'. There is a first dividend from increasing an environmental tax, the environmental improvement. A second dividend comes about from the possibility of decreasing distortionary taxes. After some initial enthusiasm, the literature is now slightly less optimistic as to net benefits of swapping narrow and broad tax bases. Thus, Goulder et al. (1997, 1999) suggest that pre-existing taxes raise the cost of environmental policies. Similar statements appear in Bovenberg and de Moijj (1994). The empirical evidence is not conclusive, however. It is possible to find studies that show a positive welfare gain from an environmental distortionary tax swap, but it is perhaps slightly easier to find studies that do not.

Our concern here is not with the existence of a double dividend, but rather some policy options that can be used to mitigate distributional concerns. The examples invariably concern results from the double dividend literature, which has focused on climate policy. The results could still give some useful indications for other policy areas as well. Table 3.6 summarises a number of options, and some empirical insights.

There is fairly substantive support in the literature for the idea that labour–carbon tax swaps are regressive. As we have seen, this conclusion is quite independent of whether or not we allow for market repercussions. However, an important motivation for such tax swaps is that they may improve the workings of labour markets. The empirical support for this proposition is, however, not very strong. Nickell and Bell (1996) show that the correlation between unit costs of labour and labour taxes is weak among the 13 different OECD countries studied. The fundamental reason why labour taxes do not seem to have a significant effect on the level of employment, is, according to the authors, that such taxes tend to be shifted towards the employees. Holmlund and Calmfors (2000) quote a number of studies that also indicate that lower labour taxes may not reduce wage costs. If correct, such results suggest that we should not expect a large impact on the labour market from a green tax swap. Bovenberg and Van der Ploeg (1993) show, however, that a 'green' tax swap can reduce unemployment, in

Table 3.6   Distributional effects of revenue recycling

Tax reduction option	Study	Distributional effect
Lowering the general tax on labour	Swedish Green Tax Commission (SOU 1997:11), Kverndokk and Rosendahl (2001) survey.	Fairly substantive support that this tax switch is regressive.
Lowering the tax on labour in the service sector	Swedish Green Tax Commission (SOU 1997:11).	Regressive (?). This reform leads expansions of service sectors and has lower welfare losses than the labour tax replacement (in the Swedish study).
Lump sum return	European Commission (CEC,1992).	Progressive (?). If all households receive the same amount, the reform might well be progressive.
Lowering the price for public transportation	Brännlund and Nordström (2004).	Regressive. The environmental benefit is hard to estimate, possibly positive.
Lowering VAT	Brännlund and Nordström (2004).	Regressive, but other models suggest that it could be progressive.
Comprehensive package, involving exemptions of pay-roll tax (up to a certain income level), across-the-board income tax cut and a refundable tax credit	Metcalf (1999).	Progressive.
A £1.1 (1992) billion once-and-for-all programme of conservation measures that saves annual energy consumption valued at £175 million (that is, a payback of 6–7 years).	Barker and Johnstone (1993).	Regressive. Energy savings relatively large for low-income groups, thus mitigating some of this impact.

Note: (?) signifies that the effect is uncertain, either because of methodological limitations or because of conflicting results in a survey of several studies.

a model where one of the factors of production is fixed, if the tax burden falls predominantly on the non-flexible factor.

The Swedish Green Tax Commission (SOU 1997, p. 11) recognised that the significant difference between the broad labour tax base and the narrow carbon tax base implies small impacts on the labour market; the available reduction of the tax on labour is very small. The Swedish Commission examined the possibility of targeting the tax reduction towards the relatively labour-intensive service sectors. Targeting a tax swap in this way comes at a price, given the fact that labour resources will be artificially induced to move to the service sectors. This entails a welfare loss, because the marginal returns of a factor are not equalized across sectors. In the long run, this policy therefore entails risks, as labour resources are 'trapped' in the service sector. Furthermore, this also means a higher burden for certain energy-intensive sectors, because they receive no tax reductions. The adjustment costs can therefore be higher under the targeted scenario, costs that are difficult to quantify. Nevertheless, according to the Commission's model (which did not include transition costs), the aggregate welfare loss was smaller under this selective tax cut.

A lump sum return of revenues from carbon/energy taxation could have progressive effects overall, as exemplified by in the European Commission study of climate policy (CEC, 1992, p. 136). Kverndokk and Rosendahl (2001) reach a similar conclusion. They summarise experience from models shedding light on the costs of reducing carbon emissions in Denmark, Finland, Ireland, Norway, Sweden and the United Kingdom.

Some arguments could be made to the effect that using environmental tax revenues to reduce the cost of public transportation might well be progressive. This, inter alia, depends on the consumption pattern, that is, the budget shares for public transportation across households. Brännlund and Nordström (2004) have studied this case for Swedish data, finding that such a reform is probably regressive on the average. However, it is a boon to urban households, but hits the rural households. In turn, this is a function of the particular structure of Swedish public transportation systems. In other countries, it is easy to see that other results may be found. It is to be noted that the VAT for public transportation has been lowered as a part of Sweden's reform restructuring the taxation system towards greater reliance on energy and environmental taxes.

Some findings suggest that a lowering of the general VAT is less regressive, which is not inconsistent with findings from household studies. However, it should be kept in mind that most CGE models only include a rudimentary description of the tax system. Consequently, findings with respect to the regressivity/progressivity of the tax system should be interpreted with some care in those cases.

4.2 Exemptions and Grandfathering

A slightly different, but quite popular, approach is to use exemptions for certain sensitive sectors. There is ample evidence on the use of exemptions in OECD countries. Exemptions imply that a certain environmental target cannot be reached at minimum cost. Furthermore, depending on how tax revenue is returned to the economy, emissions might actually increase in certain sectors. Studies of exemptions appear in, for example, Fullerton and Metcalf (1997) for the United States, Jensen (1998) for Denmark and Harrison and Kriström (1999) for Sweden.

There are several ways in which policy may be designed that are similar to the commonly used exemptions, but that may be less costly. Consider the use of grandfathered pollution permits. The advantage with such a system is that it will provide an efficient allocation of emissions reductions, since the marginal cost of abatement will be equalised across sources. Thus a system with permits based on grandfathering will provide efficiency benefits, without increasing the relative cost of production in the competitive industry. In a way, it is a subsidy in disguise. The discussion here is to some extent supported by the results reported by Jensen (1998). In a numerical general equilibrium model for the Danish economy, he finds that the permit system gives lower welfare costs, compared to an exemption policy.

If the choice is between exemptions and permits, then a country that would like to act unilaterally may prefer to use the permit system. If such a system is used, the question of whether or not it is dynamically efficient arises. Indeed, as noted earlier, grandfathering permits to a subset of the productive sectors tend to make entry more costly. An entrant must buy a part of the endowment that has been handed over to sectors that happened to be active when the system started. If the permit market is thin, one would expect that incumbents may be able to use permits strategically, for example, by increasing the cost of entry.

Exemptions conveniently target certain sectors and the logic behind using them is transparent in certain cases. If the underlying environmental problem is global, there is an environmental argument in favour of exemptions. This follows from an assumption that emissions would otherwise move to other countries, leaving environmental quality potentially worse than without a single country's exemption. Furthermore, exemptions can be fairly well targeted on sensitive sectors and can sometimes be viewed as part of regional policy. It is nevertheless the case that exemptions are costly, because, by definition, they make it impossible to equalise marginal costs across sources.

If exemptions are used, these nullify to some extent the double dividend possibilities. Given that the exempted sectors are handed a lower tax on labour, they will typically expand their production. Consequently, given that the exemptions target pollution-intensive sectors, the increase of emissions in those sectors may well dwarf the reductions elsewhere. In a way, this can be viewed as the price to be paid for distributional policy, since the exemptions are often motivated by equity concerns in the first place.

In summary, the tax system provides ample opportunities for a government to reduce undesirable distributional consequences of environmental policy. Current theoretical and empirical evidence suggests that a double dividend might not exist, although this should not be a major concern. Rather, it seems prudent to examine the benefits and costs of improving environmental quality. Such analysis may usefully include presentation of distributional impacts as a way of broadening the information set.

4.3   Subsidies and Regulations

There are a number of ways in which subsidies can be combined in environmental policy packages. Targeted subsidy schemes are notably used in the energy sector.[39] They could include energy savings subsidies in various forms, investment grants to plants producing electricity from renewables and district heating plants. Policies occasionally include investment programmes to reduce carbon dioxide emissions. An example is the almost 1 billion euro scheme Sweden has introduced to promote investments that reduce carbon dioxide. Evaluations (yet to be published) suggest, as one would expect, differences in the marginal cost of reductions across projects. This difference translates into efficiency losses. For example, some projects apparently provide carbon reductions at a cost per kilo of 10 or 100 times the carbon tax.

Price contests have been used to spur innovations in energy-saving appliances. One may debate whether such contests are efficient relative to the standard economic instruments. The distributional impact is unclear. Suppose a contest spurs the introduction of a new energy-saving device that otherwise would not have seen the light of day. The market price of the device would reflect its relative energy efficiency (and other relevant dimensions, including security, ease of use and so on and so forth). It is possible that high-income earners reap most of the initial subsidy, although this conclusion is rather speculative.

There are additional possibilities, including the reduction of VAT for eco-labelled goods. This has been discussed by a number of countries and is considered by the EU. In this author's view, this policy option has many drawbacks. Standard theory holds that it is better to attack the problem as close to the source as possible; a stick is better than a carrot provided that the stick is used 'early on'. Furthermore, many practical problems arise, not the least the definition of which good that should be allowed lower VAT. While we have some empirical evidence on the price elasticity, scarcely any is available on the income elasticity of eco-labelled goods. As we have noted, intuition suggests that such goods have an increasing budget share, when plotted against income. Thus, pending empirical evidence, this author believes that an ecological VAT will have progressive impacts.

5. CONCLUSIONS

Our survey of the costs of environmental policy in a distributional context leads to the following conclusions. First of all, environmental policy must have distributional impacts in order to be successful. Empirical evidence tends, on balance, to suggest that environmental policy is regressive (on a gross basis). However, there are numerous ways of mitigating unwanted distributional effects by, for example, judicious use of parameters in the tax system. Yet, the important question of what exactly it is that should be distributed must be answered before proceeding to the compensation stage. For example, conclusions regarding the distributional impact may well depend on whether annual income or lifetime income is considered to be the most relevant measure. Furthermore, any distributional analysis should be carried out with a fixed baseline of comparison in mind.

Turning then to the practical issues, we have elaborated on the OECD (1994) study and suggested a three-stage approach (household/firm, market, sector/economy) to provide insights into the costs of environmental policy when markets are interrelated. Thus, a distributional study could include:

- Examining the distributional impacts at the firm and household levels.
- Detailing the effects of different policy instruments at the market level, assuming that there are no repercussions on other markets.
- Buttressing how environmental policy affects markets within a particular sector of the economy, allowing a certain number of markets to be interrelated.
- Analysing the costs of environmental policy in economy-wide models, allowing for interactions between all markets in the economy.

To this, one could add the economy–environment links. We showed how this can be done in a general framework using a Social Accounting Matrix. It consistently handles links between the economy and the environment, and provides an integrative framework for distributional studies in environmental policy settings.

Our overall conclusion is rather simplistic, yet it may at the end of the day prove to be the most important. We firmly believe that it is important to disentangle the distributional impacts of environmental policy, not least because it is beneficial to public debate and general understanding of how environmental policy affects human well-being. While environmental economists have been focusing on efficiency issues, the fact that equity is important in shaping environmental policy is increasingly being appreciated. A priority in the process of shaping environmental policy should be comprehensively to evaluate its distributional impacts.

NOTES

1. See for example, Persson and Tabellini (1994) and Perotti (1996).
2. See for example, Carneiro et al. (2002) and Heckman et al. (1997).
3. For example, Harrison et al. (2002) find that trade policy changes may be progressive in Brazil. This includes tariff reductions within MERCOSUR, trade agreements with the EU and other reforms.
4. Traditional economics holds that there exists an efficiency–equity trade-off; some efficiency gains may be sacrificed for efficiency reasons.
5. It has been argued, for example, that removing harmful environmental subsidies is a win-win policy. This is true almost by definition, provided that distributional concerns do not enter the picture. We comment on such subsidies below.
6. If resources are expended on cleaning up the environment, say via a publicly-funded clean-up programme, it might be argued that national income actually increases. Since we begin at an efficient point A, resources must be taken from other sectors in the economy, decreasing the value of output in those sectors. To repeat, the point here is that we cannot improve the environment without sacrificing some resources; there are other indicators of this loss.
7. Hourcade (2001) argues strongly that the importance of this fact has not been sufficiently appreciated (by economists) in the shaping of environmental policy.
8. One could use a variety of empirical models for comparing the costs of different policy options, given a fixed environmental goal. For example, one could compute the level of environmental taxes that guarantees the same environmental quality as a prevailing system of regulations.
9. While utility is not measurable, willingness to pay measures are 'money measure of utility change'. If a person is asked to pay x for an improvement that is worth $y > x$ to him, he must be better off with the change. The reverse is true when $y < x$. Thus, the maximum amount the individual would be willing to pay is the case when $x = y$. Taken together this suggests that willingness to pay is a money measure of utility change.
10. There are two strands of the literature disentangling the welfare properties of certain indices. One is based on expanded version of national product, that is, a 'green' national product. See Dasgupta et al. (1995). There is a related literature based on the change in wealth as a welfare measure. Weitzman (1976) provided the key insight and showed under what assumptions comprehensively measured national product is equal to the return on wealth. Heal and Kriström (2005) propose a similar idea, but based on an infinite-dimensional version of the fundamental separation theorem in a Arrow–Debreu type of framework. There is some agreement today that the wealth-based measures are to be preferred over linear indices such as 'green NNP'. Extending these new ideas in a

formal way to include distributional matters has not been a focal point of the now very significant theoretical literature on this issue.

11. In so far as the costs are included in the analysis, most studies in this literature focus on valuing the benefits of improvements. Carson et al. (1994) include more than 1600 references to valuation studies. It should be noted that most studies focus on estimating the benefits and seldom include the costs.

12. There are a number of technical problems with the Kaldor–Hicks criteria. For example, the 'winners can compensate the losers' interpretation does not hold water in a general equilibrium context according to the well-known Boadway paradox. See, for example, Johansson (1993).

13. If compensation is paid and nobody is worse off in the new equilibrium, the issue is moot, because the policy satisfies the Pareto criterion.

14. One can separate production and consumption decisions according to the so-called Fisher separation theorem. A related question is if the size of the cake depends on how it is cut. Macroeconomic studies suggest that economic growth is not independent of the distribution of income, although there seems to be no consensus on the exact relationship. In general, consumption patterns are not independent of how income is distributed in society. This has implications, for example, for carbon emissions as developing countries become richer. See, for example, Ravallion et al. (2000). Some studies find that a more even distribution of income will help economic growth over the long run. The reverse result is also found.

15. I am grateful to Karl-Göran Mäler for this example.

16. Stiglitz (1995) argues that the separation between efficiency and equity is not possible if there are information failures. If there are increasing returns to scale, Brown and Heal (1979) show that efficiency and equity cannot be separated. In general, such cases suggest non-convexities.

17. In the cost–benefit analysis literature, the debate on whether or not weights different from unity should be used have been long-standing. See, for example, Dreze and Stern (1987), who also defend the possibility of using weights different from unity. As shown by Kanninen and Kriström (1992) it is not necessary to fix a particular weighting scheme. Rather, they illustrate which system of weights flips the decision either way. Such information is often useful.

18. For an overview of the economics of the Endangered Species Act, see Brown and Shogren (1998). A cost–benefit analysis of the spotted owl (using the Kaldor–Hicks criteria) is presented in Rubin et al. (1991).

19. EPA (2002).

20. See, for example, Heal (1998) or Dasgupta (2001) for surveys of intertemporal issues, including, but not limited to, sustainability discussions.

21. Economists often adopt envy as the basic concept in discussions of equity. Thus, an allocation is envy-free if no individual envies any other individual's consumption bundle, see for example, Varian (1974). For example, if equality is defined as the allocation where everybody has the same consumption bundle, the equal allocation is envy-free. Furthermore, one could also include process-based equity criteria, so that equity also relates to the process of the particular distribution of income. How did a particular person become rich or poor?

22. Needless to say, exactly what 'equals' is supposed to mean is not clear (that is, in which dimensions is this supposed to hold?).

23. Thus, there are different income concepts suitable for different purposes. Some are suitable for tax purposes, other for macroeconomic analysis, yet others for sustainable income. For a review, see Heal and Kriström (2005).

24. Fullerton and Rogers (1993, p. 19) suggest that the regressive impacts of taxes, in general, appear 'muted' in a lifetime context.

25. A survey of studies using lifetime income measures is in Metcalf (1999).

26. For example, Executive Order 12898, 'Federal Actions to Address Environmental Justice in Minority Populations and Low-Income Populations' (11 February 1994) states that 'no person or group of people should shoulder a disproportionate share of the negative

environmental impacts resulting from the execution of this country's domestic and foreign policy programs'.

27. The cost is defined as the amount of money that would make the individual indifferent between having and not having the policy.
28. See for example, the reviews by Been (1993) and Hite (2000).
29. The Frisch parameter has been used in many distributional studies. It is, however, an ordinal concept, see McKenzie (1986). Thus, it is not invariant to monotonic transformations of an underlying utility function.
30. This is because a coefficient on an interaction term with price and income is positive.
31. This analysis is similar to, inter alia, Fullerton (2001).
32. This follows from the definition of a distortionary tax. If the tax was not distortionary, the social cost of 1 euro in tax revenue would be 1 euro.
33. For further discussion about this, see Johnstone and Alavalapati (1998) and Box 3.5.
34. This illustrates the Marshallian dictum of 'the importance of being unimportant' when considering the approximating features of partial equilibrium analysis.
35. For a mathematical treatment, see Brännlund and Kriström (1996).
36. A brief overview of such models is in Heal and Kriström (2002).
37. Surveys of this literature can be found in Freeman (1993).
38. Thanks to Ari Rabl for providing this information.
39. Barker and Johnstone (1993) include a particular subsidy in a package targeted at saving energy. They structure this package so that low-income earners could actually gain from the reform, because of the energy savings.

REFERENCES

Atrostic, B.K. and J.R. Nunns (1990), 'Measuring Tax Burden. A Historical Perspective', in E.R. Berndt and J.E. Triplett (eds), *Fifty Years of Economic Measurement: The Jubilee of the Conference on Research in Income and Wealth*, Chicago: University of Chicago Press, pp. 343–408.

Barde, J.-P. and N.A. Braathen (2002), 'Environmentally Related Levies', paper prepared for the conference on excise taxation, 11–12 April, Ministry of Finance, The Hague, The Netherlands.

Barker, T. and N. Johnstone (1993), 'Equity and Efficiency in Policies to Reduce Carbon Emissions in the Domestic Sector', *Energy and Environment*, 4(4), 335–61.

Baumol, W. and W. Oates (1988), *The Theory of Environmental Policy*, Cambridge: Cambridge University Press.

Been, V. (1993), 'What's Fairness Got to Do With It: Environmental Justice and the Siting of Locally Undesirable Land Uses', *Cornell Law Review*, **78**, 1001–85.

Bergman, L. and M. Hill (2000), 'Productivity and Growth Effects of Acidification: A Dynamic CGE Modelling Study of Sweden', discussion paper, Stockholm School of Economics.

Bostedt, G. (2002), 'Samordnat nyttjande ger bättre samhällsekonomi – exemplet skogsbruk och renskötsel', Fakta Skog Nr. 7/02 (in Swedish).

Bovenberg, L. and L. Goulder (2001), 'Addressing Industry Distributional Concerns in U.S. Climate Change Policy', http://weber.ucsd.edu/~carsonvs/papers/810.pdf.

Bovenberg, L. and R. de Moijj (1994), 'Environmental Levies and Distortionary Taxation', *American Economic Review*, **84**, 1085–9.

Bovenberg, L and F. Van der Ploeg (1993), 'Consequences of Environmental Tax Reform for Involuntary Unemployment and Welfare', mimeo, Tilburg University, The Netherlands.

Brännlund, R. and B. Kriström (1993), 'Assessing the Impact of Environmental

Charges: A Partial General Equilibrium Model of the Swedish Forestry Sector', *Environmental and Resource Economics*, **3**, 297–312.

Brännlund, R. and B. Kriström (1996), 'Welfare Measurement in Single and Multimarket Models: Theory and Application', *American Journal of Agricultural Economics*, **78**, 157–65.

Brännlund, R. and B. Kriström (2001), 'Too Hot to Handle? Benefits and Costs of Stimulating the Use of Biofuels in the Swedish Heating Sector', *Resource and Energy Economics*, **23**, 343–58.

Brännlund, R. and J. Nordström (2004), 'Carbon Tax Simulations Using a Household Demand Model', *European Economic Review*, **48**(1), 211–33.

Brown, D.J. and G. Heal (1979), 'Equity, Efficiency, and Increasing Returns', *Review of Economic Studies*, **46**(4), 571–85.

Brown, G.M. and J.F. Shogren (1998), 'The Economics of the Endangered Species Act', *Journal of Economic Perspectives*, **12**(3), 3–20.

Burtraw, D., A. Krupnick, K. Palmer, A. Paul, M. Toman and C. Bloyd (2001), 'Ancillary Benefits of Reduced Air Pollution in the United States from Moderate Greenhouse Gas Mitigation Policies in the Electricity Sector', RFF Discussion Paper 61.

Bye, B., S. Kverndokk and K.E. Rosendahl (2001), 'Mitigation Costs, Distributional Effects and Ancillary Benefits of Carbon Policies in the Nordic Countries, the UK and Ireland: A Survey', draft paper, Statistics Norway.

Carneiro, P., K.T. Hansen and J.J. Heckman (2002), 'Removing the Veil of Ignorance in Assessing the Distributional Impacts of Social Policies', Working Paper, Department of Economics, University of Chicago.

Carson, R.T. et al. (1994), 'A Bibliography of Contingent Valuation Studies and Papers', Natural Resource Damage Assessment, Inc., La Jolla, California.

Chichilnisky, G. and G. Heal (1994), 'Who Should Abate Carbon Emissions? An International Viewpoint', *Economic Letters*, **44**(4), 443–9.

Commission of the European Communities (CEC) (1992), 'European Economy: The Climate Challenge – Economic Aspects of the Community's Strategy for Limiting CO_2 Emissions', *European Economy*, **51**, May, Luxembourg: Office for Official Publications of the EC.

Cornwell, A. and J. Creedy (1997), 'Measuring the Welfare Effects of Tax Changes Using the LES: An Application to a Carbon Tax', *Empirical Economics*, **22**, 589–613.

Dasgupta, P. (2001), *Human Well-being and the Natural Environment*, Oxford: Oxford University Press.

Dasgupta, P., B. Kriström and K.-G. Mäler (1995), 'Current Issues in Resource Accounting', in P.-O. Johansson, B. Kriström and K.-G. Mäler (eds), *Current Issues in Environmental Economics*, Manchester: Manchester University Press, pp. 94–137.

Deaton, A. (2003), 'Health, Inequality, and Economic Development', *Journal of Economic Literature*, **41**, 113–58.

Dreze, J. and N. Stern (1987), 'Theory of Cost–Benefit Analysis', in A.J. Auerbach and M. Feldstein (eds), *Handbook of Public Economics, Vol 2*, Amsterdam: North-Holland, pp. 909–90.

EPA (2002), 'Distributional Analyses: Economic Impact Analysis and Equity Assignments', exhibit 9–2, p. 145.

Feldstein, M. (1972), 'Distributional Equity and the Optimal Structure of Public Prices', *American Economic Review*, **62**(1), 32–6.

Freeman, A.M. III (1993), *The Measurement of Environmental and Resource Values*, Washington DC: Resources for the Future.

Fullerton, D. (2001), 'A Framework to Compare Environmental Policies', NBER Working Paper 8420, Massachusetts, USA.

Fullerton, D. and D.L. Rogers (1993), *Who Bears the Lifetime Tax Burden?*, Washington DC: The Brookings Institution.

Fullerton, D. and G.E. Metcalf (1997), 'Environmental Controls, Scarcity Rents and Pre-Existing Distortions', working paper, University of Texas, Austin.

Goulder, L.H., I.W.H. Parry and D. Burtraw (1997), 'Revenue Raising versus other Approaches to Environmental Protection: The Critical Significance of Existing Distortions', *RAND Journal of Economics*, **28**(4), 708–31.

Goulder, L.H., I.W.H. Parry, R.C. Williams and D. Burtraw (1999), 'The Cost-effectiveness of Alternative Instruments for Environmental Protection in a Second-best Setting', *Journal of Public Economics*, **72**(3), 329–60.

Gravelle, H. (1998), 'How Much of the Relation between Population Mortality and Unequal Distribution of Income is a Statistical Artefact?', *British Medical Journal*, **316**, 382–5.

Harrison, G.W and B. Kriström (1999), 'General Equilibrium Effects of Increasing Carbon Taxes in Sweden', in R. Brännlund and I. Gren (eds), *Green Taxes: Theory and Practice*, Cheltenham, UK and Northampton, MA: Edward Elgar, pp. 59–108.

Harrison, G.W., T.F. Rutherford, D.G. Tarr and A. Gurgel (2002), 'Regional, Multilateral and Unilateral Trade Policies of MERCOSUR for Growth and Poverty Reduction in Brazil', working paper, The World Bank.

Heal, G. (1998), *Valuing the Future: Economic Theory and Sustainability*, New York: Columbia University Press.

Heal, G.M. and B. Kriström (2002), 'National Income in Dynamic Economies', working paper, Columbia University, http://www.ssrn.com.

Heal, G.M. and B. Kriström (2005), 'National Income and the Environment', in J. Vincent and K.-G. Mäler (eds), *Handbook of Environmental and Resource Economics*, Amsterdam: North-Holland (forthcoming).

Heckman, J.J., J. Smith and N. Clements (1997), 'Making the Most of Programme Evaluations and Social Experiments: Accounting for Heterogeneity in Programme Impacts', *Review of Economic Studies*, **64**, 487–555.

Helfand, G. (1999), 'Standards versus Taxes in Pollution Control', in Jeroen C.J.M van den Bergh (ed.), *Handbook of Environmental and Resource Economics, Vol. 1*, Cheltenham, UK and Northampton, MA, USA: Edward Elgar, pp. 223–34.

Herrington, P.R. (2003), 'Distribution of Costs and Environmental Impacts of Water Services in OECD States: Affordability Measures and Policies', paper prepared for the OECD workshop on the Distribution of Benefits and Costs of Environmental Policies, 4–5 March.

Hite, D. (2000), 'A Random Utility Model of Environmental Equity', *Growth and Change*, **31**(1), 40–58.

Holmlund, B. and L. Calmfors (2000), 'Unemployment and Economic Growth – A Partial Survey', *Swedish Economic Policy Review*, **1**, 107–53.

Hourcade, J.-C. (2001), 'Articulating National, Regional and International Policy: Simple Signals in an Heterogeneous World', IPIECA Symposium, 15–16 October, Cambridge, MA.

Jensen, J. (1998), 'Carbon Abatement Policies with Assistance to Energy Intensive Industry', MobiDK Project, Ministry of Business and Industry Denmark, http://www.mobidk.dk/mobi_p.htm.

Johansson, P.O. (1993), *Cost-Benefit Analysis of Environmental Change*, Cambridge: Cambridge University Press.

Johnstone, N. and J. Alavalapati (1998), 'The Distributional Effect of Environmental Tax Reform', Environmental Economics Programme, IIED, London, DP 98-01.

Kanninen, B.J. and B. Kriström (1992), 'Welfare Benefit Estimation and Income Distribution', Beijer Discussion Paper series No. 20, Beijer International Institute of Ecological Economics, The Royal Swedish Academy of Sciences, Stockholm.

Klinge-Jacobsen, H., K. Birr-Pedersen and M. Wier (2001), 'Fordelningsvirkninger af Energi- og Miljöavgifter' [Distributional Impacts of Environmental and Energy Charges], Risö National Laboratory, November (in Danish with English summary).

Kriström, B., R. Brännlund, J. Nordström, and S. Wibe (2003), 'Fördelningseffekter av Miljöpolitik' [Distributional Effects of Environmental Policy], Supplement 11 to the Medium Term Survey of Sweden 2003 (in Swedish. www.finans.regeringen.se).

Künzli, N., R. Kaiser, S. Medina, M. Studnicka, O. Chanel, O. Filliger, M. Herry, F. Horak Jr, V. Puybonnieux-Texier, P. Quénel, J. Schneider, R. Seethaler, J.-C. Vergnaud and H. Sommer (2000), 'Public Health Impact of Outdoor and Traffic-related Air Pollution: A European Assessment', *The Lancet*, **356**(9232), 782–801.

Kverndokk, S. and K. Rosendahl (2001), 'Greenhouse Gas Mitigation Costs and Ancillary Benefits in the Nordic countries, the UK and Ireland: A Survey', working paper, Ragnar Frisch Centre for Economic Research, Oslo, Norway.

Labandeira, X. and J.M. Labeaga (1999), 'Combining Input–Output Analysis and Micro-Simulation to Assess the Effects of Carbon Taxation on Spanish Households', *Fiscal Studies*, **30**(3), 305–20.

Lutter, A. and J. Shogren (2002), 'Tradable Permit Tariffs: How Local Air Pollution Affects Carbon Emissions Permit Trading', *Land Economics*, **78**(2), 159–70.

Lynch J.W., G.A. Kaplan, E.R. Pamuk, R.D. Cohen, K.E. Heck, J.L. Balfour and I.H. Yen (1998), 'Income Inequality and Mortality in Metropolitan Areas of the United States', *American Journal of Public Health*, **88**(7), 1074–80.

Markandya, A. (1998), 'Poverty, Income Distribution and Policy Making', *Environmental and Resource Economics*, **11**(3–4), 459–72.

Martinez-Alier, J. (2002), *The Environmentalism of the Poor: A Study of Ecological Conflicts and Valuation*, Cheltenham, UK and Northampton, MA: Edward Elgar.

McKenzie, G. (1986), 'Applied Welfare Economics and Frisch's Conjecture', in D. Bös, M. Rose and C. Seidl (eds), *Welfare and Efficiency in Public Economics*, Berlin: Springer Verlag, pp. 1–20.

Metcalf, G.E. (1997), 'The National Sales Tax: Who Bears the Burden?', Cato Policy Analysis, No. 289, http://www.cato.org/pubs/pas/pa-289.html.

Metcalf, G.E. (1999), 'A Distributional Analysis of Green Tax Reforms', *National Tax Journal*, **52**, 655–81.

Nickell, S. and B. Bell (1996), 'Would Cutting Payroll Taxes on the Unskilled Have a Significant Impact on Unemployment?', Centre for Economic Performance, London School of Economics, Discussion Paper 276.

O'Brien, P. and A. Vourc'h (2001), 'Encouraging Environmentally Sustainable Growth. Experience in OECD Countries', OECD Economics Department Working Papers 293, Paris: OECD.

OECD (1994), *The Distributive Effects of Economics Instruments for Environmental Policy*, Paris: OECD.

Panayotou, T. (1998), *Instruments of Change: Motivating and Financing Sustainable Development*, London: UNEP, Earthscan Publications.

Parks, P.J., G. Bostedt and B. Kriström (2002), 'An Integrated System for Management and Policy Analysis – Theoretical Results for Forestry and Reindeer Husbandry in Sweden', *Environmental and Resource Economics*, **21**, 203–20.

Perotti, R. (1996), 'Growth, Income Distribution, and Democracy: What the Data Say', *Journal of Economic Growth*, **1**, 149–87.

Persson, T. and G. Tabellini (1994), 'Is Inequality Harmful for Growth?', *American Economic Review*, **51**(84), 600–21.

Pope, C.A., R.T. Burnett, M.J. Thun, E.E. Calle, D. Krewski, K. Ito and G.D. Thurston (2002), 'Lung Cancer, Cardiopulmonary Mortality and Long-term Exposure to Fine Particulate Air Pollution', *Journal of the American Medical Association*, **287**(9), 1132–41.

Poterba, J.M. (1991), 'Is the Gasoline Tax Regressive?', *Tax Policy and the Economy*, vol. 5, pp. 145–64.

Rajah, N. and S. Smith (1993), 'Distributional Aspects of Household Water Charges', *Fiscal Studies*, **14**(2), 86–108.

Ravallion, M., M.T. Heil and J. Javal (2000), 'Carbon Emissions and Income Equality', *Oxford Economic Papers*, **54**(4), 651–69.

Roback, J. (1982), 'Wages, Rents and the Quality of Life', *Journal of Political Economy*, **90**(6), 1257–78.

Roberts, D., J. Farrington, D. Gray and S. Martin (1999), 'The Distributional Impacts of Fuel Duties: The Impact on Rural Households in Scotland', *Regional Studies*, **33**(3), 281–8.

Rose, A., B. Stevens and G. Davis (1988), *Natural Resources Policy and Income Distribution*, Baltimore, MD: Johns Hopkins University Press.

Rubin, J., G. Helfand and J. Loomis (1991), 'A Benefit–Cost Analysis of the Spotted Owl', *Journal of Forestry*, **89**, 25–30.

Russell, C.S. and P.T. Powell (1999), 'Practical Considerations and Comparison of Instruments of Environmental Policy', in Jeroen C.J.M van den Berg (ed.), *Handbook of Environmental and Resource Economics*, Cheltenham, UK and Northampton, MA: Edward Elgar, pp. 307–28.

Sieg, H., V.K. Smith and H.S. Banzhaf (2001), 'Estimating the General Equilibrium Benefits of Large Changes in Spatially Delineated Public Goods', working paper, Carnegie Mellon University, 20 February.

Sipes, K. and R. Mendelsohn (2001), 'The Effectiveness of Gasoline Taxation to Manage Air Pollution', *Ecological Economics*, **2**(36), 299–309.

Smith, S. (1992), 'The Distributional Consequences of Taxes on Energy and the Carbon Content of Fuels', *European Economy*, Special Edition, **1**, 241–68.

Smith, Z. (2000), 'The Petrol Tax Debate', Briefing Note 8/2000, Institute for Fiscal Studies, London.

SOU (1997), *11 Skatter, Miljö och Sysselsättning, slutbetänkande från skatteväxlingskommittén*, Stockholm: Fritzes förlag (final report from the Green Tax Commission, with English summary).

Stiglitz, J.E. (1995), *Whither Socialism?*, Cambridge, MA: MIT Press.

Sutherland, R.J. (1994), 'Income Distribution Effects of Electric Utility DSM Programs', *Energy Journal*, **15**(4), 103–16.

Sturm, P. (1995), 'The Efficiency of Greenhouse Gas Emissions Abatement and International Equity', Discussion Paper No 95.9, June, School of Applied and International Economics, Massey University, New Zealand.

Symons, E., J. Proops and P. Gay (1994), 'Carbon Taxes, Consumer Demand, and Carbon Dioxide Emissions: A Simulation Analysis for the UK', *Fiscal Studies*, **15**(2), 19–43.

Tietenberg, T. (1996), *Environmental and Natural Resource Economics*, 4th edn, New York: HarperCollins.

Tiezzi, S. (2001), 'The Welfare Effects of Carbon Taxation on Italian Households', Working Paper 337, Dipartimento di Economica Politica, Universita degli Studi di Siena.

Varian, H.R. (1974), 'Equity, Envy, and Efficiency', *Journal of Economic Theory*, **9**(1), 63–91.

Walls and Hanson (1999), 'Distributional Aspects of an Environmental Tax Shift: The Case of Motor Vehicle Emissions Taxes', *National Tax Journal*, **1**, 53–65.

Weitzman, M.L. (1976), 'On the Welfare Significance of National Product in a Dynamic Economy', *Quarterly Journal of Economics*, **90**(1), 156–62.

West, S.E. (2004), 'Distributional Effects of Alternative Vehicle Pollution Control Policies', *Journal of Public Economics*, **88**(3–4), 735–57.

West, S.E. and R.C. Williams (2002), 'Estimates From a Consumer Demand System: Implications for the Incidence of Environmental Taxes', Working Paper No. 9152, NBER, http://www.nber.org/papers/w9152.

Whalley, J. (1984), 'Regression or Progression: The Taxing Question of Incidence Analysis' (The Innis Lecture), *Canadian Journal of Economics*, **17**(4), 654–82.

Zimmerman, K. (1986), 'Distributional Considerations and the Environmental Policy Process', in A. Schnaiberg, N. Watts and K. Zimmerman (eds), *Distributional Conflicts in Environmental Resource Policy*, Aldershot: Gower, pp. 95–105.

PART II

Evidence on the Distributional Effects of
Environmental Policies

4. Distributional effects of the ecological tax reform in Germany: an evaluation with a microsimulation model

Christhart Bork

1. INTRODUCTION

The German Government introduced several tax reforms during the period 1998 to 2002. One of them was an income tax reform that decreased the burden for nearly every taxpayer, while abolishing some tax exemptions and deductions (for details, see Petersen and Bork, 2000). Another was an ecological tax reform, the aim of which was not only to protect the environment but also to use the revenue in order to reduce social security contributions, for example, the contributions to the old-age pension scheme. This revenue is supposed to promote employment by reducing the cost of labour. The ecological tax reform consists of an increase in tax rates on motor fuels as well on a few other types of energy use (see Kohlhaas, 2000).

In the policy debate, the distributional effects of the ecological tax reform are a key issue. A comprehensive analysis of environment-related distributive effects should include variables such as the direct and indirect financial impacts, effects on pollution, and consequences for human health (see, for example, Johnstone and Alavalapati, 1998). In general, the direct financial effects of energy taxes are said to be income-regressive, but the degree of regressivity is weak (OECD, 2001, p. 87).

As regards the ecological tax reform in Germany, several major questions are raised. What kind of distributional effects will the reform result in? Who gains and who loses when comparing to the situation before the reform? By how much does the impact of the reforms vary? Literature on the distributional effects of the German tax reforms is scarce but one extensive analysis does show that the ecological tax reform tends to have some small regressive effects (Bach et al., 2001 and 2002).

There are many ways of examining the distributive impact of green taxes (see OECD, 1994). For an analysis of the impact on competitiveness, employment, prices and growth, a macroeconomic model is useful (Meyer and Ewerhart, 1998). In order to take macroeconomic feedback effects and long-run effects into account, one can use a computable general equilibrium model (see for example, O'Ryan et al., 1999; and Böhringer et al., 2001). But for an investigation of short-term effects on individuals, a microsimulation model is usually the best approach. This type of model focuses either on households or on enterprises.

Most of the studies on the distributional incidence of environmental taxes identify weak to mild regressive effects on average, regardless of the models used, the countries reviewed, or the specific questions examined. For instance, in the case of Denmark, a study finds that distributional effects are mildly regressive and that they vary according to the different environmental taxes (see Klinge-Jacobsen et al., 2002). Aasness and Larsen (2002) investigated the distributional effects of taxes on transportation for Norway and reached the same conclusion. However, other studies have also detected a progressive impact. For developing countries like Pakistan, mildly progressive effects of environment-related taxes have been found (Baranzini et al., 1998). According to a cross-country study, taxes on motor fuels could be weakly progressive (Barker and Köhler, 1998). Other studies extend the distributional analysis to general welfare effects. According to an examination of the effects of carbon taxation on Italian households, for example, there is a substantial welfare loss (Tiezzi, 2001).

One comprehensive study of the distributional effects of environmental taxes includes every conceivable effect that may have an impact on households, enterprises and the government (see Kriström, Chapter 3 in this volume). In the following analysis we concentrate on first-order effects of ecological taxes on private households. Enterprises are excluded for lack of data. Our primary goal is to present an integrated analysis of the changes in the burden of both the ecological taxes and the social security contributions. We also investigate the distributional effects of the other major reform: the income tax reform that includes increased child benefits. For this purpose, we use a microsimulation model inspired by the models developed first by Orcutt (1957). The model is conceived so as to analyse direct taxes, indirect taxes and social security contributions simultaneously. This chapter also updates a previous study by Bach et al. (2002). It is organised as follows. First we briefly describe the model, the data and the set-up of the integrated microdata file used to represent the actual population. Then we give a brief description of the ecological tax reform in Germany and its distributional effects. Finally, we present the results of the simulation and conclude with a discussion of the distributional incidence of the reform on households.

2. THE MODEL

The microsimulation model has a static and mostly deterministic structure. At the current stage of development, the model is able to analyse first-order effects of nearly all types of indirect and direct taxes (for comparable models, see Harding, 1996; or Drabinski, 2002). The model has a modular structure which includes modules for direct and indirect taxes, for social security contributions, and for transfers. Figure 4.1 gives a systematic overview of the microsimulation model, from raw data sets to the calculation modules.

The direct tax module consists of patterns for the income tax, the tax on cars and the property tax. Value added tax, taxes on gasoline, electricity, tobacco, insurance and on alcoholic beverages are parts of the indirect tax module. The social security contributions module contains old-age pensions, health services, unemployment insurance and nursing care insurance. The module for transfers covers child and housing benefits, education, social aid and old-age benefits.

2.1   The Data

For the construction of a tax and transfer microsimulation model, detailed information is needed about the personal income distribution and expenditures of the households. In Germany, only a few microdata sets are suitable for analysing the underlying issue. Furthermore, not all existing data sets are available for scientific analysis. The first accessible one is the Income and Expenditure Survey carried out by the German Federal Statistical Office in 1993 on a sample of 40 230 households, with 779 variables. The variables cover extensive socio-economic information, such as the composition, the income and expenditures of households. Since 2001, the Federal Statistical Office provides data based on the 1998 survey, but we could not use them because the new sample contains only quarterly income data. This means that only 25 per cent of the households in the sample receive additional payments such as Christmas or seasonal bonuses. This is inappropriate for our analysis.

For issues relevant to taxation, we use a microdata set which was generated by a regional tax authority in 1992. It contains 88 460 cases and 253 variables. This income tax data set includes information about tax exemptions and deductions and takes into account negative incomes, in particular from rents and leasing. This is important as the overall sum of this type of income is negative in Germany. All other sources provide data whose total is overall usually positive. However, we could not access an up-to-date data file from the tax authority. As the Income and Expenditure Survey dates from 1993, it makes sense to use a tax data set of a more recent year as well.

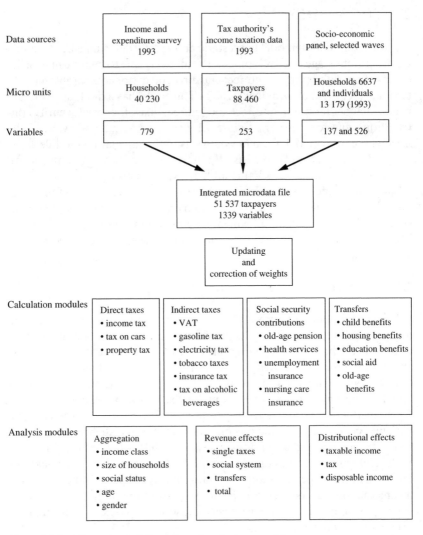

Figure 4.1   Overview of the microsimulation model

A problem arising when analysing distributional effects is the absence of data from upper-income classes in the basic data set. Our basic data set covers only household incomes of less than 17 900 euros per month after tax. We solve this problem by tripling all cases with an income over 100 000 euros per year. The income information from the tax authority's data set without income limitations is merged with the cases we have multiplied in the basic data set. We consider only the main income source. In addition, we use the German Socio-Economic Panel established by the German Institute of Economic Research. For the year 1993, this includes 6637 households and 13 179 persons.

While the Income and Expenditure Survey provides our basic data set, the information from the Socio-Economic Panel is mainly used for time allocation of the individuals. We have to merge the three data sets into one integrated microdata file which should adequately represent the German population.

2.2 The Integrated Microdata File

With these three data sets, we construct one integrated microdata file. First we have to transform the household units of the Income and Expenditure Survey into taxpayer units so that we can merge this second file in the basic data set.[1] Capital income and income from rents and leasing are not assigned to individuals. Therefore, we distribute these sources of income among members of the household. We assume that the distribution of this category of income is identical to the per capita distribution of the other sources of income. To assign the expenditures, we follow the same procedure.

Now we can merge the data from the tax authority with our basic data set. We look for similarities and build clusters containing comparable micro-units. Common characteristics are distributed across seven income classes, seven main income sources, marital status and the number of children of each taxpayer. As a result of this process, we obtain approximately 290 clusters for the Income and Expenditure Survey and the tax data. Each case in each cluster of the basic data set is randomly assigned a corresponding case from the second data set.[2]

Time allocation data from the Socio-Economic Panel is merged in a similar fashion.[3] The clusters are built only for taxpayers receiving an income from work. They are broken down by gender and ten income classes. After the second merging, we can calculate the monthly working hours for wage-earners. Our integrated microdata file now contains 51 537 taxpayers in 40 799 households and 1339 variables, representing 40 income sources.[4]

In order to account for changes in employment over time, we use the overall German unemployment rate to represent the probability of becoming unemployed. Those people already unemployed in 1993 are assumed to stay unemployed through 2003. The overall increase in unemployment is matched randomly to other individuals for whom unemployment benefits are computed.

Moreover, it is necessary to update the integrated microdata file from 1993 to 2003. This is straightforward for the expenditures: we use the inflation rates for nearly 200 different commodities. By doing this, the effects of the ecological tax reform on prices are included. But we cannot quantify them because a decomposition is not possible. To update the different incomes of our sample of taxpayers, we choose various growth rates provided in the national accounts and other statistical information. The variance of income growth for different income groups is not taken into account because national accounts do not provide such data. The enlarged data set is now ready for simulation. We compute almost every regulation of the tax law, social security contributions and benefits for each taxpayer in the data set. Once these computations are done, we aggregate the data on taxpayers back to households (for details, see Bork, 2000). We can now analyse the financial effects of taxes and benefits broken down into a large spectrum of variables. Thanks to the capacity of cross-sectional data, we can examine the distributional effects on an annual basis. There is a wide range of studies discussing the distributional effects of taxes by differentiating between a lifetime view and an annual view (compare Fullerton and Rogers, 1993). The result of this research, which mostly uses expenditure as a proxy for lifetime income, is that regressive effects observed on an annual basis become milder when considered over a lifetime. Politicians primarily look at first-order effects because that is what households directly face. However, there are so many uncertainties about future developments that opting for an annual perspective to examine the first-order effects of changes in a tax system seems justified. Before exploring distributional effects, it is worth making some assumptions. For our analysis, we suppose that suppliers can shift the whole tax burden on to consumers. For the energy sector, this is a pragmatic approach because this market is essentially monopolistic or oligopolistic where firms can set prices.

The analysis of distributional effects will tell whether taxes are 'regressive' or 'progressive'. The definition we use here depends on the average tax rate. A tax is said to be regressive if the average tax rate falls with income. It is proportional if the average tax rate is constant and it is progressive if the average tax rate rises with income. Low-income households pay a higher (lower) fraction of their income in taxes if the tax is regressive (progressive) (Metcalf, 1998).

Compared with macroeconomic models, the strength of the microsimulation model is that it enables us to compute almost every tax rule for every case in the sample in detail. For instance, by providing consumers' spending on natural gas, diesel, petrol or electricity, the data enable us to calculate the ecological taxes for each household. Furthermore, as the data contain information about exemptions and deductions, the German income tax can be calculated quite precisely. Together with the socio-economic information, we can differentiate the impacts of the reform in many cases.

Table 4.1   Energy consumption by households, 1993

Energy	Microsimulation model (million tons)	Energy balances (mineral coal units)	Difference (%)
Electricity	15.52	15.50	100.1
Natural gas	24.24	27.30	88.8
Heating oil	30.14	32.30	93.3

Source: Arbeitsgemeinschaft Energiebilanzen (1999), Table 2.8.2.1; own calculations.

The microsimulation model also enables measurement of the variance which the distributional effects of a reform could have. The distributional impact of taxes can be measured across different dimensions such as the distribution of households over income groups, among different household types, categorised by social status, size of family, residential area (rural/urban) and age of the head. In contrast to macroeconomic models, the microsimulation model does not work with equilibrium equations. This means that behavioural effects derived from supply-and-demand equations are not included in the microsimulation model which looks primarily at the financial first-order effects of policy changes.

2.3   Suitability of the Model

The simulation matches the actual tax revenue well. The simulated revenue of the model in most cases equals the value of the revenue published by the Federal Statistical Office in Germany. Furthermore, we have to check energy consumption in the simulation model against total actual consumption. Table 4.1 provides an example of the results. In fact, the results for the simulated consumption of electricity, natural gas and heating oil are close to the actual consumption. In the case of fuel, it is not possible to check the validity of the model because energy balances do not break down consumption between households, enterprises and the public sector (for the suitability of the model for taxes and social security contributions, see Bork, 2000).

3.   THE ECOLOGICAL TAX REFORM

The German government implemented its ecological tax reform shortly after the political change in 1998. A new electricity tax was then introduced. Taxes on petroleum and gas have been gradually increased from 1999 to 2003 in five steps. Table 4.2 provides the tax rates before and after the reform. For storage heaters installed before April 1999, there is a rebate for the electricity tax of 40 per cent. For energy-intensive industries, there are also many rebates.

The revenues from ecological taxes are transferred to the pension scheme and the contribution rates to the scheme were reduced from 20.3 per cent to 19.5 per cent of gross income in 2003. In the proposed tax reform, a further reduction of the contribution rates to 18.4 per cent in 2003 was assumed. This reduction of the social security contributions should partly relieve households from the additional burden of ecological taxes.

The importance of environment-related taxes in Germany has grown since 1998. The revenues of taxes on gas, motor fuels and heating oil are published together by the Federal Statistical Office as the 'taxes on mineral oil'. But the revenue of the latter consists essentially of taxes on motor fuels. As a result of the ecological tax reform, the revenue grew from 34.1 billion euros in 1998 to 49.7 billion in 2003 (Table 4.3), that is from 1.8 per cent to 2.3 per cent of GDP. Since 2001, environmental taxes have exceeded 10 per cent of total tax revenues.

Table 4.2   Tax rates on energy, 1998–2003 (euro cents per unit)

Energy (Unit)	1998	1999	2000	2001	2002	2003
Heating oil (litres)	4.09	6.14	6.14	6.14	6.14	6.14
Natural gas (kWh)	0.18	0.35	0.35	0.35	0.35	0.55
Electricity[a] (kWh)	–	1.02	1.28	1.53	1.79	2.05
Petrol (litres)	50.11	53.17	56.24	59.31	62.38	65.45
Diesel (litres)	31.70	34.77	37.84	40.90	43.97	47.04

Note: [a] There is a rebate for storage heaters.

Table 4.3   Revenue of environment-related taxes, 1998–2003 (billion euro)

	1998	1999	2000	2001	2002	2003
Tax on mineral oil	34.1	36.4	37.8	40.7	42.2	43.2
Tax on electricity	–	1.8	3.4	4.3	5.1	6.5
Environmental taxes	34.1	38.3	41.2	45.0	47.3	49.7
Percentage of total tax revenue	8.0	8.4	8.8	10.1	10.7	11.2
Percentage of nominal GDP	1.8	1.9	2.0	2.2	2.2	2.3

We do not want to discuss the reform in all its details, but rather to show its financial effects. First, changes in disposable income after the additional ecological taxation (an increase in taxes on heating oil, natural gas, electricity, petrol and diesel). Our analysis covers only the consequences of these changes for households. It required investigating all the steps of the reform and comparing the situation of private households in 1998 with their situation in 2003. Second, we look briefly at further changes to the tax system and we simulate the income tax in 2003 compared with the income tax rate of 1998. In a third step, we simulate an increase in child benefits. The reason for extending the investigation is to give a complete overview of potential compensations for higher ecological taxes, even though the government did not design the reform with special distributive concerns in mind (compare Ekins, 1999).

4.   DISTRIBUTIONAL EFFECTS

Normally, distributional effects are twofold. First, there are environmental benefits. Analysing their distribution over the population is very complicated but there are two environmental benefits generally associated with energy taxes (see Baranzini et al., 2000): one is global, the other is local, such as an improvement in local air quality. We could not investigate these different benefits because we do not have regional variables in our data set. We therefore concentrate our analysis on the other distributional effects, namely the burden due to the ecological tax reform.

The hypothesis of a regressive effect of the ecological tax can be answered first by some stylised facts. The scatterplot of the tax burden of all existing ecological taxes in 1998 in percentage of disposable income shows a left-steepness (Figure 4.2). The sum of all ecological taxes is obviously regressive. Figure 4.2 also illustrates that the tax burden is much more variable in lower-income brackets than in upper brackets. The mean tax burden in percentage of disposable income is only 2.75 per cent, while the standard deviation is 2.86. On the whole income scale, several households have a much higher tax burden than all other households with the same gross income.

To show the variation of the burden within the different income group, we plot the coefficient of variation (standard deviation divided by mean); especially for annual gross incomes up to 50 000 euros broken down by socio-economic status (Figure 4.3). For every social status, it is obvious that the variation decreases when gross income increases. Especially in the lowest income brackets, the variation is very high, but up to a gross income of 8000 euros we find only households of unemployed, students and other

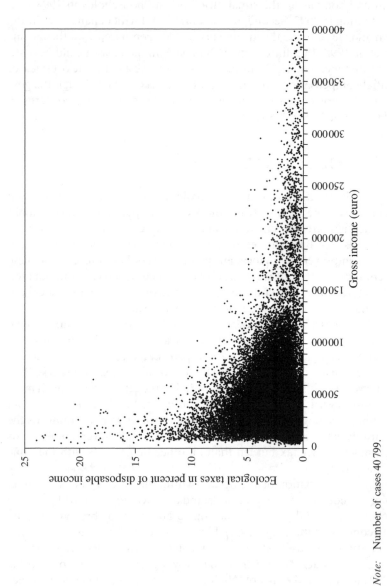

Note: Number of cases 40 799.

Figure 4.2 Ecological taxes in percentage of disposable income, 1998

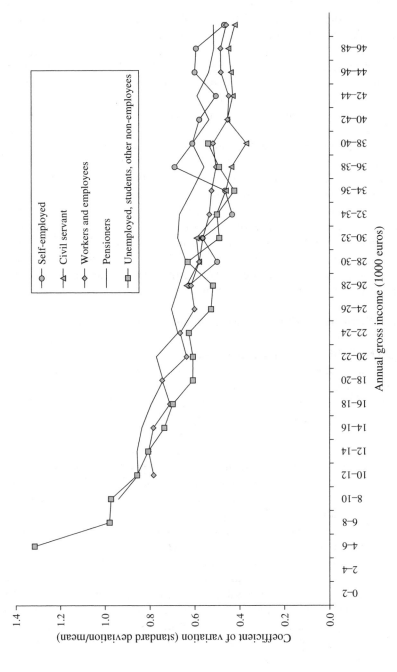

Figure 4.3   Coefficient of variation of the distributional effects of ecological taxes

149

non-employed. The variation of the distributional effects changes with the socio-economic status of the household. Households of pensioners tend to face a higher coefficient of variation than others. In most cases, the coefficient of variation for households of workers and employees is between the coefficients of the other types of households. It is interesting to note that within the income bracket from 36 000 to 50 000 euros, the variation of the environmental tax burden for civil servants is the lowest.

To perceive the size of the increase in ecological taxes since 1999, our analysis concentrates only on the changes that occurred between 1998 and 2003. First we give some stylised facts for the impact of the ecological tax reform, including the reduction of social security contributions. The burden or otherwise from the reform is – like the 1998 ecological taxes – very diversified. Figure 4.4 shows the impact of the reform in percentage of disposable income. Most households are negatively affected by the reform. Only 8.8 per cent of all households gain from the reform. The maximum gain is 0.8 per cent of disposable income. The maximum loss is about 10 per cent. Hence, gains are much smaller than losses. But, on average, the loss is small (0.7 per cent of disposable income). Also the standard deviation (0.835) is smaller than the standard deviation of the ecological taxes existing in 1998.

4.1   Distributional Effects of the Environmental Tax Reform

Impacts of different environmental taxes

Which taxes cause a higher burden and do they have different distributive effects? The previous section showed that the impact of the ecological tax reform could vary greatly. To give more detailed information about distributional effects, we reduce the variance by aggregating the sample, using gross income groups as a break variable. The first aggregation takes all cases together. Then we divide them by socio-economic status, type and size of household, residential area, and age of the head of household. In practice, all these categorisations have to be done for each head of household. Each category will be combined with the distribution of gross income which covers about 40 different types of income from work and from transfers. When looking at average changes in the tax burden from the ecological tax reform, one sees clearly regressive effects for the tax on electricity, for the tax on natural gas and for the tax on heating oil (Figure 4.5). The figure shows also that, on average, the burden of each ecological tax does not exceed 1 per cent of disposable income. For taxes on motor fuels, the result is different. Up to the income bracket 25 000 to 30 000 euros, there is an increasing tax burden as a percentage of disposable income. With a gross annual income beyond 30 000 euros, the relative tax burden decreases. By abolishing the tax rebate for storage heaters, the burden from a tax on

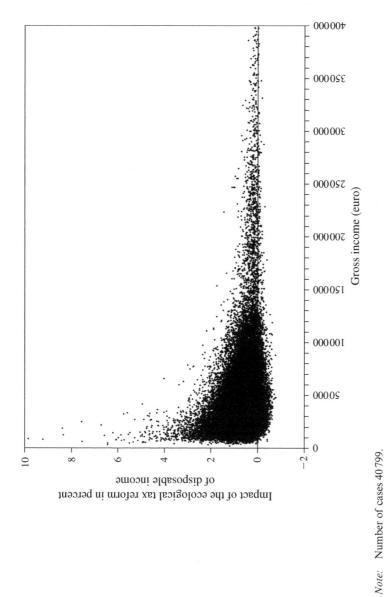

Note: Number of cases 40 799.

Figure 4.4 Impacts of the ecological tax reform in percentage of disposable income

151

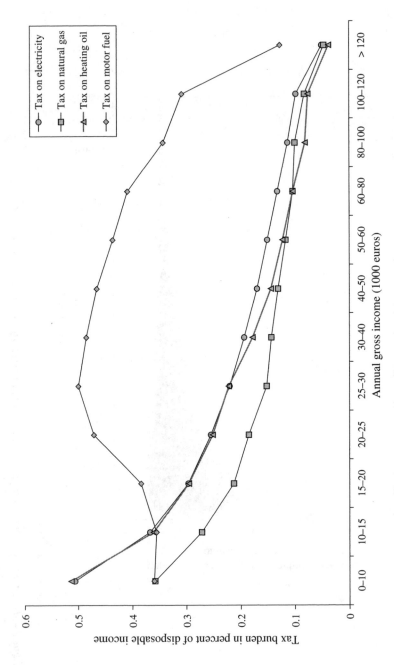

Figure 4.5 Changes in tax burden of the ecological tax reform by type of tax

electricity would rise, especially for households in lower-income brackets. This rebate mitigates the impact of taxes on electricity for about 10 per cent of all households with storage heaters.

Impacts by size of household
In addition to all the changes in ecological taxes, we also take into account the use of the revenue. This means we take the effects of reduced social security contributions into consideration. Distinguishing between the sizes of the households, nearly all of them experience a regressive effect of the reform (Figure 4.6). Only for the two-person households, we discover a small progressive effect from the lowest to the second-lowest income bracket. In this case, the progressive effect of motor fuel taxes predominates over the effects of other types of ecological taxes. In contrast to a previous analysis by Bach et al. (2001, p. 110), there is no more relief for one-person households in middle-income brackets because of higher actual contribution rates to the pension scheme than forecasted. The burden of the reform clearly increases with the size of the household.

Impacts by socio-economic status
When looking at the socio-economic status, each income group has not a sufficient number of cases to represent the whole population accurately, while the sampling error is small and tolerable. With fewer than 50 observations, the results are typically not reliable. For example, there are not enough cases of households of unemployed people, students and other non-employed with a gross income above 60 000 euros.

The impact of the ecological tax reform varies with socio-economic status (Figure 4.7). In the income bracket up to 15 000 euros, the group of pensioners is affected less than other households. In the income bracket between 15 000 euros and 30 000 euros, this group bears an increasing relative burden on average. Workers and employees with a gross income between 20 000 euros and 100 000 euros are affected on average less than all the other groups. In their case, the reduction of the social security contributions mitigates the higher tax burden. This group experiences a regressive effect of the reform over the whole income scale. The group of civil servants does not gain from the reduction of social security contributions. This is the reason for their almost always higher average tax burden. But for a gross income of 30 000 euros and more, there is a clear regressive effect for civil servants. The group of households with unemployed, students and other non-employed is confronted with a nearly proportional burden in the income range up to 25 000 euros. In addition, the negative impact of the reform is comparatively high for this social group. The burden of the reform for the self-employed is – except for the highest income bracket – the

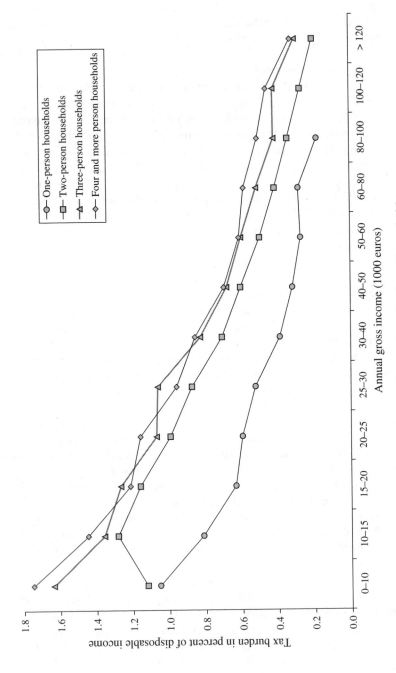

Figure 4.6   Changes in tax burden of the ecological tax reform by size of household

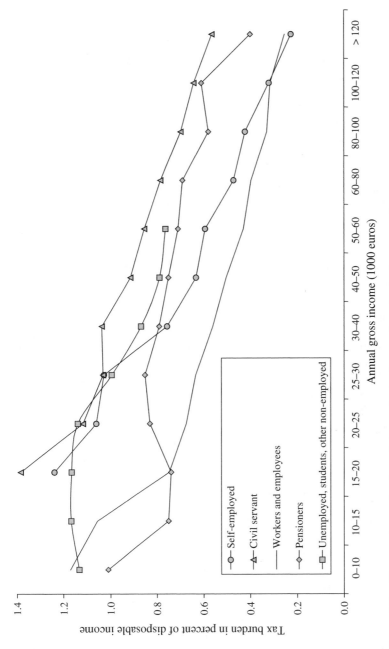

Figure 4.7   Changes in tax burden of the ecological tax reform by socio-economic status

same as for civil servants, and workers and employees. The self-employed households have on average clearly the highest gross income in the whole sample. This is especially obvious in the upper-income brackets. This is why, in the bracket with incomes of more than 120 000 euros, the average impact is very small and less than for all other social groups.

Impacts by family type
The picture of the effect of the ecological tax reform across family types is quite clear (Figure 4.8). The average burden of the reform rises across almost all income brackets with the number of people living in the household. Only in the income bracket between 10 000 euros and 15 000 euros do couples without children have a higher burden than couples with children. Without exception, couples face a clear regressive negative impact. Contrary to this finding, single persons with children have a decreasing negative impact only over the income brackets up to 40 000 euros. Between 40 000 and 80 000 euros, there is a proportional negative impact of the ecological tax reform. Obviously, single people without children have the lowest burden. The overall size of the burden is not very high. Just about 84 per cent of all households face a burden less than 1 per cent of disposable income.

Impacts by residential area
Considering that taxes on motor fuels are the main source of revenue, the distributional effects classified by residential area of the household merit a special analysis. Our data allow us to distinguish between households living in a city with a population over 100 000 people and other households living at a given distance from such cities. Households in a city bear the lowest burden from the ecological tax reform (Figure 4.9). Obviously, cars are used less by these households than by others, and the distributional effect is almost regressive on average. If we look at other households living outside a city with a gross income of over 30 000 euros, they bear roughly the same relative burden. However, the distributional effects for these groups of households differ in the lower-income brackets. The highest burden is borne by households in the lowest income bracket when they live at between 25 km and 60 km from a city. Surprisingly, the burden of the reform is lighter for households in this income bracket when they live still further away from a city. In the income brackets between 10 000 and 20 000 euros, the heaviest burden is faced – as expected – by households who live more than 60 km away from a city.

Impacts by age of the head of household
Finally, age does not have any influence on the distributional effects of the ecological tax reform in the income brackets between 25 000 euros and

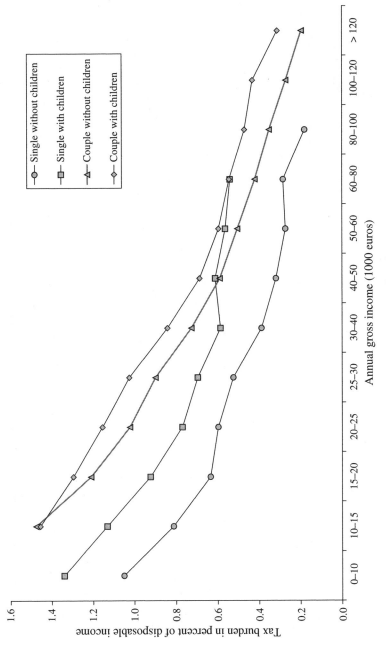

Figure 4.8 Changes in tax burden of the ecological tax reform by family type

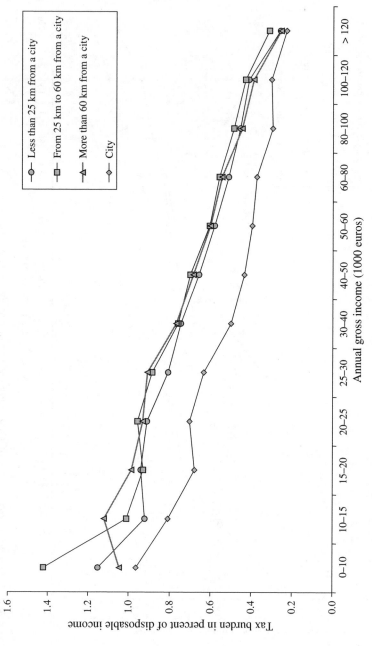

Figure 4.9   Changes in tax burden of the ecological tax reform by residential area

40 000 euros. In this range, almost all households experience on average the same weakly regressive effect (Figure 4.10). For the income brackets up to 25 000 euros, the results differ by age of the head of household. Especially, the 'oldest' category pays less than the others. Also the degree of regressivity is lower than for 'younger' categories, although in the income brackets up to 15 000 euros for 'younger' categories, and for households whose head is over 65 in the income bracket between 15 000 and 25 000 euros, the reform has a small progressive effect. In the upper-income brackets, we find the burden is reversed. The relative burden increases with the age of the head of household. For the category of households whose head is over 65, the burden is relatively constant, ranging between 0.6 and 0.8 per cent of disposable income for the wide income bracket between 10 000 and 80 000 euros. They do not profit from the reduction in social security contributions.

4.2 Distributional Effects of the Additional Income Tax Reform

In summary, it becomes obvious that the whole population loses on average because of the ecological tax reform, even when the reduced social security contributions are taken into account. In most cases, households experience a regressive effect of the reform.

What did the government do to make up for these effects? A large reform, the income tax reform, resulted in a net relief as from the year 2000. In addition, the government increased child benefits from 112 euros per month in 1998 up to 154 euros per month in 2003 for first and second children. Although these reforms were not designed to compensate those negatively affected by the ecological tax reform, they were part of a comprehensive tax reform package. However, can these additional reforms totally compensate the losers? What are the links between the distributional effects of the ecological tax reform and those of the income tax reform and increased child benefits?

There may be some other measures the government could take to compensate or mitigate the distributional impacts of the ecological taxes. For example, there are special regulations in the public transport or environment-related support programmes which are funded from the ecological tax revenue (see Bundesministerium für Umwelt, Naturschutz und Reaktorsicherheit und Umweltbundesamt, 2003). The regulations for public transport could benefit especially households in urban areas and those in lower-income brackets if the provider of public transport passed the advantage to customers. This depends on the demand elasticity for public transport and the opportunity to use public transport. Government expenditures for the environmental protection programmes will reach

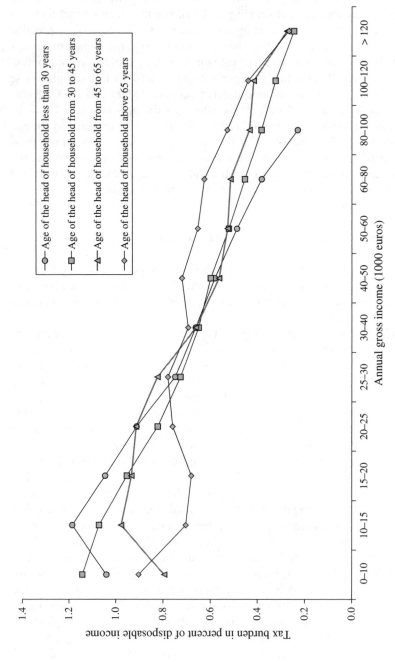

Figure 4.10 Changes in tax burden of the ecological tax reform by age

about 1.1 per cent of the revenue derived from the ecological tax reform in 2003; the distributional effects should thus be very low. In a qualitative discussion, these effects could also be progressive because individual house-owners will be the main beneficiaries of those programmes.

Before we analyse the distributional effects of the income tax reform and increased child benefits, some restrictions have to be pointed out. The two reforms are not revenue-neutral. There is a net relief for households of about 9.3 billion euros (Sachverständigenrat, 2000, p. 108). This may distort the comparability. However, the distributional effects of these two reforms compared with those of the ecological tax reform suggest there is a relationship between these two reforms. Particularly the increased lump-sum child benefit is a reform which could probably make up for the regressive effects of the ecological tax reform.

The increased rates of the environment-related taxes due to the ecological tax reform have a weak regressive effect (Figure 4.11). But the reduction in social security contributions strengthens the regressive effect. The advantages arising from the reduction in social security contributions mostly favour the middle and upper-income classes. As regards disposable income, all income classes above 15 000 euros enjoy a higher disposable income on average than with the increased ecological taxes alone. The burden of the reform is weak; hardly 1 per cent of households' disposable income.

When taking the income tax reform into the analysis, the picture of the distributional effects changes completely. Only households in the income brackets up to 20 000 euros bear the burden from the ecological tax reform in spite of the income tax reform. For these households, a marginal decrease in disposable income can be observed. All households above these income brackets pay less in taxes than before the reform. Because the income tax is progressive in Germany, the relative relief brought by the income tax reform increases up to an annual income of 60 000 euros. For almost every income class, we find a decreasing average tax burden, except for some households with a gross income between 80 000 and 120 000 euros. Some of these have to pay more after the income tax reform. This may not be visible immediately. One reason for this finding is that the government decided to cut by half the existing tax exemptions and deductions. This burdens especially households in higher-income brackets. The second reason is that in Germany, one may choose between a child benefit or a tax reduction per child. The tax authority calculates the income tax corresponding to these two options and uses whichever is more favourable for the taxpayer. Because of the increased child benefits for households in this higher-income bracket, child benefits are the favoured option after the reform.

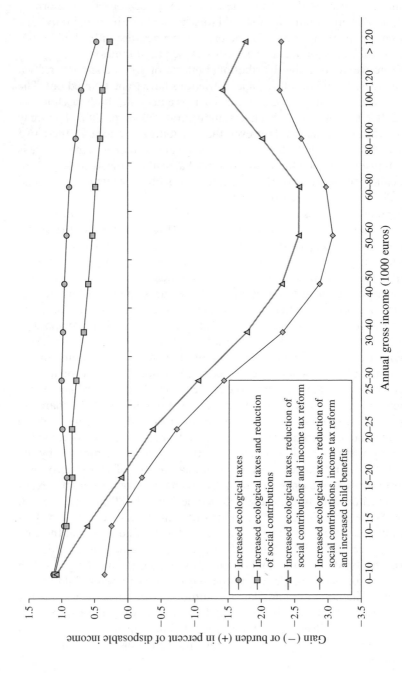

Figure 4.11   Effects of different reforms since 1998

These effects become quite clear if we include increased child benefits into the observation. Normally we would expect that increasing child benefits by the same amount across all income brackets should reduce the relief for those with a higher gross income. Because of the optional solution and the distribution of households with children across the income scale, we cannot determine these effects clearly. We find that the relief of higher child benefits is increasing in the income bracket between 60 000 and 120 000 euros. On average, only households with a gross income up to 15 000 euros are burdened by these two tax reforms, but only mildly with less than 0.5 per cent of their disposable income.

4.3 Total Distributional Effects of the Reforms

What kind of households are burdened more than others after all the reforms we discussed? When examining the results by socio-economic status, we get a clearer picture (Figure 4.12). Only some pensioners and a few households of unemployed, students and other non-employed bear on average a higher burden after all the reforms. Pensioners with an income up to 30 000 euros lose up to 1 per cent of their disposable income. The group of unemployed, students and other non-employed in the income brackets up to 25 000 euros also lose in monetary terms, though less than pensioners. Households of self-employed, civil servants as well as workers and employees enjoy on average a higher disposable income after considering all the reforms.

Finally, if we look at households differentiated by the age of their head (Figure 4.13), we see that the gains and burdens of the reforms are the same for older heads of household and for pensioners. Middle-aged heads (from 30 to 45 years) gain over the whole income. Especially in the lower-income brackets, increased child benefits more than compensate the burden of the ecological taxes. The advantages increase in parallel with gross income up to 60 000 euros because of a higher-income tax relief and the changes in child benefits. If the age of the head is between 45 and 65 years, the advantage of the reform is usually smaller than for middle-aged heads because there are fewer dependent children in these households. In the lower-income brackets of this middle-aged group, we find many households with people in early retirement. In their case, the burden is the same as for older heads of household. Younger groups benefit from all the changes, except in the income brackets up to 15 000 euros. This low-income group frequently consists of students without a taxable income; which means that they usually do not gain from the reforms implemented to reduce the burden of higher ecological tax rates.

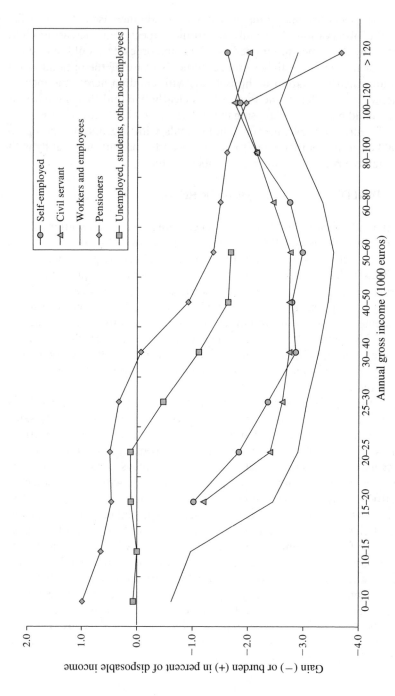

Figure 4.12   Effects of all reforms since 1998 by socio-economic status

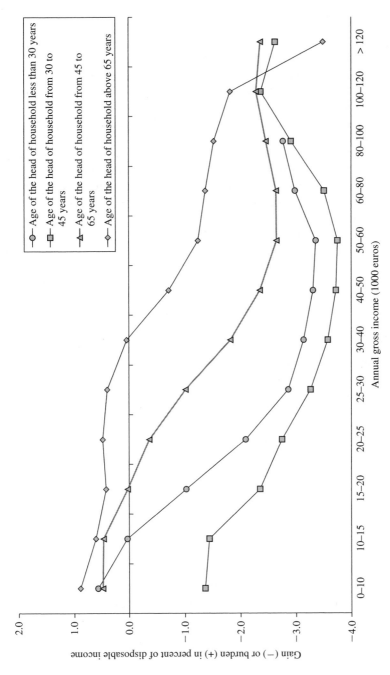

Figure 4.13   Changes in burden of all reforms since 1998 by age of the head of household

5.   CONCLUDING REMARKS

The analysis has shown that the ecological tax reform in Germany has the expected distributional effects. On average, these effects are weakly regressive, less regressive than the German value added tax, for instance. Especially for taxes on motor fuels, we find a progressive distributional effect in lower-income brackets. The reduction in social security contribution rates strengthens the regressive effects. When examining the incidence of the ecological taxes by differentiating between socio-economic status, type and size of households, residential area and age of the head of household, we find a few more cases where the changes of the reform are distributed proportionally or progressively. On average, we probably overestimate the regressive effects of the ecological tax reform because most of the behavioural changes are not included (for estimating behavioural effects, see West and Williams, 2002).

However, most households are compensated by other reforms, although the government did not implement any reform specially designed to correct the distributional effects of the ecological tax reform. In particular, increased child benefits partly alleviate the burden for households in lower-income brackets. The income tax reform neutralises the burden of the ecological taxes in most cases. Only pensioners and some older people in lower-income brackets do not gain from other reforms. They usually do not pay income taxes and are not entitled to child benefits. But because of the variance of the effects, there is no guarantee that no one will be losing through the ecological tax reform, although other reforms have net advantages.

When reforming the tax and transfer systems, it is important to study the distributional and revenue effects. Politicians, as well as taxpayers, should have an interest in the impact of such reforms. In Germany, only the revenue effects are usually calculated by the Ministry of Finance. This deficiency could be overcome by using a microsimulation model. It is a suitable instrument to analyse first-order effects of a reform or a reform proposal. The chosen methodology is likely to overestimate the regressive effects in the absence of behavioural responses. By taking the behavioural responses into account, the regressive effects would be slighter because households with a lower income will probably reduce their consumption of the taxed goods to avoid the ecological taxes. Owing to a lack of longitudinal data on the income and expenditures of households, it is not possible to estimate the individual demand elasticity for the taxed goods for each household. However, these individual elasticities could vary over the income scale and within an income bracket. In this respect, it does not make sense to use an overall demand elasticity to compute behavioural responses to the reform.

A more comprehensive approach would be to analyse whether the status quo is distributionally fair. The German tax system allows many exemptions and deductions from which only a few groups benefit. Before introducing more exemptions into the income tax system, the government should first try to compensate only people heavily affected by environmental taxes. A compensation for each household negatively affected by the ecological taxes would undermine the aim of the reform: reducing energy consumption.

NOTES

1. A taxpayer can consist of just one unmarried person or two persons if they are a married couple.
2. We have tried this merging method several times to check simulation results. The encountered differences were negligible.
3. In Germany extra pay for work on Sundays, on public holidays or for night shifts is tax-free. This factor, if not taken into account, would distort our results.
4. For income sources, see Appendix.

REFERENCES

Aasness, Jørgen and Erling Røed Larsen (2002), 'Distributional and Environmental Effects of Taxes on Transportation', Discussion Paper No. 321, Statistics Norway, Research Department.

Arbeitsgemeinschaft Energiebilanzen (ed.) (1999), *Energiebilanzen der Bundesrepublik Deutschland*, Frankfurt am Main.

Bach, Stefan, Christhart Bork, Michael Kohlhaas, Christian Lutz, Bernd Meyer, Barbara Prätorius and Heinz Welsch (2001), *Die ökologische Steuerreform in Deutschland – eine modellgestützte Analyse ihrer Wirkungen auf Wirtschaft und Umwelt*, Heidelberg: Physika-Verlag.

Bach, Stefan, Michael Kohlhaas, Bernd Meyer, Barbara Praetorius and Heinz Welsch (2002), 'The Effects of Environmental Fiscal Reform in Germany – a Simulation Study', *Energy Policy*, **30**, 803–11.

Baranzini, Andrea, José Goldemberg and Stefan Speck (1998), 'Are Carbon Taxes an Alternative to Prevent Climate Change?', International Academy of Environment, Background Paper 4, Geneva, Switzerland.

Baranzini, Andrea, José Goldemberg and Stefan Speck (2000), 'A Future for Carbon Taxes', *Ecological Economics*, **32**, 395–412.

Barker, Terry and Jonathan Köhler (1998), 'Equity and Ecotax Reform in the EU: Achieving a 10 per cent Reduction in CO_2 Emissions Using Excise Duties', *Fiscal Studies*, **19**, 375–402.

Böhringer, Christoph, Anna Ruocco and Wolfgang Wiegard (2001), 'Energy Taxes and Employment: A Do-it-yourself Simulation Model', Discussion Paper No. 01–21, Centre for European Economic Research.

Bork, Christhart (2000), *Steuern Transfers und private Haushalte – Eine mikroanalytische Simulationsstudie der Aufkommens- und Verteilungswirkungen*, Frankfurt am Main: Peter Lang.

Bundesministerium für Umwelt, Naturschutz und Reaktorsicherheit und Umweltbundesamt (2003), 'Distributional Effects of Environmental Policy in Germany', Germany's Contribution to the OECD Workshop on Distributional Effects, Paris, 4–5 March.

Drabinski, Thomas (2002), 'Taxation, Incidence and Microsimulation: An Approach to Germany', Lorenz-von-Stein-Institut für Verwaltungswissenschaften, Kiel.

Ekins, Paul (1999), 'European Environmental Taxes and Charges: Recent Experience, Issues and Trends', *Ecological Economics*, **31**, 39–62.

Fullerton, Don and Diane Lim Rogers (1993), *Who Bears the Income Tax Burden?*, Washington DC: Brookings Institution.

Harding, Ann (ed.) (1996), *Microsimulation and Public Policy*, Amsterdam/ London/New York/Tokyo: North-Holland.

Johnstone, Nick and Janaki Alavalapati (1998), 'The Distributional Effects of Environmental Tax Reform', London, IIED Working Paper 98–01.

Klinge-Jacobsen, Henrik, Katja Birr-Pedersen and Mette Wier (2002), 'Distributional Implications of Environmental Taxation in Denmark', *Fiscal Studies*, **24**(4), 477–99.

Kohlhaas, Michael (2000), 'Ecological Tax Reform in Germany from Theory to Policy', American Institute for Contemporary German Studies, Johns Hopkins University.

Metcalf, Gilbert E. (1998), 'A Distributional Analysis of an Environmental Tax Shift, Department of Economics', Tufts University, Discussion Paper 98–01.

Meyer, Bernd and Georg Ewerhart (1998), 'Multisectoral Policy Modelling for Environmental Analysis', in Kimio Uno and Peter Bartelmus (eds), *Environmental Accounting in Theory and Practice*, Amsterdam: Kluwer, pp. 395–406.

OECD (1994), *The Distributive Effects of Economic Instruments for Environmental Policy*, Paris: OECD.

OECD (2001), *Environmentally Related Taxes in OECD Countries – Issues and Strategies*, Paris: OECD.

Orcutt, Guy (1957), 'A New Type of Socio-economic Systems', *Review of Economics and Statistics*, **58**, S773–97.

O'Ryan, Raúl, Sebastian Miller and Carlos J. de Miguel (1999), 'Environmental Taxes, Inefficient Subsidies and Income Distribution in Chile: A CGE Framework', Documentos de Trabajo No. 98, Centro de Economía Aplicada, Universidad de Chile.

Petersen, Hans-Georg and Christhart Bork (2000), 'Revenue and Distributional Effects of the Current Tax Reform Proposals in Germany – An Evaluation by Microsimulation', in Hans-Georg Petersen and Patrick Gallagher (eds), *Tax and Transfer Reform in Australia and Germany*, Berlin: Berliner Debatte Wissenschaftsverlag, pp. 219–36.

Sachverständigenrat zur Begutachtung der gesamtwirtschaftlichen Entwicklung (2000), *Chancen auf einen höheren Wachstumspfad, Jahresgutachten 2000/01*, Stuttgart: Metzler-Pöschel.

Tiezzi, Silvia (2001), 'The Welfare Effects of Carbon Taxation on Italian Households', Dipartimento di Economica Politica, University of Siena.

West, Sarah E. and Robert C. Williams III (2002), 'Estimates from a Consumer Demand System: Implications for the Incidence of Environmental Taxes', NBER Working Paper 9152.

APPENDIX: DEFINITION OF GROSS INCOME IN THE MODEL

1. Income from agriculture and forestry
2. Income from business
3. Income from self-employment
4. Income from employment
5. Income from capital assets
6. Income from renting and leasing
7. Redundancy payments, lay-off benefits, tide-over allowance
8. Premium payments, share in profits, rewards
9. Old-age pensions from the statutory pension insurance from own employment
10. Widow and widower pensions from the statutory pension insurance
11. Orphan's pensions from the statutory pension insurance
12. Old-age pensions from supplementary insurance of public employees and workers from own employment
13. Widow and widower pensions from supplementary insurance
14. Orphan's pensions from supplementary insurance
15. Injury pensions from statutory accident insurance
16. Widow and widower pensions from statutory accident insurance
17. Orphan's pensions from statutory accident insurance
18. Sickness benefits from statutory health insurance
19. Unemployment benefits
20. Short-time workers' payments, bad weather payments
21. Other permanent transfer payments from public employment pro-grammes
22. Maternity benefits
23. Social aid
24. Child-care benefits/grants from the federal education act
25. Permanent transfers from the federal training assistance act (*Bafög*)
26. Disability pension from the war victims' welfare service
27. Survivor's pension from the war victims' welfare service
28. Other permanent transfers from the regional authority
29. Unemployment aid
30. Early retirement payments, old-age transition payments
31. Public pensions and pensions from public enterprises from own employment as civil servants
32. Public pensions and pensions from public enterprises for widows and widowers
33. Public pensions and pensions from public enterprises for orphans
34. Company pensions from own employment

35. Company pensions from other claims
36. Permanent transfers from private health, damage and accident insurance
37. Strike support payments (from unions to their members)
38. Other permanent transfers from non-profit organisations (churches, labour unions)
39. Other permanent transfers from private households
40. Child benefits.

5. The distributive effects of direct regulation: a case study of energy efficiency appliance standards

Ronald J. Sutherland

In short, the best way to understand any regulatory scheme is to answer the twin questions, who wins and who loses.[1]

1. INTRODUCTION

Analyses of economic policy and economic regulation typically focus on efficiency implications, such as benefits, costs and net benefits. The rationale for this focus is that economic analysis contains a powerful set of optimisation tools designed specifically to analyse the efficiency of resource allocation. Distributional effects are less often considered. This is not surprising since there is no commonly accepted definition of optimum equity; certainly nothing analogous to maximum net benefits from economic efficiency.

However, the distributional implications of environmental policies are now attracting significant interest. One concern is the effect of environmental quality (EQ) on households relative to their income level. A second issue is the impact of economic instruments on households relative to their income level. A large literature has appeared in the last decade that provides reasonably consistent evidence on each issue (see Kriström, Chapter 3, and Pearce, Chapter 2, in this volume). The literature indicates that quite frequently – but certainly not always – both the distribution of environmental quality and the costs of environmental policy are regressive. That is, higher-income households receive a proportionately larger share of the environmental benefits and a lower share of the financial costs of environmental policy. As stated by Tollison (1991), regulations can be explained by winners and losers. In the regulations considered here, a consortium of interest groups is the winner, and the poor and middle-income households are the losers, hence such energy efficiency regulations are politically feasible.

Existing studies of the distributional effects of environmental policies typically focus on short-run costs and benefits. For example, energy/carbon taxes have immediate but unequal effects on households with different income levels. However, environmental policies, both taxes and direct regulations, require investments with initial costs but long-term benefits. Mandated investments of environmental and energy programmes can produce adverse equity effects because low-income households discount the subsequent flow of benefits very highly.

The main purpose of this chapter is to present evidence on the distributional effects of some direct regulations that directly affect individual households. The analysis is a case study of energy efficiency (EE) regulations that affect energy-using appliances and technologies purchased by households. The approach used here emphasises the investment aspect of policies, which in turn reflect the relationship between income level and discount rates. Empirical evidence is provided on the (adverse) equity effects of these EE standards. Technical efficiency standards are compared to financial rebates and to energy/carbon taxes in terms of their equity and efficiency effects. EE standards and subsidies typically reduce both equity and efficiency. However, subsidies tend to benefit high-income households, while indirectly and adversely affecting low-income households. In contrast, EE standards impose a cost on low-income households, while not necessarily affecting high-income households. Energy/carbon taxes are found to have regressive effects, because of the regressive (and immediate) burden of the tax. The present analysis suggests an additional regressive effect. The investment element of such taxes includes upfront costs and long-term benefits, which adversely affects those who highly discount future benefits.

Overall, this analysis supports Kriström's (Chapter 3) view that equity and efficiency should be studied together, because the underlying cause of regulatory inefficiency also produces inequity. The linkage between environmental quality, environmental regulation and equity can be studied within larger conceptual frameworks that have already found widespread use in analysing similar issues. Relevant bodies of knowledge include public finance, the theory of economic regulation and public choice theory.

The public finance literature documents the incidence and ultimate burden of various taxes and also subsidies. The results are immediately applicable to environmental taxes and subsidies. For example, investment subsidies benefit those households which make investments, at the expense of those who do not. High-income households save and invest a larger share of their income than low-income households, and hence benefit from investment subsidies. The imposition of costly but technically efficient EE standards on household appliances does no harm to those who would have invested in energy-efficient appliances without standards (the rich), but adversely affects those who prefer lower-cost and less technically efficient models (the poor). EE standards affecting household appliances, and subsidies for EE investments, are inevitably regressive.[2] Public choice theory and the theory of economic regulation indicate that the cost of such government regulations is borne by those unable to affect the regulatory process.

2. ENERGY EFFICIENCY APPLIANCE STANDARDS AND ASSERTED BENEFITS

In 1978, the United States Congress authorised the Department of Energy to set mandatory standards of minimum EE for 13 household appliances.[3] The Reagan Administration opposed setting national EE standards, and this opposition delayed the promulgation of standards for several years. The American Council for an Energy Efficient Economy (ACEEE) continuously lobbies for increasing energy efficiency standards, and such standards were adopted in several states, such as California, Florida and others.[4] The variations in state standards motivated the appliance manufacturers to support uniform mandated national standards. As explained by Geller (1995, p. 1), of the ACEEE, 'manufacturers and energy efficiency advocates then directly negotiated what became the National Appliance Energy Conservation Act (NAECA)'. This 1987 act set the first national energy efficiency standards for refrigerators, freezers, furnaces, air-conditioners, dishwashers and other appliances, and deadlines for mandatory review of these standards.[5]

The Energy Policy Act of 1992 (EP Act) expanded the initial coverage of standards to common types of incandescent and fluorescent reflector lamps and to some commercial and industrial technologies. As noted by Geller (1995, p. 3), the standards in the 1992 act, like the 1987 act, were negotiated agreements between manufacturers and energy efficiency advocates. The nine residential appliances, along with the years in which their EE standards became effective, are as follows: refrigerators 1990, freezers 1990, room AC 1990, central AC 1992, clothes washers 1988, clothes dryers 1988, dishwashers 1988, water heaters, 1990 and gas furnaces, 1992.

The US Department of Energy (DOE) administers the energy efficiency programme which affects household appliances. Lawrence Berkeley National Laboratory (LBL) is the DOE laboratory that has conducted engineering and economic analyses of appliance standards since 1982.[6] These studies consistently show enormous net benefits. In numerous articles and reports, LBL analysts provide quantitative estimates of the costs and benefits of standards. The LBL study by Meyers et al. (2003) is used here because it is recent and was published in a peer-reviewed journal. Meyers et al. conclude that residential appliance standards will produce a reduction in residential primary energy consumption and carbon dioxide (CO_2) emissions of 8 to 9 per cent in 2020 compared with levels expected without any standard. Further, these standards will save a cumulative total of between 26 and 32 EJ (25–30 quads) by the year 2015, and 63 EJ (60 quads) by 2030. The estimated cumulative net present value of consumer benefit amounts to nearly $80 billion by 2015 and grows to $130 billion by 2030 ($150 billion by 2050), and the overall benefit–cost ratio of cumulative consumer impacts in the 1987–2050 period is 2.75:1. The cumulative cost of the DOE's programme to establish and implement standards is in the range of $200–$250 million. These estimates reflect the summary estimates of LBL on net benefits, and the benefit–cost ratio.

Most of the empirical analyses on costs and benefits of EE appliance standards are sponsored by the US DOE and conducted by LBL. Mainstream economists have shown little interest in applying cost–benefit analysis to EE appliance standards. Hausman and Joskow (1982) present qualitative arguments that EE appliance standards probably do not reduce market failures, and the DOE analysis in support of standards has serious flaws. Consequently, such standards are unlikely to produce benefits in excess of costs, but are likely to 'bite' most at low-income levels, and hence are regressive. The short Hausman and Joskow paper is a rare exception where economists comment on EE appliance standards, and their paper is seldom cited in the energy efficiency literature.

Mandated EE appliance standards are designed to reduce the use of energy in targeted appliances. The benefits are estimated as the reduced energy costs to consumers over the lifetime of the appliance. In the LBL analyses, net benefits of EE appliance standards are estimated by first estimating energy consumption over future years with new standards in place. Next, energy consumption per year is estimated over the same time period assuming that standards are not implemented. The estimated increment in energy consumption in each future year is the difference between projected energy consumption with standards in effect and energy use that would have occurred in the absence of standards. These estimated energy savings are multiplied by a projected price of energy to obtain an estimate of dollar savings in energy costs. The estimated future cost savings are then discounted to the present.

Mandated EE standards require manufacturers to increase their investment in developing technologies. Those costs are reflected as an increased purchase price of new appliances. Consumers thus face higher prices for appliances affected by EE standards. This one-time increase in purchase price is compared to the present value of the energy cost saving to estimate net benefits.

The key variables that determine the net benefits of increased EE standards include the investment cost required to improve technical efficiency as reflected in a higher purchase price, the reduction in future energy use resulting specifically from the new standard, and the appropriate consumer discount rate used to value these future cost reductions. The net benefits of standards will be high if the new appliance has a low incremental investment cost; if the appliance substantially reduces energy use relative to the base case; if the price of energy increases in the future; and if consumers use a low discount rate. Similarly, net benefits will be low if consumers use a higher discount rate than assumed by LBL; if the energy saving is smaller than estimated; if energy prices decline, or if the investment costs of standards are higher than expected.

3. UNRAVELLING THE COST–BENEFIT CLAIMS FOR ENERGY EFFICIENCY STANDARDS

This chapter focuses on estimated future energy savings, and on the appropriate household discount rates for valuing these savings. Existing data on costs and benefits are used as a base case, but revised estimates of energy saving and discount rates are used, as suggested by available evidence. New evidence indicates that significant technical improvements in appliances occur without standards, hence energy saved is less than typically estimated. Further, the discount rates used in current B/C analyses are too low. Adjusting for over-estimating energy saving and under-estimating discount rates produces negative net benefits from EE standards.[7]

The application of EE appliance standards and other conservation regulations were based on the assumption that market barriers discouraged technology adoption. However, the correct rationale for introduction of such policies is the presence of market failures, and not barriers. The absence of significant market failures implies that EE standards will retard and not enhance economic efficiency. Although the issue of market barriers versus market failures is not pursued here, the benefits of efficient appliances are primarily internal to appliance purchasers and mandated standards do not reduce market failures.[8]

Empirical evidence establishes that energy use in appliances has declined in the absence of standards. The Association of Home Appliance Manufacturers (AHAM) publishes annual historical data regarding the energy consumption of new appliances. Figure 5.1 shows the trend in energy consumption per year of new refrigerators, freezers and room

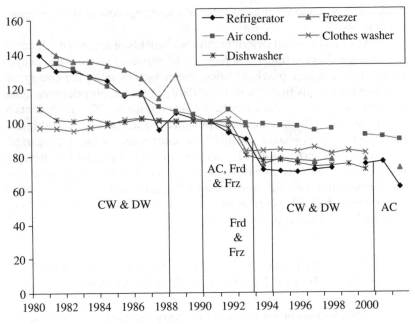

Note: Vertical bars correspond to years when standards were introduced.

Source: American Home Appliance Manufacturers, Washington, DC.

Figure 5.1   *Energy use by selected residential appliances for years*
              1980–2001

air-conditioners. This figure also uses AHAM data to show the trend in energy use (kWh) per cycle for new dishwashers and clothes washers since 1980. The year in which standards are imposed or/and revised is indicated by the vertical lines.

The time trends in each appliance depicted in Figure 5.1 reveal declining energy use throughout the 1980s and 1990s in each appliance. The energy use in 1990 by refrigerators, room AC and freezers appears more consistent with time trends than standards imposed in 1990. However, the significant decline in energy use in refrigerators and freezers in 1993 could result from revised standards rather than underlying factors producing technical change. The time trends in energy use in new clothes washers and dishwashers do not suggest when standards were imposed or revised.

A visual inspection of energy use trends in five appliances provides little clue when standards took effect. The historical trends in energy use of these appliances cast serious doubt about the energy-saving effects of appliance standards. Generally, energy use declined in new appliances well before standards came into effect. This decline in energy use of new units was no doubt motivated by the energy price increases during the 1970s. Further, we find no decline in energy use in dishwashers and clothes washers after the first imposition of standards in 1988. These trends suggest that increases in EE since 1980 were probably caused by energy price increases of the 1970s, and not by EE standards of the 1990s. The EE trends in dishwashers and clothes washers before and after 1988 also suggest that technical improvements were not affected by EE standards.

A visual correlation does not prove causation, and variables in addition to the price of electricity contribute to energy use in refrigerators and other appliances. Newell et al. (1998 and 1999) analysed energy use trends in room air-conditioners, central air-conditioners and gas water-heaters. They tested the induced innovation hypothesis of technical change, which posits that energy prices induce efficiency improvements by encouraging manufacturers to develop more efficient models. Further, technical improvements in appliances are also autonomous, just like much of the technical change in the US economy. An autonomous increase in observed EE reflects inherent market tendencies and not energy price changes or appliance standards. Changes in EE in these appliances result from three sources: autonomous technical changes resulting from a normal market process, price-induced technical change resulting from energy price increases, and from energy efficiency standards. The evidence presented by Newell et al. (1998 and 1999) differs among the three appliances, but overall indicates that autonomous changes in technology had the largest effect on energy intensity, followed by energy price effects which induced technical improvements. Appliance standards had the least overall effect on energy use, but had the greatest effect on gas water-heaters.

The LBL analyses include projections of EE coefficients in future new units in the absence of EE standards, but these projections are not based on a technical analysis such as Newell et al.'s. In describing the calculation of energy use in the absence of standards, McMahon et al. (2000, p. 2) state: 'the unit energy consumption is based upon historical (pre-standards) trends in unit energy consumption'. Meyers et al. (2002, p. 11) derive base case energy trends using their 'subjective estimates' and 'judgement' as to how technology may be improved without standards. With this approach, LBL researchers predict that eight appliances will experience constant energy use in the absence of standards and three appliances will experience declines in energy use in the absence of standards.

The LBL projections are inconsistent with the Newell analysis which found that less than one-third of the energy savings attributed to standards by LBL is actually due to federal standards. If the Newell evidence is correct – that only about one-third of the reduction in energy use is due to standards – then the LBL dollar consumer costs saved should also be reduced to only one-third of their reported values. LBL researchers are over-estimating the effect of standards to reduce energy use.

4. THE DISCOUNT RATES CONTROVERSY

Estimates of consumer benefits from EE investments are highly sensitive to the choice of consumer discount rate. Accordingly, the choice of discount rates is controversial; especially the discount rates used to value government-mandated investments. The critical role of discount rates in calculating the present value of future benefits suggests a restatement of the principle of the discount rate. The theory of discount rates is well developed for business investments, and finance textbooks provide a detailed analysis. Brealey and Myers (2003, p. 15) in their corporate finance textbook, express the criterion for selecting a discount rate.

To calculate present value, we discount expected pay-offs by the rate of return offered by equivalent investment alternatives in the capital market. This rate of return is often referred to as the discount rate, hurdle rate or opportunity cost of capital. It is called the *opportunity cost* because it is the return forgone by investing in the project rather than investing in securities. As explained by Brealey and Myers, the opportunity cost of capital determines the discount rate for business decisions. Investments in the stock market yielded an average rate of return of 13 per cent from 1926 through 2000.[9] Consumers who invest in common stocks must apply a discount rate of at least 13 per cent to EE investments because this is their appropriate opportunity cost. However, LBL researchers typically use a 7 per cent real rate when calculating the present value of consumer benefits from investing in EE affected by standards. The various LBL reports simply apply this rate with limited discussion.[10] Meyers et al. (2003, p. 764) go even further and assume a 3 per cent discount rate when calculating the present value of net savings from federal EE standards from 1987 to 2000. The stated rationale by Meyers et al. is that this rate approximates the average return on long-term government bonds. However, it is doubtful that the long-term government bond rate correctly reflects the opportunity cost for households, because households do not forgo the purchase of such bonds to make EE investments.

The present value of benefits is estimated here with a simple equation that assumes constant revenues in perpetuity. This assumption is roughly consistent with the LBL approach of estimating benefits up to year 2050. An investment occurs when the present discounted value exceeds its investment cost. If the initial investment cost is I, the discount rate is r, and annual revenue in perpetuity (reduced energy cost) is R, the net present value (NPV) is:

$$NPV_t = \int_0^\infty Re^{-rt}dt - I_t,$$

where the present value of revenue is the benefit, and the initial investment, the cost. Evaluating the integral produces the simplified equation:

$$NPV_t = R/r - I_t, \qquad (5.1)$$

which assumes that the reduction in energy cost is a constant per year in perpetuity. The benefit of an investment is its present value, estimated as R/r.

Equation (5.1) offers the insight that a consumer's present value of future energy saving is proportional to the consumer's discount rate. A doubling of the consumer's discount rate implies a 50 per cent reduction in the value of future energy saving. Consumers who value future cost saving highly implicitly have low discount rates. Analogously, consumers who have low discount rates will value future cost saving highly.

Recall that Meyers et al. (2003) calculated benefits of appliance standards using a 7 per cent and a 3 per cent discount rate. To put these rates into perspective, consider the question: 'How much would a household with a 7 per cent discount rate be willing to pay for an investment that reduces future energy costs by $20 per year in perpetuity?' Applying equation (5.1) indicates that $20 received per year in perpetuity, discounted at a 7 per cent rate, is worth $286 today. Consumers that have a Meyers-assumed discount rate of 3 per cent would be willing to pay $667 to receive just $20 per year. If a standard model clothes washer cost $500, consumers with 7 per cent and 3 per cent discount rates would be willing to pay $786 and $1167 to purchase the EE models. Consumers who are not willing to pay $667 or even $286 for $20 per year revenue stream must have higher discount rates. Evidence that consumers have discount rates in excess of 3 per cent and 7 per cent implies that the LBL analyses over-estimate the benefits of appliance standards to households.

The net present value of EE investments depends on the higher initial cost, the assumed discount rate and on the assumed future energy cost saving resulting from the imposition of standards.[11] Table 5.1 examines the present value of an $85.7 billion investment in EE with alternative discount rates and assumed future energy savings. The first row reproduces the LBL result where a 7 per cent discount rate produces $235.7 billion in present value to consumers for saving energy. This row is the LBL estimate of net benefits equal to $150 billion ($235.7 − $85.7). Some LBL analyses allow

*Table 5.1   The present value of investments in EE appliances with
            alternative assumptions*

Case	Discount rate (%)	Autonomous energy efficiency (%)	LBL results, or Newell results	PV of investment (bill. $)	Net PV investment (bill. $)
1	7	0	LBL model	235.7	150
2	7	50	Newell result	117.85	32.15
3	14	0	LBL model	117.85	32.15
4	14	50	Newell result	58.93	−26.77
5	21	0	LBL model	78.57	−7.13
6	21	50	Newell result	39.29	−46.41
7	28	0	LBL model	58.93	−26.77
8	28	50	Newell result	29.46	−56.24
9	35	0	LBL model	47.14	−41.44
10	35	50	Newell result	23.57	−62.13

Notes: These calculations use the equation $NPV = R/r − I$, where an investment of $85.7 billion for EE produces a present value of energy saving of $235.7 billion. Where $r = 0.07$, annual energy saving is $16.5 billion. The base case is the LBL result where the B/C ratio is 2.75/1, $B − C = \$150$ billion, and $r = 0.07$. The Newell result assumed here is that one-half of the increase in EE assumed by LBL is determined by market forces.

for small increases in EE in the absence of standards. Using the Newell result that two-thirds of the EE increases are market-induced, standards should account for one-third of the EE increases. To be conservative, we assume that only one-half rather than two-thirds of the EE increases are market-determined. Hence, 50 per cent of the EE assumed by LBL occurs as a result of technical change caused by market forces, rather than from appliance standards. The second row in Table 5.1 shows that if energy saving is reduced by half, the present value of consumer benefits is likewise reduced by half.

As indicated in cases 6 and 5 in Table 5.1, consumers with a 21 per cent discount rate value future energy cost saving at a net loss of $46.41 billion with the Newell result and at a net loss of $7.13 billion without the Newell result. Consumers with a 28 per cent discount rate receive a net loss of $56.24 billion for EE standards. Consumers would not make such an investment without government mandates. If consumers discount future energy cost saving by 14 per cent in the Newell case or by 21 per cent or more, EE appliance standards would make consumers worse off.

Kenneth Train (1985), in his review of the empirical evidence on consumer discount rates for EE, indicates a wide range of empirical estimates, with many estimates falling in the 20–30 per cent range. A more recent review of the literature by Johnstone et al. (2002) concludes that households must have discount rates well in excess of 20 per cent to account for consumer choices of EE in durable goods. Discount rates in this range indicate that consumers experience a net financial loss when making EE investments affected by appliance standards. Even without the Newell effect of autonomous and induced technical improvements in appliances, standards produce negative net benefits to consumers. Allowing for 50 per cent market-driven technical improvements in appliances approximately doubles the net losses from appliance standards.

5. DISCOUNT RATES AND HOUSEHOLD INCOME

According to Train's (1985) survey, low-income households require much higher discount rates than high-income households to make similar investments. The net losses to consumers from appliance standards are therefore much greater for low-income consumers than for high-income consumers. This conclusion follows from empirical studies of revealed discount rates that consistently conclude that consumer discount rates are inversely related to household income.

The data in Tables 5.2 to 5.5 demonstrate that a discount rate of 20–30 per cent may be a rough average for all households. More pertinently, the evidence indicates consistently that low-income consumers require much higher discount rates than higher-income households to make the same investments. Because the Train (1985) survey article refers to previous studies, the income classes in Tables 5.2 to 5.5 are low by current income levels. However, the findings are not challenged and the estimated discount rates should reflect relative income levels today. Although the four

Table 5.2 Consumer discount rates and income (space heating system)

Household income ($)	Discount rate (%)
1000	56
5000	46
10 000	38
25 000	25
40 000	19
60 000	14

Source: Berkovec et al. (1983), cited in Train (1985, p. 1251).

Table 5.3   *Consumer discount rates and household income (air-conditioners)*

Household income ($)	Discount rate (%)
6000	89.0
10 000	39.0
15 000	27.0
25 000	17.0
35 000	8.9
50 000	5.1

Source: Hausman (1979), cited in Train (1985, p. 1251).

Table 5.4   *Consumer discount rates and income (automobiles)*

Household income ($)	Discount rate (%)	
	(1)	(2)
10 000	59	36
20 000	35	30
25 000	31	29
30 000	29	29
50 000	24	28

Sources: (1) discount rates are obtained from Beggs et al. (1981), cited in Train (1985, p. 1251); (2) discount rates are obtained from Beggs and Cardell (1980) cited in Train (1985, p. 1251).

tables are merely a sample from Train's survey, the results are consistent with all 14 studies that he reviewed. As stated by Train (1985, p. 1261): 'The results . . . show that discount rates were found in all 14 studies to fall as income increases.' Lower-income households are observed consistently to place a lower economic value on future cost savings than high-income households.

Hartman and Doane (1986) revisited the household discount rate issue and began by developing a discount rate based on standard economic theory. They estimate the discount rate empirically for household energy conservation choices, and by household characteristic. The main result is that low-income households reveal high discount rates of 87.8 per cent, 79.0 per cent and 52.8 per cent for the lowest three income classes. In add-

Table 5.5   Discount rates and household income (space heating systems)

Household income ($)	Discount rate (%)
4000	51.0
8000	25.0
12 000	17.0
16 000	13.0
20 000	10.0
25 000	8.0
35 000	5.8
50 000	4.1

Source: Goett and McFadden (1984), cited in Train (1985, p. 1251).

ition, estimated discount rates are higher for elderly persons than for others and higher for renters than home-owners. Hartman and Doane conclude 'Use of the market rate of interest *simply will not do*' (italics original). On the basis of evidence by Kenneth Train, Hartman and Doane and others, this chapter concludes that the LBL use of discount rates is rejected by finance theory and by the empirical evidence on discount rates.

The inverse relationship between discount rates and household income is expected. As stated by Brealey and Myers, a consumer's discount rate is determined by his opportunity cost, which is what the consumer must forgo to make the investment. High-income consumers save a share of their income in the form of investments. High-income consumers may forgo an investment in common stocks to invest in EE, and hence require a discount rate in excess of 13 per cent per year. However, household appliances have the unattractive investment properties of being irreversible, whereas common stocks are highly liquid. Metcalf and Rosenthal (1995) and Hassett and Metcalf (1996) explain how this irreversibility property warrants discount rates of at least two or three times higher than may be expected. Allowing for the irreversibility property of such investments, a required rate of return of at least 20 per cent appears reasonable for high-income households.

In a previous paper, I suggested that the high discount rates characteristic of low-income households were the result of the risk and illiquidity associated with EE investments, and the inability to diversify away risk.[12] An even more obvious explanation begins by noting that poor people do not invest in common stocks or EE, simply because they are poor.

Low-income households have low and even zero savings. The opportunity cost of an EE investment for low-income households is the basic necessities of life: food, clothing and shelter. The high opportunity cost of forgoing these basic necessities requires very high discount rates. In economic terms, low-income households have a high marginal rate of time preference, and hence allocate most if not all of their income to current consumption. Consequently, such households do not hold large amounts of common stocks or government bonds, nor would they make EE investments without government mandates.

Government EE mandates remove appliances from the market that poor people would prefer to purchase, and require such persons to make unattractive investments that are not in their self-interest. Appliance standards thereby impose an economic burden that weighs particularly heavily on low- and middle-income people.

6.   EQUITY EFFECTS OF APPLIANCE STANDARDS

Appliance EE standards usually affect market choices by removing the low-end and less energy-efficient units from the market. For instance, Meyers et al. (2003) state that for new units sold in 1987–99, actual EE exceeded the minimum required by the standard, sometimes by a significant amount. They assert further that standards removed the less efficient models which increased the average EE of units sold.[13]

The data in Table 5.1 above present different benefit–cost ratios from those offered by LBL and different estimates of net benefits. The main result from Table 5.1 is that consumers with high discount rates, coupled with the Newell results, receive negative net benefits from appliance standards. The average consumer discount rate should exceed the average corporate cost of capital (about 13 per cent), which implies that EE standards produce negative benefits. As a rough average, it appears that appliance standards produce a net loss to consumers from −$46.41 billion (Case 6) to −$56.04 billion (Case 8) depending on choice of discount rate.

Comparatively wealthy consumers apparently purchase about the same appliances as they would in the absence of EE standards, and hence suffer minimal losses. However, comparatively poorer consumers find their preferred choices eliminated from the market via government EE standards, which necessarily makes these customers worse off. The high discount rates of lower-income consumers imply that such consumers prefer to purchase appliances requiring less investment in EE. The adverse equity effects of appliance standards result first because the restricted choices affect mostly low- and middle-income households. Second, the evidence that low-income households have very high discount rates indicates that these households bear large net costs, as implied by the results in Table 5.1.

7. EQUITY EFFECTS OF SUBSIDIES AND TAXES

Direct regulations (EE standards) are not the only measures used to achieve energy efficiency objectives. Subsidies and energy taxes can also be used to achieve policy objectives with respect to energy efficiency. As with direct regulations, subsidies are inequitable because they impart relative financial benefits to high-income households. Direct regulations require the poor to make welfare-retarding investments; subsidies encourage the rich to make investments that enhance their own welfare. Investment subsidies are less appealing to the poor because of the high opportunity cost, and hence discount rates, of meeting basic needs with limited income.

During much of the 1990s, electric utilities in the US offered various energy conservation subsidy programmes. The equity effects on households, documented by Sutherland (1994), are noted here. The 1990 Residential Energy Consumption Survey of the EIA identifies participation rates in utility conservation programmes by income class. Using data from Sutherland (1994), Table 5.6 depicts household participation in rebate programmes and any programme. The main result is that participation is low for the lowest two income groups and highest for the highest income group, for both rebate programmes and any programme.

Part of the story is that rebates and other conservation subsidies reduce equity across household income levels. Rebates, and other subsidy programmes, are investment subsidies that are received about eight times more frequently by high-income households than low-income households. These subsidies are paid disproportionately by low-income households through their electricity bills since these households typically use a much larger share of their income for necessities, such as electricity, than high-income households.

An econometric analysis by Sutherland (1994) shows that participation in rebate programmes or other programmes, is not statistically associated with energy use. Participants tend *ceteris paribus* to reside in homes that are well insulated and newer than average, with newer and more efficient heating and cooling equipment, and homes that have more than average conservation features. Apparently, households that participate in conservation programmes tend to substitute one energy conservation investment for another which is encouraged by a rebate. This substitution results in no net energy savings, as observed, and accounts for the preferences of rebate recipients for other conservation investments.

Table 5.6   Participation in electric utility conservation programmes by income class

Income class	1990 income (number)	1990 income (percentage in income class)	Rebate programmes (percentage participation)	Any programme (percentage participation)
Less than $5000	133	4.0	0.34	1.05
$5000–$9000	329	9.8	0.76	1.95
$10 000–$14 000	393	11.7	1.24	5.68
$15 000–$24 000	602	17.9	1.23	5.85
$25 000–$34 999	588	17.5	1.97	5.40
$35 000–$49 999	651	19.3	1.38	5.70
$50 000 or more	671	19.9	2.21	8.84
Total	3367	100	1.49	5.79

Source: Sutherland (1994, p. 107).

The observed household response to EE rebate programmes follows directly from the economic assumption that consumers maximise utility. Households maximise consumer surplus (free money), which they obtain by requiring as little of the rebate as possible to encourage a change in behaviour. Those consumers who change their behaviour the least receive the most consumer surplus from participating in rebate programmes. Such utility maximising consumers are the most likely participants in a subsidy programme. The simple but unfortunate principle is that rebates have their greatest appeal to exactly the wrong participants. An implication of this principle is that rebates and subsidies are unlikely to be cost-effective in encouraging a change in behaviour. With evidence that rebates are obtained by the rich and financed by the poor, rebate EE programmes also reduce income equity.

An example of a more recent subsidy programme is the Climate Change Technology Initiative (CCTI), proposed in 1998 by then President Clinton. The proposed CCTI contained a tax credit to encourage the adoption of new energy-efficient technologies and thereby reduce carbon emissions. The CCTI included a tax credit of 20 per cent for the purchase of residential-size electric heat pumps and air-conditioners.[14] The costs and benefits of the proposed CCTI are illustrated by a hypothetical demand curve for efficient heat pumps. The cost of the typical current model of heat pump is $4400, while that of a more efficient model is $5500. President Clinton's CCTI included a 20 per cent tax credit that would cover the full price

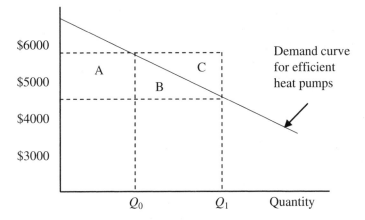

Figure 5.2   Internal benefits and costs of a super efficient heat pump

differential of $1100 (Sutherland, 2000). Consumer demand for the more energy-efficient heat pump is depicted in Figure 5.2, where initially a small number of units (Q_0) are purchased at a price of $5500. When purchasers of the heat pump receive a tax credit of $1100, the effective price of the more efficient heat pump declines to $4400 and the quantity demanded increases to Q_1. The total cost of the rebates is $1100 times the total number of rebates provided, which is area $A + B + C$ in Figure 5.2.

The total consumer benefit from purchasing the more efficient heat pump is defined as total willingness to pay (WTP) and is measured as the area under the demand curve up to the quantity purchased. Net benefits to consumers are equal to total WTP minus actual payments. The increase in net benefits to consumers from the tax credit is the area under the demand curve between the initial and new price, area $A + B$. Some rebate recipients are free-riders, who would purchase the heat pump without the subsidy. The benefit received by free-riders is equal to the dollar amount of the rebate they receive (area A). The rebate also encourages additional purchases of the heat pump, which is its purpose. The dollar benefit of the rebate to the adopters encouraged by the rebate is the triangle area under the demand curve (area B). In this example, the cost of the rebates provided to new adopters is the price of the rebate times the quantity of rebates, which is area $B + C$. For a linear demand curve, the cost of the rebate provided to new adopters will be twice the benefits as measured by the change in consumer surplus.[15] In the absence of an externality benefit, rebates will retard economic efficiency.

A rebate provides a larger benefit to free-riders than to new adopters. To the free-riders, the entire rebate is consumer surplus, hence a pure net benefit. However, this rebate is merely a redistribution of wealth and does not have the intended effect of encouraging technology adoption. In contrast, new adopters require part of the rebate as compensation for an otherwise unattractive investment. Hence to new adopters a rebate conceptually has two components: a bribe to change behaviour, and consumer surplus, which is the remainder of the rebate. Rebates provide the greatest amount of consumer surplus to those who minimise the bribe component and change their investment behaviour the least. Those who can obtain a rebate by substituting a subsidised conservation investment for a non-subsidised conservation investment will be big winners. Households that make these easy substitutions and thereby maximise consumer surplus are the most likely participants in rebate programmes. The inherent incentive of rebate programmes is to minimise cost-effectiveness.

As depicted in Table 5.6, low-income households are unlikely to participate in rebate programmes to make EE investments, including in super efficient heat pumps. High-income households typically make EE investments even without subsidies. Tax credits and rebates require minimal change in investment from some high-income households, while offering little appeal to low-income households. High-income households maximise their consumer surplus by receiving the tax credit; poor people maximise their consumer surplus by using fans and by going without central air-conditioning. High-income households may invest in EE units because such households have relatively low discount rates. Hence the inherent tendency of rebate or tax credit programmes is to attract participants from high-income households; but only from those households that change their behaviour the least and thereby use most of the rebate as consumer surplus (free money).[16]

As noted above, participants in electric utility energy conservation programmes come disproportionately from the highest income class, with negligible participation from the lowest income classes. However, energy expenditures are a larger share of the income of lower-income groups. Utility conservation subsidies have regressive effects because the benefits are received disproportionately by the highest income groups and paid for by lower- and middle-income groups. Tax credits for purchasing heat pumps and other investments encouraged by former President Clinton's Climate Change Technology Initiative are likely to benefit mostly the high-income households.

The analysis thus far considers only private benefits, but the objective of a climate policy, focusing on technology adoption, is to obtain 'external benefits' from reducing carbon emissions. In a previous paper (Sutherland, 2000) I calculated the reduction in carbon emissions from Clinton's proposed CCTI programme. An estimate of $510 per tonne of carbon reduced is a tenable, mid-case estimate. This cost per tonne is much higher than the cost characterising other programmes of about $25 to $50, implying that the tax credits are not as cost-effective as a climate change mitigation strategy.

At least in a qualitative sense, we may suggest the relative distributional effects of direct regulation, subsidies and energy/environmental taxes. The source of the regressivity emphasised here derives from the low value that future benefits convey to low-income households. This low value is expressed as a high discount rate, or as a high marginal rate of time preference.

Direct EE regulations of household appliances produce regressive effects because they distort the purchases mostly of low- and middle-income households and require an investment with negative value. Household subsidies, including tax credits, are regressive because they bestow disproportionate benefits on high-income households.

The equity effects of energy taxes have been studied numerous times, often focusing on the equity effects of energy/carbon taxes. The usual finding is that energy taxes are regressive because energy purchases are a larger share of income of low-income households than of high-income households. Consideration of how the taxes are used, or recycled, complicates the analysis and introduces uncertainty, but generally does not reverse the overall finding of regressive effects.

Direct regulations and energy taxes increase the cost of the final good to consumers. The equity effect typically considered is the burden of this cost relative to income level, with the largest relative burden being inversely related to income. The equity effect emphasised in this study is in addition to, or over and above, the initial equity effect. The increased cost of the final good, from either direct regulation or a tax, is an investment with a flow of subsequent benefits. These benefits are internal in the case of EE regulations and external in the case of carbon taxes. However, in each case, the policy tool has regressive effects because of the low value that future benefits bestow on low-income households. Hence energy/carbon taxes, and direct regulation, are regressive first, by the incidence of the cost, and second, by the time value of the flow of benefits.

8. AN INTEREST GROUP EXPLANATION OF EE APPLIANCE STANDARDS

The environmental equity literature estimates the equity effects of regulation, and concludes quite typically that many regulations have regressive distributional implications. However, this literature typically does not explain why such regulations were promulgated.

The distributional effects of specific policies are determined in economic markets characterised by supply, demand and market outcomes. However, environmental regulation and environmental policy are determined in political markets, which are characterised by the supply and demand for regulation, and market outcomes. This section explains the continued ratcheting up of EE appliance standards as an outcome in a political market where the winners have more influence than the losers.

Applying public choice theory (Stigler, 1971; Buchanan and Tullock, 1975; Buchanan, 2003), it can be argued that EE appliance standards result from a political process where the interest group that supports EE standards has more political influence than the interest group that opposes the standards. Further, EE standards will be supported by some segments of industry in order to compete more effectively against other segments of industry. The consortium of interest groups that supports EE appliance standards includes the US DOE, Lawrence Berkeley National Laboratory (LBL), the American Council for an Energy Efficient Economy (ACEEE) and the American Home Appliance Manufacturers (AHAM). ACEEE is just one EE interest group supporting standards. There are other supporting interest groups, such as the Alliance to Save Energy and the Natural Resources Defense Council, as well as numerous environmental interest groups. Residential households are not part of this consortium of interest groups.

In the US, EE standards for household appliances result from federal energy legislation, where the proposed standards are specified. The EE community includes numerous energy efficiency and environmental organisations that provide political support for the continuous ratcheting up of standards. The American Council for an Energy Efficient Economy (ACEEE) receives DOE funding and advocates various efficiency programmes, including increased federal standards. Interest group theory asserts that interest groups use the political process to achieve their objectives.[17]

The appliance manufacturers, represented by their trade association, the American Home Appliance Manufacturers, can be an important political ally to the EE community. The appliance manufacturers sometimes (but not always) benefit financially from increased EE standards. The initial motivation of manufacturers to support federal energy efficiency standards was to obtain national uniformity in standards which would replace various state requirements.

Appliance EE standards are sometimes supported by one manufacturer to obtain a competitive advantage over rivals. A proposed new standard on central air-conditioners and heat pumps, for instance, would increase the Seasonal Energy Efficiency Ratio (SEER) to 13 in 2006. As of early 2001, Goodman Co., a large privately-owned manufacturer, was lobbying in favour of the higher standards, while the other large manufacturers – Carrier, Trane, Lennox and York – were lobbying against the new standard and have filed lawsuits accordingly. An interest group explanation is that Goodman Company is motivated by profit. Goodman currently markets a heat pump with a SEER rating of 14, well above the proposed standard.[18] An increase in the EE standard would increase Goodman's profits at the expense of competitors who market heat pumps with lower SEER ratings. The behaviour of Goodman and its competitors is consistent with interest group theory, and specifically with Stigler's view of industry-seeking regulation.

In 2001, the DOE issued EE standards affecting clothes washers. Schleede (2001) explains these standards as the result of rent-seeking behaviour of a consortium of interest groups. The consortium included the DOE, LBL, ACEEE and the appliance manufacturers, as well as some supporting US senators. Supporting legislation included a proposed tax credit for manufactures of super efficient clothes washers. General Electric Co., a large manufacturer of washing machines, is located in Iowa, and the legislation was sponsored by an Iowa senator. According to Schleede (2001, p. 7) the proposed tax credit would shift from $75 million to $150 million from taxpayers to Iowa manufacturers of clothes washers.

In addition to this political support, the DOE obtained support for its proposed new standards from a 'Joint Stakeholders Comment'. These stakeholders included representatives from nine clothes washer manufacturers and eight EE organisations. The manufacturers are obvious financial beneficiaries of national standards. The various EE organisations receive financial support from the DOE and lobby Congress for DOE EE budgets and legislation. As noted by Schleede (2001, p. 12), the Joint Stakeholders Comment did not represent the interests of consumers, who of course are directly affected by such standards.

9. CONCLUSION

This chapter estimates the net present value of the EE standards affecting household appliances to be about negative $46.4 billion to $56.2 billion, with B/C much less than 1. The DOE has sponsored numerous studies that conclude that EE standards provide positive and large net benefits. Recent evidence that energy efficiency increases are the result of autonomous effects and price-induced technology effects means that previous estimates are attributing energy saving to regulation rather than to market forces. The use of artificially low discount rates, in the presence of extensive evidence to the contrary, also means that the monetary value of energy saving to consumers was being overstated.

Although EE standards cannot pass an economic cost–benefit test, such standards pass a political cost–benefit test and have thereby been continuously ratcheted up and expanded in scope. Viewing appliance standards as the political outcome of rent-seeking interest groups, the winners are the environmental and energy interest groups, for example ACEEE, and the appliance manufacturers. The losers are residential households, especially those with low or moderate incomes. The winners have a high willingness to pay for EE regulations; the losers have a negligible willingness to pay to oppose these regulations. Lower- and middle-income households are 'rationally ignorant' of the burden of standards and are not politically organised.

This chapter does not revisit the issue of whether market barriers are actually market failures (see Hausman and Joskow, 1982; Sutherland, 1991). However, it is apparent that – in contrast to environmental quality – the benefits of future cost reduction are largely internal to consumers. A qualification is that electricity generation results in carbon dioxide emissions that are associated with global warming. This external cost could warrant a downward adjustment in private discount rates. The adjusted discount rate would be applied to low- and middle-income households that are affected by EE standards. The adjustment could possibly have efficiency implications, but not equity implications. The equity effects result from low-income households having a high opportunity cost of investing, not from some market characteristic affecting these households. The literature on the market for durable goods alleges various market failures that may justify government action. However, as Wolf (1991) explains and this chapter emphasises, the choice between market outcomes and government mandates is a choice between imperfect alternatives.

Direct regulations in the form of EE standards have different effects from EE subsidies, but each is inefficient and regressive. The inefficiency arises from the internality of benefits and lack of significant market failure. The inequity arises from the high opportunity cost of poor people to invest, as reflected in their discount rates. Indeed, emphasis in this case study is on the investment element of the environmental policy – the upfront costs with long-term benefits. The time profile of benefits characterises direct regulations, as well as energy/carbon taxes. The equity implications of a required investment are in addition to the initial incidence of the cost on households by income level.

The inefficient market outcome of EE standards should not be generalised to environmental regulations that achieve externality benefits. However, the equity results can be generalised to environmental regulations which require households to make investment decisions with expected future benefits. For instance, corporate average fuel economy standards (CAFE) require an increased investment with subsequent decline in operating costs. This increased investment cost, along with the discounted value of long-term benefits, should have regressive effects.[19]

Analysts frequently relate equity effects to the income elasticity of the good affected by regulation. For instance, taxing luxury goods is equity-enhancing; taxing inferior or normal goods is equity-retarding. In contrast, this chapter emphasises the time value of benefits. Government regulations, including environmental and EE, result in an initial investment followed by a subsequent flow of benefits. Equity effects result from households placing a different value on the flow of future benefits depending on their income level. The inverse relationship between household income and discount rates implies that the poor place a low value on future benefits, including energy cost savings and environmental quality. The implication is that environmental policies and regulations, including EE standards, that require household investments are likely to be inequitable.

NOTES

1. Tollison (1991, p. 66).
2. The required qualification is the income elasticity of the goods that are subject to regulation. Investment subsidies generally benefit high-income households, but investment subsidies of inferior goods could benefit low-income households.
3. Energy efficiency standards require that each regulated appliance use a minimum specified amount of energy per unit of output: US Congress, National Energy Policy Conservation Act, 1978.
4. State standards by California, Florida and other states are noted and cited by Howard Geller (1995).
5. US Congress (1987).
6. See the LBL website www.lbl.gov, and search under energy efficiency appliance standards.
7. Much of the first part of this chapter is based on Sutherland (2003).
8. See Sutherland (1991) for a discussion.
9. Brealey and Myers (2003, p. 155) note that the average annual rate of return on common stocks (S&P 500) from 1926–2000 was 13 per cent per year nominal and 9.7 per cent per year in constant dollars. Year 2000 reflected highly valued internet stocks. This long-term rate of return would likely be closer to 12 per cent if calculated in year 2003.
10. A defence of the LBL use of discount rates is provided by Richard B. Howarth and Alan H. Sanstad (1995).
11. This analysis implicitly uses the same investment cost, and the same forecast of energy prices, as used by LBL.
12. See Sutherland (1991), and for a critique see Stoft (1993).
13. See Meyers et al. (2003, Figure 2, and p. 760).
14. The document describing this initiative is a press briefing, Clinton (1998).
15. If the demand curve is linear, benefits to new adopters will equal one-half their cost. If the demand curve is concave, as is typical, benefits are less than one-half of costs to new adopters.

16. My analysis is comparative static; Kriström (Chapter 3) points out that subsidising nega-
     tive externalities may over time encourage an increase in emissions. My analysis suggests
     that subsidy recipients would try over time to game the subsidy process by claiming emis-
     sions reductions, but minimising actual behavioral changes.
17. Howard Geller, of the ACEEE, confirms this theory (see Section 2 above) when he states
     that the EE standards contained in both the 1987 and 1992 federal legislation were nego-
     tiated directly by the manufacturers and energy efficiency advocates. The 1987 Act, as
     stated by Geller (1995, p. 1): 'was adopted by the U. S. Congress with virtually no oppo-
     sition'. The assertion that EE standards are the result of negotiations with the EE com-
     munity confirms the interest group theory. The 'losers' from EE standards – lower- and
     middle-income households – were not part of the negotiation process.
18. Goodman's website address is www.goodmanmfg.com, and see 'CLQ Series 14 SEER
     2 to 5 Ton'.
19. Equity is also affected by the income and price elasticity of demand for automobiles. Bae
     (2003, p. 12) notes that the poor do not buy new cars. However, automobile transporta-
     tion is a necessity in the US, and low- and middle-income households purchase vehicles
     (new or second-hand) that include fuel economy investments. Although price and
     income elasticities influence equity, the increased cost of automobiles to achieve fuel
     economy is equity-retarding.

REFERENCES

Bae, Christine (2003), 'The Distributional Impacts of Air Quality Regulations:
    Smog Controls in Los Angeles and Toxic Air Releases in Houston and Los
    Angeles', paper prepared for the OECD Workshop on the Distribution of
    Benefits and Costs of Environmental Policies, March 4–5.
Beggs, S. and N. Cardell (1980), 'Choice of Smallest Car by Multi-vehicle
    Households and the Demand for Electric Vehicles', *Transportation Research*,
    14A, 389–404.
Beggs, S., N. Cardell and J. Hausman (1981), 'Assessing the Potential Demand for
    Electric Cars', *Journal of Econometrics*, **17**, 1–19.
Berkovec, J., J. Hausman and J. Rust (1983), 'Heating System and Appliance
    Choice', Report Number MIT-EL 830004WP, MIT Energy Laboratory, MIT
    Cambridge, MA.
Brealey, Richard A. and Stewart C. Myers (2003), *Principles of Corporate Finance*,
    7th edn, New York: McGraw Hill.
Buchanan, James M. (2003), 'Public Choice: Politics without Romance', *Policy*,
    19(3), Spring, 13–18.
Buchanan, James M. and Gordon Tullock (1975), 'Polluters' Profits and Political
    Response: Direct Controls Verses Taxes', *American Economic Review*, **65**(1),
    March, 139–47.
Clinton, William (1998), 'The President's Climate Change Technology Initiative',
    The White House.
Geller, Howard (1995), 'National Appliance Efficiency Standards: Cost Effective
    Federal Regulations', Washington DC, American Council for an Energy Efficient
    Economy, November.
Goett, A. and D. McFadden (1984), 'Residential End-use Energy Planning System
    (REEPS)', Report EA-2512, Electric Power Research Institute, Palo Alto.
Hartman, R.S. and M.J. Doane (1986), 'Household Discount Rates Revisited',
    Energy Journal, **7**(1), 139–48.

Hassett, Kevin and Gilbert Metcalf (1996), 'Can Irreversibility Explain the Slow Diffusion of Energy Saving Technologies?', *Energy Policy*, **24**(1), 7–8.

Hausman, J. (1979), 'Individual Discount Rates and the Purchase and Utilization of Energy Using Durables', *Bell Journal of Economics*, Spring, **10**, 33–54.

Hausman, Jerry A. and Paul L. Joskow (1982), 'Evaluating the Costs and Benefits of Appliance Efficiency Standards', *American Economics Review, Papers and Proceedings*, **72**(2), May, 220–25.

Howarth, Richard B. and Alan H. Sanstad (1995), 'Discount Rates and Energy Efficiency', *Contemporary Economic Policy*, **XIII**, July, 101–9.

Johnstone, Nick, Nadia Caid and Yse Serret (2002), 'Decision Making and Environmental Policy Design for Consumer Durables', Discussion Paper, Organisation for Economic Co-operation and Development, ENV/EPOC/ WPNEP(2002)7/Final, November.

McMahon, James E., Peter Chan and Stuart Chaitkin (2000), 'Impacts of U.S. Standards to Date', LBNL-45825, available on lbl.gov and published in the Proceedings of the 2nd International Conference on Energy Efficiency in Household Appliances and Lighting, Naples, Italy, September 27–29.

Metcalf, Gilbert and Donald Rosenthal (1995), 'The "New" View of Investment Decisions and Public Policy Analysis: An Application of Green Lights and Cold Refrigerators', *Journal of Policy Analysis and Management*, **14**(4), 517–31.

Meyers, S., J.E. McMahon, M. McNeil and X. Liu (2003), 'Impacts of US Federal Energy Efficiency Standards for Residential Appliances', *Energy*, **28**, 755–67.

Meyers, S., J.E. McMahon, M. McNeil and X. Liu (2002), 'Realized and Perspective Impacts of U.S. Energy Efficiency Standards for Residential Appliances', Lawrence Berkely National Laboratory, LBNL-49504, June.

Mitchell, William C. and Randy T. Simmons (1994), 'Beyond Politics: Markets, Welfare and the Failure of Bureaucracy', Oakland, CA, Independent Institute.

Newell, Richard G., Adam B. Jaffe and Robert N. Stavins (1998), 'The Induced Innovation Hypothesis and Energy Saving Technological Change', Resources for the Future, Discussion Paper, October.

Newell, Richard G., Adam B. Jaffe and Robert N. Stavins (1999), 'The Induced Innovation Hypothesis and Energy Saving Technological Change', *Quarterly Journal of Economics*, **114**(3), 941–75.

Schleede, Glenn (2001), 'Will Congress or the New Administration Protect Consumers from DOE, Clothes Washer Manufacturers and Self-Appointed Energy Efficiency Advocates?', Energy Market & Policy Analysis, Inc. Reston VA, July, and http://www.consumeralert.org/issues/enviro/2SchleedeWash.htm.

Stigler, George (1971), 'The Theory of Economic Regulation', *Bell Journal of Management and Science*, **2**(1), Spring, pp. 1–21; and in George Stigler (ed.) (1988), *Chicago Studies in Political Economy*, Chicago: The University of Chicago Press, pp. 209–33.

Stoft, Steven (1993), 'Appliance Standards and the Welfare of Poor Families', *Energy Journal*, **14**(4), 123–8.

Sutherland, Ronald J. (1991), 'Market Barriers to Energy Efficiency Investments', *Energy Journal*, **15**(4), 15–34.

Sutherland, Ronald J. (1994), 'Income Distribution Effects of Electric Utility DSM Programs', *Energy Journal*, **15**(4), 103–18.

Sutherland, Ronald J. (2000), 'No Cost Efforts to Reduce Carbon Emissions in the U.S.: An Economic Perspective', *Energy Journal*, **21**(3), 89–112.

Sutherland, Ronald J. (2003), 'The High Cost of Federal Energy Efficiency

Standards for Residential Appliances', The Cato Institute, Washington DC, No. 504, December.

Tollison, Robert D. (1991), 'Regulation and Interest Groups', in Jack High (ed.), *Regulation: Economic Theory and History*, Ann Arbor: University of Michigan Press, pp. 59–76.

Train, Kenneth (1985), 'Discount Rates in Consumers' Energy Related Decisions: A Review of the Literature', *Energy*, **10**(12), 1243–53.

US Congress, National Appliance Energy Conservation Act of 1987, P.L. 100-12, March 17, 1987.

US Congress, Energy Policy Act of 1992, P.L. 102-486, October, 1992.

Wolf, Charles Jr (1991), *Markets or Government: Choosing Between Imperfect Alternatives*, Cambridge, MA: MIT Press.

PART III

Evidence on the Distribution of Environmental Quality

6. Exposure to environmental urban noise pollution in Birmingham, UK

**Julii S. Brainard, Andrew P. Jones,
Ian J. Bateman and Andrew A. Lovett**

1. INTRODUCTION

Recent decades have seen increased recognition that biases within environmental policy-making and regulatory processes, combined with discriminatory market forces, may lead to disproportionate exposures to environmental disamenities amongst certain population groups. In the context of examining such discrepancies, the terms 'environmental equity' and 'environmental justice' are sometimes used synonymously (Harding and Holdren, 1993), although distinctions can be made. Lavelle (1994) suggests that environmental equity implies an equal sharing of risk burdens, but not necessarily a reduction in the total burden of pollution. Cutter (1995) argues that environmental justice implies much more, including remedial action to correct an injustice imposed upon a specific subgroup of society. Perlin et al. (1995) further advocate that environmental justice should achieve adequate protection from harmful hazardous agents for everyone, regardless of ethnicity, age or socio-economic status.

Potential effects of high noise on human welfare can include nuisance, disrupted sleep patterns, hearing loss, perceptions of poor well-being and loss of quality of life or impaired mental health. Furthermore, stress-related health effects can be psychological, behavioural or physical in manifestation (Stansfield et al., 2000; Passchier-Vermeer and Passchier, 2000). Haines et al. (2001) reported that children attending four schools located in high aircraft noise areas showed evidence of impaired reading comprehension and high levels of noise annoyance. Evans and Maxwell (1997) also found that 6–8 year olds exposed to chronic aircraft noise were more likely to suffer from deficits in language skills, whereas speech communication may be impaired for the elderly at ambient noise levels as low as 45 dB L_{Aeq} (Berglund, 1996). Ng (2000) reported a direct correlation between exposure to building-site noise and sleep disruption, inability to concentrate and difficulty in relaxation among adults. More seriously, the effect of traffic and other noise sources on cardiovascular risk factors in adults has been documented. Babisch et al. (1999) reported that long-time male residents of homes exposed to high traffic noise had a relative risk of 1.6 for ischemic heart disease. Among a sample of 1542 young children, Regecova and Kellerova (1995) found that individuals attending nursery schools situated in areas with high traffic noise (>60 dB(A)) had higher mean systolic and diastolic blood pressures and lower mean heart rate than children in quiet areas. In a study of exposure to local road and rail transport noise in Austrian villages, Evans et al. (2001) observed effects on infant cardiovascular health; children in the noisier areas had elevated resting systolic blood pressure and higher levels of stress hormones in urine samples. The children from noisier neighbourhoods also showed elevated heart rate reactivity to a discrete stressor (reading test) in the laboratory and rated themselves higher in perceived stress symptoms on a standardised index.

While we have a good understanding of the manner in which environmental noise pollution may affect the health of exposed populations, there is rather less evidence available on the degree of equity by which different populations are exposed to it. A few studies (Baum et al., 1999; Hoffmann et al., 2003) find that lower socio-economic groups are unfairly exposed to noise, but we have little information concerning the distribution of exposure among other (possibly) disadvantaged groups such as ethnic minorities, the very young or old. Baum et al. (1999) argued that apparent health disadvantages of lower socio-economic groups may actually be largely attributable to environmental stresses, including noise pollution.

This chapter examines whether inequities in exposure to noise pollution are apparent among certain population groups in a large English city. Research on distributional inequities with respect to environmental pollution and amenities is relatively new in the UK, and the authors have undertaken several studies to investigate whether such inequities exist. We previously found evidence that deprived and ethnic communities were more exposed to poor air quality (Brainard et al., 2002). Our research has also indicated that access to a publicly-funded environmental amenity, such as a public park, also may be much better for wealthier income groups. We are in the process of investigating how provision of other services, public and private, may vary between social groups, and whether those afflicted by seemingly inferior services and environmental quality perceive other compensations for their apparent disadvantages. The work presented in this chapter is grounded within the context of European developments and legislation on noise control. A Green Paper from the European Commission published in the mid-1990s (CEC, 1996) claimed that about 20 per cent (80 million) of the population in the European Union experience noise levels that are believed to have detrimental effects on human health. A further 42 per cent of the EU population was believed to reside in so-called 'grey areas', where noise pollution, if not hazardous to human welfare, is severe enough to cause occasional serious nuisance.

The Commission Green Paper suggested that the mapping of noise levels should be undertaken within local contexts to serve as both a planning tool and input to further debate on public policy. Subsequent developments, including consultations with member countries (CEC, 1999), led to the issue of a Draft Framework Directive on the Assessment and Reduction of Environmental Noise by the EU in December 2000 (CEC, 2000). The Directive calls on member states to generate noise maps for all European conurbations with populations greater than 250 000 by 2005, with corresponding maps to be drawn up for urban areas with populations in excess of 100 000 by the end of 2009. The draft directive further stipulates that local authorities managing these conurbations should generate action plans that both analyse the noise maps and detail intended corrective measures.

In November 2000 the UK government issued a White Paper on Rural England (DETR and MAFF, 2000), announcing plans to consult on a national noise strategy in 2001 and map the main sources and areas of noise in England by 2004. The council of the city of Birmingham, England, was involved with European Union (EU) level discussions on noise reduction from an early stage, contributing to consultations on the 1996 Green Paper and the subsequent development of noise mapping and abatement guidelines. Birmingham, the UK's largest city after London, was subsequently chosen as the trial site for noise mapping in the United Kingdom. Hence the work undertaken in the city has been subject to a considerable amount of empirical effort and is of both national and European significance. For our purposes, Birmingham is also interesting because it is culturally diverse, with non-whites making up 30 per cent of the population (in the 2001 Census), compared to 28 per cent in London, and around 12 per cent on average in other large cities (population > 200 000) of England and Wales. In other respects, Birmingham's social profile may be more deprived than most other British cities. In the 2001 Census, 27.8 per cent of Birmingham residents were in council ('public') or council-approved housing and unemployment was 5.7 per cent, while the average city-wide ward-level rank in the 2000 Index of Multiple Deprivation (IMD) was 23. In other large cities in England and Wales (including London), 26 per cent of residents are in council/council-approved housing and unemployment was 4.3 per cent in the 2001 Census, while the 2000 IMD rank average is 91 (that is, less deprived on average than Birmingham).

The work presented in this chapter uses data from the Birmingham noise mapping project to make assessments of possible inequities in noise exposure between different population groups. Although no specific legislation regarding ambient environmental noise exists, there is explicit guidance from HM Treasury (2003) that consideration of distributional impacts should be included within cost–benefit analyses, environmental impact assessments and policy implementation in the UK. Using a Geographical Information System (GIS), a methodology is developed whereby measures of noise exposure and population age, ethnicity and socio-economic characteristics are calculated for neighbourhoods in the city. Using a combination of descriptive statistics, Kolmogorov–Smirnov tests, and mapping techniques, the distributions of noise and population characteristics are then tested and compared. Finally, the implications of our findings for noise pollution legislation and future research into inequities in exposure are discussed.

2. METHODS

2.1 The Study Area

The boundaries of the city of Birmingham were used to define the study region area (see inset map on Figure 6.1). Birmingham is the most urban of seven metropolitan local authorities that form the West Midlands region in western England. The 1991 UK Census of Population recorded just under one million residents in the city.

2.2 Data Sources

Information on demographic structure of the study area population was extracted from the UK Census records held in the archive available on the Manchester Information & Associated Services (MIMAS) supercomputer service. The demographic details were compared to modelled levels of both day and night-time noise values emitted from roads, rail and air sources so that measures of exposure to noise could be calculated.

2.3 Population Characteristics

Measures of spatial variations in the socio-economic characteristics of neighbourhood populations in Birmingham were taken from the 1991 Census at enumeration district (ED) level. These were the most recent date and the smallest area for which data were available. In total, there were 1950 EDs within the study area. However, due to national confidentiality requirements, complete information was not available on the population of 10 EDs. Hence, 1940 EDs, with a median population of 496 residents and a typical area of about 8.5 ha, were included in the final analysis.

A variety of socio-economic indicators were directly extracted or derived from the census (Table 6.1). These focused on age, ethnicity and indicators of poverty. There was no explicit income question in the 1991 Census, but a number of variables, such as levels of unemployment or car ownership, can be considered as proxy indicators of relative affluence or deprivation. As a general indicator of the level of socio-economic deprivation within each ED, census variables indicating the level of male unemployment (unemployed male residents over 16 as a proportion of all economically active male residents aged over 16), overcrowding (persons in households with one and more persons per room as a proportion of all residents in households), non-car ownership (residents in households with no car as a proportion of all residents in households) and low social class (residents in households with an economically active head of household in social class 4 or 5 as a proportion of all residents in households)

Table 6.1   *Variables extracted or derived from the 1991 Census, for each ED*

Variable name	Description	Range of observed values		
		Min.	Median	Max.
Ethnicity				
BANG	Bangladeshi population (%)	0	0	35.96
INDN	Indian population (%)	0	1.54	67.38
PAK	Pakistani population (%)	0	0.40	85.11
BLACK	Black population (%)	0	3.32	43.43
WHITE	White population (%)	4.95	92.10	100.0
Social characteristics				
MUNEM	Male unemployment (%)	0	15.98	65.63
NOCAR	Households without a car (%)	0	47.87	93.75
OVERCR	Overcrowded households (>1.5 persons per room) (%)	0	6.42	55.57
LOWSC	Population of social class 4 and 5 (%)	0	23.08	100
RET	Pensioners (women >= 60 years and men >= 65 years old) (%)	0.92	17.71	84.51
U5	Infants under 5 years (%)	0	7.16	22.97
U15	Children aged 5–14 years (%)	0	21.80	60.17
Deprivation				
CARST	Carstairs deprivation index scores (value)	−5.50	−0.29	9.66

were obtained from the census. These were used to calculate Carstairs Deprivation Index (Carstairs and Morris, 1989) scores, a composite measure of social deprivation in the city of Birmingham. The Carstairs index is standardised using Z-scores such that the mean value centres at zero. Within the index, negative scores indicate less deprived (and hence more affluent) areas, whilst positive scores denote neighbourhoods with higher levels of deprivation.

The term 'race' may be treated as a distinct phenomenon which is linked to physical features or racial categorisation (Rex, 1970), but the analytical validity of the categorisation has been questioned (Miles, 1980). Ethnicity, on the other hand, is associated with a sense of belonging to a particular group (Anthias, 1992). As the categorisations in the UK Census are based on self-reported characteristics, we considered ethnic rather than racial divisions in this research. White, Asian (particularly persons of Indian, Pakistani or Bangladeshi ancestry) and black (predominantly Caribbean but also African ancestry) ethnic groups are particularly represented in Birmingham, and information on the population of each group was extracted for every ED from the census.

Age groups extracted for ED populations from the census included the number of children under 5 years old, children under 15 years, and retired persons (aged over 60 years for women and 65 years for men).

2.4   Noise Pollution

Information on modelled noise levels, based on values for 1998, was supplied by Birmingham City Council. Using a proprietary computer software package (Lima™), maps of noise levels at reception points were derived by estimating noise levels from road, rail and air sources at points regularly spaced at 10-metre intervals across the city. Here we give only a brief overview of the generation of the noise maps. A more detailed discussion can be found in Hinton (2000).

Noise estimates were utilised for both day and night-time periods, and for road noise alone or road combined with that from the other sources. There were several reasons for assessing the sources of noise independently. The amount of noise that a population is exposed to can vary substantially by source and throughout the day. For example, although noise levels will generally be lower at night, aircraft noise may be most disruptive in the late evening, while disturbance associated with road traffic noise may be highest in the late afternoon. Particular emphasis was placed on road noise in this research, as road traffic is the overwhelming source of noise in the city and its estimation was based upon the highest quality input data in the noise generation model.

The main requirement for the estimation of road noise was a digital representation of the location of roads, and estimates of their associated traffic flows. For most of Birmingham, road centrelines, elevations and cuttings were extracted from digital Ordnance Survey data. Some additional roads not included in that database were digitised manually. It was assumed that all road surfaces consisted of impervious bitumen. Separate estimates of vehicle movements for day (7am–11pm) and night-time periods (11pm–7am) were available for the 1900 individual road sections within the study area. Estimates of the proportion of heavy good vehicles (HGVs) on each segment of road were available, but these data were not broken down by time of day, nor were details available on temporal variations in vehicular speeds. Thus, the percentage of HGVs and average speeds were treated as constant throughout both day and night. The lack of information on temporal variations in road traffic may influence our findings if vehicles driven at night were driven at higher speeds and were hence noisier. Furthermore, sporadic and sudden loud vehicular sounds on an otherwise quiet road may be more disturbing than a constant background of traffic noise.

The gradient of each road link was incorporated into the estimation of noise values. Aside from elevated road sections, the base height of roads was assumed to be the same as ground height contours. The effect of road parapets, screens and embankments greater than 0.5 metres was also incorporated into the model. Calibration of the road noise generation was achieved by undertaking field measurements at two Birmingham sites (Walmley Golf Club and Sutton Park). The field measurements enabled an empirical formula to be derived that described sound/power relationships between the proportion of HGVs on a road link, and measured noise levels at a distance of 25 metres from the road.

For the estimation of the contribution of rail noise to the overall noise profiles, details of passenger train services, including the number, type, length of units, and average speed between stations were used. Information on freight train movements was also utilised, although no specific data could be obtained on the length, type or average speed of these units. All sections of track in Birmingham were assumed to have insignificant gradients, and to be composed of identical materials. Furthermore, all trains of a particular type (for example, electric or diesel, passenger or freight) were assumed to have identical engines. No allowance was made for the effect of railway cuttings or embankments. Subsequent estimated noise levels were again calibrated using field assessments.

The mapping exercise undertook no independent modelling of aircraft noise. Rather, three decibel (dB) noise contours for a noise 'footprint' area affected by the city's airport in 1998 were supplied by Birmingham Airport for the time periods 7am to 11pm (Figure 6.1), and 11pm to 6am. No data

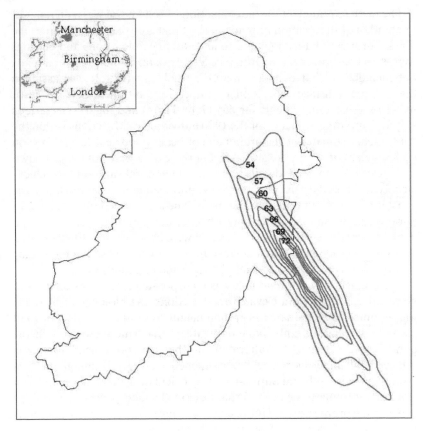

Figure 6.1   Noise footprint (dB) around Birmingham airport

were available for 6am to 7am, and so no estimates of aircraft noise were made for this period. Interpolation between contours was not attempted, but rather the areas between contours were categorised using estimates of noise levels according to the contour boundaries. It is important to note that the data for the airport footprint only refers to noise contributions at 54 (day) or 48 (night) decibels and above. These cut-off values were chosen because they approach the background levels of transport-generated noise in most cities (Kurra et al., 1999). The consequence is likely to be some under-estimation of total noise levels just outside the designated airport footprint area. However, the effect of the omission will be small because noise is added logarithmically. For instance, the addition of a 52 dB source into an environment that already contains an average of 51 dB of noise increases the total only slightly to 53 dB.

All emissions sources were input to the Lima™ package produced by Stapelfeldt Ingenieurgesellschaft mbH in Germany (Brüjer and Kjær, undated) for the estimation of sound propagation. In addition to land contours, the modelling incorporated Ordnance Survey digital Landline data for the perimeters of 184 500 buildings and other structures (heights were partly estimated using aerial photography). The output estimates were generated on a 10 × 10 metre grid for reception points across Birmingham, in 5 dB bandwidths, for both day and night periods. The mapped values show continuous outdoor sound levels for the designated areas (Figure 6.2). The greatest single source of noise in Birmingham is the M6 motorway, with noise generation from air traffic also being quite significant close to the airport. The measurements are denoted as dB L_{Aeq}. 'A'-weighting refers to correction by factors that weight sound to correlate with the sensitivity of the human ear to sounds at different frequencies (Fidell et al., 2002). Because values have been generalised so as to indicate an average sound level over the entire designated period (that is, day or night), the noise estimates are assumed to be continuous and refer to modelled noise levels at a height of 4m above ground level. This height was chosen to comply with European standards for noise pollution modelling (CEC, 1996). The combined noise source maps in Figure 6.2 were produced by logarithmic addition of the different noise sources. Field verification of the model outputs at eight sites suggested no significant over- or under-predictions (Hinton, 2000).

So that the noise data was consistent with the population data set used in the research, the initial 10 metre resolution noise maps were resampled using the Arc/Info Geographical Information System package (ESRI, 1999) to derive levels for 20m × 20m cells. This conversion procedure required the generation of a surface in the form of a triangulated irregular network (TIN) from the 10m × 10m cell data. A new grid of 20m × 20m cells was overlain onto this map and interpolated estimates of noise levels at the centre of each new 20m × 20m cell were assigned as the average value for that entire cell.

2.5   Population-weighted Average Noise Exposures for Each ED

In order to use the noise exposure estimates to predict population dose, it was necessary to obtain a detailed estimate of the spatial distribution of the population of Birmingham. A data set that was derived from the 1991 UK Census of Population providing estimates of the number of persons residing in 200m × 200m grid cells across the study area was employed (Martin, 1996). These data were subsequently resampled to give the estimated number of persons in 20m × 20m cells by dividing the original 200m population values by 100. ED area average noise estimates were calculated by multiplying the noise value for each 20m × 20m grid cell by the

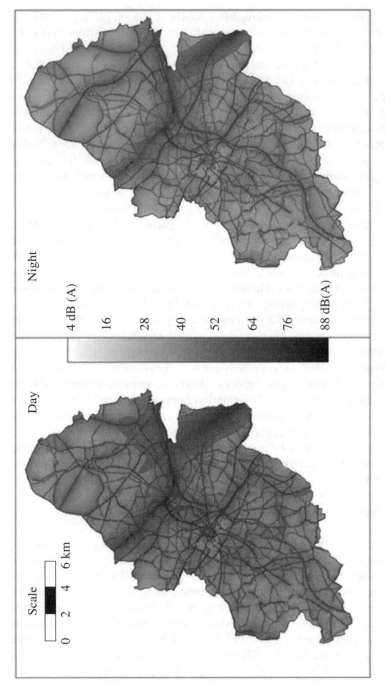

Figure 6.2   Noise levels from combined (rail/road/airport) sources, for day and night-time, in A-weighted decibels (L_{Aeq})

population in that same cell. Summing these values for the entire ED, and dividing by the ED's total population gave a population-weighted average exposure estimate.

2.6 Statistical Analysis

The statistical analysis focused on the elucidation of possible differences in noise pollution exposures related to variations in population ethnicity, poverty and age. To examine these relationships, descriptive statistics including means, median, percentages and quartiles were calculated. In order to determine how the estimates of exposure were distributed across the different population groups under study, Kolmogorov–Smirnov (KS) tests were also undertaken.

3. RESULTS

3.1 The Distribution of Exposures Based upon Age Profile

The analysis of noise exposure by age concentrated on the proportion of ED populations below the age of five years, between 5 and 14 years, and at pensionable age. To compare levels of noise exposure across these populations, the percentage of the total Birmingham population in each age group was determined for each ED. For example, the ED labelled CNFA10 had 56 children aged between 5 and 14 years. This equates to 0.012 per cent of the total 45 140 persons within this age range residing in Birmingham in 1991. Calculating this percentage of the total for each ED allowed the proportion of each age group that was exposed to various noise levels to be determined. These proportions can be used to plot the cumulative frequency (proportion of population) against noise. Table 6.2 shows the

Table 6.2 Median estimated noise exposure for age cohorts in Birmingham (decibels)

Source and period	Age cohort			
	0–4 yrs	5–14 yrs	Pensioners	City average
Road, day	46.6	46.4	46.8	46.7
Road, night	37.9	38.8	39.1	38.0
Combined, day	49.8	49.6	50.1	49.8
Combined, night	41.8	41.5	41.9	41.8

median estimated noise exposures for various sources and times for each age cohort. Differences in apparent doses for each group are small, although pensioners appear to experience slightly higher noise levels than other population groups at night.

Figure 6.3 shows the cumulative frequency curves for daytime road noise. The 'under 5', '5 to 14' and 'pensioners' lines are all virtually coincident, suggesting that there is no strong difference in estimated noise exposures experience between the different age cohorts. If the lines were divergent this would suggest that some populations were receiving disproportionate exposure. The equivalent plots of age against night-time road noise and combined source sound levels were extremely similar, and are not given here for the sake of brevity.

In order to confirm the apparent lack of differences in estimated noise exposure between groups, two-sample Kolmogorov–Smirnov (KS) tests were run to compare each of the age subgroups for each permutation of noise exposure. The KS test was used to determine the degree of difference in the shape of the exposure lines in the figures. Here, the size of the KS statistic makes it possible to determine how strongly the pattern of exposure to noise differs between the various age groups considered in this analysis, where larger KS scores represent more strongly divergent exposure lines. This statistical measure is non-parametric and only requires that the data belong to a continuous distribution. Problems of multi-collinearity, non-Gaussian distribution and unequal variances in subsets of the noise exposure estimates made parametric statistical analyses (such as regression

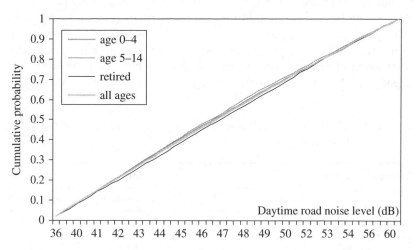

*Figure 6.3   Cumulative probability distributions for specified age
cohorts against exposure to daytime road noise in Birmingham*

or t-tests) inappropriate. The non-parametric alternatives to analysis of variance (Kruskal–Wallis or Friedman tests) describe differences between group medians, whereas the measures of interest are the differences at any point between population groups. More information on KS tests is given in Connover (1999).

Critical values for the Kolmogorov–Smirnov statistic vary with sample intervals; in this case, frequencies were broken down into 2 per cent quantiles, giving 50 intervals. Between the specified age groups, none of the KS scores reached statistical significance at a $p = 0.1$ level, confirming that there is little evidence of age-related disparities in noise exposure in Birmingham.

3.2 The Distribution of Noise Exposure Based upon Ethnic Profile

In the 1991 Census, the population of Birmingham was reported as being 78.49 per cent white, 14.13 per cent Asian and 5.85 per cent black. The percentage of each ethnic group in each ED was determined so that comparisons between these groups could be made. Table 6.3 shows the median estimated noise exposure for various sources and times for each ethnic group. The table suggests that disparities in noise exposure are greater between ethnic groups than was apparent for age, with the Indian and Pakistani subgroups tending to experience somewhat lower exposure than the city average, and blacks somewhat higher levels. These differences are plotted as a cumulative frequency graph in Figure 6.4.

Two-sample KS tests were again run to compare each of the ethnic subgroups for each permutation of noise exposure and the results of these are given in Table 6.4. We omit results for road noise alone, as no KS test scores were statistically significant at $p = 0.1$ or better. For combined sources, during the day or at night, Table 6.4 shows weak evidence of disparate experiences. Looking at Tables 6.3 and 6.4, the Indian and Pakistani communities appear to have less daytime noise exposure than black populations

Table 6.3   Median estimated noise exposure for ethnic groups in Birmingham (decibels)

Source and period	Ethnic group					
	Indian	Pakistani	White	Bangladeshi	Black	City average
Road, day	45.9	45.8	46.6	47.1	47.6	46.7
Road, night	37.2	37.0	37.9	38.5	38.5	37.9
Combined, day	48.1	48.9	50.0	50.4	51.0	50.8
Combined, night	41.3	41.8	41.8	42.3	43.3	41.8

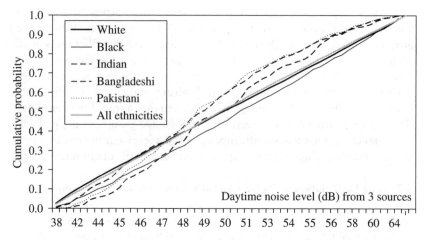

Figure 6.4   Cumulative probability distributions for specified ethnic groups and modelled daytime noise exposure from combined road/rail/airport sources

Table 6.4   Kolmogorov–Smirnov statistics for two-sample tests comparing cumulative probability distributions for ethnic groups and noise from combined sources

(a) Day

	Indian	Pakistani	Black	Bangladeshi
White	0.1214	0.1327	0.0731	0.1227
Indian		0.0521	**0.1611**	0.0974
Pakistani			**0.1734**	0.0962
Black				0.1173

(b) Night

	Indian	Pakistani	Black	Bangladeshi
White	0.0973	0.0892	0.0957	0.1094
Indian	–	0.0893	**0.1608**	0.1344
Pakistani		–	0.1270	0.0546
Black			–	0.1013
Critical values	$p = 0.1$	$p = 0.05$	$p = 0.01$	
	0.1513	0.1923	0.2305	

Note: Values exceeding the critical $p = 0.1$ threshold are highlighted in bold.

at a confidence level of 90 per cent (p = 0.10). The discrepancy is repeated between Indian and black populations for night-time noise, but is less strong between Pakistani and black communities. Neither the white nor the Bangladeshi populations are significantly advantaged over the other ethnic groups with regard to day or night-time noise from the combined sources.

Further explanations for the above findings of disparities in exposure between ethnic groups were sought by examining geographical distribution of ethnic minority populations in the city. Figure 6.5 maps enumeration districts in the city centre (where the ethnic minority populations are heavily concentrated) with specified proportions of various ethnic groups. The population of twenty EDs were at least 25 per cent Indian and 25 per cent black or Pakistani, whereas 71 were at least 25 per cent black, but less than 25 per cent Indian or Pakistani. The remainder were predominantly Indian, Pakistani or white. Grid cells that were receiving at least an estimated value of 60 dB (L_{Aeq}) noise are also shown on the figure.

The city centre is marked by the presence of high noise in the middle of the map, as it is apparent that roads become more closely congested in this area. Although the centre itself is a predominantly white area, with more than 80 per cent of residents being reported as white in the census, it is relatively unpopulated with around only 3500 residents. Hence, high city centre exposures contribute little to the overall residential noise exposure profile for white Birmingham residents. Figure 6.5 shows a ring of EDs around the centre with relatively large concentrations of black populations. To the north-west are mixed and Indian areas, whilst south-east of the city centre are the neighbourhoods with the highest concentrations of Pakistani residents. It is apparent that the closer proximity of black populations to the city centre and its associated traffic noise may explain their higher estimated noise exposures compared to other ethnic groups. Although still rather central, both the Indian and Pakistani communities are far enough away from the high density roads, the M6 motorway, and the airport to be less affected.

3.3 The Distribution of Noise Exposure Based upon Deprivation

To compare the measures of noise exposure for different levels of deprivation, EDs were categorised into Carstairs quartile groups. The lowest group refers to the least deprived (and hence most affluent) 25 per cent of EDs according to their Carstairs score. The fourth quartile is the most deprived 25 per cent of EDs.

Ethnicity was found to be closely associated with Carstairs index scores; the percentage of each ED population classified as black has a correlation coefficient of 0.541 (p < 0.001) with the Carstairs index. The equivalent

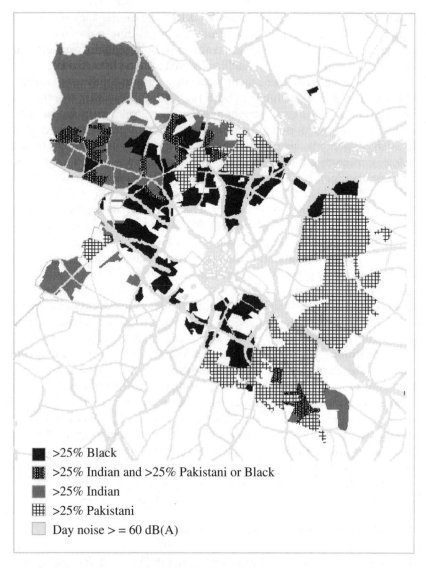

>25% Black

>25% Indian and >25% Pakistani or Black

>25% Indian

>25% Pakistani

Day noise > = 60 dB(A)

*Figure 6.5   Location of highly ethnic neighbourhoods (concentrations
             of these groups is negligible outside the city centre) and high
             noise areas*

*Table 6.5   Percentage of each ethnic group in each Carstairs deprivation
index quartile (top decile also included)*

Ethnicity	1st quartile	2nd quartile	3rd quartile	4th quartile	10th decile
White	30.2	27.5	26.0	16.2	4.8
All Asian	8.6	10.7	16.7	64.0	34.2
Bangladeshi	1.9	2.7	7.5	87.8	55.3
Indian	17.2	19.6	22.3	40.9	17.0
Pakistani	2.7	5.3	13.8	78.3	44.1
Black	7.2	15.4	25.8	51.7	23.0

*Table 6.6   Median estimated night-time noise (decibels) from combined
road/rail/airport exposure for Carstairs index deprivation
cohorts*

Cohort	1st quartile	2nd quartile	3rd quartile	4th quartile	10th decile	City average
	41.25	42.1	41.8	42.5	42.7	41.83

correlation for the Asian community is 0.528 ($p < 0.001$). The strong association between poverty and ethnicity is illustrated by Table 6.5, which shows the proportion of ethnic group populations in each Carstairs quartile. The final column of the table gives the proportion of each ethnic group in the 10 per cent most deprived EDs. A clear gradient is apparent whereby the proportion of the population reported as white declines with increasing deprivation, while the proportion of the other ethnic groups increases. Although only 4.8 per cent of white populations reside within the top 10 per cent of deprived EDs, 34.2 per cent of Asians, and 23 per cent of blacks live in these areas.

Cumulative proportions of populations in different deprivation categories were compared to estimated noise exposures, and KS statistics were calculated to assess the magnitude of any disparities between groups. These statistics showed no statistically significant disparities for the road-only noise map data, either at day or night-time levels. Furthermore, no significant differences in exposure were apparent between the deprivation groups for daytime noise from the combined source map. However, some discrepancies were evident in estimated exposure to night-time noise from the combined sources. Table 6.6 shows median estimated exposure levels for night noise from rail/road and airport sources, while Figure 6.6 depicts

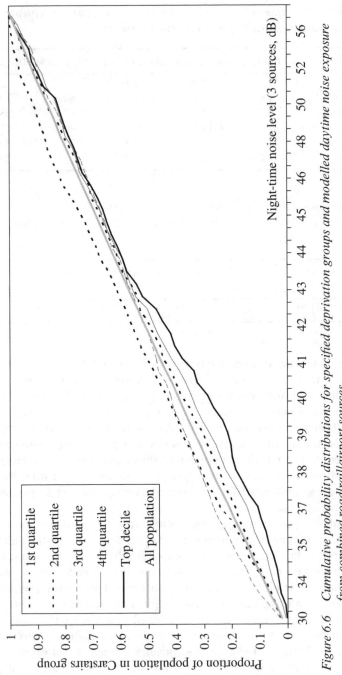

Figure 6.6   Cumulative probability distributions for specified deprivation groups and modelled daytime noise exposure from combined road/rail/airport sources

*Table 6.7   Kolmogorov–Smirnov statistics for two-sample tests comparing
             cumulative probability distributions for night-time noise
             exposure between deprivation groups*

	2nd quartile	3rd quartile	4th quartile	10th decile	City average
1st quartile	0.0920	0.1052	0.1011	**0.1664**	0.0706
2nd quartile		0.0783	0.0439	0.1003	0.0320
3rd quartile			0.1186	**0.1583**	0.0575
4th quartile				0.0745	0.0635
10th decile					0.1235
Critical values	p = 0.1	p = 0.05	p = 0.01		
	0.1513	0.1923	0.2305		

Note: Values exceeding the critical p = 0.1 threshold are highlighted in bold.

cumulative proportions of populations in different deprivation categories
against estimated night-time noise levels.

Table 6.7 shows the KS statistics for each cumulative frequency exposure
curve in Figure 6.6. Tables 6.6 and 6.7 show that, at night, the first and
third quartiles (most affluent, and second most deprived quartiles) experience estimated noise levels that are lower than those in the most deprived
10 per cent of enumeration districts at a p = 0.1 level. The differences are
not statistically significant between the top decile and the second or fourth
quartile, however. Nor are there strong differences between the quartiles
with each other or the city-wide average. The top decile has a higher mean
noise level (Table 6.6), but this level is only just above the quartile values.
The most deprived 10 per cent of EDs may therefore receive a slightly
unfair share of noise, but the disadvantage is very small. No generally positive relationship between deprivation and noise emerges from this part of
the analysis.

To investigate the association between deprivation and noise exposure
further, Figure 6.7 was produced which maps the top (most deprived)
Carstairs quartile EDs with the noise data. For cartographic purposes,
sixty dB(A) was again chosen as the threshold to differentiate lower and
higher noise areas. The most deprived areas with high noise levels are
shaded in the darkest tones. Deprived areas with noise levels below 60
dB(A) are presented in lighter tones.

Figure 6.7 depicts many EDs with high levels of deprivation outside the
city centre. Most of these do not experience particularly high noise exposure. Indeed, as was found for different ethnic groups, the map suggests that

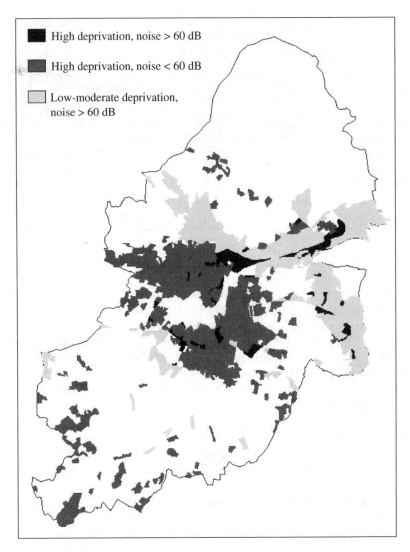

Figure 6.7   Location of deprived neighbourhoods (as noted by Carstairs score) and high noise areas

levels of noise pollution are quite variable between high deprivation areas. Moreover, there are sizeable areas of land near the M6 motorway and city airport that do not have significantly deprived populations according to the Carstairs index, but do experience high noise levels. These communities may be accepting noise nuisance in exchange for lower housing costs and better transport links. In the absence of the motorway and the airport, inner city exposures would predominate and the deprivation-related disparities in noise exposure would be greater than those observed here.

4. DISCUSSION

Little previous research has addressed the question of the differential impact of noise pollution upon the diverse communities residing in urban areas. Using a case study of the city of Birmingham, England, this study has sought to go some way to rectify this deficiency by assessing the distribution of exposure to noise from road traffic, rail and aircraft sources among a diverse urban population.

Our findings illustrate considerable diversity in both the sources and magnitude of noise exposure in Birmingham. For example, we found that spatial patterns of A-weighted environmental noise from road, rail and aircraft sources ranged from under 20 to over 80 decibels in the study area. Our results indicate that some inequalities may exist, but not strong ones. We found that blacks tended to experience higher noise exposure than other ethnic groups, particularly that generated during the daytime. Conversely, Indian and Pakistani communities appear to reside in areas with noise sound exposure slightly lower than that generally experienced by other ethnicities. We also found some indication of inequality in noise exposure associated with deprivation. In particular, estimated exposure to night-time noise from the combined sources was highest amongst the populations of the most deprived EDs.

A strong association exists between deprivation and ethnicity, making it difficult to discern the independent effects of the two factors. Similarly, there are many deprived areas without especially high noise levels, and many non-deprived areas with apparently high noise problems. To some communities, the benefits of living near good transport links (or associated urban services; Tiebout, 1956) may compensate for high noise pollution. Indeed, we found that some comparatively affluent populations receive high levels of aircraft and motorway noise. Similarly, environmental nuisance may sometimes be mitigated by lower housing costs (Oakes et al., 1996), or improved access to urban services and lower housing costs (Hite, 2000). Ballestero et al. (2003) tried to explicitly model the possible trade-offs between nuisance and benefits offered by various transport development options. However, there is not strong evidence that the marginal benefits received by individuals do reflect the trade-off between urban service levels and environmental nuisance or pollution (Bewley, 1981; Hoyt and Rosenthal, 1997; Hite, 2000). Moreover, unacceptable noise levels may lead to claims for compensation which have legitimacy in law, regardless of other benefits that may exist from living in noisy areas (Lake et al., 2000).

There are caveats to note regarding the data and methodology underlying our analysis. Our findings are based on a detailed analysis undertaken in a socially and environmentally diverse, yet singular, urban area. We chose to study Birmingham due to the interest generated by this diversity, coupled with availability of very high quality data in the city. From our analysis it is not possible to determine whether similar associations would be apparent elsewhere. However, our research has demonstrated the application of a methodological framework that could be readily applied in other contexts.

We used a detailed methodology to produce maps of community variations in noise exposure across Birmingham. However, the results of this analysis only provide estimates of average rather than individual population exposures. It is impossible to compare true noise exposures between populations without detailed and large surveys of individual exposure. Such exposures can be highly dependent on lifestyle factors such as occupation, or the amount of time spent outdoors. And while indoor and outdoor noise levels may be partially associated, some people may receive differential indoor and outdoor exposures due to the presence of significant indoor sources or noise insulation features in buildings. Moreover, our estimates are based on modelled rather than measured noise levels. They refer to values averaged over the entire day or night period, and hence give no indication of areas where noise may be especially elevated for relatively brief periods. Such sporadic but loud noise may be perceived as more annoying than constant low level emissions (NPL, 1998). The models also assume that all age, ethnic and deprivation groups are equally geographically distributed within each ED but this may not be the case.

Our analysis was only concerned with noise levels across the place of residence while, in reality, most people are not at home all day. Although we were able to differentiate between day and night-time noise levels, data on individual activity patterns was not available at a high enough spatial resolution to allow us to assess how the population composition changed during these periods. Ideally, we would like to know both where the residents (according to the census) of any particular area are to be found during day and night, weekdays and weekends. Noise exposure during commuting (Koushki et al., 2002) may also be significant. The use of relatively detailed information, varying by time of day or week for populations would be an innovative and welcome development in future noise exposure assessments.

The 1991 Census was the most recent information source available at the time of our analysis. It may be that the geographical distribution of the population groups in 1991 do not match the noise patterns generated for this project in 2001. However, while absolute noise levels may well have increased in the decade since the census, there is no reason to believe that the distribution of this noise would have changed significantly.

We chose particular population groups on the basis of vulnerability, mobility and likeliness of social prejudice. Of course, individual and cultural factors, as well as those influencing noise exposures, may affect noise tolerance (Heinonen-Guzejev et al., 2000). To assess disturbance, it is ultimately necessary to survey residents in areas with apparently elevated exposure to determine the perceived disturbance from ambient noise levels. This need is highlighted in a review commissioned by the UK Government. It discusses inconsistencies and controversy with regard to research on noise nuisance levels and the setting of public guidelines (NPL, 1998). The report cites the work of Fidell et al. (1991), who derived a dose-effect relationship between noise levels and nuisance response. The research highlighted considerable disparities in individual tolerances to exposure to loud noise; while 50 per cent of the studied population were 'highly annoyed' by levels above 80 dB, almost all reported noise levels above 90 dB to be highly annoying. Similar relationships have been derived for specific types of effect, such as sleep and activity disruption (Miedema and Vos, 1998). However, while these person-specific findings can be helpful in identifying threshold values for particular effects from specific sources, they are less useful for the creation of broad-based standards from all noise sources (NPL, 1998).

It was not our aim to develop a policy framework of remediation measures of environmental inequities. However, it is useful to consider the policy implications of our findings. The NPL report did not issue specific guidelines on exceedence thresholds. Instead it called for work to develop an agreed method to consider multiple source noises, cumulative noise exposure, and other risk factors or modifiers in order to assess overall health impacts. The report notes that ideally a framework should be provided for the practitioner or decision-maker to consistently and effectively assess the impact of noise, and which may be used to inform noise control decisions. We would argue that one aspect of this framework should be the possible disparate effects of any mitigation measures on the different segments of the community, as distinguished by ethnic or socio-economic character.

As noted previously, vehicle traffic and aircraft noise are the main sources of differentials in population noise exposure in Birmingham. Ongoing technical improvements in the aviation industry may reduce noise from the airport in the future. Similar advances should be possible with regard to both automobile design and road surface materials (Nelson and Phillips, 1997). However, increasing levels of car ownership and transport of freight by road can easily act to erode gains made from the introduction of technical innovations. Since the noise data were generated, some regeneration has occurred in the city centre, including new shopping centres and cultural facilities, and these attractions may have lead to increased traffic levels and related noise.

There is a need to consider whether biases against certain social groups exist within the mechanisms driving changes in land-use patterns, urbanisation and the development of transportation corridors. Davoudi and Atkinson (1999, p. 232) had little doubt that such biases exist, arguing that 'there has been a decline in attempts by planners to reduce spatial inequalities and social segregation. Indeed it may be argued that, since 1980, the planning system actually operated in a manner which intensified the situation of deprived groups and played a role in exacerbating the growth of poverty, social polarisation and inequality.' In Birmingham the situation is complex, and the contemporary distribution of ethnic, deprived groups within the city is a result of the interplay between personal preferences and forces operating in the public and private housing markets. Undoubtedly, discriminatory housing practices have been important. A significant proportion of ethnic groups in Birmingham live in the rented sector (Henderson and Karn, 1987), and there is historical evidence of widespread practices whereby landlords and housing agencies discriminated ethnic groups away from 'white' areas (Smith, 1977). Hence a racial steering process took place, accentuated by the preference of white members of Birmingham's population for suburban dwellings away from the city centre.

The previous housing policies of Birmingham City Council may also have contributed to the observed inequities in the city whereby families from ethnic minority groups tended to be allocated older local authority housing, and this type of housing stock is located towards the city centre in Birmingham. By the late 1960s, the concentration of West Indians and Asians in the inner and middle rings of Birmingham had become an issue of considerable concern to the City Council, particularly in terms of service provision in those areas (City of Birmingham, 1968). As a consequence, a policy of dispersing council tenants was adopted. However, the policy faced implementation problems, particularly associated with the unwillingness of different ethnic groups to cohabit neighbourhoods. Consequently, it resulted in a pepper-pot distribution of allocations that tended only to accentuate the development of predominantly ethnic neighbourhoods.

Factors such as economic restructuring across cities undoubtedly hold important social consequences for immigrant and impoverished populations. Such people, induced to migrate by changing economic circumstances, find growing ghettoisation, isolation, cultural antipathies and environmental degradation in their new settings (Laws, 1997). In Birmingham, the situation is complex, and the present day geography of ethnicity and poverty within the city is a result of the interplay between personal preferences and external forces operating in the public and private housing markets. It will be an important challenge for the city authorities and those involved with public housing to consider environmental equity issues in the future.

ACKNOWLEDGEMENTS

Three anonymous referees gave constructive and insightful comments on an earlier draft of this manuscript. We are indebted to staff at Birmingham City Council, who were involved with the original noise pollution mapping and supplied us with the data used in this analysis. We also thank Dr Iain Lake of UEA who helped coordinate data acquisition. 1991 Census data are crown copyright, ESRC purchase.

REFERENCES

Anthias, F. (1992), *Ethnicity, Class, Gender and Migration*, Aldershot: Avebury Publishers.
Babisch, W., H. Ising, J.E.J. Gallacher, P.M. Sweetnam and P.C. Elwood (1999), 'Traffic Noise and Cardiovascular Risk: The Caerphilly and Speedwell Studies, 10 Years Follow-up', *Epidemiology*, **10**, 4150–60.
Ballestero, E., J.M. Anton and C. Bielza (2003), 'Compromise-based Approach to Road Project Selection in Madrid Metropolitan Area', *Journal of the Operations Research Society of Japan*, **46**, 99–122.
Baum, A., J.P. Garofalo and A.M. Yali (1999), 'Socio-economic Status and Chronic Stress – Does Stress Account for SES Effects on Health?', *Annals of the New York Academy of Sciences*, **896**, 131–44.
Berglund, B. (1996), 'Aircraft Noise and Health', The Proceedings of the Second Airport Regions Conference (ARC), Vantaa, Finland, pp. 111–19.
Bewley, T.F. (1981), 'A Critique of Tiebout's Theory of Local Public Expenditures', *Econometrica*, **49**, 713–40.
Brainard, J.S., A.P. Jones, I.J. Bateman, A.A. Lovett and P.J. Fallon (2002), 'Modelling Environmental Equity: Access to Air Quality in Birmingham UK', *Environment and Planning A*, **34**, 695–716.
Brüjer and Kjær (undated), Product Data: Lima™ Environmental Noise Calculation and Mapping Software Version 4.0 – Types 7812 A/B/C, Nærum, Denmark: Brüjer and Kjær.
Carstairs, V. and R. Morris (1989), 'Deprivation, Mortality and Resource Allocation', *Community Medicine*, **11**, 364–72.
CEC (Commission of the European Communities) (1996), *Green Paper: Future Noise Policy*, Brussels, Com (96) 540 Final.
CEC (Commission of the European Communities) (1999), *Position Paper on EU Noise Indicators: Working Group on Noise Indicators*, Brussels: European Commission.

CEC (Commission of the European Communities) (2000), *Draft Directive Proposal for a Directive of the European Parliament and of the Council Relating to the Assessment and Management of Environmental Noise* (COM(468) Final – 2000/0194 (COD)), Brussels: European Commission.

City of Birmingham (1968), *Report to the General Purposes Committee on Immigration*, Birmingham: Birmingham City Council.

Connover, W.J. (1999), *Practical Nonparametric Statistics*, New York and Chichester: John Wiley and Sons.

Cutter, S. (1995), 'Race, Class and Environmental Justice', *Progress in Human Geography*, **19**, 111–22.

Davoudi, S. and R. Atkinson (1999), 'Social Exclusion and the British Planning System', *Planning Practice and Research*, **14**, 225–36.

DOE (Department of the Environment) (1995), *1991 Deprivation Index – a Review of Approaches and a Matrix of Results*, London: HMSO.

DETR (Department of the Environment, Transport and the Regions) (2000), *Indices of Deprivation 2000*, London: DETR.

DETR and MAFF (Department of the Environment, Transport and the Regions and Ministry of Agriculture, Food and Fisheries) (2000), *Our Countryside: The Future*, CM 4909, London: HMSO.

ESRI (Environmental Systems Research Institute Inc.) (1999), *Getting Started with Arc-Info*, Redlands, California: ESRI.

Evans, G.W. and L. Maxwell (1997), 'Chronic Noise Exposure and Reading Deficits – The Mediating Effects of Language Acquisition', *Environment and Behavior*, **29**, 638–56.

Evans, G.W., P. Lercher, M. Meis, H. Ising and W.W. Kofler (2001), 'Community Noise Exposure and Stress in Children', *Journal of the Acoustic Society of America*, **109**, 1023–7.

Fidell, S., D.S. Barber and T.J. Schultz (1991), 'Updating a Dosage Effect Relationship for the Prevalence of Annoyance Due to General Transportation Noise', *Journal of the Acoustic Society of America*, **89**, 221–33.

Fidell, S., M. Sneddon, K. Pearsons and R. Howe (2002), 'Insufficiency of an Environmental Sound's Power Spectrum as a Predictor of its Annoyance', *Noise Control Engineering*, **50**, 12–18.

Forest, R. and D. Gordon (1993), *People and Places: A 1991 Census Atlas of England*, University of Bristol: SAUS.

Haines, M.M., S.A. Stansfield, R.F. Job, B. Berglund and J. Head (2001), 'Chronic Aircraft Noise Exposure, Stress Responses, Mental Health and Cognitive Performance in School Children', *Psychology and Medicine*, **31**, 265–77.

Harding, A.K. and G.R. Holdren (1993), 'Environmental Equity and the Environmental Professional', *Environmental Science and Technology*, **27**, 1990–93.

Heinonen-Guzejev, M., H.S. Vuorinen, J. Kaprio, K. Heikkila, H. Mussalo-Rauhamaa and M. Koskenvuo (2000), 'Self-report of Transportation Noise Exposure, Annoyance and Noise Sensitivity in Relation to Noise Map Information', *Journal of Sound and Vibration*, **234**, 191–206.

Henderson, J. and V. Karn (1987), *Race, Class and State Housing: Inequality and the Allocation of Public Housing in Britain*, Aldershot: Gower Publishing.

Henrique, P., T. Zannin, F.B. Diniz, A. Calixto and W.A. Barbosa (2001), 'Environmental Noise Pollution in Residential Areas of the City of Curitiba', *Acustica*, **87**, 625–8.

Hinton, J. (2000), *A Report on the Production of Noise Maps of the City of Birmingham*, London: HMSO.

Hite, D. (2000), 'A Random Utility Model of Environmental Equity', *Growth and Change*, **31**, 38–56.

HM Treasury (2003), *The Green Book Appraisal and Evaluation in Central Government*, London: HMSO.

Hoffmann, B., B.P. Robra and E. Swart (2003), 'Social Inequality and Noise Pollution by Traffic in the Living Environment – An Analysis by the German Federal Health Survey', *Gesundheitswesen*, **65**, 393–401.

Hoyt, W.H. and S.S. Rosenthal (1997), 'Household Location and Tiebout: Do Families Sort According to Preferences for Locational Amenities?', *Journal of Urban Economics*, **42**, 159–78.

Jarman, B. (1984), 'Underprivileged Areas: Validation and Distribution of Scores', *British Medical Journal*, **289**, 1587–92.

Koushki, P.A., M.A. Ali, B.P. Chandrasekhar and M. Al-Sarawi (2002), 'Exposure to Noise Inside Transit Buses in Kuwait: Measurements and Passenger Attitudes', *Transport Reviews*, **22**, 295–308.

Kurra, S., M. Morimoto and Z.I. Maekawa (1999), 'Transportation Noise Annoyance – A Simulated-environment Study for Road, Railway and Aircraft Noises, Part 1: Overall Annoyance', *Journal of Sound and Vibration*, **220**, 251–78.

Lake, I.R., A.A. Lovett, I.J. Bateman and B.H. Day (2000), 'Improving Land Compensation Procedures via GIS and Hedonic Pricing', *Environment and Planning C*, **18**, 681–96.

Lavelle, M. (1994), 'Environmental Justice', in World Resources Institute, *The 1994 Information Please Environmental Almanac*, Boston MA: Houghton-Mifflin, pp. 234–65.

Laws, G. (1997), 'Globalization, Immigration, and Changing Social Relations in US Cities', *Annals of the American Academy of Political and Social Science*, **551**, 89–104.

Martin, D. (1996), 'An Assessment of Surface and Zonal Models of Population', *International Journal of GIS*, **10**, 973–89.

Miedema, H.M.E. and H. Vos (1998), 'Exposure-response Relationships for Transportation Noise', *Journal of the Acoustic Society of America*, **104**, 3432–45.

Miles, R. (1980), 'Class, Race, and Ethnicity: A Critique of Cox's Theory', *Ethnic and Racial Studies*, **3**, 130–43.

Nelson, P.M. and S.M. Phillips (1997), *Quieter Road Surfaces*, Crowthorne, Berkshire: Transport Research Laboratory Limited.

Ng, C.F. (2000), 'Effects of Building Construction Noise on Residents: A Quasi-experiment', *Journal of Environmental Psychology*, **20**, 375–85.

NPL (National Physical Laboratory) (1998), *Noise and Nuisance Policy: Health Effect Based Noise Assessments Methods: A Review and Feasibility Study*, London: HMSO.

Oakes, J.M., D.L. Anderton and A.B. Anderson (1996), 'A Longitudinal Analysis of Environmental Equity in Communities with Hazardous Waste Facilities', *Social Science Research*, **25**, 125–48.

Passchier-Vermeer, W. and W.F. Passchier (2000), 'Noise Exposure and Public Health', *Environmental Health Perspectives*, **108**, 123–31.

Perlin, S., R. Setzer, J. Creason and K. Sexton (1995), 'Distribution of Industrial Air Emissions by Income and Race in the United States: An Approach Using the Toxic Release Inventory', *Environmental Science and Technology*, **29**, 69–80.

Regecova, V. and E. Kellerova (1995), 'Effects of Urban Noise-pollution on Blood Pressure and Heart Rate in Preschool Children', *Journal of Hypertension*, **13**, 405–12.

Rex, J. (1970), *Race Relations in Sociological Theory*, London: Weidenfeld and Nicolson.

Rex, J. and S. Tomlinson (1979), *Colonial Immigrants in a British City*, London: Routledge.

Smith, D. (1977), *Racial Disadvantage in Britain*, Harmondsworth: Penguin.

Stansfield, S., M. Haines and B. Brown (2000), 'Noise and Health in the Urban Environment', *Reviews in Environmental Health*, **15**, 43–82.

Tiebout, C. (1956), 'A Pure Theory of Local Expenditures', *Journal of Political Economy*, **64**, 416–24.

Townsend, P., P. Phillimore and A. Beattie (1988), *Health and Deprivation: Inequality and the North*, London: Croom Helm.

7. Environmental equity and the siting of hazardous waste facilities in OECD countries

James T. Hamilton

1. INTRODUCTION

Measuring environmental equity entails as many challenges as defining it. Pearce (Chapter 2) reveals how economics can be used to explain and evaluate the distribution of environmental quality across socio-economic groups. This chapter looks at a particular type of environmental hazard, the siting of hazardous waste facilities, from the perspective of environmental equity. Section 1 reviews the nature of the data available, the methodologies of analysis used, and the comparability of studies within and across OECD countries. Section 2 reviews and discusses the studies of hazardous waste facilities and focuses in particular on the distribution of potential risks by demographic group, including different income groups. Section 3 discusses the determinants of disparities in exposure. Section 4 reviews the policy actions taken to address the disparities in the distribution of exposure to environmental impacts from hazardous waste facilities. Though the majority of the studies analysed in each section focus on the United States, the available research published in English from other OECD countries is included in each part of the analysis.

Conclusions about the distribution of risks from hazardous waste facilities depend in part on how these hazards are defined. Studies of facility siting, operation and clean-up indicate that the greatest hazards appear to be distributed in some countries as if the environment were a normal good. Risks are greater for those with lower incomes. During the 1980s and early 1990s, many of the policies dealing with hazardous waste focused on how to site new facilities and how to clean up older plants. The explicit incorporation of environmental equity concerns came in later policies. This means that while efforts to focus attention on the distribution of risks by income class have recently succeeded in generating new policies in some countries, it is too early to determine the actual efficacy of these policies.

2.   DATA AND METHODS IN HAZARDOUS WASTE STUDIES

Assessing how risks arising from hazardous waste facilities vary by demographic group involves defining risks, wastes, facilities and demographic groups. The definition of a 'facility' offers numerous options: plants that generate hazardous waste, facilities that treat, store or dispose (TSDs) of hazardous waste, or even sites now abandoned that once generated or managed these materials. The operation of the facility can be judged in the siting stage (for example, who will be exposed to new risks?), during its operation (for example, which facilities violate environmental regulations?) and during remediation (for example, how has environmental contamination been handled?) Risks can be characterised in a number of ways. Some studies use a simple indicator variable approach, where a facility either does or does not handle specific wastes, is or is not in violation of rules, or contains or does not contain a particular type of environmental contamination. Risks are also proxied by function of facility, so that plants are categorised by whether they generate and manage their own hazardous waste or whether they receive shipments from other facilities and process the waste for a fee. In countries with detailed data on waste management, plants are often grouped by the amount of hazardous waste stored or treated. More sophisticated assessments describe risks by tracking amounts of waste released to the environment, such as air emissions or underground injections. Databases that track reported and/or detected chemical spills at a facility are another source of risk information.

The advent of geographic information systems (GIS) technology has allowed risk assessments to be conducted at the facility level for some types of hazardous waste sites. This involves a number of judgements, starting with the radius of externalities generated by a plant. Modelling how far out risks extend requires assumptions about dispersion of air emissions or the likelihood of groundwater contamination and migration. Calculation of risks posed by groundwater contamination entails assumptions about ingestion, chemical toxicity and the population around a facility. Some analyses focus on determining the lifetime excess cancer risks arising from exposure to a particular chemical for an individual. Though these estimates are generally made with a standard set of assumptions, more sophisticated analyses do use Monte Carlo analysis (which uses multiple values for individual parameters) to generate a range of risks arising from exposure to a given chemical. Multiplying individual risk levels by likely populations exposed offers a way to characterise risks by estimating the likely number of cancer cases arising from the presence of a site. Non-cancer health effects are harder to quantify since an analyst often lacks slope factors that enable a given level of exposure to be translated into an estimated probability of experiencing a non-cancer effect. These non-cancer risks are more often expressed in terms of the degree to which exposure exceeds the level of exposure generally associated with no adverse health effects.

Defining the radius of risks around a plant is most often an exercise in modelling. Exposure routes are estimated and health effects are calculated by modelling. An alternative methodology used in some studies of hazardous waste sites draws on epidemiology. The health of residents living around a site is monitored and calculations are made to determine whether higher than expected levels of disease are noted. The multiple sources of risks make it difficult to isolate the separate effect of a plant's operation on residents, however. If residents close to a plant have lower incomes, for example, higher rates of illness may come from poor diet, inadequate health care, and exposure to toxics from a facility. The turnover in residents may also make it difficult to detect effects through epidemiology, since there may be a long lag time between the exposure and the onset of cancer. Another drawback of using a single radius to assess risks is that this will often ignore the transportation risks that arise in a community if wastes are transported to a facility by truck or rail. Defining risks by plant location also misses another set of stakeholders, those individuals who have an existence or bequest motive to value the environment surrounding a plant. Individuals may care about natural resource damages in an area even if they never visit it. People distant from a plant may also have a willingness to pay value that they attach to living in a just society. These existence values may become important in siting conflicts where residents may be willing to trade risks for jobs but others outside the community may wish to block the siting because of perceived injustice.

Studies of environmental equity also entail decisions about what reference points to use in analysing exposure and what demographic categories to use in comparing risks. Researchers may focus on a single site or a small group of facilities and analyse how demographics change as distance from the hazard increases. This type of approach uses the residents within a given radius as the population to study. Other studies take the city as the geographic unit to analyse and explore how city neighbourhoods that contain hazardous waste sites differ from those without. Some analyses view the country as a whole as the potential site of hazardous plants and compare how geographic units such as counties, cities, census tracts or even zip code areas compare for those with and without facilities. The demographic categories that researchers use to examine variations in exposure include race, income, education and age. Population density is also factored into comparisons of areas with and without hazardous waste facilities.

A snapshot of facility locations across a country can reveal what factors are correlated with risks, but more information is required to tell a causation story about how exposures arise. For example, if one observes a hazardous waste facility located in a neighbourhood with low-income residents, several scenarios could explain the association of income and pollution. A plant might locate in a given neighbourhood because of factor price considerations. The plant's negative externalities could lower housing prices, and low-income residents might move in because of their willingness (due to constrained budgets) to trade environmental quality for housing costs. Or a facility might target its location in a low-income neighbourhood because anticipated political opposition might be lower. To see the relation between pollutants and people, some studies analyse census data for a number of years to see the change over time in neighbourhood demographics and facility location. Other works use plans about the expansion of hazardous waste facilities to determine what types of areas are targeted by plants. Researchers also analyse how the current composition of an area affects the enforcement of environmental regulations at facilities and the clean-up of hazardous waste sites. These approaches, which go beyond a simple snapshot of exposure, allow researchers to explore the degree to which disparities in environmental quality are driven by differences in race, income, political power or education.

A final way to analyse the disposition of hazardous waste is to examine the flow of hazardous materials across borders. This analysis takes the country as the unit of observation and explores how trade in waste varies with differences in income levels and environmental policies across states. The literature reviewed here focuses on the analysis of environmental equity within a given country. Most of the detailed studies on hazardous waste facility siting and operation are conducted using data from the United States. For each section, however, I compare results from the United States with those studies published in English that examine the operation of plants in other North American countries, Europe and Asia.

Studies of environmental equity in the US have evolved rapidly with the decline in computing prices, increase in data availability, and growth in the sophistication of spatial analysis software. Research in the US in the early 1990s on hazardous waste facilities focused on the state or county as the unit of geographic analysis. Investigators next explored how risks varied by zip code area or census data tract. The ease of GIS analysis in the mid-1990s made explicit modelling of risks possible at plants and hazardous waste sites. In the next section I will review the environmental equity literature on hazardous waste facilities using the following strategy. I will not attempt to summarise every article on disparities in exposure to hazardous waste, since detailed research summaries are available in Bryant and Mohai

(1992), Bullard (1996), Mohai (1996), Foreman (1998) and Bowen (2002). Instead I will discuss in detail representative results from a subset of the most sophisticated analyses. I will divide the results based on the geographic unit of analysis adopted in the report, the degree to which the research focuses on exposure versus causation, and whether the analysis uses data from the United States versus other OECD countries. Overall, this review of the literature indicates that in general low-income residents face the higher risks from hazardous waste facilities.

3. LITERATURE REVIEW ON THE DISTRIBUTION OF HAZARDOUS WASTE FACILITIES

3.1 Exposures within the United States

The US Environmental Protection Agency (EPA) generally defines hazardous waste as waste that is ignitable, corrosive, reactive or toxic. Facilities that generate hazardous waste or manage hazardous waste through treatment, storage or disposal (TSDs) register with the EPA under the Resource Conservation and Recovery Act (RCRA) and often supply regulators with quantity data through shipping forms or regular surveys. Early research on environmental equity used information from the EPA's hazardous waste programme to examine how potential risks are distributed across demographic groups. In 1987 the Commission for Racial Justice issued a report that found that when communities with commercial hazardous waste facilities were compared with their surrounding county, the community with the facility had a higher minority percentage, lower household income, more sites contaminated by previous exposure to hazardous waste, lower house values, and higher levels of waste generated per person. The study sparked a debate still continuing in the United States over equity and the environment, a debate which involves concepts such as environmental racism, environmental equity, and environmental justice. In this subsection I review four types of studies generated by this debate: national studies of commercial TSDs, reports that focus primarily on hazardous waste sites in a given city, research that uses company self-reported pollution figures from the US Toxics Release Inventory, and information on environmental cleanups in the US Superfund Program. Box 7.1 contains a summary of studies dealing with the distribution of exposure to hazardous waste facilities.

Anderton et al. (1994a, b) use the census tract, a county subdivision they indicate averages about 4000 individuals, as the unit of observation in their national study of hazardous waste distribution. The authors first compare the 408 census tracts in 1980 with commercial hazardous waste facilities

BOX 7.1   EVIDENCE ON THE DISTRIBUTION
OF HAZARDOUS WASTE FACILITIES

Sample of US Studies

Anderton et al. (1994 a, b)
408 census tracts (around 4000 residents each) with commercial
TSDs had slightly higher percentage poverty than other tracts in
the nation in 1980. Within the top 25 cities, tracts with commercial
TSDs do not have statistically significant differences in poverty
percentage compared to other tracts in the areas. If one compares
408 tracts with 4239 tracts within 2.5 miles of a facility, tracts closer
to the plant have a higher percentage of workers in precision occupations and a lower percentage of families in poverty. If one compares the location and nearby tracts (4647) with other national
tracts, the tracts affected by TSDs have higher percentage of families below poverty (19 per cent versus 13 per cent) and lower
housing prices ($45 876 versus $60 291).

Atlas (2001a)
In 1997, 108 commercial TSDs (in sample if accounted for at least
0.2 per cent managed wastes). For half-mile ring around facility,
mean low-income population percentage (150 per cent of poverty
level) was 29.6 per cent, and 30.4 per cent for two-mile ring; nation-
wide 21.7 per cent. On a population weighted basis: 25.9 per cent
of residents within half a mile, and 30.4 per cent for two-mile ring
were low-income populations.

Hamilton (1995)
Of 207 zip codes with commercial hazardous waste facilities in
1987, 84 areas had plans for expansion in capacity. Mean percentage of families in poverty higher in zips targeted for expansion
(14 per cent versus 11 per cent) and average of median household
income was lower ($15 750 versus $17 060). Expansion planned
in areas with lower populations, more minorities, poorer populations and less politically active individuals.

Hamilton and Viscusi (1999)
For 1173 hazardous waste sites being cleaned up under the
Superfund programme, site-level mean household incomes lower
at the one-mile ring ($36 930) and four-mile ring ($37 690) than
national average ($38 450, 1990 census). At 61 per cent of sites,

mean household income lower in zero to one-mile ring than one to four-mile ring. Site-level mean house values for residents within one mile ($98 590) or within four miles ($103 900) were lower than the US mean ($112 660). Also calculated individual cancer risks, expected cancer cases, current land use at 150 sites. Found some evidence that minority groups account for a larger fraction of the estimated cancers than the national population, evidence that population weighted mean maximum individual cancer risk higher for minorities, and strong evidence that minorities bear larger current risks arising from present land uses at sites.

Studies in Other OECD Countries

Friends of the Earth (1999)
Examined postcode location of industrial plants registered under Integrated Pollution Control programme and household income distribution by postcode. Findings:

> All across England and Wales the poorest families (reporting average household income below £5000) are twice as likely to have a polluting factory close by than those with average household incomes over £60 000 . . . Overall, almost two-thirds of the most polluting industrial facilities are to be found in areas of below-average income.

Friends of the Earth (2001)
Analyses distribution of 156 plants in England emitting more than 1000 kilogrammes of carcinogens in 1999. Found '66 per cent of carcinogen emissions are in the most deprived 10 per cent of wards; 82 per cent of carcinogen emissions are in the most deprived 20 per cent of wards; only 8 per cent of carcinogen emissions are in the least deprived 50 per cent of wards'.

Jerrett et al. (1997)
Examine Canada's National Pollutant Release Inventory. Model county aggregate pollution as function of four variables: median income per household, average dwelling value, total population, manufacturing employment. All statistically significant, with income, population, and manufacturing positive, and housing negative.

Harrison and Antweiler (2002)
Using Canadian NPRI at facility level, 'generally do not find significant impacts of community income on either the current releases or changes in releases over time'.

(that is, privately-owned plants that receive waste from other firms) to the 31 595 other census tracts. They find no statistically significant differences in the mean percentage of black residents in the tracts with TSDs (14.54 black percentage) versus the other tracts (15.20 per cent). They did find statistically significant differences between the TSD tracts and others for the mean percentage of Hispanic residents (9.41 per cent versus 7.74 per cent), the mean percentage of families below the poverty line (14.50 per cent versus 13.94 per cent), mean value of housing stock ($47 120 versus $58 352), and mean percentage employed in precision occupations (38.60 per cent versus 30.61 per cent). When they restrict the analysis to tracts in the 25 largest metropolitan areas in the USA, they find, when comparing the 150 census tracts with commercial TSDs with the other 17 406 tracts, that those with TSDs had statistically significant differences in means for percentage black (12.23 per cent in tracts with TSDs versus 16.43 per cent without), percentage Hispanic (13.88 per cent versus 10.05 per cent), percentage employed in precision occupations (37.08 per cent versus 28.95 per cent), and mean value of housing stock ($55 980 versus $65 764). There was no statistically significant difference in the mean percentage of families below the poverty line (12.46 per cent versus 13.53 per cent). The authors also compared the 408 tracts with commercials TSDs to the immediately surrounding tracts, defined as 4239 tracts where at least 50 per cent of the area is within a 2.5-mile radius of the TSD tract. They find statistically significant differences in the mean percentage black (14.54 per cent for TSDs versus 25.70 per cent other), percentage of families below the poverty line (14.50 per cent versus 19.48 per cent), and percentage employed in precision occupations (38.60 per cent versus 35.41 per cent). There were no statistically significant differences in mean percentage Hispanic (9.41 per cent versus 10.79 per cent) or mean value of housing stock ($47 120 versus $45 754).

Anderton et al. go on to combine the tracts with commercial TSDs with the nearby tracts to form a new set of TSD and nearby tracts (N = 4647) to compare to the other tracts (27 356) in the nation. Here they find that the TSD and nearby tracts had statistically different means in terms of percentage black residents (24.72 per cent versus 13.57 per cent), Hispanic residents (10.67 per cent versus 7.27 per cent), percentage of families below the poverty line (19.04 per cent versus 13.08 per cent), percentage employed in precision occupations (35.69 per cent versus 29.87 per cent), and mean value of housing stock ($45 876 versus $60 291). One's assessment of environmental equity thus depends in part on how far one believes the negative externalities generated by plants extend. If the harms extend to nearby tracts, then those minority and low-income residents appear to bear higher risks than residents living in other areas. If the harms extend primarily to the census tract with the TSD, then poor families and Hispanic residents appear to be more exposed. Relative to nearby tracts, those that contain the actual TSD have lower percentages of black residents or poor families. A consistent pattern is the association of employment in industrial facilities (denoted by percentage employed in precision occupations) with the presence of commercial TSDs.

Atlas (2001a) makes several contributions to the analysis of national TSD locations. He reviews the evidence on the actual risks posed by current hazardous waste TSDs and concludes (p. 952) that:

> There is no evidence that TSDFs pose, much less have produced, meaningful harm to surrounding populations. The strict regulations under which they operate, the types and quantities of substances that they manage, the minimal potential exposure paths from them to people, and their compliance records all make the risks that they pose pale in comparison to other environmentally regulated facilities, such as those with air emissions.

He puts the waste handled by TSDs in perspective by noting that of 1.1 trillion pounds of hazardous waste generated in the USA in 1995, less than 2 per cent (21 billion pounds) were transported off-site for management. The focus on commercial hazardous waste facilities thus can miss the 98 per cent of waste that is managed on site by generators. The EPA estimated that in 1997 there were between 700 000 and 950 000 generators of hazardous waste and 2025 TSDs. Atlas focuses his analysis on those TSDs that received waste from other facilities and accounted for at least 0.2 per cent of the managed hazardous wastes tracked in surveys by the EPA. This results in a set of 97 TSDs in 1991, 104 in 1993, 101 in 1995, and 108 in 1997.

Using GIS technology and 1990 census data, Atlas determined there were 65 736 individuals living within a radius of half a mile of the TSDs he examined in 1991 and 1 690 505 within a two-mile radius. For 1997, there were 71 079 individuals living within half a mile of the TSDs in the sample and 1 494 231 within two miles. Looking at the mean of the percentage of minorities living within a given ring, Atlas found mean minority percentages of 27.0 for the half-mile ring and 28.4 for the two-mile ring in 1991, and 23.8 for the half-mile ring and 26.1 for the two-mile ring in 1997. These means are generally higher than the 24.2 minority percentage in the national population in the 1990 census. For low-income populations (defined as those with incomes less than 150 per cent of the poverty level), in 1991 the mean low-income population percentage for the half-mile ring was 23.8 per cent and 26.1 per cent for the two-mile ring; for 1997 it was 29.6 per cent for the half-mile ring and 30.4 per cent for the two-mile ring. These mean percentages are higher than the 21.7 per cent figure for the national low-income population. By looking at the mean percentages, one sees some evidence that TSDs operate in neighbourhoods with higher minority and low-income residents.

If one weights the means by population, a stronger association between race, income and exposure appears. Of the total populations within a given ring, for 1991 at the half-mile radius 29 per cent were minorities, and 44.1 per cent minorities at the two-mile ring. In 1997, the figures were 23.4 per cent minority population at the half-mile ring and 41.4 per cent at the two-mile ring. In terms of income, 25.3 per cent of the population living within half a mile of TSDs in 1991 were low-income and 27.9 per cent within the two-mile ring. In 1997, 25.9 per cent of the population within half a mile were low-income residents and 30.4 per cent for the two-mile ring. Atlas notes that, although on an aggregate basis minority and low-income residents have a greater likelihood of living near a TSD, this is because of the presence of a small subset of TSDs in heavily populated areas that have a high percentage of minority or low-income residents. He finds that half of the total minority population living within a given radius of a TSD are concentrated at between 2 per cent and 7 per cent of all TSDs. Analysing the data in another way, he generally finds a negative correlation between the minority population percentage in a ring and the amount of hazardous waste managed at the TSD. This negative correlation also held for the percentage of low-income population and the amount of waste generated.

The expansion plans of hazardous waste facilities provide another way of looking at potential exposure by demographic group. Hamilton (1995) uses a 1987 EPA national survey of TSD capacity plans and matches facility decisions with census data on the zip-code neighbourhood surrounding a plant. Of 207 zip codes with commercial hazardous waste facilities, net positive expansions in capacity were planned in 84 areas, against no net expansion in 123 zip codes. The difference of means tests comparing the areas targeted for expansion to the other zip codes was statistically significant for a number of demographic variables. The mean percentage of families in poverty was higher in zips targeted for expansion (14 per cent versus 11 per cent), the average of the median household incomes was lower ($15 750 versus $17 060), the mean non-white population percentage was higher (25 per cent versus 18 per cent), the average zip code population lower (18 700 versus 24 000), and the mean voter turn-out in the county (a proxy for collective action potential) was lower (51.8 versus 54.8). Commercial hazardous waste facilities were thus planning expansions in areas with lower populations, more minorities, poorer populations, and less politically active individuals.

Many authors analysing environmental equity have examined the populations surrounding hazardous waste sites slated for clean-up in the EPA's

Superfund Program (see Zimmerman, 1993; Hird, 1993, 1994; Anderton et al., 1997). Hamilton and Viscusi (1999) use 1990 census data to determine that overall 50.9 million people live within four miles of the 1173 sites they examine on the Superfund's National Priorities List. Overall, minorities account for 28.9 per cent of residents living within four miles of the sites, 35.1 per cent of on-site populations, and 24.2 per cent of the US population. The percentage of most non-white populations and minority groups as a whole declines as one moves farther from the sites, indicating that these groups bear more of the potential exposures from Superfund sites. Viewed in terms of probability of living within one mile of a site, minorities had a 0.05 probability compared to 0.03 for whites. At the four-mile range, a minority resident had a 0.24 probability of living in this area compared to a 0.20 probability for white residents. The probability of living within four miles was particularly high for Asians (0.31) and Hispanics (0.29), while the probability for blacks (0.21) is close to that for US residents as a whole (0.20).

Hamilton and Viscusi (1999) show the dangers of focusing on a single measure of environmental equity in assessing the distribution of exposure. For example, they find that the average white population percentage at Superfund sites is 85.6 per cent, which is larger than the national white percentage of 80.3 per cent. This comparison, however, is not weighted by population and misses the fact that sites with higher minority percentages tend to be more populous. Less than one-third of the sites (347 out of 1173) accounts for 89 per cent of the minority residents living within one mile of the National Priorities List (NPL) sites. Sites with 0 to 10 per cent minority populations in the one-mile ring around a site have a mean population of 3966, while sites with 40 to 50 per cent minorities in the one-mile ring have a mean population of 22 396. Thus on a site basis Superfund, problems are concentrated in neighbourhoods with lower minority population percentages than the national minority population percentages. The location of some sites in highly populous minority neighbourhoods, however, means that the overall set of residents surrounding Superfund sites are more likely to be minorities than one would predict on the basis of their national population percentages.

Looking at site level (that is, unweighted by population) means, Hamilton and Viscusi find that site-level mean household incomes are lower at the one-mile ring around Superfund sites ($36 930) and the four-mile ring ($37 690) than the mean household income for the nation as a whole ($38 450). Note that mean household income steadily increases as one moves from one-mile to four-mile to ten-mile rings. At 61 per cent of the sites, the mean household income is lower in the zero to one-mile ring than in the one to four-mile ring. The increase in income levels with distance from the site is consistent with the prediction that the environment is a normal economic good. The site-level mean house values for residents living within one mile ($98 590) or within four miles ($103 900) were lower house values than the US mean ($112 660). Such differences would be consistent with the location of NPL sites in industrial working-class neighbourhoods. The ring trend is generally consistent with the theory that the negative externalities associated with the sites will drive down housing values. At 62 per cent of the sites, the mean housing value is lower for the zero to one-mile ring than for the one to four-mile ring. For populations living within one mile, the percentage of residents with less than a high-school education (25.5 per cent) is higher than the national figure (24.8 per cent) and the percentage of residents with higher education levels (16.5 per cent) is lower than the national figure (20.3 per cent). If one weights the results by population or household, the ring trends generally remain evident. As distance from a site increases, the mean household income for the populations potentially exposed increases, the mean housing values increase, and the percentage of highly educated residents increases. However, on a population weighted basis, residents within four or ten miles of Superfund sites have higher mean household incomes and greater housing values than those for the United States as a whole. Such income differences may arise because of the high concentration of sites in urban areas, where both incomes and housing values are higher.

For a subset of 150 Superfund sites, Hamilton and Viscusi conducted risk assessments to determine the potential cancer and non-cancer risk arising over a 30-year period. They estimate that there would be 731 expected cancer cases arising from contamination at these sites. The breakdown by demographic group of the percentage of the 731 estimated cancer cases was minorities 43 per cent, whites 68 per cent, other race 9 per cent, Hispanic 22 per cent, black 4 per cent, Asian 18 per cent, and American Indian 1 per cent. If the site (that is, the Westinghouse site in Sunnyvale California) with the largest number (652) of cancers is dropped from the analysis, however, the results are reversed. Minorities would account for 16 per cent of the remaining cancer cases, while whites (including Hispanic whites) would account for 87 per cent of the expected cases. The conclusion that minorities bear a disproportionate share of the expected cancers must be tempered by the fact that this result is driven primarily by one extremely hazardous site. The EPA's risk assessments at NPL sites focus on individual lifetime excess cancer risks arising from contamination rather than the expected number of cancer cases. In terms of population weighted mean maximum individual cancer risks at sites, minorities face higher risks than white populations surrounding the 150 NPL sites in the sample. Minority populations within four miles of the sites face a mean risk of

0.142 versus 0.125 for the white population. The magnitude and distribution of the risk exposure again depends to a great extent on the Westinghouse site. If this extremely hazardous site in California is dropped from the analysis, the gap between mean risks faced by minorities (0.108) and whites (0.102) nearly disappears. These calculated risk levels are high in part because of the EPA's requirement that analyses use conservative parameter values for variables such as ingestion rate or exposure duration in the calculation of individual risks.

In the EPA's site-level risk assessment, the agency distinguishes between current risks and future risks, which are hypothetical risks that could arise if land use changed or if the likelihood of contamination changed through a mechanism such as the migration of a groundwater plume. Data on both potential exposures and estimated individual cancer levels indicate that minorities may be more likely to be exposed to current risks from Superfund sites. At sites where minorities account for more than 20 per cent of the population within one mile, the mean of the maximum current cumulative risks is 0.013, while the mean for sites where minority population percentages are 20 per cent or lower is 0.0022 (t = 1.7). Minorities make up a higher proportion of the population at sites where EPA survey data indicate current residential use. At the 165 sites where the EPA data indicate current residential land use, minorities constitute 45 per cent of the population living within a quarter mile. At the sites (N = 343) where there is no current use (for example, residential, industrial, commercial), minorities constitute 22 per cent of the populations living within a quarter mile.

The approach by Hamilton and Viscusi shows how multiple indicators can be used to assess national environmental equity outcomes when significant amounts of data are available (note that the EPA budgets over $1 million to study contamination and remediation options at each Superfund site). In terms of the estimated risks at Superfund sites, minority groups are disproportionately exposed. There is some evidence that minority groups account for a larger fraction of the estimated cancers than their national population percentage, evidence that the population weighted mean maximum cancer risks for minorities are higher than that for whites, and strong evidence that minorities bear larger current risks arising from present land uses at sites.

Though this review focuses on the siting of hazardous waste facilities, the fact that much hazardous waste is managed on-site by industrial facilities and the overlap between hazardous and toxic chemicals make research conducted on toxic emissions from plants relevant. Brooks and Sethi (1997) use information from the US EPA's Toxics Release Inventory (TRI), which contains annual self-reported figures by plants on their toxic releases and transfers. They construct an air pollution index at the zip code level that takes into account TRI emissions in and around the zip code and the toxicity of the chemicals released. Using 1990 census data for US zip codes, Brooks and Sethi find that minorities, renters, individuals with fewer years of schooling, and people with incomes below the poverty line are more highly exposed to toxic air emissions from TRI facilities. Sadd et al. (1999) use GIS technology to study TRI air releases in southern California. They find that census tracts in the metropolitan Los Angeles area that contain a facility releasing air emissions tracked in the TRI had many statistically significant differences from other Los Angeles census tracts. The TRI tracts had higher minority percentages, higher percentages of Latino residents, lower per capita incomes, lower household incomes, a higher percentage of industrial land, a higher percentage of the population employed in manu-facturing, and lower housing values. Chakraborty (2001) uses data on the amount and toxicity of hazardous chemicals stored at plants in a given area (Hillsborough County, Florida) to model the dangers arising from acute events such as the accidental releases of toxic chemicals. The study found a positive and statistically significant association between the degree of potential exposure to chemical accidents and the proportion of non-white residents and residents below the poverty line. These studies are typical of the growing environmental equity literature that uses TRI data (Cutter et al., 1996; Ringquist, 1997; Hockman and Morris, 1998; Arora and Cason, 1999; Daniels and Friedman, 1999) and/or tries to devise more direct indicators of risk exposure from air toxics (Graham et al., 1999; Morello-Frosch et al., 2001).

While recent studies often use GIS technology to link exposures with populations in one-mile rings around facilities or sites, Millimet and Slottje (2000) demonstrate the usefulness of broad assessments of equity. They develop environmental Gini coefficients to measure inequality across US states in per capita releases of different types of pollution. They find that states with relatively high proportions of women, minorities and children are 'over-represented in the upper tail of the per capita pollution distribu-tion' (p. 25) and point out that environmental policies that do not take this into account may end up increasing environmental inequity.

3.2   Exposures in Other OECD Countries

Detailed analysis of exposure to hazardous waste risks within a country requires data on waste facility location, quantities of waste handled, and the demographics of surrounding areas. The building blocks of this analy-sis are available in some OECD countries. A 1998 report by the OECD, for example, presents estimates of hazardous waste generation, export and import in the early 1990s. McDougall and Fonteyne (1999) examine waste management data from 11 European cities and find that quantitative comparisons were difficult because of variations in the definitions of waste. Prokop et al. (2000) survey the management of contaminated sites in 18 Western European countries, determine that 13 had started a systematic process to identify potentially contaminated industrial or waste disposal sites, and (while noting the wide variation in data quality) present estimates of potentially contaminated sites for most of these countries. Page (1997) describes the clean-up programmes for contaminated sites in the Netherlands, the United Kingdom and Central and Eastern Europe. Christiansen and Munck-Kampmann (2000) also note the difficulties of comparing hazardous waste generation data across OECD countries in Europe. A report by the Commission for Environmental Cooperation (1999) notes the problems associated with tracking the transborder shipments of hazardous waste between Canada, the United States and Mexico. Connor (1992) notes the problems associated with tracking the disposal of hazardous waste by Mexican facilities on the United States border. The Canadian Institute for Environmental Law and Policy (2000) uses information from Ontario's Hazardous Waste Manifest tracking system to provide a detailed description of the generation and shipment of waste in the province. Overall these studies indicate that data on hazardous waste generation or contamination at sites may be available in some OECD countries, but differences in definition of hazardous waste and lack of consistent reporting would make it difficult to compare environmental equity across countries in terms of hazardous waste exposure. As the use of Pollution Release and Transfer Registers (PRTRs) that record which facilities release particular types of pollution spreads across countries, more detailed environmental justice analyses will become available in the future. Harjula (2003) notes that countries with operating PRTRs include Australia, Canada, Ireland, Korea, Japan, the Netherlands, Norway, Mexico, the Slovak Republic, the United Kingdom and the United States. For more on PRTRs, see Johnson (2001).

There are analyses that focus on the calculation of risks at particular types of sites within a given country. Openshaw (1982) presents estimates of populations exposed and expected thyroid cancers around a set of nuclear plants in the UK. Walker et al. (2000) offer estimates of the number of residents exposed to major industrial accident hazards for a set of industrial facilities in Britain. Ragaini (1997) describes how site-level assessments can be conducted at contaminated waste sites in Central and Eastern Europe. Dolk et al. (1998) examine data from registries of congenital anomalies in five countries (Belgium, Denmark, France, Italy and the UK) to analyse at 21 hazardous waste landfills the impact of proximity to potential contamination and birth defects. The authors conclude that living within 3 km of a landfill was associated with an increased chance of congenital anomalies (after controlling for socio-economic status), that the risk decreases for residents more distant from a site, and that more research is needed to determine whether the association is caused by contamination at the sites.

The most complete studies on environmental equity from OECD countries other than the United States are from the United Kingdom and Canada (but see also the work by Kruize and Bouwman (2003) that analyses environmental justice outcomes in the Rijnmond region of the Netherlands using GIS technology). A 1999 report for Friends of the Earth used information on postcode location of industrial plants registered between 1992 and 1996 under the Integrated Pollution Control programme and household income distribution by postcode. The authors conclude (p. 1):

> All across England and Wales the poorest families (reporting average household income below £5,000) are twice as likely to have a polluting factory close by than those with average household incomes over £60,000 . . . Over ninety percent of London's most polluting factories are located in communities of below average income. London is just the most extreme example. A similar pattern is found throughout England and Wales. Overall, almost two-thirds of the most polluting industrial facilities are to be found in areas of below average income.

A 2001 report by Friends of the Earth examines the distribution of the 156 plants in England emitting more than 1000 kilogrammes of carcinogens in 1999. Using the government's Index of Multiple Deprivation that ranks wards by indicators such as health, income, education, employment, housing and access to services, the authors found that the polluting facilities were primarily located in the most deprived wards. They note (p. 1) that of the 11 400 tonnes of carcinogenic chemicals emitted in 1999 by the factories in the study: '66 per cent of carcinogen emissions are in the most deprived 10 per cent of wards; 82 per cent of carcinogen emissions are in the most deprived 20 per cent of wards; only 8 per cent of carcinogen emissions are in the least deprived 50 per cent of wards'.

Three studies focus on the exposure to particular air pollutants by demographic group. Brainard et al. (2002) use modelled emissions from vehicles and measured emissions from monitoring sites to estimate exposures to carbon monoxide (CO) and nitrogen dioxide (NO_2) in Birmingham, England. Using GIS technology and 1991 census data at the enumeration district level, the authors conclude that: 'both ethnicity and poverty are associated with pollutant emissions in Birmingham, with the highest emissions being recorded for populations with the highest proportions of minority ethnic groups and impoverished residents' (p. 707). Note that census forms did not provide an explicit question about income, so the authors use questions about occupation of the household head (for example, works in a professional and managerial position versus a partly skilled or unskilled position). McLeod et al. (2000) used monitoring data on sulphur dioxide, nitrogen dioxide and fine particulates to estimate exposures at the local authority district level in England and Wales in 1994. They find in regression analysis that pollution decreases as their social class index increases. Once they control for population density, however, they find that: 'the concentrations of all three air pollutants are higher in higher social class areas' (p. 82). Pye et al. (2001) use data on air pollution, GIS technology and demographic data at the ward level to study four areas: Greater Belfast in Northern Ireland, Cardiff City Council in Wales, Greater London and Birmingham City District in England. They conclude that (p. iii):

> Greater London, Birmingham City District and Greater Belfast appear to show a positive correlation between air pollution and social deprivation, with higher pollutant concentrations of NO_2 and PM_{10} found in areas exhibiting higher levels of deprivation. Cardiff City Council does not appear to show any significant relationship between air pollution and social deprivation.

Canada's National Pollutant Release Inventory, which contains self-reported data on facility emissions similar to those collected in the US Toxics Release Inventory programme, has generated research on environmental equity. Jerrett et al. (1997) aggregate 1993 facility air, water and land emissions to the county level in Ontario and model the county emissions total as a function of four county characteristics: median income per household, average dwelling value, total population, and manufacturing employment. They found that the coefficient on median income per household is positive and statistically significant (as are the population and manufacturing variables) and that the housing variable is negative and statistically significant. They note that the positive relation between income and pollution may arise if high wages are part of compensation for pollution exposure, and note that their use of interaction terms suggests that housing value is a 'more important explanator of the location of pollution emissions than income' (p. 1793). Harrison and Antweiler (2002) examine at the facility level on-site releases (that is, air, water, land and underground injection) and off-site transfers. Modelling the level and changes across time in releases and transfers as a function of plant and community characteristics, they 'generally do not find significant impacts of community income on either the current releases or changes in releases over time' (p. 22). They measure average community income based on census figures for the enumeration districts within a 50 km^2 area around each plant.

4. LITERATURE REVIEW OF THE DETERMINANTS OF EXPOSURE TO HAZARDOUS WASTE FACILITIES

4.1 Influences on Siting and Exposure in the United States

Studies that link pollution data with demographic information provide snapshots of who is exposed to potential risks from hazardous waste facilities at a given point in time. Research that focuses on the current location of plants and people, however, cannot determine causation. Because the externalities generated by facilities change the landscape and perceptions of an area, the actual operation of hazardous waste plants may change the desirability of living in an area, affect housing values, and lead to shifts in population characteristics. The key to isolating what determines exposures to risk is to gather information on the demographics of a community when the decisions of interest are taken. In this section I review a number of different approaches used in environmental research in the USA to examine what causes exposures to risk to vary across demographic groups. These approaches include analysing which communities are targeted by firms when they plan to expand hazardous waste capacity, how regulators respond to communities as they clean up hazardous waste sites, the impact of neighbourhood characteristics on the reduction of carcinogenic air emissions by facilities, the change in area demographics over time as plants locate, the response of housing prices to changes at waste sites, and the reported reactions of individuals when they are queried about siting hazardous facilities. Box 7.2 contains a summary of studies dealing with the determinants of exposure.

Hamilton (1993, 1995) examines the expansion plans for 1987–92 submitted by commercial hazardous waste facilities to the US EPA. The study of planned changes has the advantage of being prospective, so that the effects of the proposed expansion of the facilities are unlikely to be reflected in changes in neighbourhood demographics. The work tests three theories of why race may be associated with the location of hazardous waste facilities. In the pure discrimination model, owners of waste facilities may trade off profits for prejudice and gain utility from exposing minority communities to potential risks. According to standard interpretations of the Coase Theorem (1960), a polluting plant such as a hazardous waste facility may locate where it does the least damage, *ceteris paribus*, because this is where compensation is the least. The firm takes into account the physical and demographic characteristics of the surrounding neighbourhood which influence the 'cost' of its externalities: the number of people affected, incomes, property values, and residents' willingness to pay for

BOX 7.2 DETERMINANTS OF EXPOSURE TO HAZARDOUS WASTE FACILITIES

Sample of US Studies

Hamilton (1993, 1995)
In expansion plans of commercial hazardous waste facilities, zip code areas targeted for expansion had lower voting rates, fewer people and higher percentage of renters.

Hamilton (1999)
Uses Toxics Release Inventory data to analyse reduction in air carcinogen emissions between 1988 and 1991. Plants reduced emissions more the greater the expected cancers generated by the facility and the higher the voting rate around the plant, a proxy for collective action. Median household income and minority percentage in the zip code were not statistically significant.

Viscusi and Hamilton (1999)
At clean-up of hazardous waste sites, when cancer risks are low, more stringent clean-ups are chosen if surrounding residents are more politically active. The higher the average income in the one-mile ring around a site, less stringent the clean-up chosen (though this may be because wealthier residents can take more preventive measures on their own). Higher voter turn out at a site, greater cost per cancer case averted implied in EPA clean-up. Income level of residents had no impact on clean-up expenditure levels.

Been and Gupta (1997)
Examined census tract data for 1970, 1980, 1990. Found that when TSDs originally sited, they were not located in areas with high concentrations of the poor or African Americans. Locations did have a disproportionate share of Hispanics.

Lambert and Boerner (1997); Pastor et al. (2001)
Mixed evidence on whether TSDs sited in poor areas originally or whether poor residents moved to areas after plants were located.

Sample Studies in Other OECD Countries: Surveys and Case Studies

Frey and Oberholzer-Gee (1996, 1997); Frey et al. (1996)
Survey interviews in Switzerland in 1993 before referendum on nuclear waste repositories. Willingness to have repository located in a resident's community declined as perceived risks or negative economic impacts were larger. Compensation offers in the survey reduced willingness to accept the nuclear waste site. Compensation offers can crowd out a feeling of civic duty.

Lesbirel (1998)
Compensation facilitates siting of energy plants in Japan.

Fischer (1995)
Examines successful siting of hazardous waste treatment plant in Alberta, Canada. Ascribes approval to early local plebiscite on accepting siting, regional government's provision of funds for local community to hire experts to analyse plant impacts, government's provision of compensation for infrastructure costs and more experts, and formation of local committee to monitor plant operation.

Numerous case studies in Europe
Emphasise role of compensation, unemployment, public participation in explaining success/failure of siting.

---

environmental amenities. To the extent that low incomes and education are related to low willingness to pay for the environment and low expected damages in liability cases, and these variables are associated with race, profit-maximising firms may choose to locate in minority areas because compensation demands and expected liabilities from operation are lower there. In the actual process of siting facilities, compensation demands are typically voiced through the political process. Firms will care about the expressed opposition to siting, which depends on a combination of political activity and willingness to pay. If collective action is required to lead a firm to internalise its externalities, then differences in political participation may help explain why minority neighbourhoods would be less costly locations for polluting firms.

Of the 205 zip codes with commercial hazardous waste facilities operating in 1986, Hamilton finds that 83 had net planned expansions in processing capacity. He uses a logit model to predict where firms will decide to expand which includes community demographic variables and market variables relating to processing capacity surplus in the county and state importation and generation of hazardous waste. The results demonstrate that firms care about compensation and political involvement. Consistent with the collective action theory, voter turn-out in the county associated with the zip code is negative and statistically significant. The higher the county voter turn-out, the less likely that a zip code neighbourhood will be targeted for additional capacity. The Coasean compensation variables generally have the expected sign. The number of people in the zip code and the percentage of renters are both statistically significant. The more people in the zip code (a factor in compensation demands and liability calculations), the less likely a firm is to expand in the area. The higher the percentage of renters, the more likely firms are to expand capacity, in part because compensation may be lower where residents have fewer sunk costs associated with living in a particular area. The higher the average house price or percentage of adults with a high school education, the less likely the area would be chosen as a site for expansion (though these effects are not statistically significant). The higher the income in the zip code, the greater the probability of expansion. This result, which is statistically significant in one of two expansion specifications, may be due to the fact that areas with expanding waste capacity are areas with expanding industry and higher incomes. The non-white population figure is not statistically significant. Though zip codes with planned expansions do have a higher non-white population percentage, once one controls for other community characteristics, race is not a predictor of where firms target expansions.

Decisions by firms to reduce their toxic emissions offer another avenue to examine how differences in risks arise across demographic groups. Hamilton (1999) examines at the facility level the change in air releases between 1988 and 1991 of 16 carcinogens. For a set of 2788 plants tracked in the Toxics Release Inventory, he uses GIS technology to calculate the expected cancer risks arising around a plant and the nature of the community bearing these risks. He finds that controlling for the level of air pollution emitted in 1988, a facility with a higher expected number of deaths due to the release of the carcinogen had greater reductions in emissions between 1988 and 1991. In other words, the most hazardous plants in terms of human carcinogenic risks reduced their emissions more. As voter turn-out in the area surrounding a facility increased, emissions declined. This indicates that for a given level of pollution, facilities may be more likely to engage in reductions if they believe that the affected parties are likely to engage in collective action to force firms to internalise the cost of their pollution. The impact of collective action is evident even after one controls for other socio-economic measures, such as median household income, percentage of college graduates, or percentage vote for the Republican presidential candidate in 1988. None of the community variables other than voting was consistently statistically significant. Median household income and percentage of the zip code population that was black were not statistically significant. While plants do take into account the nature of who bears the risks of their contaminants, it is the likelihood that residents will engage in collective action and thereby force plants to consider the costs of their pollutants that affects plant decision-making.

A growing literature (see Zimmerman, 1993; Hird, 1994; Gupta et al., 1996, Hamilton and Viscusi, 1999; Atlas, 2001b) examines how the US EPA responds to hazardous waste sites depending on the nature of the surrounding community. Viscusi and Hamilton (1999) provide a detailed analysis using risk assessments conducted at a sample of 150 Superfund sites. They analyse in regression analyses the target risk levels that regulators choose to remain after clean-ups and the cost per cancer case avoided implied by the remediation decisions. Looking first at the risk pathway targets chosen, they divide the risks into two sets – those where the original risk posed by a given pathway of exposure to a chemical was greater than or equal to 10^{-4} (that is, high-risk pathways) and those where the unremediated risk was less than 10^{-4} (that is, low-risk pathways). The higher the voter turn-out in an area, *ceteris paribus*, the more stringent the target risk chosen to remain after remediation when the original risks are low. When risks are high, political activity has no effect on clean-up standards. It is only when risks are low that political activity matters. The higher the average income level in the one-mile ring around a site, the less stringent the risk target that will be chosen. This result may be because regulators believe wealthier residents are less likely to be exposed as assumed in risk assessments (for example, groundwater exposures assume well-water consumption, while wealthier residents may be connected to public systems). A higher minority percentage in the area leads to the selection of a more stringent risk target. This could be evidence that regulators were concerned with environmental equity or might believe that calculated risks were more likely to arise in minority communities (for example, if minorities were more likely to consume contaminated groundwater). In terms of the cost per cancer case avoided at Superfund sites, Viscusi and Hamilton find that variables such as the minority population percentage within a one-mile ring of a site or the mean income of residents within one mile had no impact on the clean-up expenditures chosen by the EPA. The higher the voter turn-out in the county, however, the greater the cost per cancer averted implied by the EPA's clean-up decision. Clean-ups at hazardous waste sites appear in part to follow a 'fire-alarm' process (McCubbins and Schwarz, 1984), where regulators respond to the likelihood that residents will complain about the nature of site remediation.

Another explanation for demographic variations in exposure to hazardous waste facilities is that facilities may generate negative externalities that lower surrounding housing prices. Lower housing prices in turn may attract lower-income residents, whose budget constraints limit their ability to pay for a clean and safe environment. Economists have used a variety of hedonic methods to see how housing prices react to the presence of 'locally undesirable land uses' (see Nelson et al., 1992; Kiel and McClain, 1995; Hite, 2000). Farber (1998) summarises the results of 25 studies on the impact of undesirable facilities on housing prices. He finds for ten studies of the impact of hazardous waste or Superfund sites that housing prices do increase with distance from these sites. For three studies that estimated the housing price impacts after a site had been placed on the Superfund's NPL list, Farber finds a consistent effect that housing prices increased by approximately $3500 (in 1993 values) per mile from the site. Gayer et al. (2000) find that residents' willingness to pay to avoid risks actually declines after the release of remedial investigation studies at Superfund sites, suggesting that the information in the EPA studies lowers the perceived risks at sites. Gayer (2000) uses estimates of cancer risks at a set of Superfund sites and analyses what housing prices imply about the marginal valuation of risk reduction in different neighbourhoods. He finds that the price–risk trade-off is greater for households in areas with residents with higher education and residents with higher incomes. The price–risk trade-off implied in housing sale data is lower in neighbourhoods with a higher proportion of non-white residents.

Research about the current patterns of exposure to hazardous waste facilities has generated significant debate and controversy (see Been, 1995; Mohai, 1995; Yandle and Burton, 1996; Boer et al., 1997; Liu, 1997; Boyce et al., 1999). One of the most direct ways to analyse exposure causation is to examine the nature of communities at the time of facility siting. Been (1994) examined four hazardous waste landfills studied in a 1983 General Accounting Office environmental report and concluded 'at the time the facilities were sited . . . the host communities were home to a considerably larger percentage of African-Americans and were somewhat poorer than other communities within the host states. The analysis therefore suggests that the siting process had a disproportionate effect on the poor and people of color.' In examining ten landfills and incinerators first studied by Robert Bullard (1983, 1990), Been found that when they were originally sited, five of the ten facilities were in areas with higher percentages of minority residents than the surrounding county and that three out of ten were in areas with higher poverty rates. By 1990 the neighbourhoods had changed so that nine out of ten had greater than average proportions of minorities and seven out of ten had relatively higher poverty rates. Been and Gupta (1997) conducted a national study of 544 communities that in 1994 contained active commercial hazardous waste TSDs. Using census data at the tract level for 1970, 1980 and 1990, they examined the nature of neighbourhoods at the time sitings occurred and the changes in demographics for these areas across time. They found (p. 9):

> no substantial evidence that the facilities that began operating between 1970 and 1990 were sited in areas that were disproportionately African American. Nor did we find any evidence that these facilities were sited in areas with high concentrations of the poor; indeed, the evidence indicates that poverty is negatively correlated with sitings. We did find evidence that the facilities were sited in areas that were disproportionately Hispanic at the time of siting. The analysis produced little evidence that the siting of a facility was followed by substantial changes in a neighbourhood's socio-economic status or racial and ethnic composition.

Environmental equity studies focused on causation have also begun to look at historical relationships between facilities and neighbourhoods within a given city. Baden and Coursey (2002) examine the distribution of hazardous facilities and waste sites across time in Chicago. By matching facility siting dates with community demographic data (often at the census tract level), they determine that (p. 87):

> past waste-generating activities tended to be in less populous, lower income areas with good access to highways and waterways. Present waste sites tend to be located in less populous, wealthier neighbourhoods, with convenient access to transportation infrastructure. There is no good evidence that African Americans of any income class are more likely to live in areas with more concentrated waste sites in the city of Chicago, or that they have been targeted to be disproportionately exposed to more hazardous waste. Several of the 1990 regressions found that the percentage Hispanic in a community was significant in describing the presence of a site in, or near, a community.

Lambert and Boerner (1997) examine changes over time in the city of St Louis for census tracts with hazardous facilities or waste sites. They find that between 1970 and 1990 the percentage of residents below the poverty line and the percentage of minority residents increased disproportionately in neighbourhoods with TSDs, hazardous waste sites, and non-hazardous landfills and incinerators. They determine that mean real family incomes fell in these tracts (while the mean for St Louis as a whole was rising) and that median real housing values increased at a less rapid pace around the hazardous sites. Pastor et al. (2001) examine the historical siting patterns of high-capacity TSDs in Los Angeles by matching siting dates with census tract data from 1970 through 1990. They find more evidence to support disproportionate exposure of minorities at the time of siting than a later increase of minorities once a TSD is located in an area.

A final way to analyse why hazardous waste facilities are distributed in current patterns is to examine the results of surveys on siting, risk perception and compensation (see Bord and O'Connor, 1992, Groothuis and Miller, 1994; Rogers, 1997; Halstead et al., 1999). A significant literature exists on how individuals in surveys differ in their expressed support for the siting of hypothetical or actual NIMBY (not in my backyard) facilities. Summarising the role of potential compensation in facility siting, Oberholzer-Gee and Kunreuther (1999) note that compensation appears to increase support for siting of facilities such as prisons or airports but has little impact on prospective acceptance of projects perceived as highly risky such as incinerators or nuclear waste repositories; they note that for projects perceived as very risky, compensation can in some cases reduce support for siting if it is perceived as a bribe. Smith and Kunreuther (1999) estimated in a study of compensation and mitigation for four hypothetical facilities that there is a core of respondents who view a siting as unacceptable even under a wide range of compensation/mitigation. They estimated this core of opponents to be 11.7 per cent for a prison siting, 13.4 per cent for a municipal landfill, 26.9 per cent for a hazardous waste incinerator and 40.2 per cent for a disposal repository for high-level radioactive waste. Mitchell and Carson (1986) report that to reach a cumulative percentage of 50 per cent of respondents accepting a facility, a large factory or coal plant would have to be five miles from residents but that a hazardous waste facility would not reach this level of acceptance until it was nearly 50 miles from residents. Mansfield et al. (2001) find that those who are more likely to oppose nuisance facilities are also more likely to vote or participate in other forms of collective action, which suggests that political siting processes may engender more participation from opponents. Focusing on the role of trust in siting, Groothuis and Miller (1997) find that younger respondents and those with lower incomes express more distrust of waste disposal firms and the government, that people who distrust the media, government and business express a higher estimate of the risks of hazardous waste disposal facilities, and that distrust affects the willingness to accept a facility siting. Swallow et al. (1994) show the importance of using contingent-valuation surveys to estimate different willingness to pay measures in siting disputes for different demographic groups (for example, on the basis of age or income). Much of the research on siting attitudes comes from surveys relating to the siting of a high-level nuclear waste repository in Nevada (see Kunreuther and Easterling, 1990, 1996; Easterling, 1992; Dunlap et al., 1993). This research shows residents more willing to support a facility the lower the perceived risks to future generations, the better the mitigation efforts taken to limit risks from a facility, and the more residents view the siting as the best policy outcome.

4.2   Influences on Siting and Exposure in Other OECD Countries

Most of the literature that explains siting patterns for hazardous waste facilities in OECD countries other than the USA focuses on individual-level survey data or case studies of particular siting mechanisms. A series of papers focus on survey interviews done in Switzerland in 1993 a week before a referendum on nuclear waste repositories (see Frey and Oberholzer-Gee, 1996, 1997; Frey et al., 1996). The researchers find the expected results that willingness to have a nuclear waste repository located in a resident's community declined as perceived risks or negative economic impacts were larger. The authors determine, however, that compensation offers reduce the willingness to accept a nuclear waste site. They report (1997, p. 749): 'While 50.8 per cent of the respondents agreed to accept the nuclear waste repository without compensation, the level of acceptance dropped to 24.6 per cent when compensation was offered'. They determine that compensation reduces acceptance not because it signals more risk but because it crowds out a feeling of civic duty. Once monetary rewards are introduced, respondents are less likely to view siting acceptance as related to civic duty and less likely to accept the facility. Respondents viewed compensation as bribes to be rejected (though note that rejecting compensation in votes or surveys is relatively costless, compared to rejected compensation in actual market settings). If a proposed siting process was seen as fair by respondents, they were more likely to accept the facility. Research by Renn et al. (1996) on siting of a Swiss landfill showed via focus groups that notions of fair siting involved considerations of the amount of waste generated in an area, whether an area was already exposed to hazardous facility, and the need to prevent unacceptable levels of risk.

   A different assessment emerges in research on the role of compensation in siting in Japan. Lesbirel (1998) examines the siting of energy plants in Japan and finds that compensation packages facilitated the siting of these facilities. Lesbirel notes that the Ministry of International Trade and Industry (MITI) has set up structures to facilitate bargaining between utilities and community interests, that adjacent areas to locations are involved in negotiations, that risk mitigation strategies are pursued, and that powerful fishing co-operatives are able to strike bargains with prospective plants. Broadbent (1998) examines the general impact of protest on environmental politics in Japan and finds that national party politics, bureaucratic constraints, the influence of big business interests and (at times) local protest influenced the location of polluting plants and landfills. Kleinhesselink and Rosa (1994) use survey evidence from college students in the United States and Japan to demonstrate the similarities in risk perception across the two countries. In both countries perceptions of the risks from particular sources are governed by characteristics such as the degree the risk is seen as involuntary or infrequent. They note that the Japanese respondents: 'rated the technological risks associated with nuclear power as older and risks of which they had individual or scientific knowledge, whereas US students rated these as newer and risks for which they had significantly less individual or scientific knowledge' (p. 116).

Studies of waste siting in Canada stress the role of participation. Fischer (1995) discusses the successful siting of a hazardous waste treatment plant in Alberta and ascribes the final approval to the high level of public participation designed into the process, including an early local plebiscite on accepting the siting, the regional government's provision of funds for the local community to hire experts to help analyse and discuss the plant's impacts, the government's provision of funds once the plant was sited to compensate for infrastructure costs and retain more experts, and the formation of a local committee to advise the facility on community concerns about its operation and review monitoring data. Huitema (1998) reviews studies of hazardous waste disposal facilities in Canada and the USA and concludes that voluntary approaches mixed with compensation may be the most effective, though he notes that few new facilities have actually been sited overall, that capacity is underutilised at the sites, that communities outside the host community may be left out of the process, and that it is difficult to generate high levels of sustained public participation. Baxter et al. (1999) analyse landfill siting in Canada and note that environmental suitability and community control played much larger roles in the siting procedures than equity considerations, that considerations of fair procedure were often crowded out, and that the importance attached to public participation meant that some 'residents were successful in their opposition to the siting process in part because they had the financial and educational means to mount sophisticated opposition' (p. 520).

Explanations for siting difficulties are also the topic of research in many European countries. Linnerooth-Bayer and Fitzgerald (1995) found in a survey of 111 residents of Lower Austria that there are wide variations in what the concepts of fairness in siting are, with support for hierarchical, market and lottery approaches among some segments of the population. They note (p. 6):

> When the respondents were asked if they would disregard all features of the host communities (whether they are already burdened by other industrial hazards, whether they are poor and vulnerable, whether they have benefited from industrial production, etc.), if experts reported that the proposed site was technically superior or posed the lowest overall risk to the public, 53 per cent of the respondents answered positively (and 70 per cent of the industrial experts). This shows remarkable deference to expert authority and an acceptance of Austrian hierarchical political procedures.

Schneider and Renn (1999) describe how a structured discussion process involving ten groups of citizens was used to elicit rankings of sites for waste facilities in the Northern Black Forest Region of Germany, though the political process ultimately did not draw upon the reports written. Gaussier (2001) analyses the actual location of garbage dumps in the Provence-Alpes-Côte d'Azur region of France and demonstrates the influence of transportation costs and NIMBY forces on the spatial distribution of dumps. Sjoberg et al. (1999) describe how debates in Sweden at the municipal level over the desirability of initiating a feasibility study in a given municipality for siting a national high-level nuclear waste repository often focus on the benefits and costs of the repository rather than of the study. In terms of jobs brought by a future repository, they note (p. 5):

> unemployment, while certainly unpleasant, is not economically disastrous in Sweden. The social welfare benefits are generous . . . The jobs promised at a repository are in a rather distant future and may not be, in themselves, very attractive to the young people of today who would be the ones to get them.

Vari (1996) conducted 24 interviews with individuals involved in a disputed siting in Hungary of a low-level radioactive waste facility and found that perceptions of fairness depended in part on questions about whether those who generate waste bear its risks and a desire to avoid targeting of those who are economically or socially disadvantaged. Snary (2002) finds that the public participation process involved in the potential siting of a waste-to-energy incinerator in Portsmouth, Hampshire, UK was flawed in part because participants were directed to focus on technical questions rather than on broader waste management issues. Coenen (1998) describes how the process of participation in 'green planning' at the national and province level in the Netherlands can lead to improved decision-making about pollution because of communication and learning sparked by the planning process.

5. SITING POLICIES AND ENVIRONMENTAL EQUITY

5.1 General Siting Policies for Hazardous Waste Facilities in the United States

The difficulties associated with siting commercial hazardous waste TSDs in the United States has generated large literatures on theories of siting noxious facilities (Sullivan, 1990, 1992; Gregory et al., 1991; Swallow et al., 1992; O'Sullivan, 1993; Ingberman, 1995; Fredriksson, 2000; Quah and Tan, 1998; Lejano and Davos, 2002; Minehart and Neeman, 2002; Waehrer, 2003) and on lessons learned from attempts to locate NIMBY projects (O'Hare and Sanderson, 1993; Gerrard, 1994, 1997; Wheeler, 1994; Miranda et al., 2000; Richman, 2001). Understanding the potential role for equity concerns to play in siting policies entails an understanding of how siting practices and the siting literature evolved in the USA and the limitations evident in siting procedures.

Facilities that process hazardous waste attracted growing attention during the 1980s from environmentalists, state legislators and academics. Incidents of chemical contamination such as the highly publicised unravelling of a dump site in Love Canal, New York and the abandonment of an entire town because of dioxin exposure in Times Beach, Missouri raised public awareness of dangers posed by hazardous waste and increased scrutiny of facilities dealing with such waste. Legislation such as the Resource Conservation and Recovery Act of 1976, which established cradle to grave monitoring of hazardous wastes, and the Comprehensive Environmental Response, Compensation, and Liability Act of 1980, which established the Superfund ex post liability system for cleaning up waste sites, marked the beginning of an era of more stringent regulation. Attempts to site new facilities to treat, store or dispose of hazardous wastes (TSDs), however, were often halted by public opposition. Public hearings during the permitting process for these facilities became a forum for debate over potential adverse impacts: groundwater contamination from accidental releases; airborne contamination from spills and incineration of wastes; noise and odours from plant operation and traffic; and threats to neighbourhood property values. A survey of state hazardous waste officials in 1987 noted that nearly half of the commercial facilities that were rejected were stopped by public opposition (Mason, 1989). The gridlock in siting led to continual revision of state laws governing location of such 'locally undesirable land uses' (LULUs). By 1988, 41 states had enacted specific laws dealing with the siting of hazardous waste facilities (National Governors' Association, 1989). During the same period, legal scholars, economists and political scientists produced models aimed at breaking the siting impasse and easing the location of facilities that entailed concentrated costs and dispersed benefits (see Morell and Magorian, 1982; O'Hare et al., 1983).

The Coase Theorem offers a framework for understanding both the details of state siting laws and the design of academic siting models. Coase focused on the relationship between property rights and externalities in his seminal 1960 article 'The Problem of Social Cost' (often referred to as Coase II, to distinguish it from an earlier influential 1937 piece, 'The Nature of the Firm'; hereafter referred to as Coase I). He noted that in a world of zero transaction costs, property rights would be fully defined, contracts could be costlessly negotiated and enforced, and trades would be easily consummated so that resources would flow to their highest valued use. In this model, the definition of property rights leads to a market for pollution. If individuals in a community enjoyed the right to be free from pollution, then a firm such as a hazardous waste facility that generated externalities would consider the impact of its location on communities. The firm would end up locating, *ceteris paribus*, where its environmental damage would be the least because that is where the compensation for pollution it would have to pay to affected communities would be the lowest. The market for pollution rights, where either individuals enjoy the right to be free from pollution and must be compensated by firms, or firms possess the right to pollute and must be paid by affected neighbours to restrict their pollution, creates a market for the location of polluting facilities.

State laws adopted during the 1980s that dealt with siting hazardous waste facilities were often viewed as establishing markets for locating these facilities. Though the statutes varied in format, the basic provisions involved defining the specific property rights of facility operators, affected communities, and state and local governments. The statutes were interpreted as facilitating negotiations in a world where transaction costs did matter. Explicit compensation mechanisms were established, so that a locality targeted for a facility would be able to extract some compensation for hosting a facility. Technical assistance grants were provided to communities so that they could conduct their own studies to determine risks posed by a facility. Public hearings were designed to educate potential neighbours, who would then negotiate on the basis of information about particular operations at the proposed facility. Some states even considered the spillover effects on communities close to the community with the facility, so that some compensation would be paid to areas which did not enjoy the larger compensation package that came with hosting a facility but did bear some additional risk because of the transportation of waste through their area.

Academic models of the siting process generally recommended making the market elements of siting mechanisms even more explicit. Many proposals for breaking the NIMBY gridlock in siting unwanted facilities involved auctions in which communities submitted bids to receive compensation for hosting a hazardous waste facility. Though the formats of the proposed auctions differed, economists and political scientists who made these recommendations generally focused on the siting problem as an exercise in demand revelation, that is, in determining the demand for environmental amenities across communities. The community was generally the unit of observation, though sometimes individual preferences were also aggregated within each community through procedures such as referendums on siting compensation. The models stressed that if a community's rights to compensation were well defined and firms had to pay compensation through a system such as an auction for the right to locate in a particular community, then a firm could end up choosing to locate where citizens place a lower value on the environmental risks posed by the facility's operation. In the models, clearer property rights and an auction system would lead to the Coasian solution.

Despite the attention devoted by legislators and scholars to resolving locational conflicts, few commercial hazardous waste facilities were sited under the newly revised laws. Models and statutes that view the location of a hazardous waste facility as an exercise in auctioning a facility among communities focus on one strand of the law and economics literature (Coase II) while ignoring other insights from this literature. Specifically, lessons from at least four separate literatures are useful in understanding the current regime of US siting laws: Coase's early work on the firm versus the market (Coase I); the theories of collective action; evidence on the psychology and political economy of risk perception; and the positive political theory of institutions. These disparate literatures in law, economics and political science offer explanations of why previous understandings of siting statutes and previous versions of siting models are inadequate and, in part, unlikely to succeed as long as they are based primarily on establishing a 'market' for locally noxious facilities.

One key to understanding the design of the current siting literature is to see how the evolution of siting statutes parallels the discussion of institutional design in Coase I. In 'The Nature of the Firm', Coase (1937) determined that whether a decision would be made within a firm or through the marketplace depended on the relative transaction costs of using the particular mode of operation. If the centralised decision-making power that constitutes a firm can reach a decision more easily because of transaction costs of market exchange, then the production step will take place within the firm. The evolution of decision-making power about siting hazardous waste facilities shows a shift from market to firm, a shift associated with a rise in transaction costs. In the era of less intense scrutiny of hazardous wastes, firms that treated hazardous substances enjoyed the right to locate freely within the constraints imposed by local zoning ordinances. As local opposition to such facilities increased with heightened perceptions of hazards, however, the operation of the 'market' for location broke down as protests, zoning battles and litigation slowed the siting of hazardous waste facilities. These siting battles led state legislatures in the United States to clarify and redefine property rights involving facility location. Some of the states adopted provisions which did attempt to establish a market in siting through better definition of the rights of the parties involved, a solution in the spirit of Coase II. But some legislatures opted instead to create a decision-making process similar to that of a firm to site LULUs such as hazardous waste facilities. Ultimate authority to site a facility was given to the state, or the state was given the right to override local attempts to block a facility. At times, this use of centralised decision-making was supplemented by a process that would elicit preferences within communities about proposed siting, much like firms may attempt to use market-like mechanisms internally to establish the appropriate transfer prices in production decisions. Whether the state actually possesses sufficient centralised decision-making power to overrule a locality and place a facility where it is not wanted is an empirical question. The important point in understanding the legislation that emerged to deal with the siting gridlock, however, is that it was not necessarily trying to establish a market in well-defined pollution rights across communities (Coase II). State laws are better understood as designed to make a decision (where to locate a facility) given a set of transaction costs that may vary by state, with some states choosing a system that resembles a market and some states choosing a mechanism that resembles a firm in its reliance on centralised authority to select a site.

Theories of collective action provide another set of qualifications to current siting statutes and models, which generally treat 'the community' as the relevant unit of observation in siting disputes. In legislation, compensation schemes are often based on negotiations between the elected officials of a locality and developers. In academic models, auctions are conducted where a 'community' names its compensation fee for accepting a facility, though the details of arriving at such a figure are often ignored or are seen as a preference revelation problem. Yet Olson (1965) pointed out long ago the dangers of equating group interests with group action. Current models assume that compensation demands expressed by communities vary only because of the individuals' differences in valuing environmental risks and willingness to pay for the environment. Often, however, individuals will vary in the degree to which they are able to overcome free-rider problems and engage in collective action. If communities vary in the degree to which they engage in the collective action necessary to force a locating firm to pay compensation, then facilities which generate externalities will choose to locate where the expressed compensation demands are the least (*ceteris paribus*). Further complications arise when one considers the principal–agent relationships in models where elected representatives announce the compensation figures. Depending on the strength of monitoring by the electorate and the state of local political competition, the compensation figures announced by elected representatives may or may not relate to the preferences of affected constituents. Compensation may flow directly to representatives, to representatives' favoured constituents, or to those put at risk by the facility. The 'community' affected by a facility is often viewed as those residents whose activities are physically affected by the potential operation of the facility, for it is their 'use value' of the environment that is threatened. Individuals also have existence values and bequest motives over the environment, however, which means that affected parties who may be active in siting disputes also include those people who place a value on knowing that the environment is undisturbed by the risks of such a facility and those who wish to transfer an environment to future generations which does not entail the risks posed by such facilities. Thus the theories of collective action indicate the importance of starting the modelling process and statutory design with individuals rather than 'the community' as the basic unit of observation.

The literature on risk perception provides a third set of qualifications to the market models of locating hazardous waste facilities, which generally are based on an expected utility framework where individuals' preferences over facility siting are driven by expected values for outcomes calculated from the available information about a facility's risk. Many of the siting statutes provide for public education programmes to inform citizens about the risks associated with particular technologies. State officials often view part of the NIMBY gridlock as arising from a tendency of environmentalists' and citizens' perceived risks to outrun the actual risks posed by facility operations. This ignores, however, the fact that most citizens will remain rationally ignorant of hazardous waste policy and that risk regulation policies are more likely to be driven by perceived risks than actual risks. Noll and Krier (1990) have assembled the evidence from cognitive psychology about behaviour that indicates risk perceptions may diverge from the expected utility model: individuals reason by relating situations to previous experiences (representativeness heuristic); valuations are determined by how a choice is presented (framing effect); estimates of probabilities are influenced by whether a similar event readily comes to mind (availability heuristic); people act as if they believe small-probability events are more likely than their own beliefs would suggest; and people have preferences over how probabilities arise. The implications for siting a hazardous waste facility are that public reactions to a facility will not simply be based on the risk analyses presented for an individual facility's technology. Acceptance of the facility will in part be path-dependent, in that previous experiences with similar technologies will drive assessments of newly proposed facilities. Assessments of the dangers posed may depend on general world views of participants (for example, their interpretations of past experiences with the ability of market incentives and regulatory scrutiny to affect corporate health and safety decisions). Participants in siting battles will also react to how probabilities are generated, for example, what process ultimately results in the expected outcomes at particular facilities.

The positive political theory of institutions also provides insights for understanding the operation of siting statutes and the design of siting models. Discussion of the decision-making procedures used to select a site often portray the design of the procedure itself as a question of how to incorporate scientific criteria into the process so that the 'best' site is chosen. Positive political theory, however, implies that just as legislators have preferences over the outcomes of siting battles, they will have explicit preferences over the types of institutional designs likely to lead to particular outcomes. Legislators who wish for a facility to be sited may attempt to delegate the decision to a separate board and raise the transaction costs of overturning the board's decision, an exercise in blame-shifting (to the delegated decision-makers) and in commitment strategy (the costs of overturning a decision may make future legislative intervention less likely). Though it is often assumed that legislators make decisions about siting procedures behind a veil of ignorance that hides whose districts may be likely candidates, some legislators will have general preferences over whether any facility is sited and thus preferences over particular features of the siting procedures. Those concerned with discouraging siting may include substantial public participation requirements that provide activists with the ability to use litigation to halt siting activity, while those concerned with facilitating location may provide the state siting authority with the ability to override local objections to a facility. Separate from the outcomes likely with a particular decision-making process, individuals may also have preferences over such elements as whether a process is fair, open, and incorporates public participation. Preferences over procedure allow opponents of facilities to combine multiple issues into opposition to a facility, so that the debates are framed both in terms of risks posed by technology and the fairness of procedures used to narrow down possible sites. Though discussions of siting laws often proceed as if the goal were to site a facility, the positive theory of institutions offers warnings on how preferences over outcomes can map backwards into preferences over the design of institutions and how people may value the details of

institutions because they relate to broader notions of democracy, participation and equity.

In 1977 three states in the United States had statutes that dealt with the
siting of hazardous waste facilities; by 1988, 41 states had passed such laws.
The evolution of these laws demonstrates how more resources are devoted
to structuring property rights as the returns to well-specified rights in a
given area increase. While plants such as commercial hazardous waste facilities have always generated nuisances such as odours and truck traffic, vehe-
ment opposition to such facilities did not coalesce around most proposed
sitings until the later part of the 1970s and the early 1980s. Few new facilities that treated hazardous waste generated at another site (for example,
commercial facilities) were sited in the 1980s, according to the permit data
for the facilities in an EPA survey of hazardous waste TSDs (Hamilton,
1993). Demand for off-site waste treatment increased as more wastes were
declared hazardous under federal legislation and companies that treated
waste on-site were subject to strict regulatory scrutiny. Yet public opposition to commercial facilities led to siting gridlocks. Environmentalists used
local zoning power to halt attempted sitings across the country, buttressed
by additional litigation over whether proposed facilities violated environmental statutes. Against this background of public protest, state legislatures passed laws specifically detailing the procedures governing the siting
of hazardous waste facilities. These laws spelled out with clarity the property rights of developers, localities and state government in terms of the
power to initiate sitings, compensate affected localities, and finalise the
location of a particular facility. This marked a shift in the previous siting
method that was often referred to as the 'Decide–Announce–Defend'
model in which developers simply attempted to place the facility in a given
locality without an extended public selection process.

Academic articles and models written during this period concentrated on
breaking siting impasses through compensation mechanisms aimed at
reducing local opposition. These models typically used the community as
the unit of observation and proposed siting mechanisms that involved communities submitting compensation bids in an auction for siting a facility.
The community with the lowest compensation figure announced or submitted would be the host to the facility. The details of the auctions varied,
including sealed-bid auctions in which communities submitted a compensation figure, a reverse Dutch auction in which the first community to
accept a declared compensation package would 'win' the facility, and public
referendums in which citizens would vote on particular compensation
packages. A common thread throughout these models is the focus on siting
battles as a demand revelation problem, for example, how can the facility
operator or state government determine which community places the

lowest value on the potential environmental risks and would demand the least compensation for hosting a hazardous waste facility.

These siting models differed in whether they emphasised strategic factors in securing approval for a facility, equity considerations in the distributional impact, or efficiency in matching a plant with an area which demanded the lowest compensation for its externalities. Works by O'Hare (1997) and O'Hare et al. (1983) emphasised how compensation mechanisms could contribute to the probability of successfully siting a facility with concentrated costs and diffuse benefits. These models focused not on questions of efficiency but on how to overcome local opposition. Methods for securing local support for a noxious facility included a community referendum on a single proposed compensation offer from a developer, a vote on different bids, or the use of the existing political structure such as the town government to negotiate on behalf of the affected community. These models also stress the equity considerations of compensating residents whose health and safety are threatened by the operation of a facility or who experience economic losses such as property value declines because of externalities generated by the locating firm. Compensation thus becomes a method of sharing the benefits generated by the facility with those experiencing the costs. Sullivan (1990) has explored the interaction between equity and efficiency considerations in the design of compensation mechanisms. He notes that if victims are in part compensated for their exposure to pollution, then they may be less likely to take averting actions, and he explores the conditions under which these schemes may make residents less likely to locate away from polluting facilities.

A third type of compensation model emphasises the use of an auction process as an instrument to reveal where the facility's externalities will result in lower disamenities. Models by Kunreuther and Kleindorfer (1986) and Kunreuther et al. (1987) approach the NIMBY process as a demand revelation process in which the challenge is to structure an auction that will cause communities to reveal truthfully the compensation they would demand for receiving a facility. These models are in the tradition of public finance mechanisms that attempt to elicit true preferences for public goods. An auction process is designed in which a community submits the payment it would demand to be a host site, the community with the lowest bid wins, and other communities pay it compensation based on their submitted bids. The community is the unit of observation, although the authors point out that if one views individuals' preferences in each community as quasi linear in site value and income, then one can view the community's bids as aggregations of residents' willingness to accept compensation figures. Though the auction process is typically described as a sealed-bidding process, Inhaber (1992) proposes a 'reverse Dutch' auction in which the government would announce a figure that would increase over time which would be paid to compensate a host community. The first community to accept the proffered compensation package would end up with the facility.

Discussion of these siting statutes and models often centres on the creation of a 'market' for the location of hazardous waste facilities. The notion is that if property rights are well defined, then the operation of the market will lead a firm to locate where its risks involve the lowest compensation to affected neighbours. Some siting articles explicitly cite Coase II as evidence that if property rights can be specified better, then the siting gridlock can be eased. Mitchell and Carson (1986) state that the often ambiguous nature of property rights in siting disputes results in protracted disputes; they recommend that a community be given the explicit right to refuse a proposed siting through a referendum process in which residents would vote on a proposed compensation package. They point out that if each individual in the community had the right to block sitings, then the transaction costs of negotiating with the developer of a facility could be prohibitive. Bacow and Milkey (1982) point to the compensation negotiations provided for in the Massachusetts siting statute as evidence that Coasian transactions can be facilitated through the explicit arrangement of property rights. They say that the Massachusetts process, where developers negotiate compensation with potentially affected communities, is 'more efficient because developers must consider the full social cost when choosing where to site a facility'.

The evolution and details of the state siting laws, however, are also consistent with Coase's earlier article, 'The Nature of the Firm'. In that work, Coase points out that whether a particular production decision is made within the firm or across a market will depend on the transaction costs of using one method of organisation versus another. When costs of negotiation and contract enforcement in a market are high relative to the costs of internal production, then a good will be produced within a firm. Numerous factors associated with negotiating compensation contracts between a community and a developer make such agreements costly to arrive at: the problem of how elected officials can bind their successors to honour particular agreements; the possibility that disgruntled residents within the community or environmental groups outside the community may attempt to use legal means to delay construction even after community officials have reached an agreement; the difficulty of specifying exact payments depending on environmental outcomes, especially since a firm may be bankrupted by adverse outcomes; and the danger that explicit compensation contracts will be interpreted as bribes by residents. The key advantage of using a firm-like structure to make the production decision is that the use of centralised decision-making authority reduces the problems of breach and hold-up that are associated with incomplete contracts in a market.

The changes in siting regimes for hazardous waste facilities are consistent with Coase's insight about the relative transaction costs of different institutional arrangements. In an era when the perceived risks of waste handling were low, firms that operated hazardous waste facilities were free to site their facilities within the normal constraints on the market for industrial location imposed by zoning. As public opposition mounted, however, negotiations over siting became increasingly protracted and expensive. The transaction costs of siting battles became a weapon used by environmentalists to raise the costs of location to firms. State legislatures responded to a perceived need to increase available treatment capacity by drafting laws that explicitly dealt with siting of hazardous waste TSDs. Though the laws across states were similar in that they attempted to specify the particular property rights of developers, localities and state government, they varied in the degree to which they left the location decision to institutions that resembled a market versus a firm (National Governors' Association, 1989). States that adopted a market model typically left the initiation of siting to a private developer, specified a process of explicit negotiation between the developer of the facility and the targeted community, and provided for compensation mechanisms that transferred payments to affected localities. In a 1988 National Governors' Association survey of state siting regimes, at least 13 of the states had laws that mandated the provision of compensation to host communities. Compensation took various forms, including a tax on gross receipts at the facility whose proceeds went to the locality, per ton tipping fees that went to the community, licence fees, or general compensation packages that included money and in-kind contributions of goods and services. Twenty-two states had programmes that entailed direct negotiations between developers and communities affected by proposed facilities. Sixteen states provided technical assistance grants to allow communities selected as potential sites to develop the expertise and information necessary to participate in negotiations over siting.

Other states relied on a siting process that resembled a firm's decision-making process in reliance on centralised decision-making power to ultimately determine the location of the facility. In 11 states, the state itself had authority to initiate the siting process for a new hazardous waste facility. Fourteen states gave their state governments pre-emption power, where the state essentially pre-empts the delegated zoning power of localities in this case and simply makes the siting decision. In this process, the state assumes zoning power and excludes the targeted community from the decision-making process. The NGA study found that twenty-two states provided state government with override power, so that a state agency or board could override a local decision that attempted to block a siting. The state would not initiate the siting, but the threat of using state power remained in the background so that it could be used to resolve siting disputes. Note that even where the firm model was adopted, often provisions for negotiation with the community and for compensation were included in the siting statute. Local representatives from affected communities may be provided with membership on state siting boards. Such procedures are similar to mechanisms within a firm that help establish 'transfer prices' for internal transaction. Though the location decision has been moved within a central decision-making authority (in this case a state agency or board with ultimate decision-making power), there is still a need to elicit information on how communities vary in the value they place on environmental amenities.

Statutes that provide a state agency or board with pre-emption or override power are attempts to solve the NIMBY gridlock by creating a firm-like structure in which centralised decision-making power makes the resource allocation decision, that is, where the facility should be located. It remains an empirical question, however, whether such decision-making power can be effectively exercised. For even if the state nominally has the right to locate a facility in an area where opposition runs deep, local governments may possess sufficient power to frustrate the developer and the state so that the attempt is ultimately unsuccessful. Local governments determined to block a siting have used police powers to slow traffic to sites to a standstill, disrupted roads leading into facilities for long-term construction, and established zoning requirements that generate further litigation. Environmentalists have also been successful in appealing to state legislatures to remove sites selected by agencies from consideration once they are targeted. In at least one state, the backlash against a siting process directed by a state commission caused the legislature to halt all funding for the commission. The leverage of local governments and possibility for appeal back to state legislatures thus weaken the actual exercise of 'centralised' decision-making power in states with pre-emption and override provisions. Morell and Magorian (1982) captured the essence of this operation of siting mechanisms in their book title, *Siting Hazardous Waste Facilities: Local Opposition and the Myth of Preemption*. Bacow and Milkey (1982) have also pointed out that a state's use of pre-emption power may simply lead facility opponents to turn to litigation to slow the construction of a facility.

No one configuration of property rights has become dominant across states or proved successful in facilitating the siting of commercial hazardous waste facilities. Most of the models of the siting process emphasise the use of market mechanisms such as auctions to solve the problem of determining where facilities will elicit the lowest demand for compensation. Discussions of the siting laws which have clarified property rights in this area often assume that the definition of property rights is the same thing as the establishment of a market for location of facilities, a market where firms internalise their externalities in the manner described in Coase II (1960), 'The Problem of Social Cost'. Yet a review of the siting statutes reveals that the procedures employed resemble both the arm's-length transactions of a market and the centralised decision-making power of the firm. Coase still provides insight into the structure of these laws, but it is the insight from Coase I that relative transaction costs determine the institutional framework used for making a decision that explains the evolution of siting laws.

To see how siting progressed after the debate in the academic literature and state legislatures over effective procedures, Ibitayo and Pijawka (1999) conducted a national survey of state environmental agencies to analyse the siting of hazardous waste facilities over the previous decade. For the 42 states responding, they found five states had successfully sited hazardous waste facilities, 12 states had mounted efforts that did not work, 13 had ongoing siting processes, and 12 had not attempted to site such facilities. Contrasting the procedures in the five states with successful sitings with the efforts of other states, they conclude (p. 387):

The success of any strategy depends on the extent to which the strategy deals with issues such as public trust, early and continuous public involvement in the siting process, public education on hazardous waste, empowerment of host communities, and the incorporation of citizens' concerns into risk mitigation plans.

5.2   General Siting Policies for Hazardous Waste Facilities in Other OECD Countries

The concentrated costs and generally diffuse benefits of facilities that treat and dispose of hazardous waste have made their sitings controversial and relatively rare recently in most OECD countries. The literature on siting policies generally focuses on case studies within a given country and assessments by the authors of what factors led to siting success or failure in a particular case. The successful sitings of hazardous waste facilities in the Canadian provinces of Alberta and Manitoba have generated much research (Rabe, 1994; Castle and Munton, 1996; Richards, 1996). The voluntary siting process used there involved the stages of an expression of local interest by a community, hosting of open houses to discuss the facility with residents, creation of local citizen advisory committees funded by the proponent to investigate the process and plant, a referendum on the proposal, and a negotiation stage where facility operation issues and local input are discussed. This gives a community multiple points at which to veto a project. In terms of the socio-economic characteristics of the two towns

(Swan Hills and Montcalm) that accepted facilities, Castle and Munton note (p. 78):

> The evidence to support the argument that the Alberta or Manitoba volunteer siting process singled out poor or otherwise disadvantaged communities to host hazardous waste treatment facilities seems . . . lacking. . . . The town of Swan Hills had an average household income of $44,023 in 1986, significantly higher than the Alberta norm ($36,796). Unemploy,ment in Swan Hills in 1986 was 7%, one of the lowest in the province. Montcalm is much poorer than Swan Hills, but the community is not economically disadvantaged compared to other rural areas in Manitoba.

The jobs associated with the plants were a considerable factor in public acceptance. In the case of Swan Hills, a town of approximately 2000 residents, a '1991 report concluded that the facility provides more than ninety full-time jobs in Swan Hills that contribute $2.7 million a year to the local economy in salaries and makes an overall impact of $6 million on the economy each year'(Rabe, 1994, p. 76). Additionally, proponents in Alberta stressed that the waste would come primarily from within the province so that the siting was seen as solving a local problem rather than creating an outlet for waste from across the country. Additional research on siting waste facilities (Lawrence, 1996) and toxic disposal facilities (Ristoratore, 1987; Richards, 1996) in Canada analyses the use of voluntary process, the role of compensation or jobs in generating support, and the importance of ensuring a minimum level of safety in the operation of facilities.

Research on hazardous waste facility siting in European countries reveals wide variety in public participation and reaction. Linnerooth-Bayer (1997) notes that survey evidence from Austria indicates multiple views on fairness in siting, with some stressing support for hierarchical processes based on expert opinion, others favouring market mechanisms, a segment objecting on distributive justice grounds to siting in economically or socially disadvantaged communities, and still others believing in spreading the burdens of waste management broadly across communities. Lidskog (1993) emphasises the role that economic benefits played in leading a local government to host a disposal facility in Sweden. Seeliger (1996) examines four case studies of siting waste facilities in Germany and stresses the large role of state governments in initiating the siting process and the experimentation with public consultation in more recent policies. Describing the lack of opposition in one neighbourhood hosting an incinerator, he notes (p. 241):

> The GSB facility is located not in the town of Ebenhausen itself but a subsection called Ebenhausen-Werk . . . Ebenhausen-Werk is about a kilometer from the town proper, and home to a working-class population of 400–500, of low social

status. The proportion of foreign and migrant workers living in Ebenhausen-Werk is also said to be high . . . It is possible that this social setting is not conducive to the emergence of a local environmental initiative.

Analysing lessons from siting disputes in Europe overall, Kunreuther et al. (1996) describe variations in siting policies by two main characteristics, the degree to which the process is open, versus closed, to public participation and the degree to which decision-making authority rests with the local community rather than with the national/state government or developer. They note examples of efforts taken to increase public support for proposed facilities, such as the case in Austria where local citizens were involved in the selection of experts chosen to assess risks from a facility, and the use of substantial compensation (that is, a promise of 2.5 million Swiss francs for 25 years for a town of 500 households) in the siting of an underground nuclear waste repository in Switzerland.

Dente et al. (1998) review successful sitings of waste facilities in France, Hungary, Italy, the Netherlands, Slovenia, Spain and Switzerland. Their findings emphasise that many factors related to equity are involved in the siting of facilities in these European countries. In areas with higher unemployment rates, residents appear more likely to accept facilities because of the employment opportunities provided. In successful sitings, those trying to locate the plants are more likely to succeed if they can transform the debate from a zero sum game in which one area gains and another loses to a situation where compensation in some form comes along with the risks of a facility. The distance the waste travels appears to matter to residents, for if the waste is seen as local, then disposal is interpreted as more equitable. Fewer communities appear willing to accept waste generated far away. Siting attempts overall worked more easily in industrial areas for at least three reasons: the waste is seen as local; residents are more likely to work in plants generating the waste; and residents are used to the risks posed by industrial pollution. A final equity consideration emerges in the design of the siting process, with procedures involving more public participation being seen as more equitable.

Huitema (2002) develops in depth three case studies of hazardous waste siting attempts in each of three different countries: Canada, the Netherlands and the United Kingdom. In terms of procedure, he finds all three countries provide an increasing role for citizen participation, though this does not overwhelm the prominent roles played by experts and elected officials. Environmental impact assessments are now common elements of siting in each country. Overall, the market plays a greater role in sitings in the UK and Canada and a lesser role in the Netherlands. Huitema notes that there are distinct procedural differences across the three countries, differences which may help explain outcomes in sitings. In the Netherlands siting disputes are much more likely to spill over into the courts. In the UK, the inquiry system (a quasi-judicial investigation procedure) generates substantial dialogue about siting issues, though Huitema finds overall that regulations in the UK are likely to limit the ability of government to block the actions of private developers. Looking across the three countries, he concludes that debates about siting are more likely to involve notions of managerialism (for example, importance of experts) and conservative pluralism (for example, right of private parties to pursue development) than ideas of distributive equity.

Research on Japan notes the role of rewards used in the siting process. Shaw (1996) describes how laws in Japan smoothed the siting of power plants by providing communities with compensation without having to prove damages. Electricity is taxed, and the revenues are redistributed to local communities in the form of expenditures on public facilities such as roads, schools or sewage systems. Ohkawara (1999) discusses compensation in the case of siting of nuclear power plants. Munton (1996) reviews the siting of hazardous waste facilities in Japan and notes problems similar to that found in the USA: NIMBY opposition to construction, declining capacity and illegal dumping. Attempts to overcome opposition to siting included a policy of offering side payments to communities, which would receive public works projects from the national government in return for hosting a treatment facility.

Probst and Beierle (1999) stress how facility operation is embedded in a larger regulatory structure affecting hazardous waste generation and management. They examine hazardous waste management systems in Germany, Denmark, the United States, Canada, Malaysia, Hong Kong, Thailand and Indonesia. Their results stress the time needed to establish a comprehensive system to regulate waste, the need to create a culture of compliance, and the expense of constructing hazardous waste treatment facilities. To encourage the development of treatment capacity, the countries studied had tried a range of ownership for the facilities (for example, public, private, mixed). Initial subsidies from some governments encouraged generators to use the facilities, a step in creating compliance with hazardous waste management.

A substantial legal and policy literature exists on international trade and hazardous waste (see Engfer et al., 1991; Walsh, 1992; Murphy, 1994; Pinzon, 1994; Kummer, 1995; Marbug, 1995; Bradford, 1997; Sundram, 1997; OECD, 1998; Park, 1998; Belenky, 1999; Verchick, 1999; O'Neill, 2000; Waugh, 2000). Part of this literature focuses on notions of fairness in the export of waste and risks across borders. Lofstedt (1996) analyses the literal spillover of risks across borders in the case of a nuclear power plant in Sweden sited close to the border with Denmark. Explicit consideration of the impact of siting on risk exposure by income or ethnicity is less prevalent in much of the European literature, though Johnson (2001) notes that analysis of such disparities is growing as more detailed information on pollution incidence becomes available in OECD countries. A European Commission March 1997 Council Directive on environmental impact assessment does specifically encourage the analysis of how waste disposal installations dealing with hazardous waste will affect the environment. The European Commission (2001) has also encouraged greater use of public participation mechanisms in environmental decision-making.

5.3   Incorporating Environmental Equity Considerations into Siting: US Perspective

In 1994 President Clinton issued Executive Order 12898, 'Federal Actions to Address Environmental Justice in Minority Populations and Low-Income Populations', which required federal agencies to create environmental justice strategies and examine whether their policies have disproportionate impacts on minority or low-income populations. In response to this order, the EPA began to develop guidance documents to incorporate environmental equity considerations into government decision-making. The EPA's Administrator, Christine Todd Whitman, noted in 2001 that the agency's programme includes:

(a)   Conducting our programmes, policies, and activities that substantially affect human health and the environment in a manner that ensures the fair treatment of all people, including minority populations and/or low-income populations;

(b)   Ensuring equal enforcement of protective environmental laws for all people, including minority populations and/or low-income populations;

(c)   Ensuring greater public participation in the Agency's development and implementation of environmental regulations and policies; and

(d)   Improving research and data collection for Agency programmes relating to the health of, and the environment of all people, including minority populations and/or low-income populations.

The agency's efforts to define and implement environmental equity have attracted significant legal research (see Georges, 1999; Johnson, 1999; Mank, 1999; Foster, 2002; Yang, 2002). Yet the number of permitting or enforcement actions specifically taken on environmental justice concerns is so small that to date no statistical investigations have analysed the agency's implementation. In the most famous case to date, the transaction costs generated by the EPA's environmental justice investigation of the Shintech plant in part led the company to shift the plant's proposed location from a predominantly African-American community to a white community (see Lambert, 2000). The EPA's consideration of environmental justice concerns in permitting facilities (see EPA, 2000) has generated controversy among industry participants concerned about the freedom to locate facilities, officials in economically depressed areas who want to attract plants to stimulate the economy, and activists concerned that the EPA's consideration of disparate impacts will not alter the location and operation of polluting facilities. The greatest lessons to date for considering equity in the siting of hazardous waste facilities may lie in examining two sets of environmental equity guidance instructions adopted by the EPA.

Under the National Environmental Policy Act (NEPA), EPA must often create an environmental impact statement (EIS) or environmental assessment (EA) of agency actions. In 1998 the EPA issued its guidance documents for incorporating environmental justice considerations into developing an EIS or EA. The guidance encourages analysts to look at affected populations using detailed census data; take into account how differences in diet might result in different exposure; look for cumulative effects (for example, what other sources of pollution are already in the area); examine local health outcomes data; be cognizant of local literacy rates, especially when communicating complex risk information; consider occupational exposures; and determine whether community representatives are involved in local decision-making. The guidance encourages analysts to use GIS technology to analyse potential exposures. Mitigation measures are also to be incorporated into the analysis, including monitoring of emissions, encouraging participation of affected communities, reducing pollutants to lessen cumulative exposures, and requiring mitigation of pollution as part of a permitting process.

The operations of many environmental regulatory programmes are delegated to the states by the EPA, so that state environmental agencies will end up writing permits needed for the construction and operation of polluting facilities. The most controversial EPA environmental equity rules concern the guidance documents issued that define when a permit may be challenged under Title VI of the 1964 Civil Rights Act, which relates to discrimination involving disparate impacts by entities that receive federal funding (such as funding for state environmental programmes). These rules have attracted great attention among legal scholars (see Lazarus and Tai, 1999; Lyle, 2000; Guana, 2001; Mank, 2000, 2001; Cody, 2002; Santiago, 2002). The guidance documents set forth what types of evidence the EPA would expect when parties file a civil rights complaint with the EPA about a state or local permitting decision. The guidance states that for evidence of disparate impacts, the agency expects detailed information on the exposed population, which may include census data on racial composition in an area, GIS analysis of exposure to pollutants, information on reported chemical releases, monitoring data, and health outcomes information. The guidance notes that the EPA's Office of Civil Rights (OCR) is unlikely to find an adverse health impact when cumulative risks of cancer calculated in the analysis are less than 10^{-6} and much more likely in cases where the cancer risk is 10^{-4} or higher; the higher the non-cancer hazard index for a chemical is above one the more likely the OCR is to find an adverse health impact. The rules indicate that in determining whether a plant generates a disparate impact, the comparison population can be the general surrounding population (for example, city or state) or the non-affected segment of the local population. The guidance documents suggest that a denial of a permit solely on environment justice grounds is unlikely. Rather, if the EPA finds a violation, the agency will focus on mitigating the impact of a facility, such as reducing permissible pollution levels or requiring stricter monitoring.

6.   CONCLUSIONS

Statistical studies in the United States suggest that low-income and minority populations are often exposed to greater risks arising from the siting and operation of hazardous waste facilities. Less detailed information exists on the exposure of residents by income to hazardous waste risks in other OECD countries, though the evidence suggests that in some countries disparate exposures may exist by income (in part because of the draw of jobs and compensation programmes in siting procedures). Concerns about environmental equity may involve dissatisfaction with disparate exposure or dismay at how these differences arise across demographic groups. Thinking about policies to address environmental equity (see Box 7.3) requires definitions of equity, an assortment of policy tools that take into account how disparate impacts arise, and a recognition of the prospect that market dynamics may make equity policies hard to implement in the long run.

Consider first how to define a fair siting process. Been (1993, p. 1008) notes at least seven ways of defining a fair siting: even distribution of NIMBY sites across neighbourhoods; compensation to those affected paid by neighbourhoods that do not host facilities; progressive siting, where areas with more income bear more sitings or pay more in damages; equal vetoes by communities to bid in excluding facilities; siting where those who benefit pay the cost; no intentional discrimination against minorities; and a process that shows 'equal concern and respect' for all communities.

Hampton (1999) adds the complication that concepts of fairness reside in procedures and outcomes, so fair policies may involve meeting standards of participation, information provision, trust in the decision-making process and expression of public values.

The tool-box of policy options to promote equity in siting is large. Site permitting could involve an analysis of whether a plant involves a disparate impact on low-income or minority communities, with impact defined by the radius of externalities and risks modelled using GIS technology and information on emissions or adverse health outcomes. If differences in collective action give rise to disparities, authorities may take such steps as technical assistance grants to communities involved in siting, information provision, or attentive enforcement of rules in areas less likely to call upon regulators for help. The process of negotiation in siting and permitting may give rise to mitigation efforts, which may include reductions in emissions or increases in monitoring for ambient exposures. Compensation for siting may come in numerous forms, such as the jobs provided by plants, tax payments that reduce tax burdens in a community, or expenditures on public goods such as roads or schools. If disparate impacts arise from racism in housing markets or job market outcomes that limit incomes, then attempts to address discrimination in these markets will provide minority residents with greater freedom to avoid environmental hazards. Greater research on how cumulative risks arise and vary across demographic groups would aid the design of these programmes.

At least three problems may arise with equity policies. In the short run, some compensation may offset damages for current residents when a facility is sited. Yet in the long run a facility may generate externalities that end up lowering property values and attracting more low-income residents to an area. These low-income individuals may be willing because of their constrained budgets to accept a larger risk for a lower housing price, though this offends the values of individuals who do not believe environmental quality should be traded like a normal good. A related point is that, in some areas poor residents may be willing to accept a facility because of the jobs provided, which again may generate dissatisfaction among those who have preferences about the distribution of risk across demographic groups. If plants are channelled outside current industrial areas because of equity concerns, this raises the likelihood that new environments will be diminished. In devising environmental equity policies, there are few easy and obvious choices. Selection of programmes to pursue environmental equity involves potential trade-offs between equity and efficiency, across demographic groups, and among values relating to procedures, outcomes and self-determination.

BOX 7.3   CONCLUSIONS

How can environmental equity be incorporated in siting policies? Analysis of impact; technical assistance grants to communities to analyse facilities; mitigation efforts, including reductions in pollution or increases in monitoring; compensation mechanisms (for example, payments for community infrastructure).

Example   In the United States, Executive Order requires agencies to incorporate environmental justice considerations (for example, exposure by race and income) into their policies.

EPA guidance documents on when permit may be challenged on civil rights grounds:

- For evidence on disparate exposure, expect detailed information. Examples would include GIS analysis of census population, potential routes of exposure, monitoring data on cumulative impacts and health outcomes information.
- Agency unlikely to find adverse health impact if cumulative risks of cancer calculated are less than 10^{-6}, more likely if 10^{-4}.
- Comparison population: general population, or non-affected local population.
- Guidance suggests unlikely EPA would deny permit solely on environmental justice grounds. Rather, agency would focus on reducing pollution levels or requiring stricter monitoring.

Challenges to incorporating equity in siting:

- Residents may accept risks in return for jobs provided by facilities. Policies that steer facilities away from poor/minority areas may discourage development/employment.
- Even if local residents who are poor are willing to accept facility, those outside the area may have existence/bequest motives of justice that hold this trade-off is unfair. Whose preferences matter more? How to incorporate existence values (contingent valuation)? Related point: procedures have intrinsic and instrumental fairness values.
- If compensation is involved in siting, where does it flow? How can you avoid principal–agent problems between representatives and residents in compensation negotiations?

- Will environmental equity policies force more sitings into green fields? Where is marginal damage of plant greater, already polluted area or new environment?
- What are the long-term impacts on the poor of cleaning up an area? Rise in housing prices that causes them to relocate?

These are the types of concerns that make debates over environmental equity difficult to resolve.

BIBLIOGRAPHY

Anderton, Douglas L., Andy B. Anderson, John Michael Oakes and Michael R. Fraser (1994a), 'Environmental Equity: The Demographics of Dumping', *Demography*, **31**(2), 229–48.

Anderton, Douglas L., Andy B. Anderson, Peter H. Rossi, John Michael Oakes, Michael R. Fraser, Eleanor W. Weber and Edward J. Calabrese (1994b), 'Hazardous Waste Facilities: "Environmental Equity" Issues in Metropolitan Areas', *Evaluation Review*, **18**(2), 123–40.

Anderton, Douglas L., John Michael Oakes and Karla L. Egan (1997), 'Environmental Equity in Superfund: Demographics of the Discovery and Prioritization of Abandoned Toxic Waste Sites', *Evaluation Review*, **21**(1), 3–26.

Arora, Seema and Timothy N. Cason (1999), 'Do Community Characteristics Influence Environmental Outcomes? Evidence from the Toxics Release Inventory', *Southern Economic Journal*, **65**(4), 691–716.

Atlas, Mark K. (2001a), 'Safe and Sorry: Risk, Environmental Equity, and Hazardous Waste Management Facilities', *Risk Analysis*, **21**(5), 939–54.

Atlas, Mark K. (2001b), 'Rush to Judgment: An Empirical Analysis of Environmental Equity in US Environmental Protection Agency Actions', *Law and Society Review*, **35**, 633–82.

Bacow, Lawrence S. and James R. Milkey (1982), 'Overcoming Local Opposition to Hazardous Waste Facilities: The Massachusetts Approach', *Harvard Environmental Law Review*, **6**, 265–305.

Baden, Brett M. and Don L. Coursey (2002), 'The Locality of Waste Sites within the City of Chicago: A Demographic, Social, and Economic Analysis', *Resource and Energy Economics*, **24**, 53–93.

Baxter, Jamie W., John D. Eyles and Susan J. Elliott (1999), 'From Siting Principles to Siting Practices: A Case Study of Discord among Trust Equity, and Community Participation', *Journal of Environmental Planning and Management*, **42**(4), 501–25.

Been, Vicki (1995), 'Analysing Evidence of Environmental Justice', *Journal of Land Use and Environmental Law*, **11**(1), 1–36.

Been, Vicki (1994), 'Locally Undesirable Land Uses in Minority Neighbourhoods: Disproportionate Siting or Market Dynamics?', *Yale Law Journal*, **103**(6), 1383–422.

Been, Vicki (1993), 'What's Fairness Got to Do With It? Environmental Justice and the Siting of Locally Undesirable Land Uses', *Cornell Law Review*, **78**, 1001–85.

Been, Vicki and Francis Gupta (1997), 'Coming to the Nuisance or Going to the Barrios? A Longitudinal Analysis of Environmental Justice Claims', *Ecology Law Quarterly*, **24**, 1–56.

Belenky, Lisa T (1999), 'Cradle to Border: US Hazardous Waste Export Regulations and International Law', *Berkeley Journal of International Law*, **17**, 95–137.

Boer, J. Tom, Manuel Pator Jr, James L. Sadd and Lori D. Snyder (1997), 'Is There Environmental Racism: The Demographics of Hazardous Waste in Los Angeles County', *Social Science Quarterly*, **78**(4), 793–810.

Bord, Richard J. and Robert E. O'Connor (1992), 'Determinants of Risk Perceptions of a Hazardous Waste Site', *Risk Analysis*, **12**(3), 411–29.

Bowen, William (2002), 'An Analytical Review of Environmental Justice Research: What Do We Really Know?', *Environmental Management*, **29**(1), 3–15.

Boyce, James K., Andrew R. Klemer, Paul H. Templet and Cleve E. Willis (1999), 'Power Distribution, the Environment, and Public Health: A State-level Analysis', *Ecological Economics*, **29**, 127–40.

Bradford, Mark (1997), 'The United States, China, and the Basel Convention on the Transboundary Movements of Hazardous Wastes and their Disposal', *Fordham Environmental Law Journal*, **8**, 305–49.

Brainard, Julii S., Andrew P. Jones, Ian J. Bateman, Andrew A. Lovett and Peter J. Fallon (2002), 'Modelling Environmental Equity: Access to Air Quality in Birmingham, England', *Environment and Planning A*, **34**, 695–716.

Broadbent, Jeffrey (1998), *Environmental Politics in Japan: Networks of Power and Protest*, New York: Cambridge University Press.

Brooks, Nancy and Rejiv Sethi (1997), 'The Distribution of Pollution: Community Characteristics and Exposure to Air Toxics', *Journal of Environmental Economics and Management*, **32**, 233–50.

Bryant, Bunyan and Paul Mohai (eds) (1992), *Race and the Incidence of Environmental Hazards: A Time for Discourse*, Boulder, CO: Westview.

Bullard, Robert D. (1983), 'Solid Waste Sites and the Black Houston Community', *Social Inquiry*, **53**, 273–88.

Bullard, Robert D. (1990), *Dumping in Dixie: Race, Class and Environmental Quality*. Boulder, CO: Westview Press.

Bullard, Robert D. (1996), 'Environmental Justice: It's More Than Waste Facility Siting', *Social Science Quarterly*, **77**(3), 493–9.

Canadian Institute for Environmental Law and Policy (2000), 'Ontario: Open for Toxics – Hazardous Waste Becomes a Growth Industry in Ontario', Toronto, Ontario: Canadian Institute for Environmental Law and Policy.

Castle, Geoffrey and Don Munton (1996), 'Voluntary Siting of Hazardous Waste Facilities in Western Canada', in Don Munton (ed.), *Hazardous Waste Siting and Democratic Choice*, Washington, DC: Georgetown University Press.

Chakraborty, Jayajit (2001), 'Acute Exposure to Extremely Hazardous Substances: An Analysis of Environmental Equity', *Risk Analysis*, **21**(5), 883–95.

Christiansen, Kim Michael and Birgit Munck-Kampmann (2000), 'Waste: Annual Topic Update 1999', European Environment Agency topic report 2/2000.

Coase, Ronald (1937), 'The Nature of the Firm', *Economica*, **4**, 386–405.

Coase, Ronald (1960), 'The Problem of Social Cost', *Journal of Law and Economics*, **3**, 1–44.

Cody, Brendan (2002), 'South Camden Citizens in Action: Siting Decisions, Disparate Impact Discrimination, and Section 1983', *Ecology Law Quarterly*, **29**, 231–62.

Coenen, Frans H.J.M. (1998), 'Participation in Strategic Green Planning in the Netherlands', in Frans Coenen, Dave Huitema and Laurence J. O'Toole Jr, (eds), *Participation and the Quality of Environmental Decision Making*, Dordrecht: Kluwer Academic.

Commission for Environmental Cooperation (1999), 'Tracking and Enforcement of Transborder Hazardous Waste Shipment in North America', Canada.

Commission for Racial Justice, United Church of Christ (UCC) (1987), *Toxic Wastes and Race in the United States: A National Report on the Racial and Socioeconomic Characteristics of Communities With Hazardous Waste Sites*, New York: United Church of Christ.

Connor, Michael (1992), 'Maquiladoras and the Border Environment: Prospects for Moving from Agreements to Solutions', *Colorado Journal of International Environmental Law and Policy*, 3, 683–710.

Cutter, Susan L., Danika Holm and Lloyd Clark (1996), 'The Role of Geographic Scale in Monitoring Environmental Justice', *Risk Analysis*, 16(4), 517–26.

Daniels, Glynis and Samantha Friedman (1999), 'Spatial Inequality in the Distribution of Industrial Toxic Releases: Evidence from the 1990 TRI', *Social Science Quarterly*, 80(2), 244–62.

Dente, Bruno, Paolo Fareri and Josee Ligteringen (eds) (1998), *The Waste and the Backyard: The Creation of Waste Facilities in Six European Countries*, Dordrecht: Kluwer Academic Publishers.

Dolk, H., M. Vrijheid, B. Armstrong, L. Abramsky, F. Bianci, E. Garne, V. Nelen, E. Robert, J.E.S. Scott, D. Stone and R. Tenconi (1998), 'Risk of Congenital Anomalies near Hazardous-waste Landfill Sites in Europe: The EUROHAZCON Study', *The Lancet*, 352, 423–7.

Dunlap, Riley E., Michael E. Kraft and Eugene A. Rosa (1993), *Public Reactions to Nuclear Waste*, Durham, NC: Duke University Press.

Easterling, Douglas (1992), 'Fair Rules for Siting a High-level Nuclear Waste Repository', *Journal of Policy Analysis and Management*, 11(3), 442–75.

Engfer, Victoria L., Gilbert A. Partida, Thomas C. Vernon, Alejandro Toulet and David A. Renas (1991), 'By-products of Prosperity: Transborder Hazardous Waste Issues Confronting the Maquiladora Industry', *San Diego Law Review*, 28, 819–51.

Environmental Protection Agency (1998), 'Final Guidance for Incorporating Environmental Justice Concerns in EPA's NEPA Compliance Analyses', Washington DC: US EPA.

Environmental Protection Agency, Office of Environmental Justice (2000), 'Environmental Justice in the Permitting Process: A Report from the National Environmental Justice Advisory Council's Public Meeting on Environmental Permitting – Arlington, Virginia, November 30–December 2, 1999', Washington DC: US EPA.

European Commission (1997), 'Council Directive 97/11/EC, Amending Directive 85/337/EC of 27 June 1985 on the Assessment of the Effects of Certain Public and Private Projects on the Environment'.

European Commission (2001), 'Proposal for a Directive of the European Parliament and of the Council, Providing for Public Participation in Respect of the Drawing Up of Certain Plans and Programmes Relating to the Environment and Amending Council Directives 85/337/EEC and 96/61/EC'.

Farber, Stephen (1998), 'Undesirable Facilities and Property Values: A Summary of Empirical Studies', *Ecological Economics*, 24, 1–14.

Fischer, Frank (1995), 'Hazardous Waste Policy, Community Movements and the Politics of Nimby: Participatory Risk Assessment in the USA and Canada', in Frank Fischer and Michael Black (eds), *Greening Environmental Policy: The Politics of a Sustainable Future*, New York: St Martin's.

Foreman, Christopher H. (1998), *The Promise and Peril of Environmental Justice*, Washington, DC: Brookings Institution.

Foster, Sheila (2002), 'Environmental Justice in an Era of Devolved Collaboration', *Harvard Environmental Law Review*, **26**, 459–98.

Fredriksson, Per G. (2000), 'The Siting of Hazardous Waste Facilities in Federal Systems', *Environmental and Resource Economics*, **15**, 75–87.

Frey, Bruno S. and Felix Oberholzer-Gee (1996), 'Fair Siting Procedures: An Empirical Analysis of their Importance and Characteristics', *Journal of Policy Analysis and Management*, **15**(3), 353–76.

Frey, Bruno S. and Felix Oberholzer-Gee (1997), 'The Cost of Price Incentives: An Empirical Analysis of Motivation Crowding-out', *American Economic Review*, **87**(4), 746–55.

Frey, Bruno S., Felix Oberholzer-Gee and Reiner Eichenberger (1996), 'The Old Lady Visits Your Backyard: A Tale of Morals and Markets', *Journal of Political Economy*, **104**(6), 1297–313.

Friends of the Earth (1999), McLaren, Duncan, Olivier Cottray, Mary Taylor, Susan Pipes and Simon Bullock, 'The Geographic Relation between Household Income and Polluting Factories', Friends of the Earth, London.

Friends of the Earth (2001), 'Pollution and Poverty: Breaking the Link', London: Friends of the Earth.

Gaussier, Nathalie (2001), 'The Spatial Foundations of Obnoxious Goods Location: The Garbage Dumps Case', *Regional Studies*, **35**(7), 625–36.

Gayer, Ted (2000), 'Neighborhood Demographics and the Distribution of Hazardous Waste Risks: An Instrumental Variables Estimation', *Journal of Regulatory Economics*, **17**(2), 131–55.

Gayer, Ted, James T. Hamilton and W. Kip Viscusi (2000), 'Private Values of Risk Tradeoffs at Superfund Sites: Housing Market Evidence on Learning About Risk', *Review of Economics and Statistics*, **82**(3), 439–51.

Georges, Elizabeth (1999), 'If I Had a Hammer: Why Permitting Challenges Do Not Fit in the Fight for Environmental Justice', *Fordham Environmental Law Journal*, **10**, 347–57.

Gerrard, Michael B. (1994), *Whose Backyard, Whose Risk: Fear and Fairness in Toxic and Nuclear Waste Siting*, Cambridge, MA: MIT Press.

Gerrard, Michael B. (1997), 'Territoriality, Risk Perception, and Counterproductive Legal Structures: The Case of Waste Facility Siting', *Environmental Law*, **27**, 1017–33.

Graham, John D., Nancy Dean Beaulier, Dana Sussman, March Sadowitz and Yi-Ching Li (1999), 'Who Lives Near Coke Plants and Oil Refineries? An Exploration of the Environmental Inequity Hypothesis', *Risk Analysis*, **9**(2), 171–86.

Gregory, Robin, Howard Kunreuther, Douglas Easterling and Ken Richards (1991), 'Incentives Policies to Site Hazardous Waste Facilities', *Risk Analysis*, **11**(4), 667–75.

Groothuis, Peter A. and Gail Miller (1994), 'Locating Hazardous Waste Facilities: The Influence of NIMBY Beliefs', *American Journal of Economics and Sociology*, **53**(3), 335–46.

Groothuis, Peter A. and Gail Miller (1997), 'The Role of Social Distrust in Risk–Benefit Analysis: A Study of the Siting of a Hazardous Waste Disposal Facility', *Journal of Risk and Uncertainty*, **15**, 241–57.

Guana, Eileen (2001), 'EPA at 30: Fairness in Environmental Protection', *Environmental Law Reporter*, **31**, 10528.

Gupta, Shreekant, George VanHoutven and Maureen L. Cropper (1996), 'Paying for Permanence: An Economic Analysis of EPA's Cleanup Decisions at Superfund Sites', *Rand Journal of Economics*, **27**(3), 563–82.

Halstead, John M., Joanna L. Whitcomb and Lawrence C. Hamilton (1999), 'Economic Insights into the Siting Problem: An Application of the Expected Utility Model', *Agricultural and Resource Economics Review*, **28**(1), 65–75.

Hamilton, James T. (1993), 'Politics and Social Costs: Estimating the Impact of Collective Action on Hazardous Waste Facilities', *RAND Journal of Economics*, **24**(1), 101–25.

Hamilton, James T. (1995), 'Testing for Environmental Racism: Prejudice, Profits, or Power?', *Journal of Policy Analysis and Management*, **14**(1), 107–32.

Hamilton, James T. (1999), 'Exercising Property Rights to Pollute: Do Cancer Risks and Politics Affect Plant Emission Reductions?', *Journal of Risk and Uncertainty*, **18**(2), 105–24.

Hamilton, James T. and W. Kip Viscusi (1999), *Calculating Risks? The Spatial and Political Dimensions of Hazardous Waste Policy*, Cambridge, MA: MIT Press.

Hampton, Greg (1999), 'Environmental Equity and Public Participation', *Policy Sciences*, **32**, 163–74.

Harjula, Henrik (2003), Email from Henrik Harjula (Principal Administrator, Environment Directorate, OECD) to the author, March 11.

Harrison, Kathryn and Werner Antweiler (2002), 'Incentives for Pollution Abatement: Regulation, Regulatory Threats, and Non-governmental Pressures', working paper, University of British Columbia, Vancouver.

Hird, John A. (1993), 'Environmental Policy and Equity: The Case of Superfund', *Journal of Policy Analysis and Management*, **12**(2), 323–43.

Hird, John A. (1994), *Superfund: The Political Economy of Environmental Risk*, Baltimore: Johns Hopkins University Press.

Hite, Diane (2000), 'A Random Utility Model of Environmental Equity', *Growth and Change*, **31**, 40–58.

Hockman, Elaine M. and Charles M. Morris (1998), 'Progress towards Environmental Justice: A Five-year Perspective of Toxicity, Race and Poverty in Michigan, 1990–1995', *Journal of Environmental Planning and Management*, **41**(2), 157–76.

Huitema, Dave (1998), 'Hazardous Decisions: The Siting of Hazardous Waste Disposal Facilities in Canada and the United States', in Frans Coenen, Dave Huitema and Laurence J. O'Toole Jr, (eds), *Participation and the Quality of Environmental Decision Making*, Dordrecht: Kluwer Academic.

Huitema, Dave (2002), *Hazardous Decisions: Hazardous Waste Siting in the UK, the Netherlands and Canada. Institutions and Discourses*, Dordrecht: Kluwer Academic.

Ibitayo, O.O. and K.D. Pijawka (1999), 'Reversing NIMBY: An Assessment of State Strategies for Siting Hazardous Waste Facilities', *Environment and Planning C: Government and Policy*, **17**, 379–89.

Ingberman, Daniel E. (1995), 'Siting Noxious Facilities: Are Markets Efficient?', *Journal of Environmental Economics and Management*, **29**, S20–S33.

Inhaber, Herbert (1992), 'Of LULUs, NIMBYs, and NIMTOOs', *Public Interest*, **107**, 52–64.

Jerrett, M., J. Eyles, D. Cole and S. Reader (1997), 'Environmental Equity in Canada: An Empirical Investigation into the Income Distribution of Pollution in Ontario', *Environment and Planning*, **29**, 1777–800.

Johnson, Stephen M. (1999), 'Economics v. Equity: Do Market-based Environmental Reforms Exacerbate Environmental Injustice?', *Washington and Lee Law Review*, **56**, 111–66.

Johnson, Stephen M. (2001), 'Economics v. Equity II: The European Experience', *Washington and Lee Law Review*, **58**, 417–86.

Kiel, Katherine A. and Katherine T. McClain (1995), 'House Prices During Siting Decision Stages: The Case of an Incinerator from Rumor through Operation', *Journal of Environmental Economics and Management*, **28**, 241–55.

Kleindorfer, Paul R., Howard C. Kunreuther and David S. Hong (1996), *Energy, Environment, and the Economy: Asian Perspectives*, Cheltenham, UK and Brookfield, USA: Edward Elgar.

Kleinhesselink, Randall and Eugene A. Rosa (1994), 'Nuclear Trees in a Forest of Hazards: A Comparison of Risk Perceptions between American and Japanese University Students', in Thomas C. Lowinger and George W. Hinman (eds), *Nuclear Power at the Crossroads: Challenges and Prospects for the Twenty-first Century*, Boulder, CO: International Research Center for Energy and Economic Development.

Kruize, Hanneke and Arno Bouwman (2003), 'The Distribution of Benefits and Costs of Environmental Policies: A Case Study on the Distribution of Environmental Impacts in the Rijnmond Region, the Netherlands', paper prepared for OECD Environment Directorate Workshop, March.

Kummer, Katharina (1995), *International Management of Hazardous Wastes: The Basel Convention and Related Legal Rules*, Oxford: Clarendon Press.

Kunreuther, Howard and Douglas Easterling (1990), 'Are Risk-benefit Tradeoffs Possible in Siting Hazardous Facilities?', *American Economic Review*, **80**(2), 252–6.

Kunreuther, Howard and Douglas Easterling (1996), 'The Role of Compensation in Siting Hazardous Facilities', *Journal of Policy Analysis and Management*, **15**(4), 601–22.

Kunreuther, Howard and Paul R. Kleindorfer (1986), 'A Sealed-bid Auction Mechanism for Siting Noxious Facilities', *American Economic Review*, **76**, 295–9.

Kunreuther, Howard, Paul R. Kleindorfer, Peter J. Knez and Rudi Yaksick (1987), 'A Compensation Mechanism for Siting Noxious Facilities: Theory and Experimental Design', *Journal of Environmental Economics and Management*, **14**, 371–83.

Kunreuther, Howard, Joanne Linnerooth-Bayer and Kevin Fitzgerald (1996), 'Siting Hazardous Waste Facilities: Lessons from Europe and America', in Paul R. Kleindorfer, Howard C. Kunreuther and David S. Hong (eds), *Energy, Environment, and the Economy: Asian Perspectives*, Cheltenham, UK and Brookfield, USA: Edward Elgar.

Lambert, Thomas (2000), 'EPA's "Revised Guidance" for Implementing Title VI: Environmental Justice on Faulty Legal Footing', Washington University Center for the Study of American Business Policy Brief 206.

Lambert, Thomas and Christopher Boerner (1997), 'Environmental Inequity: Economic Causes, Economic Solutions', *Yale Journal on Regulation*, **14**, 195–234.

Lawrence, D.P. (1996), 'Approaches and Methods of Siting Locally Unwanted Waste Facilities', *Journal of Environmental Planning and Management*, **39**(2), 165–87.

Lazarus, Richard and Stephanie Tai (1999), 'Integrating Environmental Justice into EPA Permitting Authority', *Ecology Law Quarterly*, **26**, 617–68.

Lejano, Raul P. and Climis A. Davos (2002), 'Fair Share: Siting Noxious Facilities as a Risk Distribution Game under Nontransferable Utility', *Journal of Environmental Economics and Management*, **43**, 251–66.

Lesbirel, S. Hayden (1998), *NIMBY Politics in Japan: Energy Siting and the Management of Environmental Conflict*, Ithaca, NY: Cornell University Press.

Lidskog, R. (1993), 'Whose Environment? Which Perspective? A Critical Approach to Hazardous Waste Management in Sweden', *Environment and Planning A*, **25**, 571–88.

Linnerooth-Bayer, Joanne (1997), 'Siting Hazardous Waste Facilities: Issues of Fairness', in R.C. Ragaini (ed.), *Risk Management Strategies Applied to Environmental Clean-up in Central and Eastern Europe*, Singapore: World Scientific.

Linnerooth-Bayer, Joanne and Kevin B. Fitzgerald (1995), 'Conflicting Views on Fair Siting Processes: Evidence from Austria and the US', *Risk: Health, Safety and Environment*, **7**, 119–34.

Linnerooth-Bayer, Joanne and Ragnar E. Lofstedt (1996), 'Fairness and Siting: Introduction to a Symposium', *Risk: Health, Safety and Environment*, **7**, 95–8.

Liu, Feng (1997), 'Dynamics and Causation of Environmental Equity, Locally Unwanted Land Uses, and Neighbourhood Changes', *Environmental Management*, **21**(5), 643–56.

Lofstedt, Ragnar E. (1996), 'Fairness across Borders: The Barseback Nuclear Power Plant', *Risk: Health, Safety, and Environment*, **7**, 135–44.

Lowinger, Thomas and George Hinman (1994), *Nuclear Power at the Crossroads: Challenges and Prospects for the Twenty-first Century*, Boulder, CO: International Research Center for Energy and Economic Development.

Lyle, June (2000), 'Reactions to EPA's Interim Guidance: The Growing Battle for Control over Environmental Justice Decision-making', *Indiana Law Journal*, **75**, 687–709.

Mank, Bradford (1999), 'Is There a Private Cause of Action under EPA's Title VI Regulations? The Need to Empower Environmental Justice Plaintiffs', *Columbia Journal of Environmental Law*, **24**, 1–60.

Mank, Bradford (2000), 'The Draft Title VI Recipient and Revised Investigation Guidance: Too Much Discretion for the EPA and a More Difficult Standard for Complainants?', *Environmental Law Reporter*, **30**, 11144.

Mank, Bradford (2001), 'Proving an Environmental Justice Case: Determining an Appropriate Comparison Population', *Virginia Environmental Law Journal*, **20**, 365–430.

Mansfield, Carol, George Van Houtven and Joel Huber (2001), 'The Efficiency of Political Mechanisms for Siting Nuisance Facilities: Are Opponents More Likely to Participate than Supporters?', *Journal of Real Estate Finance and Economics*, **22**, 141–61.

Marbug, Hugh (1995), 'Hazardous Waste Exportation: The Global Manifestation of Environmental Racism', *Vanderbilt Journal of Transnational Law*, **28**, 251–97.

Mason, G. Stephen Jr (1989), 'Closure and Rejection of Waste Facilities: What Effect Has Public Pressure', *Hazardous Material Control*, July/August, 54–8.

McCubbins, Mathew and Thomas Schwarz (1984), 'Congressional Oversight Overlooked: Police Patrols versus Fire Alarms', *American Journal of Political Science*, **28**, 165–79.

McDougall, Forbes and Jacques Fonteyne (1999), 'Towards an Integrated Approach to Waste Management: The Lessons Learned from Case Studies of European Waste Management Systems', *International Directory of Solid Waste Management*, London: James and James.

McLeod, H., I.H. Langford, A.P. Jones, R.J. Day, I. Lorenzoni and I.J. Bateman (2000), 'The Relationship between Socio-economic Indicators and Air Pollution in England and Wales: Implications for Environmental Justice', *Regional Environmental Change*, **1**(2), 78–85.

Millimet, Daniel and Daniel Slottje (2000), 'The Distribution of Pollution in the United States: An Environmental Gini Approach', working paper, Southern Methodist University, Dallas, Texas.

Minehart, Deborah and Zvika Neeman (2002), 'Effective Siting of Waste Treatment Facilities', *Journal of Environmental Economics and Management*, **43**, 303–24.

Miranda, Marie Lynn, James N. Miller and Timothy L. Jacobs (2000), 'Talking Trash about Landfills: Using Quantitative Scoring Schemes in Landfill Siting Processes', *Journal of Policy Analysis and Management*, **19**(1), 3–22.

Mitchell, Robert Cameron and Richard T. Carson (1986), 'Property Rights, Protest, and the Siting of Hazardous Waste Facilities', *American Economic Review*, **76**(2), 285–90.

Mohai, Paul (1995), 'The Demographics of Dumping Revisited: Examining the Impact of Alternate Methodologies in Environmental Justice Research', *Virginia Environmental Law Journal*, **14**, 615–52.

Mohai, Paul (1996), 'Environmental Justice of Analytic Justice? Reexamining Historical Hazardous Waste Landfill Siting Patterns in Metropolitan Texas', *Social Science Quarterly*, **77**(3), 500–507.

Morell, David and Christopher Magorian (1982), *Siting Hazardous Waste Facilities: Local Opposition and the Myth of Preemption*, Cambridge, MA: Ballinger.

Morello-Frosh, Rachel, Manuel Pastor and James Sadd (2001), 'Environmental Justice and Southern California's "RISKSCAPE": The Distribution of Air Toxics Exposures and Health Risks among Diverse Communities', *Urban Affairs Review*, **36**(4), 551–78.

Munton, Don (1996), 'Siting Hazardous Waste Facilities, Japanese Style', in Don Munton (ed.), *Hazardous Waste Siting and Democratic Choice*, Washington, DC: Georgetown University Press.

Murphy, Sean D. (1994), 'Prospective Liability Regimes for the Transboundary Movement of Hazardous Wastes', *American Journal of International Law*, **88**(1), 24–75.

National Governors' Association (1989), *Siting New Treatment and Disposal Facilities*, Washington, DC: NGA.

Nelson, Arthur C., John Genereux and Michelle Genereux (1992), 'Price Effects of Landfills on House Values', *Land Economics*, **68**(4), 359–64.

Noll, Roger G. and James E. Krier (1990), 'Some Implications of Cognitive Psychology for Risk Regulation', *Journal of Legal Studies*, **19**, 747–79.

Oberholzer-Gee, Felix and Howard Kunreuther (1999), 'Social Pressure in Siting Conflicts: A Case Study of Siting a Radioactive Waste Repository in Pennsylvania', paper presented to the international workshop on Challenges and Issues in Facility Siting, Institute of Economics, Academia Sinica, Taipei, Taiwan.

O'Hare, Michael (1977), ' "Not on My Block You Don't": Facility Siting and the Strategic Importance of Compensation', *Public Policy*, **25**, 407–58.

O'Hare, Michael and Debra Sanderson (1993), 'Facility Siting and Compensation: Lessons from the Massachusetts Experience', *Journal of Policy Analysis and Management*, **12**(2), 364–76.

O'Hare, Michael, Lawrence Bacow and Debra Sanderson (1983), *Facility Siting and Public Opposition*, New York: Van Nostrand Reinhold Company.

Ohkawara, Toru (1999), 'Nuclear Power Plant Siting Issues in Japan: Relationships between Utilities and Host Communities', paper presented at the International Workshop on Challenges and Issues in Facility Siting, Taipei, Taiwan.

Olson, Mancur (1965), *The Logic of Collective Action*, Cambridge, MA: Harvard University Press.

O'Neill, Kate (2000), *Waste Trading among Rich Nations: Building a New Theory of Environmental Regulation*, Cambridge, MA: MIT Press.

Openshaw, S. (1982), 'The Siting of Nuclear Power Stations and Public Safety in the UK', *Regional Studies*, **16**, 183–96.

OECD (Organisation for Economic Co-operation and Development) (1998), 'Trade Measures in the Basel Convention on the Control of Transboundary Movements of Hazardous Wastes and their Disposal' (COM/ENV/TD(97)41/ FINAL), Paris.

O'Sullivan, Arthur (1993), 'Voluntary Auctions for Noxious Facilities: Incentives to Participate and the Efficiency of Siting Decisions', *Journal of Environmental Economics and Management*, **25**, S12–S26.

Page, G. William (1997), *Contaminated Sites and Environmental Cleanup: International Approaches to Prevention, Remediation, and Reuse*, San Diego, CA: Academic Press.

Park, Rozelia S. (1998), 'An Examination of International Environmental Racism through the Lens of Transboundary Movement of Hazardous Wastes', *Indiana Journal of Global Legal Studies*, **5**, 659–709.

Pastor, Manuel Jr, Jim Sadd and John Hipp (2001), 'Which Came First? Toxic Facilities, Minority Move-in, and Environmental Justice', *Journal of Urban Affairs*, **23**(1), 1–21.

Pinzon, Lillian M. (1994), 'Criminalization of the Transboundary Movement of Hazardous Waste and the Effect on Corporations', *DePaul Business Law Journal*, **7**, 173–221.

Probst, Katherine N. and Thomas C. Beierle (1999), *The Evolution of Hazardous Waste Programmes: Lessons from Eight Countries*, Washington DC: Resources for the Future.

Prokop, Gundula, Martin Schamann and Irene Edelgaard (2000), 'Management of Contaminated Sites in Western Europe', European Environment Agency report no. 13/1999.

Pye, Steve, John Stedman, Martin Adams and Katie King (2001), 'Further Analysis of NO_2 and PM_{10} Air Pollution and Social Deprivation', AEA Technology for the Department for Environment, Food and Rural Affairs, The National Assembly for Wales, and Department of the Environment in Northern Ireland.

Quah, E. and K.C. Tan (1998), 'The Siting Problem of NIMBY Facilities: Cost–Benefit Analysis and Auction Mechanisms', *Environment and Planning C: Government and Policy*, **16**, 255–64.

Rabe, Barry G. (1994), *Beyond NIMBY: Hazardous Waste Siting in Canada and the United States*, Washington DC: Brookings Institution.

Ragaini, R.C. (ed.) (1997), *Risk Management Strategies Applied to Environmental Cleanup in Central and Eastern Europe*, Singapore: World Scientific.

Renn, Ortwin, Thomas Webler and Hans Kastenholz (1996), 'Procedural and Substantive Fairness in Landfill Siting: A Swiss Case Study', *Risk: Health, Safety and Environment*, **7**, 145–68.

Richards, Alice (1996), 'Using Co-management to Build Community Support for Waste Facilities', in Don Munton (ed.), *Hazardous Waste Siting and Democratic Choice*, Washington DC: Georgetown University Press.

Richman, Barak D. (2001), 'Mandating Negotiations to Solve the NIMBY Problem: A Creative Regulatory Response', *UCLA Journal of Environmental Law and Policy*, **20**, 223–36.

Ringquist, Evan J. (1997), 'Equity and the Distribution of Environmental Risk: The Case of TRI Facilities', *Social Science Quarterly*, **78**(4), 811–29.

Ristoratore, Mario (1987), 'Siting Toxic Waste Disposal Facilities: Best and Worst Cases in North America', in J. Feldman and Michael A. Goldberg (eds), *Land Rites and Wrongs*, Boston: Lincoln Institute of Land Policy.

Rogers, George O. (1997), 'Dynamic Risk Perception in Two Communities: Risk Events and Changes in Perceived Risk', *Journal of Environmental Planning and Management*, **40**(1), 59–79.

Sadd, James L., Manuel Pastor Jr, J. Thomas Boer and Lori D. Snyder (1999), ' "Every Breath You Take . . ."': The Demographics of Toxic Air Releases in Southern California', *Economic Development Quarterly*, **13**(2), 107–23.

Santiago, Tessa Mayer (2002), 'An Ounce of Preemption is Worth a Pound of Cure: State Preemption of Local Siting Authority as a Means for Achieving Environmental Equity', *Virginia Environmental Law Journal*, **21**, 71–113.

Schneider, Elke and Ortwin Renn (1999), 'Fairness in Public Participation: German Experiences with a Structured Public Participation Process in Regional Waste Management Planning', paper presented at the International Workshop on Challenges and Issues in Facility Siting, Taipei, Taiwan.

Seeliger, Robert (1996), 'Siting Hazardous Waste Incinerators in Germany: From Political Imposition to Public Involvement?', in Don Munton (ed.), *Hazardous Waste Siting and Democratic Choice*, Washington DC: Georgetown University Press.

Shaw, Daigee (1996), 'An Economic Framework for Analysing Facility Siting Policies in Taiwan and Japan', in Paul R. Kleindorfer, Howard C. Kunreuther and David S. Hong (eds), *Energy, Environment, and the Economy: Asian Perspectives*, Cheltenham, UK and Brookfield, USA: Edward Elgar.

Sjoberg, Lennart, Mattias Viklun and Jana Truedsson (1999), 'Attitudes and Opposition in Siting a High Level Nuclear Waste Repository', paper presented to the international workshop on Challenges and Issues in Facility Siting, Institute of Economics, Academia Sinica, Taipei, Taiwan.

Smith, Hank Jenkins and Howard Kunreuther (1999), 'Mitigation and Compensation as Policy Tools for Siting Potentially Hazardous Facilities: Evidence from Field Survey Data', paper presented to the international work-shop on Challenges and Issues in Facility Siting, Institute of Economics, Academia Sinica, Taipei, Taiwan.

Snary, Christopher (2002), 'Risk Communication and the Waste-to-energy Incinerator Environmental Impact Assessment Process: A UK Case Study of

Public Involvement', *Journal of Environmental Planning and Management*, **45**(2), 267–83.

Sullivan, Arthur M. (1990), 'Victim Compensation Revisited: Efficiency versus Equity in the Siting of Noxious Facilities', *Journal of Public Economics*, **41**, 211–25.

Sullivan, Arthur M. (1992), 'Siting Noxious Facilities: A Siting Lottery with Victim Compensation', *Journal of Urban Economics*, **31**, 360–74.

Sundram, Muthu S. (1997), 'Basel Convention on Transboundary Movement of Hazardous Wastes: Total Ban Amendment', *Pace International Law Review*, **9**, 1–56.

Swallow, Stephen, James Opaluch and Thomas F. Weaver (1992), 'Siting Noxious Facilities: An Approach that Integrates Technical, Economic, and Political Considerations', *Land Economics*, **68**(3), 283–302.

Swallow, Stephen K., Thomas Weaver, James J. Opaluch and Thomas Michelman (1994), 'Heterogeneous Preferences and Aggregation in Environmental Policy Analysis: A Landfill Siting Case', *American Journal of Agricultural Economics*, **76**, 431–43.

Vari, Anna (1996), 'Public Perceptions about Equity and Fairness: Siting Low-level Radioactive Waste Disposal Facilities in the U.S. and Hungary', *Risk: Health, Safety and Environment*, Spring 1996.

Verchick, Robert (1999), 'Critical Space Theory: Keeping Local Geography in American and European Environmental Law', *Tulane Law Review*, **73**, 739–86.

Viscusi, W. Kip and James T. Hamilton (1999), 'Are Risk Regulators Rational? Evidence from Hazardous Waste Cleanup Decisions', *American Economic Review*, **89**(4), 1010–27.

Waehrer, Keith (2003), 'Hazardous Facility Siting when Cost Information is Private: An Application of Multidimensional Mechanism Design', *Journal of Public Economic Theory*, **5**(4), 605–22.

Walker, Gordon, John Mooney and Derek Pratts (2000), 'The People and the Hazard: The Spatial Context of Major Accident Hazard Management in Britain', *Applied Geography*, **20**, 119–35.

Walsh, Maureen (1992), 'The Global Trade in Hazardous Wastes: Domestic and International Attempts to Cope with a Growing Crisis in Waste Management', *Catholic University Law Review*, **42**, 103–40.

Waugh, Theodore (2000), 'Where Do We Go From Here: Legal Controls and Future Strategies for Addressing the Transportation of Hazardous Wastes Across International Borders', *Fordham Environmental Law Journal*, **11**, 477–544.

Wheeler, Michael (1994), 'Negotiating NIMBYs: Learning from the Failure of the Massachusetts Siting Law', *Yale Journal on Regulation*, **11**, 241–91.

Whitman, Christine Todd (2001), 'EPA's Commitment to Environmental Justice', 9 August, EPA Internal Memo, available at www.epa.gov.

Yandle, Tracy and Dudley Burton (1996), 'Reexamining Environmental Justice: A Statistical Analysis of Historical Hazardous Waste Landfill Siting Patterns in Metropolitan Texas', *Social Science Quarterly*, **77**(3), 477–527.

Yang, Tseming (2002), 'Melding Civil Rights and Environmentalism: Finding Environmental Justice's Place in Environmental Regulation', *Harvard Environmental Law Review*, **26**, 1–32.

Zimmerman, Rae (1993), 'Social Equity and Environmental Risk', *Risk Analysis*, **13**(6), 649–66.

8. Distributional effects of environmental policy: conclusions and policy implications

Ysé Serret and Nick Johnstone

Government concerns about the distributional effects of environmental policies generally arise when it is felt that a policy instrument is distributionally regressive, either in the sense that its financial burden falls disproportionately on lower-income households and/or in the sense that the environmental benefits are accrued disproportionately by higher-income households.

Generally speaking, however, it is the distribution of financial effects that is likely to raise the most important political concerns. Taxes are usually perceived as being regressive and as a result are likely to face opposition from the public. The public demonstrations that resulted from planned increases in energy taxation in several European countries in 2000 are an illustration. A more recent example is the strong reaction to charges for environmental waste collection services in Ireland as well as the Irish Government's decision in 2004 to abandon the proposed carbon taxation in the face of potential social impacts (see Box 8.3 below). Thus, addressing distributional effects can be a crucial element for a government in securing the political acceptance of environmental policy.

All public policies are likely to have distributional effects of some kind, and the need to tackle distributional impacts associated with the introduction of environmental policies arises when the effects are significant. If the existing distribution of wealth and the public policy framework (tax schedules, social security schemes and so on) are thought to be 'fair', then the case for addressing distributional concerns upon the introduction of an environmental policy only arises if: a) the policy has non-trivial distributional impacts overall and/or; b) for political economy reasons, perceptions of distributional impacts represent a significant barrier to the introduction of the policy.

This final chapter reviews some of the major challenges facing policymakers as they seek to address the distributional impacts of environmental policies. An overview of some of the main aspects to consider when assessing distributional effects in both environmental and financial terms is first presented. The second section presents the various channels through which these effects can arise. In the third section, the implications of the very nature of the environmental issue for public policy are considered. Policy recommendations on the choice of mitigation options are then formulated. The desirability of alternative means of addressing distributional impacts is discussed according to the nature of the environmental issues addressed and the need to ensure that the economic efficiency and environmental effectiveness of the policy remains intact.

1. TAKING ENVIRONMENTAL AND FINANCIAL ASPECTS INTO ACCOUNT

A full assessment of the distributional effects of environmental policies requires the examination of both the distribution of environmental quality and the distribution of financial impacts. In this section, some of the key issues with respect to both of these aspects are presented.

1.1 Disparities in the Distribution of Environmental Quality

Much of the work on the distribution of environmental quality is concerned with the existing state of the environment, rather than the incremental change in that state resulting from the introduction of an environmental policy. This is in sharp contrast to much of the work on the financial effects of environmental policies, which assesses regressivity on the basis of a comparison of distributional burdens following the introduction of the policy with some counterfactual scenario (usually one in which it is assumed that the policy is not introduced).

Moreover, much of the work focuses on an assessment of the distributional impacts in terms of physical indicators of exposure or access (see Pearce in Chapter 2). Little attention is paid to differences in preferences, which can vary widely across different socio-economic groups. This can have important implications for the findings. Thus, for example, depending upon the relative income elasticity of demand for environmental quality – about which there is little evidence and considerable controversy – a particular distribution of environmental quality which may appear to be regressive in physical terms may be progressive in welfare terms (and vice versa).

A distinction can be made between an assessment of the distribution of exposure to environmental 'bads' (for example, pollution exposure) and access to environmental 'goods' (for example, urban parks), and work in these two areas has been reviewed in the preceding chapters. However, it is with respect to environmental 'bads' that the evidence is most comprehensive. Disparities can arise in the distribution of exposure to environmental hazards and this is the main focus of the available studies on 'environmental justice' undertaken in the United States. In the 1980s, empirical analysis generally focused on hazardous waste sites, and in the 1990s coverage was expanded to include assessments of toxic releases, waste sites and air pollution, as noted by Hamilton (Chapter 7 in the present volume).

The correlation of exposure to environmental hazards with neighbourhoods with a high concentration of low-income households was established by a number of early studies in the US literature,[1] and to a lesser extent in Canada (Handy, 1977). More recent US analyses providing evidence that the higher the damage, the lower the income level, include Mohai and Bryant (1992), Yandle and Burton (1996), Hamilton and Viscusi (1999) and Millimet and Slottje (2000).[2] Empirical studies in Europe are relatively few in number and have been undertaken recently. Focusing almost exclusively on data for the United Kingdom, they indicate a positive correlation between air pollution and socio-economic deprivation (see McLeod et al., 2000; Pye et al., 2001; Brainard et al., 2002b).

While not the focus of the present volume, findings from the studies on other distributional vectors are important since they can play an important confounding role with respect to income. For instance, Zimmerman (1993) shows that neighbourhoods with significant Hispanic and African-American populations are correlated with hazardous waste sites, but finds no link to income. Been and Gupta (1997) find no correlation with poverty. Hite (2000) provides evidence of racial inequity but no evidence of income inequity when examining exposure to landfills.[3] More recent and rather limited evidence in Canada, relying on the National Pollution Release Inventory, indicates that income is positively correlated with pollution (Jerrett et al., 1997). However, a more recent study shows no association between releases, transfers and income (Harrison and Antweiler, 2002).

Noise pollution is another dimension of exposure to environmental hazards which has raised some distributional concerns. Unfortunately, very few empirical studies have addressed this issue. The few studies available are European and show a positive but weak correlation between noise levels and low-income groups (see Chapter 6). Kruize and Bouwman (2004) find that in the Rijnmond region, in the Netherlands, higher income categories are exposed to lower levels of traffic noise than lower income categories, particularly with regard to railway noise. However, for aircraft noise high-income categories are exposed to higher noise levels compared to lower income categories.

As noted above, distributional considerations can also result from disparities in the distribution of access to environmental amenities such as urban parks and conservation areas. If wealthier households are the primary beneficiaries of such policies, then the use of scarce public resources for their provision can be seen as regressive.[4] Unfortunately, this question is rarely analysed in the literature. The few European studies available on access to green space tend to conclude that provision is regressive (see Brainard et al., 2002a; Kruize and Bouwman, 2004). Beyond assessments focusing on a specific aspect of environmental quality, a broader approach may be applied in which disparities in exposure to environmental hazards and access to environmental amenities are simultaneously examined, as in Kruize and Bouwman (2004) (see Box 8.1).

Overall, there is some consensus in the literature that low-income households tend to be relatively more exposed to environmental hazards. This is particularly the case for exposure to toxic releases and proximity to hazardous waste sites with relatively less ample, and more ambiguous results for exposure to noise pollution. However, most of the studies are North American, in particular from the United States. Available evidence is very limited for Europe and extremely scarce for the OECD Pacific region.

BOX 8.1   ASSESSING THE DISTRIBUTION OF ENVIRONMENTAL QUALITY IN A BROAD FRAMEWORK

In their study on the distribution of environmental quality in the Netherlands, Kruize and Bouwman (2004) consider a wide variety of measures of access to environmental quality while most studies generally look at one environmental indicator only. In the Rijnmond case study the broad definition of environmental quality indicators include air pollution (NO_2), traffic noise, presence of waste disposal facilities as well as access to public green areas (for example, parks, forest). This approach provides a more complete picture, but, more importantly, it offers the possibility to analyse the accumulation of environmental impacts for a certain neighbourhood and for a certain population group. The work by Kruize and Bouwman also provides new insights by combining objective measures of access to environmental quality with perception-based measures (for example, perceived availability and quality of green areas).

Given the existing geographical bias, some caution must be exercised when generalising the results to other countries. Moreover, while empirical studies on the distribution of environmental quality generally focus on exposure to environmental hazards such as proximity to polluting sites, different results may be obtained with a broader approach where the distribution of other environmental disamenities, such as noise, is also considered, as well as access to environmental amenities (for example, urban parks).

In addition, it should be noted that the choice of methodological framework, such as the geographical unit selected, are important when examining the distribution of environmental quality.[5] For instance, recent research[6] on distributional effects applying sophisticated spatial techniques such as Geographic Information Systems (GIS) generates useful results, as discussed by Hamilton (Chapter 7) and allows for more disaggregated analysis. The geographic scale which can be applied includes census track,[7] county level or even zip code areas[8] analysis and this choice may affect the results obtained, as underlined in the literature.[9]

And finally, as noted above, it is important to bear in mind that most studies on the distribution of environmental quality implicitly assume that preferences for environmental quality are the same across households in different socio-economic groups. However, if this is not the case, then distributions which appear to be regressive may in fact be progressive in terms of welfare (and vice versa). While there is little evidence on the income elasticity of demand for environmental quality in general, few would argue that it is likely to be the same for all aspects of environmental quality, a point to which we return below.

1.2   The Distribution of Financial Effects of Environmental Policies

As noted by Kriström (Chapter 3 in the present volume), environmental policies – indeed all public policies – have distributional effects on households in terms of financial burdens: there are likely to be winners and losers. However, for a given environmental objective, the nature of the instrument applied can have important implications for the distribution of financial impacts across households.

There is a strong predominance in the literature on the assessment of the distributional effects of economic instruments, particularly environment-related taxes. This may be partly attributed to the relative transparency of their financial impacts compared to other measures. However, alternative policy instruments such as direct regulation may also have distributional implications which are at least as important as those arising from economic instruments.

Energy/carbon taxation is one area where extensive empirical work has been undertaken. The degree of regressivity is often found to be mild to weak. For instance, Brännlund and Nordström (2004) and Cornwell and Creedy (1997) are examples of Swedish and Australian studies confirming the general view that carbon taxes are regressive. Results from other analyses are more ambiguous and sometimes inconclusive.[10] The comprehensive study by Klinge-Jacobsen et al. (2001) for Denmark concludes that gasoline taxation may be progressive, as well as registration duties for cars, while most other environmental taxes are found to be regressive.

The distributional effects of taxes will depend on the broad categories of effects taken into account in the analysis, as further discussed below. Thus, empirical evidence indicates that the degree of regressivity decreases once indirect effects are taken into account. This is particularly true of energy taxes, and arises from the fact that energy is an input into all other goods and services, and as such the regressivity associated with the direct effects of tax on a good which is income-inelastic is partly attenuated once the effect on all expenditures are accounted for.

The results on the regressivity of environmental taxation also vary to some extent according to how the tax revenues are returned to the economy. This point is discussed by Bork (see Chapter 4) who concludes that, overall, the effects of the German ecological tax reform are weakly regressive.[11] Thus, while gasoline taxes are found to be regressive in some studies (for example, Sipes and Mendelsohn, 2001), others suggest that lump-sum payments may actually make the tax package progressive (West and Williams, 2002).

The use of tradable permits can raise distributive issues as well. Their effects can be similar to those of the taxes, as noted by Kriström (Chapter 3), as long as the permits are auctioned. The distributional implications will differ, however, with the grandfathering of permits where the rent is transferred to firms. The choice of the allocation of tradable permits (auctioned versus grandfathered), as well as the precise means by which the revenue is recycled if permits are auctioned, has significant impacts on the distributional effects of a given policy (Dinan and Rogers, 2002; Parry, 2004).

Less evidently, the adoption of direct regulation is likely to create distributional concerns. However, empirical studies in this area are scant compared to the literature on the impacts of economic instruments. The issue is, however, now receiving increased attention.[12] Early studies examining the distribution of pollution abatement costs in the manufacturing sector indicate that direct regulations tend to be regressive. Assuming that the firms pass all abatement costs into prices for goods and services produced, the burden of direct regulation tends to fall disproportionately on low-income households (Robison, 1985).

More recent studies on the distributional effects resulting from the imposition of appliances performance standards for energy efficiency (see Sutherland, 1991, 2003 and Chapter 5 in the present volume; Stoft, 1993) suggest possible regressive effects. These arise from the temporal pattern of costs and savings. Since energy efficiency standards often result in higher upfront investment costs, with benefits accruing over time through lower operating costs, households with high discount rates will benefit relatively less. Evidence on the tendency of low-income households to have higher discount rates than high-income households has been revealed in purchases of energy-using consumer durables (see Dubin and McFadden, 1984; Train, 1985). In studies assessing the possible distributional effects of direct regulations to reduce motor vehicle pollution, mandated environmental equipment (for example, smog emissions equipment) are also found to have a probable regressive impact since their cost varies little with the cost of the vehicle, as emphasised by Bae (2003). On the other hand, analysis on the effects of performance standards (that is, Corporate Average Fuel Efficiency Standard[13]) indicates that the resulting decline in the price of small cars could benefit low-income car owners. Goldberg (1998) concludes that the CAFE regulation was progressive.

However, since the financial impacts of direct regulations are not as transparent as in the case of economic instruments, the distributional effects of direct regulation are less frequently analysed than the other instruments discussed thus far. However, this does not mean that they are less important. In general, while the literature on the distributional effects of command-and-control approaches is scant, there is no a priori reason why such environmental policy instruments should be immune to distributional impacts, as noted by Kriström (Chapter 3).

Distributional concerns may also arise from the use of environment-related subsidies[14] though, here again, the conclusions on their distributional impacts remain unclear in light of the paucity of empirical studies available. Just as it is important to examine public finance issues when applying environment-related taxes and auctioned tradable permits, it is important to examine such issues when allocating subsidies. However, in the case of subsidies, the distributional effects will arise from both the direct impacts of the allocation of subsidies (that is, the relative income of the beneficiaries) and the degree of regressivity or progressivity of the tax system used to raise the finance required to pay for such programmes.

Liability for environmental damages can also have distributional implications. The impacts of legal liability regimes are likely to vary widely depending upon the means by which damages are compensated when a firm (or other economic agent) is held responsible for adverse environmental consequences arising from its activities. In particular, the distributional impacts will not be the same if damages are compensated on the basis of lost earnings or production losses, or according to fixed criteria set regardless of households' economic status. Countries use very different methods to determine compensation in such cases.

In short, all environmental policies, not just economic instruments, are likely to raise distributional concerns. When revenue is raised – as in the case of taxes and auctioned tradable permits – the outcome depends largely on how the revenue is recycled. When subsidies are used, the outcome will depend upon both the relative wealth of the beneficiaries and the means by which the revenue is raised to finance the programmes. In the case of direct regulation, the effects will depend not only on the broad pattern of consumption expenditures, but in some cases on the choices made within individual commodity classes.

Assessing such impacts is by no means straightforward. The results for a given study will be affected by whether or not indirect effects are included, as well as by the treatment of behavioural responses. In addition, methodological choices such as the proxy used to measure wealth are likely to affect the results of empirical studies, as discussed earlier. This can be illustrated with the study by Walls and Hanson (1999) which concludes that emissions-based fees look more regressive than the vehicle registration fee system applied in California, when using both annual income and lifetime income, though much less so on a lifetime income basis.

To summarise, a broad assessment framework must be used in order to grasp the variety of distributional concerns that may arise, while available studies tend to focus on the distribution of a given indicator of environmental quality (for example, air pollution) or the financial effects of specific policy instruments (for example, taxes). In addition, the literature scarcely addresses simultaneously the two aspects of the discussion (distribution of environmental quality and of financial effects), thereby overlooking the possible trade-offs (for example, lower housing near polluting sites).

2. THE CHANNELS THROUGH WHICH DISTRIBUTIONAL EFFECTS ARISE

2.1 Accounting for Indirect Effects

When assessing the possible adverse distributional impacts of a given policy, the variety of channels through which these effects can arise need to be taken into account in order to reflect the complexity of the mechanisms involved as underlined earlier. Different levels of analysis may be chosen by analysts and decision-makers, depending upon the nature of the most significant effects foreseen.

Focusing on the direct financial effects of a policy can give a good picture of the most important distributional impacts arising from the implementation of certain types of environmental policy instruments. This may be the case, for example, with taxes on final products (for example, 'gas guzzler' tax applied to cars) or mandated environmental technology for final products (for example, catalytic converters). This approach can however provide a misleading picture in some cases. Accounting for indirect effects and adopting a dynamic perspective may be necessary in order to grasp the complexity of the distributional effects involved.

Assessing the indirect financial effects resulting from the implementation of environmental policy is of particular relevance to determine the distributional impacts of policy instruments targeting goods and services that serve as inputs to the production of other goods and services. These effects can arise from both direct forms of regulation and economic instruments. For instance, irrespective of whether or not the impacts of air pollution emissions from refineries take the form of technology-based standards or tradable emission permits, there will be downstream implications on the cost of fuels used by households.

Carbon taxes are another example. The carbon tax affects prices faced by households both directly, for fuels, and indirectly for energy-intensive manufactured goods. The price of goods increases in proportion to their carbon content. Such effects can be accounted for when using input–output tables which provide data on inter-industry flows. They allow for the determination of the sectors in which price increases are likely to be greatest and the distributional implications most important.

Taking such 'indirect' effects into account can have important implications for the assessment of the distributional implications of different measures. For instance, the analysis of the distributional impacts of a carbon tax in Australia suggests that the regressivity of the tax results notably from the high price increase in the fuel and power sector, combined with relatively large price increases in the food and tobacco sectors, which also form a relatively high proportion of the budget of lower-income earners (see Cornwell and Creedy, 1997).

Considering again the example of a carbon tax, some of the interrelated mechanisms involved can be disentangled as follows (see Kriström in Chapter 3). Companies with increased costs will shift some of these costs on to the buyers of their products. If agriculture uses a significant amount of fossil fuels and faces higher fuel costs because of a carbon tax, part of this increase will be shifted on to slaughterhouses and other users of agricultural products. The cost of transporting the goods on roads will also increase, with an impact on households. An examination of all these impacts is needed in order fully to assess the distributional effects of the tax.

2.2 Taking Behavioural Response into Account

In addition, as all households may not react in a similar way to the adoption of a policy, it is essential to account for any differences in behavioural response across socio-economic groups when undertaking an analysis of the distributional effects (see Box 8.2). For instance, while most analyses on the distributional effects of vehicle pollution control policies take households' behaviour as constant (Walls and Hanson, 1999), studies that take into account how household demand may vary according to household characteristics find that this can affect results significantly[15] (West, 2004). In a similar way, Halvorsen and Nesbakken (2002) underline the role of behavioural responses in their study on the distributional effects of increased household electricity taxation in Norway. Their results suggest that when allowing for household electricity consumption to change as a response to the tax increase, the positive distributional effects of the tax increase are reduced.

Variation in the degree of price responsiveness across households may be particularly significant. For instance, low-income households are expected to be more responsive to a price increase in driving costs than higher-income households, and all the more so if they have other transportation options. Poor households are more likely to respond to an increase in costs by using public transportation. However, when substitution possibilities are constrained, the effects may be very different. As an illustration, some studies indicate that the possibility for low-income households to substitute their electricity consumption for other energy sources is smaller than for high-income households (see Halvorsen and Nesbakken, 2002).

In addition to short-run responses, the consideration of longer-term behavioural adjustments to environmental measures can be important in assessing distributional impacts. For instance, in the case of vehicle pollution control policies, in addition to considering households' responses in terms of reduction in the number of miles they drive, it may be necessary to account for changes in the number or type of vehicles they own (for example, smaller, better-maintained, newer, less polluting) in response to higher operating costs.

In a similar way, it may also be useful to trace out the response of car manufacturers to such policies and whether they introduce cleaner vehicles. Analogously, when assessing the distributional effects of household electricity taxation, longer-term behavioural changes can be examined, such as

BOX 8.2   ENVIRONMENTAL TAX INCIDENCE AND BEHAVIOURAL RESPONSES

Environmental taxes often appear to be regressive since lower-income households have greater relative expenses for many of the goods and services significantly affected by such policies (for example, taxes on heating or transport fuels). However, many of the studies which find that there are regressive impacts associated with such measures assume that households do not adjust their expenditure patterns in the face of relative price changes, or that all households do so in an equivalent manner.

Taking into account the behavioural responses of households, and particularly differences in such responses across households in different socio-economic and demographic groups, can have significant implications for the degree of regressivity associated with the introduction of a given tax. For instance, if demand is more price-elastic for lower-income households than higher-income households, then the effect of the policy will be less regressive than a simple comparison of expenditure patterns would imply.

However, with respect to some goods and services, it is very likely that substitution possibilities for lower-income households will be less important than for higher-income households. For instance, if substitution requires significant investment in capital equipment – for example, for fuel substitution with respect to home heating – lower-income households may be less able to substitute out of carbon-intensive fuels.

Tiezzi (2005) reports on the effects of carbon taxation in Italy which affects mainly transport and heating fuels through increases in the excise tax rates over the period 1999–2005. Accounting for behavioural responses seems to be important. In particular, differences in car ownership across different socio-economic and demographic groups affect the nature of responses to the tax, particularly in the short and medium run. Even among car-owning households, the size of the household can have significant implications for the incidence of the tax since there seem to be household economies of scale in car ownership and use. As the author concludes 'the way people react to policy changes seems to be crucial' when estimating the distributional effects of an environmental tax.

possibly investing in more energy-efficient equipment in addition to short-term changes in their electricity consumption. In all such cases, there may be differences in substitution possibilities for relatively poor and relatively rich households.

The need to examine long-run behavioural responses is also important in assessing the distribution of environmental quality. Indeed, Hamilton (Chapter 7 in the present volume) underlines that in order to determine the causation of possible disparities in exposure to potential risks, an approach going beyond the simple snapshot of who is exposed to hazardous waste facilities (or other 'bads') at a given point in time is required. Behavioural adjustments across different socio-economic groups can result in very different indications of distributional effects. Moreover, this example illustrates the need to look at financial and environmental impacts within a single framework, a point to which we now turn.

2.3 Accounting for Effects on Associated Markets

The analytical issues described above (indirect impacts and behavioural responses) focus on the distributional incidence of environmental policy on households as consumers. Yet, household members are also taxpayers, workers and residents. Thus, the effects on associated markets may be significant, and factoring them into the distributional analysis may be necessary to get a full picture of the mechanisms involved.

First, distributional effects will vary through the channel of public finance, a point touched upon above. This might be the case, in particular, when the proceeds raised by economic instruments (such as taxes or auctioned tradable permits) are recycled. The distributional implications will not be the same depending upon how the revenue is redistributed (for example, reduction in payroll taxes for employers, in income taxes, in value added tax rate). For instance, Kriström (Chapter 3) notes that, should the proceeds from the carbon tax be used to cut labour taxes, it is reasonable to expect that goods which are relatively 'labour-intensive' will fetch a relatively lower price. Prices on haircuts and consulting services may therefore fall. Such reductions will benefit households, much in the same way as households, in the end, must pay higher taxes. Here again, it is clear that the distributional implications of environmental policy can be rather subtle.

Distributional effects may also arise through the channel of labour markets. On the one hand, some environmental policies may disproportionately affect some household members in their role as workers or as shareholders. In such cases distributional impacts will depend upon the industry structure. On the other hand, for particular socio-economic groups such as low-income households, living near dynamic active labour markets might be seen as compensation for increased exposure to environmental hazards (noise, air pollution). Other trade-offs may exist as well, such as proximity to transport networks and enjoying lower housing costs.[16]

Most studies support the hypothesis that environmental quality is an input to the real estate market.[17] Indeed, it would be surprising if this were not the case. Recent evidence includes the work by Chay and Greenstone (2004) for the United States which suggests that improvements in air quality are associated with an increase in housing values. Baranzini and Ramirez (2005) find a statistically significant impact of all sources of noise on rents. As local environmental quality affects the housing market, distributional impacts can arise as some households may bear financial costs (that is, if a park is sited nearby) or accrue financial benefits (that is, if a hazardous waste facility is sited nearby) through the real estate market.

Focusing exclusively on distributional impacts in terms of environmental quality without taking into account these countervailing financial effects would be misleading. Indeed, the distributional effects resulting from an improvement or a deterioration of environmental quality will be different according to whether households affected are home-owners or tenants. And finally, apparent distributional effects will not be the same if disparities are assessed at the point in which the facility siting decision is taken, or at some later point following the siting decision as a result of falling property values which will induce lower-income earners to move.

Thus, when assessing distributional effects of environmental policies on households, policy-makers may choose between different frameworks of analysis according to the nature of the main distributive effects expected to arise from the implementation or tightening of a policy. With some instruments, focusing on the direct effects might give a good picture while with others, accounting for indirect effects and households' responses may be necessary. In other cases, examining only the distributional effects on households as consumers might provide a misleading picture, and adopting a wider perspective where possible impacts on households as taxpayers, workers and residents may be required in order to grasp the complexity of the adjustments occurring.

3.   THE IMPORTANCE OF THE NATURE OF THE ENVIRONMENTAL ISSUE

Efforts by OECD member countries to mitigate the adverse distributional impacts of environmental policies take many forms, but the assessment of the relative efficiency of alternative means of mitigation remains to be developed further. The relative desirability of alternative means of mitigation and whether adverse distributional effects should be addressed through modifications to the environmental policy itself or through other complementary instruments has to be assessed in light of the nature of the environmental issue being considered.

3.1   Degree of 'Publicness' of the Environmental Concern

Distributional effects will differ – and need to be addressed differently – depending upon whether the environmental 'good' or 'bad' targeted is a pure public good, for which exposure or access are non-rivalrous and non-excludable, or a local 'public' good which is at least partly rivalrous and excludable. In the latter case, environmental quality has a direct financial impact on other markets, such as real estate markets.

Global air pollution such as global warming and ozone depletion would correspond to the first type of good as one person's exposure to the environmental hazard does not reduce the level of exposure of the others, there is no means of exclusion of exposure. In this case, when implementing an environmental policy, for instance to reduce carbon emissions, the benefits in terms of improved environmental quality will be shared by all.

In such cases, it is impossible to differentiate environmental quality across household income groups, as access to a pure public good (exposure to a pure public bad) is the same for all socio-economic groups. However, this is not to say that the environmental policy does not have distributional implications. On the one hand, distributional issues arise in so far as the financial costs of implementing carbon emissions reductions differ, as with any environmental policy. Some will pay more and some less. On the other hand, even with respect to environmental quality, there may be important distributional impacts. These are not associated with the distribution of impacts themselves (as with local public goods), but rather with the overall level of the impacts. Specifically, if preferences for the public environmental good (or bad) differ across socio-economic groups, distributional effects will arise from the choice of stringency of the policy (see Chichilnisky and Heal, 1994).

Thus, the only way to control the distributional effects of the environmental policy (in terms of environmental quality) across household income groups will be through its level of stringency. Whether the improvement in environmental quality will benefit low-income or higher-income groups will depend on the elasticity of 'demand' for environmental quality. For a given environmental good, if the income elasticity is greater than one, that is to say that demand for environmental quality increases as household income increases, the stricter the measures, the more regressive the policy.

There are, however, very few pure public environmental goods. Options available to deal with distributional issues differ with local 'public' goods which have excludable benefits (or costs). Policy-makers will have some capacity to design policies so that they benefit certain household groups disproportionately. For instance, measures can be taken to facilitate access to urban green space for low-income households. Similar measures may be applied for the provision of environment-related services such as water or energy services to poorer consumers.

Yet, the possible adverse effects of some policy options on environmental effectiveness and economic efficiency need to be considered, as emphasised below. In addition, targeting policies so that they address concerns about the distribution of environmental quality in the case of local 'public' goods assumes that there are only direct effects (that is, only affecting the utility function in a direct way). However, as noted above, for local 'public' goods, this is rarely the case in practice as indirect effects are likely to arise through associated markets (for example, the real estate market).

3.2   Direct and Indirect Effects on the Household's Utility Function

The means to address distributional concerns will also be affected by the extent to which the environmental impacts enter the household's utility function directly as well as indirectly. Local air pollution affects people's health directly, and relative health damage should be assessed. However, as it has been noted above, local public goods raise particular problems for the assessment of the distributional impacts of environmental policies. Environmental quality enters into other markets, with implications for relative costs and benefits borne by participants in those markets.

The public policy intervention required to deal with distributional effects is of a different nature for a policy introduced to locate a hazardous waste site, as the household utility can be affected both directly (for example, as regards health) as well as indirectly through related markets like real estate and labour markets. Local environmental quality has an influence on the housing market, but also on the labour market.

As such, indirect effects are likely to contribute to the disproportionate exposure of low-income households to environmental hazards and lower access to local public environmental goods such as parks. Even if the government intentionally seeks to provide lower-income households with preferential access to parks or reduced exposure to environmental hazards, such a policy may be self-defeating in the long run.

As noted above, there is good evidence that dwellings which are far from polluting plants and close to city parks will tend to be more expensive. Subsequent to a policy intervention (investment in green space in deprived areas or constraints on siting of industrial facilities), there will be a degree of 'sorting' as households adjust to changing market prices. Lower-income households (most often tenants) may not benefit from the intended environmental improvements, as they will be forced out of neighbourhoods in which environmental quality has improved.

The policy-maker may find himself to be 'chasing his own tail'. In such cases discretionary siting of local public environmental goods or discretionary constraints on the siting of polluting facilities for distributional reasons may prove to be ineffective. Rather than such discretionary programmes, it may be preferable to have a more general policy of ensuring minimum levels of access and limited levels of exposure. Distributionally-motivated provision of local public environmental goods or constraints on local public environmental bads may be undermined by the market in the long run.

However, if there are specific market failures which affect the efficiency of such 'sorting' there may be a case for targeted policy interventions. For instance, if there are information failures with respect to the health effects of levels of exposure faced, government provision of such information will improve efficiency. Imperfect household credit markets may also be important. Policy-makers may, for instance, adopt measures to ensure that markets for mortgages are not systematically biased against low-income households and to facilitate their access to capital markets.

3.3 Welfare Attributes of Goods

The nature of policy response to address distributional issues will also be affected by the welfare attributes of the goods considered. For instance, there will be differences depending upon whether the measures impact primarily on a 'luxury' use of the environment (for example, water to wash the car) or for a more basic necessity (for example, water for personal hygiene).

Essential goods generally refer to those goods from which individuals should not be excluded because of inability to pay, such as basic education or health services. In the environmental context, this would include the supply of water and energy services for basic needs. In addition, it may be important for policy-makers to account for inter-agent issues as there are situations where the behaviour of some agents can enter other agents' welfare function (for example, the fact that some households do not have access to environmental services such as water sanitation may affect other agents' health).

For such aspects of the environment, policy-makers may not want households to go below a given level of consumption, either because this is seen as incompatible with a 'reasonable standard of living' and/or because of inter-agent externalities. In a number of OECD countries, affordability is, for instance, perceived to be an issue for the provision of potable water services (see OECD, 2003a; Herrington, 2003). Such considerations can be reflected in the measures taken by public authorities to tackle distributional concerns.

In the case of energy and water services, a wide range of measures are available to policy-makers to deal with distributional concerns. While some apply to all households, such as changes in tariff structure (for example, progressive pricing like increasing-block tariffs for water), others can be targeted specifically at low-income households. These would include general income support measures (for example, housing allowance), tariff-based measures (for example, targeted reductions of water charges), as well as non-tariff-based financial measures such as water vouchers and billing arrangements.

However, these policy measures are not all equivalent either in terms of environmental effectiveness or with respect to economic efficiency. In a similar way, the different options do not have the same ability to meet basic needs. For instance, in order to ensure that any benefits received are actually used for home energy or water consumption, governments may choose to provide service vouchers to lower-income families rather than income support measures leaving households to decide on their level of consumption, which may not meet essential needs. Vouchers which enable low-income families to obtain rebates on their energy or water bills are used in a number of OECD countries such as the United States and France.

3.4   Institutional Aspects of Provision

The institutional characteristics of the provision of environmental quality, including such aspects as ownership (public versus private sector), as well as the competitive structure of the market, will also have an impact on the options available to decision-makers to address distributional concerns.

For instance, on the one side, the provision of urban parks is clearly in public hands. The public sector plays a direct role in determining the level of provision and the location of such amenities. The same is true for publicly-managed facilities, such as public wastewater treatment facilities, airports, and hazardous waste transport, storage and disposal facilities. On the other hand, exposure to air pollution is largely determined by activity directly within the private sector, as is exposure to noise pollution. However, even in these areas, the public sector plays an important role in determining levels of exposure for different socio-economic groups through land-use planning and the permitting process.[18]

For the provision of environment-related services like water or waste services, public–private partnerships are common in the OECD. However, the precise nature of the mix between the public and private interests involved remains very country-specific. The options available to governments to deal with distributional issues are likely to differ according to how the different interests are combined, and how the respective roles of private firms and public entities are delineated. For example, the capacity to adjust the water tariff structure in order to meet distributional concerns, may vary according to whether the private sector owns the infrastructure assets or whether its role is limited to the management of operations, with the asset ownership remaining public.

4. POLICY PRINCIPLES

If distributional impacts from the introduction of an environmental policy are potentially significant, the use of mitigation and compensation measures may be politically necessary to allow for its implementation. Even if the environmental policy is ultimately introduced, its potential distributional effects may be such as to have an influence on the stringency of the policy adopted. For instance, in Sweden it has been argued that the relatively high level of the NO_x charge that was introduced can be attributed in part to the fact that those affected were compensated – that is, distribution and stringency are endogenous (see Millock and Sterner, 2004).

However, not all means of mitigation or compensation are equivalent. In some cases, efforts to alleviate distributional impacts may have important implications for the economic efficiency of the environmental policy measure. As such, in addition to assessing the potential distributional impacts of a given policy prior to its introduction, it is necessary to assess the potential effects of their alleviation on economic efficiency.

4.1 Assess Impacts Systematically

Distributional effects are assessed in a number of OECD countries when designing policies before their introduction and/or evaluating environmental policies which are already in place (for example, environment-related taxes). The recent Irish public consultation on the proposed 'carbon' tax is an illustration (see Box 8.3). Specific institutional arrangements may be adopted by public authorities. Thus, a committee was set up in Denmark to assess the distributional impacts resulting from the implementation of the government's 'green tax reform' in 1998 (OECD, 2002). In the United States, distributional issues have been embedded in policy-making through a series of institutional arrangements since the early 1990s.[19]

BOX 8.3 CARBON TAXATION AND COMPENSATION IN IRELAND

The Irish Minister for Finance announced in 2004 that the proposed 'carbon energy' tax will not be introduced because of 'some adverse economic and social effects that would not be fully dealt with by compensatory measures' (www.finance.gov.ie/viewdoc.asp?DocID=2608). This decision illustrates the political importance of public discussion of distributional issues when designing environmental policies.

There is little question that at first glance a carbon tax hurts the poor more than the rich: the poor spend a higher share of their weekly budget on energy; they use fuels that are high emitters of carbon dioxide; and they cannot easily change their heating equipment. However, the revenue generated from a carbon tax is likely to be considerable. Indeed, a recent study for Ireland (Scott and Eakins, 2004) shows that, in principle, a tax of €20/ton of CO_2 would have allowed poor households to be fully compensated many times over.

For instance, the study investigates the implications of using about a quarter of the revenue from carbon taxes for compensation. The social welfare and income tax systems allow for compensation without imposing a significant additional administrative burden. On the one hand, income tax rates and thresholds applied to low incomes could be reduced. On the other hand, households that did not pay sufficient tax to benefit from tax reductions would qualify for the enhanced Fuel Allowance (which is conveniently targeted at the household, not the individual).

In fact, under such a proposal, households at the lower end of the income spectrum would on average be better off than before the introduction of the carbon tax (see Figure 8.1). The taller bars show the carbon tax paid by different income groups, while the shorter darker bars represent the net tax after compensation. Lower income groups end up with negative net tax, meaning that after compensation they are on average better off than before.

However, there could still be a number of 'losers', leaving aside the benign effects of recycling the remaining revenue. Indeed, 58000 households in the lower-income deciles would not be targeted using the two instruments as currently operating, partly because of low benefit take-up at present. Losers would also be

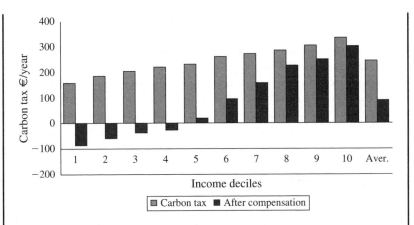

Figure 8.1 The carbon tax before and after compensation

those who use above-average amounts of energy and high-carbon fuels in particular – coal and peat. For these above-average users the proposal suggests expanding fuel switching and efficiency schemes.

After consultation, but with little public debate of alternative proposals to mitigate the potential social impacts of the carbon tax, including proposals by Combat Poverty, the tax was abandoned. Commitments to the Kyoto Protocol will be addressed, instead, through the non-tax measures in the government's National Climate Change Strategy. Whether or not the inevitable adverse distributional effects of such measures (which will not generate any revenue) will be addressed remains to be seen.

More generally, policy-makers may formalise specific guidance frameworks which factor social matters, like distributional incidence, into the design of environmental policies. For instance, in the Treasury *Green Book*, the United Kingdom has formalised central government advice on how to take account of distributional implications in policy appraisal (HM Treasury, 2003). At the level of the European Union, assessment methods incorporating distributional impacts when gauging projects or policies are being developed. These approaches include Social Impact Assessment or Sustainability Impact Assessment which are designed to assess economic, social and environmental impacts in a single coherent framework.[20]

More formally, distributionally-weighted cost–benefit analysis (CBA) may be used, as discussed in detail by Pearce (Chapter 2 in the present volume). Rather than applying equal weights to households' 'willingness to pay' (WTP) for environmental goods, greater weights can be applied to lower-income households. This will have the effect of favouring projects and programmes which are of particular value to poorer households relative to the case where WTP is aggregated in an unweighted manner (see also OECD, 2006). This can, however, be seen as being somewhat arbitrary. For example, equity is a multi-dimensional concept and there is a variety of criteria that might be used as a guide to the determination of appropriate weights, and the distributional vector across which they are applied.

4.2   Preserve Efficiency and Effectiveness

However, if it is recognised that distributional impacts are sufficiently important to warrant compensation and mitigation, it is essential to bear in mind that not all such measures are equivalent in terms of their impacts on economic efficiency and environmental effectiveness. In general, measures to address distributional concerns raised by environmental policies can have three types of potential effects in terms of economic efficiency and environmental effectiveness:

(i)   Keep the marginal incentive unchanged – for instance by implementing a tax and paying a lump sum to low-income households.
(ii)   Keep the incentive broadly the same but change its modalities to address distributional concerns (for example, differentiated tariff structures).
(iii) Exempt certain groups from the measure altogether.

In terms of efficiency, the first option is the best, but may not be politically acceptable. The third option will never be efficient or effective, but unfortunately it is the one that is often used. Indeed, in terms of strict economic efficiency, it is usually preferable to address distributional effects outside the context of the environmental policy altogether.

If the government has specific distributional objectives, these should be addressed in the least distortionary manner for the economy as a whole. By linking the realisation of a distributional objective with a specific environmental policy, the government is in effect restricting its options. However, it may be politically necessary to address environmental concerns and the social impacts which arise together as part of a single policy package.

For instance, using the revenue generated by a tax for direct financial assistance or tax refunds to vulnerable groups (for example, low-income households) may be the best option. Other channels, such as the provision of direct financial support, may also be used. While such measures may not be consistent with general principles of efficient public finance, they may allow policy-makers to overcome binding political constraints in a least-cost manner.

4.3 Ensure Access to Decision-making

The good functioning of the market with well-defined property rights is essential to ensure a direct translation between the preferences of individuals and the optimal social outcome (Coase, 1960). Assuming the owner of a hazardous waste disposal site has defined property rights, firms will have an incentive to locate where the financial costs of environmental damages are the lowest, and this will reflect in part the preferences of those who live nearby.

However, if environmental damages are not well understood by affected households, the market will not result in a situation where 'underlying' personal preferences are reflected in social outcomes. Thus, in order for the Coase theorem to hold, it is essential that households have access to information which allows them to make 'informed' decisions and to express their preferences. As underlined by Boyce (2002), distributional concerns may result from imperfect information and this can be due to the lack of knowledge about the effects of pollution, or about their causes. Right-to-know legislation can help address the first problem, while the second can be improved by environmental education.

Policy interventions that governments may take to remove information failures and barriers contributing to possible disparities in the distribution of environmental quality include the provision of information on exposure to environmental hazards and the facilitation of access to information, with specific programmes or policies targeted at low-income households.

The right of access to environmental information by the public is a principle that has been gradually adopted by almost all OECD countries through domestic legislation and/or of international legal acts (for example, the Aarhus Convention). Examples of earlier measures to promote public information on specific facilities are the Pollutant Release and Transfer Register (PRTR) in the United States since 1986, and the National Pollutant Release Inventory (NPRI) in Canada. More recent initiatives include the 1999 Law Concerning Access to Information in Japan and the Mexican environmental right-to-know legislation adopted in 2001.

However, it is equally essential that, in addition to being able to form their preferences in an informed manner, households have the opportunity to express them through facilitated access to political decision-making and/or to courts of law. Governments may encourage public participation in public hearings and decision-making procedures for the siting of environmental disamenities (for example, hazardous waste sites, airports). The consultation held in the United Kingdom, in 2003, for the design of the future airport policy in London and the south-east of England over the next 30 years provides a striking example.

In a similar way, policy measures can facilitate public participation in the decision processes associated with the provision of environmental amenities or protected areas (for example, watershed zone). In this vein, the establishment of a restricted development zone (green belt) by the Korean government illustrates the usefulness of having a consultation process at an early stage, involving the different social groups affected, and seeking to minimise possible adverse effects on some groups (Jeong and Nam, 2003). In both areas, initiatives may be taken specifically to encourage the active representation of disadvantaged interest groups (for example, low-income households) such as targeted information provision or technical assistance to communities involved in siting. Thus, the involvement of potentially affected groups is considered as a key principle in project evaluation methods such as Social Impact Assessment.

The nature of the environmental liability regime and ease of access to courts for low-income households may also have implications on the distribution of exposure to environmental hazards, even though measures are not directly targeted at them. First, tighter liability regimes (for example, strict liability principle, reversal of the burden of proof) tend to increase the propensity of affected households to sue firms responsible for excessive levels of exposure of local communities to environmental hazards. Indirect access to courts for low-income households in environmental matters may also be facilitated by public authorities through measures which extend access to justice to environmental and other community groups, as in the Finnish Environmental Protection Act which came into force in 2000. Allowing for collective action in citizen suits may also improve the access of low-income households to justice. Given the costs involved in pursuing such cases, the use of contingency fees may also increase access.

Thus, in addition to having a well-functioning market, in order to deal with concerns in the distribution of environmental quality, policy-makers may take specific measures to address possible determinants of disparities such as the existence of information failures which can prevent households from making informed choices or policy failures which can limit the possibility to express their preferences. In both cases, a well-functioning market will be ensured by policy-makers through specific institutional arrangements.

To sum up, this book has highlighted four main conclusions regarding the distributional effects of environmental policies and the means to address them. First, all environmental policies are likely to have distributional impacts. While these effects have a greater 'visibility' in the case of economic instruments, they can also arise when using alternative policy measures such as direct regulations (for example, standards). Second, although the distributive burden of environmental policies is generally assessed with a focus on direct financial effects, taking indirect effects and behavioural response into account may have significant implications on the final distributional incidence. Third, when assessing distributional effects, it is essential to consider simultaneously how different groups of individuals will be affected by the financial burden of environmental policies or by a change in environmental quality as trade-offs between the two dimensions can exist through related markets (for example, real estate). Fourth, policy-makers are confronted with important choices when considering how best to respond to these distributional concerns and whether adverse effects should be tackled through the modification of the environmental policy instrument or through other measures. In addition, and perhaps most importantly, when introducing measures to mitigate these distributional impacts, policy-makers need to maintain the effectiveness of the environmental policy, as well as its economic efficiency.

NOTES

1. Studies looking at pollutants such as SO_x (sulphur oxides), or PM_{10} (particulate matter) show that low-income groups bear higher pollution (see Freeman, 1972; Zupan, 1973; Berry, 1977; Asch and Seneca, 1978; Harrison and Rubinfeld, 1978). A review of early studies is provided in Cutter (1995), and of early and late studies in Bowen (2002). Hamilton (Chapter 7 in present volume) provides an extensive review of empirical evidence on the distribution of exposure to hazardous waste facilities.
2. See also Burke (1993), Brooks and Sethi (1997), Arora and Cason (1999) for studies on exposure to toxic releases, and Anderson et al. (1994) for exposure to transfer, storage and disposal facilities (TSDFs).
3. Other examples are provided by Boer et al. (1997) or Atlas (2001).
4. As will be discussed below, even if this is not the initial objective of the policy, effects on associated markets may result in a bias towards provision of such goods for higher-income households.
5. In addition to more general methodological issues previously discussed in this book, such as the conception of 'fairness' retained or the 'proxy' used for wealth (for example, annual or lifetime income).
6. See Chapters 6 and 7. See also Kruize and Bouwman (2004) as well as Brainard et al. (2002b), McLeod et al. (2000) and Pye et al. (2001) for the distribution of air pollution in the UK. See also Sadd et al. (1999) for the use of GIS technology to study TRI releases in southern California.
7. See, for instance, Cutter et al. (1996).
8. See, for instance, the studies of Arora and Cason (1999) and Brooks and Sethi (1997) using information from the Toxic Release Inventory (TRI) in the United States, or Kruize and Bouwman (2004).
9. See, for instance, Bae (2003). See also Lester and Allen (1999) and Hamilton (1995) for the importance of the geographical unit of analysis employed.
10. See, for instance, Labandeira and Labeaga (1999) on the neutral effect of carbon taxation across Spanish households.

11. See also the study by Symons et al. (1994) on carbon taxation of driving fuels.
12. See, for instance, Fisher (2004) for a discussion on the role of the structure of the market supply when examining the financial burden of energy efficiency standards for appliances.
13. According to the CAFE regulation which was enacted in 1975, every seller of automobiles in the USA had to achieve, by 1985, a minimum sales-weighted average fuel efficiency of 27.5 miles per gallon.
14. It should be noted that some socially-driven subsidies (for example, coal) may be environmentally harmful (see OECD, 2003b).
15. To assess the distributional incidence of alternative policies such as a miles tax, a gasoline tax, a size tax or a policy that subsidises new vehicles, key behaviour variables would include the number of vehicles, vintage, engine size, demand for vehicle-miles-travelled (VMT) or elasticities of demand for VMT.
16. See Timmins (2004) on mobility constraints and the distributional consequence of particulate matter. The role of constrained budgets on the willingness of households to trade environmental quality for housing costs is also discussed by Hamilton (in Chapter 7).
17. The study by Been and Gupta (1997) is an exception where the variable is not statistically significant.
18. However, the public sector is indirectly involved, as a land-use planner and a provider of infrastructures (for example, airports) and can be indirectly implicated through military aviation and publicly-owned civil aviation.
19. In 1992, an Office of Environmental Justice (OEJ) was established by the EPA to integrate environmental justice concerns into the environmental programmes of the agency. The National Environmental Justice Advisory Council (NEJAC) was created in 1993. In addition, the 1994 Executive Order 12898 established the Interagency Working Group on Environmental Justice (IWG).
20. The European Commission established a new integrated assessment framework to be performed for major proposals from 2004 onwards (COM(2002)276).

REFERENCES

Anderson, A., D. Anderton and J. Oakes (1994), 'Environmental Equity: Evaluating TSDF Siting over the Past Two Decades', *Waste Age*, **25**, 83–100.

Arora, S. and T. Cason (1999), 'Do Community Characteristics Influence Environmental Outcomes? Evidence from the Toxic Releases Inventory', *Southern Economic Journal*, **65**, 691–716.

Asch, P. and J. Seneca (1978), 'Some Evidence on the Distribution of Air Quality', *Land Economics*, **54**, 218–57.

Atlas, M. (2001), 'Safe and Sorry: Risk, Environmental Equity, and Hazardous Waste Management Facilities', *Risk Analysis*, **21**, 939–54.

Bae, C. (2003), 'The Distributional Impacts of Air Quality Regulations: Smog Controls in Los Angeles and Toxic Air Releases in Houston and Los Angeles', paper prepared for the OECD Workshop on the Distribution of Benefits and Costs of Environmental Policies, 4–5 March.

Baranzini, A. and J. V. Ramirez (2005), 'Paying for Quietness. The Impact of Noise on Geneva Rents', *Urban Studies*, **42**(4), 1–14.

Been, V. and F. Gupta (1997), 'Coming to the Nuisance or Going to the Barrios: A Longitudinal Analysis of Environmental Justice Claims', *Ecological Law Quarterly*, **24**(1), 1–56.

Berry, N. (1977), *The Social Burdens of Environmental Pollution*, Cambridge, MA: Ballinger.

Boer, J., M. Pastor, J. Sadd and L. Snyder (1997), 'Is there Environmental Racism? The Demographics of Hazardous Waste in Los Angeles County', *Social Science Quarterly*, **78**, 793–810.

Bowen, W. (2002), 'An Analytical Review of Environmental Justice Research: What Do We Really Know?', *Environmental Management*, **29**(1), 3–15.

Boyce, J.K. (2002), *The Political Economy of the Environment*, Cheltenham, UK and Northampton, MA, USA: Edward Elgar.

Brainard J.S., I.J. Bateman and A.P. Jones (2002a), 'Accessing Urban Park Locations: Contrasting Equity of Access with Economic Efficiency Measures', CSERGE Working Paper, University of East Anglia, UK.

Brainard J.S., A.P. Jones, I.J. Bateman, A.A. Lovett and P.J. Fallon (2002b), 'Modelling Environmental Equity: Access to Air Quality in Birmingham, UK', *Environment and Planning A*, **34**, 695–716.

Brännlund, R. and J. Nordström (2004), 'Carbon Tax Simulations Using a Household Demand Model', *European Economic Review*, **48**(1), 211–33.

Brooks, N. and R. Sethi (1997), 'The Distribution of Pollution: Community Characteristics and Exposure to Air Toxics', *Journal of Environmental Economics and Management*, **32**, 233–50.

Burke, L. (1993), 'Race and Environmental Equity: A Geographic Analysis in Los Angeles', *Geographic Information Systems*, October, 44–50.

Chay, K.Y. and M. Greenstone (2004), 'Does Air Quality Matter? Evidence from the Housing Market', Working Paper 04–19, MIT, Cambridge.

Chichilnisky, G. and G. Heal (1994), 'Who Should Abate Carbon Emissions? An International Viewpoint', *Economic Letters*, **44**(4), 443–9.

Coase, R. (1960), 'The Problem of Social Cost', *Journal of Law and Economics*, **3**, 1–44.

Cornwell, A. and J. Creedy (1997), 'Measuring the Welfare Effects of Tax Changes Using the LES: An Application to a Carbon Tax', *Empirical Economics*, **22**, 589–613.

Cutter, S.L. (1995), 'Race, Class and Environmental Justice', *Progress in Human Geography*, **19**, 111–22.

Cutter, S., D. Holm and L. Clark (1996), 'The Role of Geographic Scale in Monitoring Environmental Justice', *Risk Analysis*, **16**, 517–26.

Dinan, T.M. and D.L. Rogers (2002), 'Distributional Effects of a Carbon Allowance Trading: How Government Decisions Determine Winners and Losers', *National Tax Journal*, **55**, 199–221.

Dubin, J. and D. McFadden (1984), 'An Econometric Analysis of Residential Electric Appliance Holdings and Consumption', *Econometrica*, **52**(2), 345–62.

Fisher, C. (2004), 'Who Pays for Energy Efficiency Standards?', Discussion Paper 04–11, Resources for the Future, Washington.

Freeman, A.M. (1972), 'The Distribution of Environmental Quality', in A. Kneese and B. Bower (eds), *Environmental Quality Analysis*, Baltimore: Johns Hopkins University Press, pp. 243–80.

Goldberg, P.K. (1998), 'The Effects of the Corporate Average Fuel Efficiency Standards in the US', *Journal of Industrial Economics*, **46**(1), 1–33.

Halvorsen, B. and Runa Nesbakken (2002), 'Distributional Effects of Household Electricity Taxation', Statistics Norway.

Hamilton, J.T. (1995), 'Testing for Environmental Racism: Prejudice, Profits, or Power?', *Journal of Policy Analysis and Management*, **14**(1), 107–32.

Hamilton, J.T. and W. Kip Viscusi (1999), *Calculating Risks? The Spatial and Political Dimensions of Hazardous Waste Policy*, Cambridge, MA: MIT Press.

Handy, F. (1977), 'Income and Air Pollution in Hamilton, Ontario', *Alternatives*, **6**, 18–24.

Harrison, K. and W. Antweiler (2002), 'Incentives for Pollution Abatement: Regulations, Regulatory Threat and Non-governmental Pressure', mimeo, University of British Columbia.

Harrison, D. and D. Rubinfeld (1978), 'Hedonic House Prices and the Demand for Clean Air', *Journal of Environmental Economics and Management*, **5**, 81–102.

Herrington, P.R. (2003), 'Distribution of Costs and Environmental Impacts of Water Services in OECD States: Affordability Measurement and Policies', paper prepared for the OECD Workshop on the Distribution of Benefits and Costs of Environmental Policies, 4–5 March.

Hite, D. (2000), 'A Random Utility Model of Environmental Equity', *Growth and Change*, **31**, 40–58.

HM Treasury (UK) (2003), *The Green Book: Appraisal and Evaluation in Central Government*, London: HM Treasury, www.hm-treasury.gov.uk.

Jeong, H.S. and S.M. Nam (2003), 'Injustice Issues in the Environmental Policy Process in Korea', contribution prepared by Korea for the OECD Workshop on the Distribution of Benefits and Costs of Environmental Policies, Paris, 4–5 March.

Jerrett, M., J. Eyles, D. Cole and S. Reader (1997), 'Environmental Equity in Canada: An Empirical Investigation into the Income Distribution of Pollution in Ontario', *Environment and Planning*, **29**, 1777–800.

Klinge-Jacobsen, H., K. Birr-Pedersen and M. Wier (2001), *Fordelningsvirkninger af Energi- og Miljöavgifter* [Distributional Impacts of Environmental and Energy-charge], Risö National Laboratory, November (in Danish, with English summary).

Kruize, H. and A. Bouwman (2004), 'Environmental (In)equity in the Netherlands: A Case Study on the Distribution of Environmental Quality in the Rijnmond Region', RIVM report no. 550012003, Bilthoven, The Netherlands.

Labandeira, X. and J.M. Labeaga (1999), 'Combining Input–Output Analysis and Micro-simulation to Assess the Effects of Carbon Taxation of Spanish Households', *Fiscal Studies*, **30**(3), 305–20.

Lester, J.P. and D.W. Allen (1999), 'Environmental Injustice in the United States: Realities and Myths', paper presented at the OECD Seminar on the Social and Environmental Interface, Paris, 22–24 September.

McLeod, H., I.H. Langford, A.P. Jones, J.R. Stedman, R.J. Day, I. Lorenzoni and I.J. Bateman (2000), 'The Relationship between Socio-economic Indicators and Air Pollution in England and Wales: Implications for Environmental Justice', *Regional Environmental Change*, **1**, 78–85.

Millimet, D. and D. Slottje (2000), 'The Distribution of Pollution in the US: An Environmental Gini Approach', mimeo, Department of Economics, Southern Methodist University, Dallas.

Millock, K. and T. Sterner (2004), 'NO_x Emissions in France and Sweden: Markets Go Where Regulation Can't', in W. Harrington, R.D. Morgenstern and T. Sterner (eds), *Choosing Environmental Policy: Comparing Instruments and Outcomes in the United States and Europe*, Washington, DC: RFF Press, pp. 117–32.

Mohai, P. and B. Bryant (1992), 'Environmental Racism', in P. Mohai and B. Bryant (eds), *Race and the Incidence of Environmental Hazards: A Time for Discourse*, Boulder, CO: Westview Press, pp. 163–76.

OECD (2002), *Implementing Environmental Fiscal Reform: Income Distribution and Sectoral Competitiveness Issues*, Proceedings of a Conference held in Berlin, Germany, 27 June.

OECD (2003a), *Social Issues in the Provision and Pricing of Water Services*, Paris: OECD.

OECD (2003b), *Environmentally Harmful Subsidies – Policy Issues and Challenges*, Paris: OECD.

OECD (2006), *Cost–Benefit Analysis and the Environment: Recent Developments*, Paris: OECD (forthcoming).

Parry, I.W. (2004), 'Are Emissions Permits Regressive?', *Journal of Environmental Economics and Management*, **47**, 364–87.

Pye, S., J. Stedman, M. Adams and K. King (2001), 'Further Analysis of NO_2 and PM_{10} Air Pollution and Social Deprivation', Report AEAT/ENV/R/0865. AEA Technology, Culham.

Robison, H.D. (1985), 'Who Pays for Industrial Pollution Abatement?', *Review of Economics and Statistics*, **67**(4), 702–6.

Sadd, J.L., Manuel Pastor Jr, J. Thomas Boer and L.D. Snyder (1999), ' "Every Breath You Take . . .": The Demographics of Toxic Air Releases in Southern California', *Economic Development Quarterly*, **13**(2), 107–23.

Scott, Sue and John Eakins (2004), *Carbon Taxes: Which Households Gain or Lose?*, Johnstown Castle Estate, Wexford: Environment Protection Agency.

Sipes, K. and R. Mendelsohn (2001), 'The Effectiveness of Gasoline Taxation to Manage Air Pollution', *Ecological Economics*, **2**(36), 299–309.

Stoft, S. (1993), 'Appliance Standards and the Welfare of Poor Families', *Energy Journal*, **14**(4), 123–8.

Sutherland, R.J. (1991), 'Market Barriers to Energy-efficiency Investments', *Energy Journal*, **12**(3), 15–34.

Sutherland, R.J. (1994), 'Income Distribution Effects of Electric Utility DSM Programs', *Energy Journal*, **15**(4), 103–18.

Sutherland, R.J. (2003), 'The High Costs of Federal Energy Efficiency Standards for Residential Appliances', *Policy Analysis*, **504**, Washington, DC: Cato Institute.

Symons, E., J. Proops and P. Gay (1994), 'Carbon Taxes, Consumer Demand, and Carbon Dioxide Emissions: A Simulation Analysis for the UK', *Fiscal Studies*, **15**(2), 19–43.

Tiezzi, S. (2005), 'The Welfare and Distributive Effects of Carbon Taxation on Italian Households', *Energy Policy*, **33**(12), 1597–1612.

Timmins, C. (2004), 'Mobility Constraints and the Distributional Consequences of Particulate Matter', paper presented at the AERE Workshop on Distributional Effects and Environmental Policy, Colorado, June 13–15.

Train, K. (1985), 'Discount Rates in Consumers' Energy-related Decisions: A Review of the Literature', *Energy*, **10**(12), 1243–53.

Walls, M. and J. Hanson (1999), 'Measuring the Incidence of an Environmental Tax Shift: The Case of Motor Vehicle Emissions Taxes', *National Tax Journal*, **52**(1), 53–66.

West, S.E. (2004), 'Equity Implications of Vehicle Emissions Taxes', paper presented at the Association of Environmental and Resource Economics Workshop on Distributional Effects of Environmental Policy, Colorado, June.

West, S.E. and R.C. Williams (2002), 'Estimates from a Consumer Demand System: Implications for the Incidence of Environmental Taxes', Working Paper 9152, NBER, http://www.nber.org/papers/w9152.

Yandle, T. and D. Burton (1996), 'Re-examining Environmental Justice: A Statistical Analysis of Historical Hazardous Waste Landfill Siting Patterns in Metropolitan Texas', *Social Science Quarterly*, **77**, 477–92.

Zimmerman, R. (1993), 'Social Equity and Environmental Risk', *Risk Analysis*, **13**, 649–66.

Zupan, J. (1973), *The Distribution of Air Quality in the New York Region*, Baltimore: Johns Hopkins University Press.

Index

Abbreviations used in the index include:
EE   energy efficiency
EJ   environmental justice
SWF   social welfare function